A Social Revolution

A Social Revolution

Politics and the Welfare State in Iran

Kevan Harris

UNIVERSITY OF CALIFORNIA PRESS

University of California Press, one of the most
distinguished university presses in the United States,
enriches lives around the world by advancing scholarship
in the humanities, social sciences, and natural sciences. Its
activities are supported by the UC Press Foundation and
by philanthropic contributions from individuals and
institutions. For more information, visit www.ucpress.edu.

University of California Press
Oakland, California

Library of Congress Cataloging-in-Publication Data

Names: Harris, Kevan, author.
Title: A social revolution : politics and the welfare state
    in Iran / Kevan Harris.
Description: Oakland, California : University of
California Press, [2017] | Includes bibliographical
references and index.
Identifiers: LCCN 2016048659 (print) | LCCN 2016056132
    (ebook) | ISBN 9780520280816 (cloth : alk. paper) |
    ISBN 9780520280823 (pbk : alk. paper) | ISBN
    9780520965843 ()
Subjects: LCSH: Iran—Social conditions—1997. |
    Iran—Social conditions—1997– | Iran—
    History—1979-1997. | Iran—History—1997–
Classification: LCC HN670.2.A8 H37 2017 (print) |
    LCC HN670.2.A8 (ebook) | DDC 306.0955—dc23
LC record available at https://lccn.loc.gov/2016048659

Manufactured in the United States of America

24 23 22 21 20 19 18 17
10 9 8 7 6 5 4 3 2 1

It seems to me that we still have trouble eliminating the dichotomous concepts that we use to understand historical and social phenomena in general and Iranian political reality in particular. States are totalitarian or democratic; political regimes are ideological or rational; societies are traditional or modern; political leaders are elected or selected; constitutions are good or bad; people follow a leader or are critically-minded; leaders may be more important than institutions because they are based on a cult of personality, charisma, or autocratic tendencies, or institutions may be more important than the individuals who create and serve them. While these dichotomies give us the possibility of rapid judgment, they also place severe limitations on understanding the social and political changes occurring in Iran, the reasons why these changes happen, and the way they happen.

—*Morad Saghafi (2004b)*

Contents

Acknowledgments

This book argues that the politics of social policy and welfare organizations provides a lens through which to understand the surprising dynamics of social and political change in Iran since the 1979 revolution. This research project emerged from a simple observation. The Iran I experienced in person looked very different from the Iran I read about in journalism and scholarship. Given the dearth of secondary research on social policy in Iran, studying the postrevolutionary welfare state required a goose chase. But most fieldwork usually does, so here I wish to thank those who made the project intellectually and logistically possible.

An international dissertation fellowship from the Social Science Research Council, with funds provided by the Andrew Mellon Foundation, provided me with the opportunity for extended fieldwork. In fact, given the increasing layers of United States–led sanctions on Iran between 2007 and 2015, it was perhaps the only opportunity available. A dissertation-writing fellowship from the U.S. Institute of Peace supported me as I waded through the large amount of primary data collected from archives, interviews, and Persian-language journals. My dissertation advisor and intellectual hero, Giovanni Arrighi, and his wife, Beverly Silver, were my guides during the initial stages of this project. Giovanni unfortunately passed away in 2009. He trained me to think like an historical sociologist, who can be contrarian, but only for good reason. At The Johns Hopkins University, Joel Andreas, Rina Agarwala, Waleed Hazbun, Marc Blyth, and Michael Hanchard were vital mentors. My thanks to graduate colleagues, who kept me motivated and inspired by their own fieldwork across the world: Astra Bonini, Lu Zhang, Dan Pasciuti, Sahan S. Karataşlı, Şefika Kumral, Felipe Filomeno, Phil Hough, Nicole Aschoff, Noora Lori, Amy Holmes, Lingli Huang, and Shaohua Zhan. Additional thanks go to Ben Scully and Liz Kading for solid friendship and gentle nudging.

As a postdoctoral fellow at Princeton University, I appreciably benefited from the erudition of Michael Cook, Muhammad Qasim Zaman, Bernard Haykel, Cyrus Schayegh, Mirjam Künkler, and Hossein Modarressi. Through them, I managed to learn a great deal about Islamic studies via osmosis in the Near Eastern Studies Department. Conversations and seminars with Princeton faculty were indispensable while I wrote this monograph. My gratitude goes to Stephen Kotkin, Mark Beissinger, Amaney Jamal, Edward Telles, Mitch Duneier, Miguel Centeno, Andreas Wimmer, Alejandro Portes, and John Haldon. Thanks to Reagan Maraghy, Rose Wellman, and Mona Rahmani for research assistance and comradeship at the Princeton Center for Iran and Persian Gulf Studies, where I learned the ins and outs of how universities work. Students and fellows at Princeton were a pleasure to teach and meet, and I ran some crazy ideas by many of them: Kevin Mazur, Daniel Tavana, Eric Lob, Cole Bunzel, Zach Foster, Lindsey Stephenson, David Weil, Dan Sheffield, Sadaf Jaffer, Elvire Corboz, and Christiana Parreira.

A full list of the scholars, journalists, researchers, and academics who assisted me during this project would be exceedingly long and run the risk of self-embarrassment. Among those Iranianists outside the country, special thanks go to Ervand Abrahamian, Eric Hooglund, Arang Keshavarzian, Greta Scharnweber, Norma Moruzzi, Kaveh Ehsani, Saïd Arjomand, Touraj Atabaki, Maral Jefroudi, Farideh Farhi, Charles Kurzman, Ali Kadivar, Ahmad Ashraf, Djavad Salehi-Isfahani, Asef Bayat, Val Moghadam, John Foran, Dan Brumberg, Farhad Khosrokhavar, Afshin Matin-Asgari, and Behrooz Ghamari-Tabrizi. Inside Iran, I relied on the local knowledge and research acumen of Ali Saeidi, Ramin Karimian, Morad Saghafi, Kaveh Bayat, Fatemeh Sadeghi, Mohammad Maljoo, Parviz Sedaghat, Kamal Athari, Mostafa Azkia, Ahmad Meydari, Narges Barahoi, and countless students and professors in the universities of Tehran, Shiraz, Ahvaz, Tabriz, and Shahid Beheshti. Librarians and researchers substantially assisted me at the Majles Research Library, the Social Security Research Institute, the Planning and Budget Organization, the Imam Khomeini Relief Committee, and the Ministry of Welfare and Social Security. To hospitable people in Iran who helped me along the way, I am indebted. To inhospitable ones, all is forgiven.

When I was an early graduate student, the sociologist Erik Olin Wright told me that good scholarship is always collaborative, since it cannot be produced without wide-ranging intellectual exchange. To that end, I wish to thank some interlocutors: Peter Evans, Michael Burawoy, Patrick Heller, Ching Kwan Lee, Melani Cammett, Ishac Diwan, Vivek Chibber, Jeff Goodwin, David Harvey, Cihan Tuğal, Kiren Chaudhry, Robert Brenner, Perry Anderson, Immanuel Wallerstein, Ho-Fung Hung, Craig Calhoun, and Steven Heydemann.

Georgi Derluguian convinced me to become a sociologist. He also told me to give up my intentions of becoming a Latin Americanist and instead head to Iran. He also fed me a lot of skewered meat over the years. So I owe him quite a bit, and I hope that he sees a bit of himself in this book. Finally, my parents and sister gave me love and support over the years. Once I went to Iran, so did they on different occasions. This book is dedicated to them.

A Note on Transliteration

For purposes of readability by nonspecialists, the only diacritic used when transliterating Persian in the main text of this book is *a*-macron (*ā*), the one that connotes the long-*a* vowel in Persian. I do not use any diacritics for individuals who would likely be known to a nonspecialist audience. For example, Rouhani, Khamenei, or Ahmadinejad is rendered without diacritics, whereas Abbāsi, Rajāi, or Bāzargān use the long-*a* diacritic. For the rendering of Persian titles in endnotes and bibliography, I use the style employed in the journal *Iranian Studies*.

Introduction

In the run-up to the presidential election of summer 2013, the three-decade political improvisation called the Islamic Republic of Iran once again went off script. Just a week prior to Iran's June 14 election, according to tracking polls, former national-security adviser and chief nuclear negotiator Hassan Rouhani sat in the middle of a pack of six candidates. It seemed that no one would gain a majority of ballots, meaning that a runoff was in store. Then a coalition of centrist and reformist politicians, including former presidents Akbar Hashemi-Rafsanjani and Mohammad Khatami, announced their backing for Rouhani.

Three days of electioneering ensued, with a final day of state-mandated campaign silence before the Friday election. At some point during the week, millions of people decided to vote, and to vote for Hassan Rouhani. "I had made up my mind not to vote," said a young Tehran University student. "How could I, after our votes were taken away in 2009?" She then told me that on Thursday, all her friends scrambled to find their national identity cards in order to go to the voting booths the next morning.

Rouhani rose to frontrunner in the polls by election day. As results trickled in hourly on June 15, the outcome became clear. Rouhani won 50.7 percent of the more than 36 million votes cast (a turnout of 72.7 percent). The second-place candidate, Tehran mayor Mohammad-Bāqer Qālibāf, garnered only 16.6 percent. That evening, city streets around the country transformed into carnivals where chants of support for Rouhani resonated with huzzahs for the former 2009 presidential candidate and leader of the postelection protest wave known as the Green Movement, Mir-Hossein Mousavi, who had been held under house arrest since 2011. The few police loafing in the squares simply moved traffic along as best they could. "Yes, they are just standing there," a young man next to me yelled into a mobile phone. "I swear it's true—come out and see for yourself!"

"Iranian society surprised itself," sociologist and Khatami confidant Hamid Rezā Jalāeipour told a Tehran University crowd a week after the ballot. "Mobilizational potential turned into an electoral uprising." Jalāeipour added: "After this election, everyone was shocked." Writing in a reformist newspaper, the urban-studies scholar Parviz Pirān put it more humbly: "Iranian and non-Iranian experts alike do not know Iran well."[1] As someone who had been traveling to Iran since the 2005 election of former president Mahmoud Ahmadinejad, I knew enough, at least, to expect surprises.

For many visitors, contemporary Iran is presented through two contrasting images. No matter how rich or poor, how educated or illiterate, how connected to the state or excluded by it, people tend to talk about their daily hardships. To do so, whether in the capital city, Tehran, a provincial city such as Ahvaz, or a small village in the Iranian Plateau, individuals compare upward. Many are conscious of inequality and look to those who seem to have a wealthier lifestyle or higher social status. These comparisons can include other countries, imagined or real. Most individuals have a well-developed sense of what a fairer, more nearly equal social order could look like. Much of the time, the government is blamed as one of the main sources and generators of perceived inequality.

For some observers, all these grievances collectively put together meant that the Islamic Republic was teetering on the edge of collapse. After all, according to Jack Goldstone—a well-known scholar of modern revolutions—four elements need to be in place for a revolution to occur. There must be a weak and economically uncompetitive state, a divided internal elite, popular social groups that are mobilized to protest the regime, and an ideology, new or reinvented, that justifies rebellion against the state.[2] Iran appeared to contain all these elements. In fact, these four issues make up the vast bulk of the scholarship on contemporary Iran: economic backwardness, elite factionalism, a contentious civil society, and highly developed ideologies, both secular and religious, that challenge the Islamic Republic's orthodox state dogma. Journalists and scholars alike had been waiting for the collapse over three decades. Having been caught off-guard in 1979 by the country's "unthinkable revolution," they were determined not to make the same mistake again.[3]

There is another image of contemporary Iran, sometimes held up by journalists or scholars as a mirror opposite. By 2007, an economic boom had been under way that was spawning nouveau-riche Iranians as fast as their Indian or Chinese counterparts were appearing in their respective countries. Iranian society was messy but coherent, clumsy but ambitious, and above all, remarkably nationalistic. The population was relatively healthy and educated in comparison with most other middle-income countries. Iranians had rising expectations and were therefore unsatisfied with the status quo. Their ubiquitous criticisms were coupled with an emulation of global trends in status consumption, intellectual output, and cultural behaviors. In this view, Iranian society, or at least a growing section of it, seemed to be transforming itself in defiance of the political order of the Islamic Republic. A hidden revolution in Iran was under-way, and it had little to do with the year 1979.

Both these representations hide something important. In the former, social protection languishes because of neglect by the Iranian state, whereas in the latter, upward economic mobility occurs in spite of it. In both views, state and society rarely interact. This book argues for a dif-ferent view. We cannot understand the surprises of postrevolutionary Iran without examining interactions between state and society. The Islamic Republic was born out of a rapid upsurge in popular contention from 1977 to 1979 that led to the collapse of the previous Pahlavi mon-archy. The Islamic Republic then had to survive a protracted war with Ba'athist Iraq from 1980 to 1988—and this survival depended on another wave of popular mobilization. As the war ended, the leaders of the Islamic Republic saw themselves at the helm of an *antisystemic developmental state*. They believed that the country would have to either modernize or perish. Revolutionary Iran could catch up with wealthy states in the world economy, but the country would have to do so under duress. No foreign assistance would be forthcoming. The political elite agreed on this, but they disagreed on almost everything else.

Because of the long war that rapidly followed the 1979 revolution, the Islamic Republic diverged from other postrevolutionary states in a crit-ical dimension: it did not develop a one-party system of political rule. Rather, recurring and intense *elite competition* spilled into the public sphere. Among all sides in this domestic elite conflict, *popular mobiliza-tion* was a crucial method in gaining advantages against adversaries. As a result, the social legacies of both revolution and war were utilized and transformed through elite competition and popular mobilization over the next three decades.

These factors shaped both long-term changes and sudden events that surprised Iranians and non-Iranians alike. No one expected the 1997 election of the liberal-sounding cleric Mohammad Khatami as president. No one outside Iran had even heard of the illiberal-sounding noncleric Mahmoud Ahmadinejad before his election as president in 2005. Both men seemed to have been chosen in fair, albeit constricted, elections. Surprises in politics were coupled with surprises in society. The country's birthrate had dropped from roughly seven children per household at the time of the revolution to two children by the end of the 1990s. News reports stressed the high enrollment of women in Iranian universities—in some fields they made up 60 percent or more of postgraduate students. How were the winding dynamics of the postrevolutionary political system linked to broad transformations in people's lives? What were the consequences of the developmental project in the Islamic Republic?

THE INCONGRUITY OF WEALTH AND WELFARE

As social scientists examine countries with successful developmental trajectories, they often note the presence of states with high governing capacity. In addition, these states had "embedded" themselves, through some fashion, in a large enough segment of the population to carry out goals of economic and social transformation.[4] Beginning with the Soviet Union, antisystemic developmental states in the twentieth century tended to emerge from governments born in revolutions and steeled in war. Unlike Iran, most were avowedly socialist. Aside from revolutionary cases, developmental states came in many forms over the twentieth century. State leaders emulated policies from other countries and regions, depending on which seemed to be catching up the fastest to wealthy states. Only a handful of countries caught up, but far more countries attempted to do so.

Iran is rarely examined through the lens of the developmental state. After all, one may object, Iran returned to prerevolutionary income levels only two decades after the revolution. Perhaps the 1979 revolution was a barrier to Iran's development. Memories of the old Pahlavi monarchy, presiding over an economic boom in the 1970s, weigh heavily on perceptions of the Islamic Republic today. The political scientist Abbas Milani best summed up this common popular and scholarly view. In a 2008 interview, Milani argued that, compared with Taiwan, South Korea, and Turkey, "the state of [Iran's] economy cannot be compared with the economies of those states. . . . Iran missed an historic opportunity for leaping forward and becoming a developed country of the twenty-first century. This was the main consequence of the revolution. . . . In order to assess the consequences of the revolution, we ought to compare Iran with similar countries in 1975."[5]

Milani is correct in observing that a great leap forward in wealth and income did not materialize under the Islamic Republic. However, measuring developmental success only through wealth levels obscures other important social changes. Some of these nonincome measurements of development, such as increased access to health care, education, and other forms of social welfare, may even act as crucial inputs for future wealth creation.[6] The expansion of nonincome forms of development may also be important for political change. In certain institutional settings, a more literate and healthier population may make more forceful claims on the state.

Economic growth, usually measured by changes in GDP or income per capita, is often conflated with development. Yet this act of conflation substitutes means for ends. Growth can often be a good thing, but the relationship between income and welfare is complex. Some countries, such as parts of Latin America, experienced GDP-per-capita growth along with the widening of inequality in income and welfare outcomes. In other cases, such as parts of East Asia, growth occurred alongside a narrowing of inequality. Although some countries see nonincome-development outcomes such as life expectancy and literacy move upward along with income growth, in other cases these welfare indicators barely change at all. The opposite is also true. Among the large number of middle-income countries outside wealthy North America and Europe, there are places where wealth levels have not changed very much but welfare levels have improved quite dramatically.[7]

As Amartya Sen has indicated, "income is only one variable among many that affect our chances of enjoying life, and some of the other variables are also influenceable by economic policy."[8] Nation-states such as South Korea and city-states such as Singapore, for example, achieved rapid increases in average life expectancy through fast economic growth. For these two economies, the mechanisms linking wealth and welfare improvements were labor-intensive employment, which lowered poverty, and state expenditure, particularly on public health. Other countries, conversely, did not experience rapid economic growth but had very rapid increases in life expectancy. In Costa Rica and pre-1980 China, rapid life-expectancy increases occurred without recourse to rising incomes. Since social services such as primary health care and basic education are relatively inexpensive, these services can be provided by even the poorest states, as long as they have the capacity and motivation to do so.[9]

Instead of solely comparing Iran with countries that leapt forward in wealth levels, we should, as Milani's comment suggests, compare Iran with a wide range of countries. Like the Pahlavi monarchy, many middle-income countries circa 1975 perceived themselves as catching up with wealthy North America and Europe. How many of them made the great leap forward? Table 1 below shows changes in the relative distance in GDP per capita between wealthy member countries in the Organization for Economic Co-operation and Development (OECD) and selected middle-income countries over the past half-century. GDP per capita as a relative percentage of wealthy OECD countries may be a crude relational measurement, but it is how many people perceive their own country's development. It is also how many social scientists examine patterns of global inequality.[10]

Table 1 shows two important trends. First, Iran is not an economic outlier from the broader historical trajectory of the Middle East and North Africa (MENA, for short). Like Iran, most developing MENA countries hit their peak in wealth levels relative to high-income OECD countries in the 1970s and 1980s. The region then went into a precipitous relative decline, which reversed only in the twenty-first century. In the case of Turkey, often compared with Iran, the country has historically been closer to the OECD in relative wealth for most of the last half-century. Even so, Turkey's and Iran's trajectories over the entire period seem far more similar than divergent.

Second, with the exception of South Korea, no large country in the table came anywhere near catching up to the per-capita incomes of wealthy OECD countries. Even with economic growth during the 2000s throughout the former Third World, South Korea is still the developmental outlier, not Iran. This is why so many countries look solely at South Korea—they compare upward to a rare case of relative success. In fact, just as Iran was bestowed miracle-economy status in the 1970s by magazines such as *The Economist*, so were Brazil and Mexico. Latin American countries' paths seem no more illustrious than Iran's mediocre one. Most of the world's middle-income countries, in other words, experienced so-called lost decades and relative wealth stagnation over the past half-century. From each national perspective, many of these countries' populations blame their own governments for not catching

TABLE I   GDP PER CAPITA (FX) OF SELECTED COUNTRIES AS PERCENTAGE OF GDP
PER CAPITA (FX) OF HIGH-INCOME OECD COUNTRIES, 1965–2014

	Year					
	1965	1975	1985	1995	2005	2014
Iran	9.0	13.2	7.7	5.9	8.1	12.5
Egypt	8.2	5.4	6.4	3.8	3.5	7.3
Turkey	19.1	21.3	12.8	11.4	20.7	24.1
Middle East & North Africa	8.6	12.0	13.6	5.0	6.1	9.9
Brazil	13.2	21.6	15.3	18.9	13.9	26.1
Argentina	64.8	38	27.3	29.4	13.9	28.7
Mexico	24.8	27.6	22.7	12.3	23.3	23.7
Venezuela	54.0	46.8	31.1	13.5	16.0	no data
Latin America & Caribbean	23.5	22.5	16.9	14.8	14.2	20.8
China	5.0	3.3	2.7	2.4	5.1	17.4
Indonesia	—	4.5	4.9	4.0	3.7	8.0
South Korea	5.4	11.5	22.2	45.5	51.3	64.1
East Asia & Pacific	4.9	3.7	3.3	3.0	4.7	14.3
India	6.0	2.9	2.7	1.5	2.1	3.6
South Africa	28.2	28.2	20.1	15.3	15.3	14.9
Russia	—	—	—	10.6	15.6	29.2

SOURCE: World Bank Development Indicators (2016), except Central Bank of Iran for Iranian GDP.
Regional categories include only those countries considered "developing" by the World Bank—that is,
below a particular income level.

NOTE: *FX*, converted at exchange-rates; *OECD*, Organisation for Economic Cooperation and Development.

up with Europe and the United States. It is only in the past two decades,
and especially in the 2000s, that middle-income countries have again
experienced economic development that may be perceived as catching
up. The onus for such a generalized outcome of failure in previous decades, since it was so widespread, cannot be attributed solely to the internal political or social environment of each of these countries.[11]

Iran did not experience a spectacular rise in incomes, which would
have meant a great leap forward into the wealthy club of nations. Neither did the rest of the global South. Iran's trajectory may have been
more volatile, but small and reversible shifts should not be mistaken for
large and permanent trends. If Iran's growth trajectory can be characterized at all, it is a middling one among middle-income countries. Yet
from the evidence I just presented, we should begin to think critically

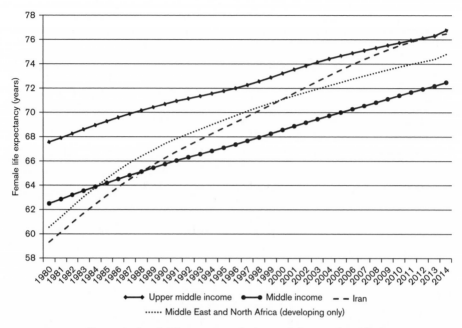

FIGURE I. Changes in female life expectancy for Iran and the rest of Middle Eastern and North African (MENA) developing countries over the past three decades (1980–2014).

about how Iran could have constituted some form of developmental state.

States face constraints on economic development in the world economy. If it were easy to grow at 10 percent per year, then every country would do so. States are less constrained, however, in matters of social policy inside their borders. These include policies on health, education, retirement pensions, labor markets, social insurance, and other enhancements in welfare. The effects of these policies are not always represented in income-measured statistics. For example, a simple welfare indicator often used to capture development outcomes in health is life expectancy. Average life expectancies tend to rise as countries get wealthier. Within middle-income countries, however, there is a wide variation in life-expectancy outcomes. In recent decades, scholars have stressed the importance of improved life expectancy for women as a separate indicator of development.

If we look beyond Iran's economic-growth record to changes in non-income measures of development, a more complex picture emerges. Figure 1 tracks changes in female life expectancy for Iran and the rest of MENA developing countries over the past three decades.

Two trends stand out in figure 1. First, MENA states on the whole have experienced improvements in female life expectancy at a much faster rate over the past three decades than the average improvement of middle-income countries. This is a trend not often noted in popular characterizations of the Middle East. For a variety of reasons, countries in this region are usually not discussed in the growing scholarship on welfare states in the global South. Second, Iran not only experienced commensurate improvements in female life expectancy over the three decades after the revolution, but the country even performed slightly better than the MENA average. Iranians live much longer today than previously, with women living slightly longer on average than men.

The inputs that increase life expectancy, however, are complex to tease out. One could argue that it was the welfare improvements and economic growth of the 1960s and 1970s, experienced under the Pahlavi monarchy before the 1979 revolution, that laid the foundation for subsequent life-expectancy gains. This is partly true, because there is a lag between social-policy implementation and an indicator such as life expectancy. To examine a welfare indicator with less of a time lag, figure 2 shows infant mortality rates in Iran and MENA countries over the past three decades. Since infant mortality measures how many children die within their first year in an entire population, it is a better measurement of welfare policy as it is being implemented instead of a lagged effect of earlier policies.

In figure 2, the same trend for MENA states stands out. The region delivered rapid improvements in infant mortality over the past several decades. For Iran, two more points can be noted. First, it is during the years 1980–96 when the fastest declines in infant mortality occurred in the postrevolutionary period. This was a period of war, economic crisis, and geopolitical isolation for Iran. As table 1 above showed, these are also the same decades in which Iran experienced a rapid decline in GDP per capita as compared with the OECD. In other words, if we just looked to GDP per capita, it might appear that Iran experienced "negative development" or, as other scholars have deemed it, "structural involution."[12] Yet by looking at nonincome measures of development, such as infant mortality, we see development improvements not only equal to or better than other MENA countries but also better than the average performance of middle-income countries as a whole. A second point to note is that, since infant mortality is a more appropriate measure of state welfare policy as it occurs, then something must have

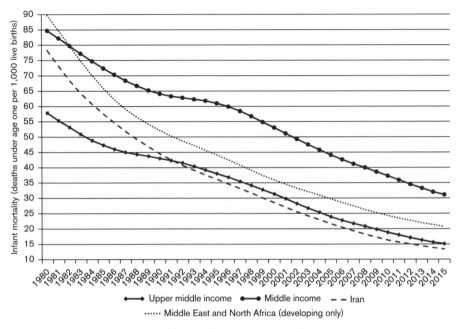

FIGURE 2. Infant mortality rates in Iran and MENA countries over the past three decades (1980–2015).

happened in the Islamic Republic to generate these improved welfare outcomes other than developmental inertia from the Pahlavi era. For certain, general improvements in health technology that spread throughout the Third World had much to do with global declines in infant mortality, as in Iran. But this meant that postrevolutionary Iran contained some system of welfare access that allowed these improvements to be distributed widely throughout the population, even during wartime. These technologies did not simply diffuse into the country to be implemented. In fact, these basic health technologies were largely available during the prerevolutionary period.[13]

Basic education outcomes are another development indicator that can be separated out from growth in income levels. Along with life expectancy and income per capita, adult literacy levels formed a major component of the United Nations Human Development Index when it was introduced, in 1990. Since female literacy usually lags behind male literacy in most of the global South, it is appropriate to look at Iran's performance since the revolution for its female population as an indicator of policy effectiveness. Also, since we want to capture a more direct

TABLE 2   YOUTH FEMALE LITERACY IN IRAN AND SELECTED COUNTRIES,
1975–2012

	Year					
	1975–76	1985–86	1990–91	1996	2005	2012
Iran	42.3	65.6	81.2	90.6	96.7	97.7
Turkey	68.3	86.0	88.4	—[a]	94	98.4
Egypt	38.1	54.0	—	66.9	78.9	86.1
Malaysia	—	86.5	95.2	—	97.2	98.5
		(1980)[b]			(2000)	(2010)

SOURCE: UNESCO statistics.

NOTE: Percentage of females aged 15–24 who were literate.

[a] Em dash (—) indicates when no data are available.

[b] Different benchmark years for Malaysia are shown in parentheses.

impact of state policy in the Islamic Republic, rather than a lagged policy effect from the prerevolutionary era, we can use literacy rates for younger females aged 15–24. In table 2, youth female-literacy levels for Iran since the late 1970s are shown along with those for Turkey, Egypt, and Malaysia.

Relative to Turkey, as table 2 shows, Iran's youth female literacy was lower before the 1979 revolution. A curious thing happened afterwards. As Iran's relative wealth levels experienced a steep decline, the country's female youth-literacy levels caught up with and surpassed those of Turkey during the 2000s. The point of these figures and tables is not to claim Iran as a spectacularly unique welfare state. Instead, given that these trends are largely ignored in studies of contemporary Iran, I show them in order to raise a point about *how* we study the country. Examining the *politics of welfare*—the process of social-policy implementation as well as its social and political effects—can lead us to reassess the consequences of the 1979 revolution as well as state-society relations in Iran.

IRANIAN STATE-SOCIETY RELATIONS IN HISTORICAL PERSPECTIVE

In 2009, I visited Iran to conduct a year-long study of the country's welfare system. My plane landed one day after the June 12 presidential election in which Mahmoud Ahmadinejad was controversially declared the winner in the first round of voting. After highly charged preelection campaigns had led supporters of opposition candidates Mir-Hossein Mousavi and Mehdi Karroubi to believe that they would at least push the election into another round, many skeptical voters did not give credence to the results. Protests shook the city that evening and the next day. Over the next several weeks, Iran experienced the largest public demonstrations since the 1979 revolution. Participants labeled themselves the Green Movement. Millions of Iranians marched in the streets, chanted slogans, made demands on the state, and captivated the attention of the world media.

On my second day in Tehran, I stepped onto the subway and got out at a scheduled demonstration, not knowing what would occur. I was swept up the train-station stairs with thousands of other metro passengers. Emerging into daylight, I saw hundreds of thousands of individuals gathered in a north-central square of the capital. They marched in silence, exhibiting high levels of self-discipline even though the movement was apparently leaderless. In a sense, the protestors were following in the tradition of not just the 1979 revolution but a hundred years of bottom-up protest in Iran that has been relatively peaceful and nonviolent.[14] As the protesters mobilized during the months of June and July, and then demobilized through the fall of 2009 and spring of 2010, I watched the unfolding of what social scientists call the "dynamics of contention."[15] The protests directed a surge of youthful emotional energy at the state's hypocritical public rhetoric about democratic fairness. The demonstrations, initially in response to a perceived fraudulent election, transcended the original demands of the opposition. Protestors drew on and reformulated the symbols and slogans of Iran's 1979 revolutionary repertoire. Nationalist calls for unity emanating from the state were matched with an equally forceful nationalism from below, which questioned the legitimacy of state elites who claimed to act in the national interest. Both sides of the struggle changed tactics in response to new opportunities, appealed to the population for support, and polarized their temperaments in relation to each other.

The effervescence of the 2009 Green Movement in the initial postelection period peaked in a multimillion-person march in Tehran on June 15th. The excitement, however, concealed weaknesses, which soon became apparent. The movement lacked any extensive autonomous organizations that could strategically coordinate a limited number of participants for maximum effect. The rallies also lacked strong connections with provincial towns across Iran, not to mention the countryside. Indeed, as I learned during travels to other provinces over the next year, the 2009 Green Movement was largely a Tehran-based event. This made the 2009 protests quite dissimilar to the 1979 Iranian revolution as well as the subsequent 2011 Egyptian revolution, both of which powerfully connected the provinces with the capital. In addition, while a broad cross-class coalition of individuals participated in the Green Movement at its peak, the core of the movement was located in the country's middle classes. In the face of these initial constraints as well as a repressive response by the state, the mobilizational wave of the Green Movement proved very difficult to maintain. Smaller protests continued to occur throughout the fall, but most original participants disengaged from the movement's public face. In some cases, individuals continued their activism in online form; in others, they returned to the less exciting struggles of daily life in Iran—pursuing jobs, spouses, business opportunities, educational credentials, private spaces of freedom away from a paternalistic state, and intellectual and cultural stimulation.

By the summer of 2010, many who had participated in the Green Movement felt that they had failed to achieve anything of lasting importance. I disagreed with their pessimism. Given the weak cohesion of Iran's political elite, the protests broke the ruling conservative coalition into even more fractured and vulnerable segments. This laid the foundation for the surprise election of Hassan Rouhani in 2013, not to mention subsequent political and diplomatic engagements with the United States. The eruption of extraparliamentary protest onto the streets in 2009 was a symbol and an expression of *social power*—ideological, organizational, and structural. If anything, the demonstrations reiterated broad public demands for social and political change to move the country onto a new, albeit uncertain track.

Another crucial theoretical question came up. Where did these new middle classes come from? As I discuss in the next chapter, most explanations of state-society relations in Iran after the 1979 revolution have relied on static theoretical formulations of the "rentier" state. Analyses of oil-producing states in the developing world stress how welfare is used as a bribe in countries in the Middle East and elsewhere. Yet if Iran was a rentier state both under the Pahlavi monarchy and the postrevolutionary government, why did the social policies that emerged from the two regimes diverge so sharply? Moreover, why did the Islamic Republic create a welfare system that benefited individuals who would go on to form a powerful base of oppositional unrest? Most broadly, what does the politics of welfare in Iran tell us about the consequences of different social policies in the global South?

Though much of the information in this book has only been available in primary-source materials, what follows is not an exhaustive accounting of all welfare organizations in Iran. Instead, this book looks at social change in postrevolutionary Iran by examining the politics of the country's welfare system in historical perspective. Rather than imagining a state totally dominant over society or, conversely, a society completely autonomous from the state, I move past a static, binary set of images. This includes the common view that posits the "charismatic authority" of state elites such as Ayatollah Khomeini or Mahmoud Ahmadinejad as an adequate explanation for the social action of millions of Iranians. Neither ideology nor repression is sufficient to account for the manner in which individuals have organized and acted in the Islamic Republic. To paraphrase Adam Przeworski, Iranian society has neither been a perpetual dupe nor a passive victim but instead has been an active force in transforming the state.[16] We must uncover and reconsider the role of social forces in shaping the Islamic Republic in order to understand the surprising dynamics of the postrevolutionary period.

AN OUTLINE OF THE ARGUMENT

The 1979 revolution and the 1980–88 war produced a state with intense *elite competition*. Unlike most postrevolutionary states, however, the Islamic Republic failed to channel this competition into an enduring single-party apparatus. Even with many internal differences, this political elite shared a common vision for an *antisystemic developmental state*. To survive war and achieve development without foreign assistance, the Islamic Republic's project of state building became necessarily intertwined with a welfare-building project. State elites created and relied upon a set of welfare institutions that channeled the *popular mobilization* of the 1979 revolution and the eight-year war with Iraq into a *warfare-welfare complex*. This broadened the social bases linked to the state while also constraining the capacity to implement technocratic, top-down projects by the political elite during the postwar period. The intertwining of *elite competition* and *popular mobilization* in subsequent decades created pathways of upward status mobility and the expansion of middle-class positions. This was the actual social revolution of the Islamic Republic, underpinning the growing power of middle classes in Iran. This power, with its associated expectations of upward mobility and political representation, was expressed in events such as the 2009 Green Movement.

TABLE 3   A COMPARATIVE TYPOLOGY OF WELFARE-STATE CHARACTERISTICS IN
THE PAHLAVI MONARCHY AND THE ISLAMIC REPUBLIC

| | Characteristic | |
Category	Pahlavi monarchy	Islamic Republic
Elite politics	Narrow Restrictive	Wide Competitive
Social-policy access	Corporatist Exclusionary	Dual-regime Inclusionary
Institutional form	Bureaucratic Limited	Fragmented Overlapping

Comparing welfare systems before and after the 1979 revolution reveals some important differences, highlighted in table 3. Like many authoritarian late-developers, the welfare system constructed by the Pahlavi monarchy from the 1930s to the 1970s took an *exclusionary* and *corporatist* form. Social-policy organizations were *bureaucratic* in structure and orientation but were *limited* in reach to a circumscribed segment of the population. This outcome was due to two factors: first, the *narrow* and *restrictive* quality of elite politics, which revolved around the shah, and second, the type of modernization project adopted by the monarchy for a development strategy.

The Islamic Republic inherited and used the corporatist welfare organizations of the Pahlavi monarchy but also created a second set of postrevolutionary welfare organizations that directly targeted those segments of the population excluded from the previous system—a "martyrs' welfare state." It was more *inclusionary* than the Pahlavi welfare system, but it also was more varied in institutional form.

This resulted in a *dual-welfare regime* of *overlapping* organizations and *fragmented* coverage. In many cases, parallel state organizations overlapped each other's welfare activities. Instead of merging various welfare organizations into a single social-policy apparatus, the state repeatedly proliferated new organizations and new activities for existing organizations. Some of these organizations, such as a primary health-care network implemented in rural villages, were bureaucratic and acquired the "embedded autonomy" that made them effective public bodies for welfare delivery and social transformation. Other organizations were more politicized and served as the vanguards of state building by the Islamic Republic, with the unintended result that the state became dependent on its own welfare organizations for crucial functions of governance. This outcome was due to the interaction between, first, a *wider* and more *competitive* form of elite politics and, second, popular mobilizations from 1979 onward, which pressured state officials to expand, adapt, and upgrade the country's social-welfare compact.

There was one important similarity and one important difference between these two Iranian political regimes. During *both* the Pahlavi monarchy *and* the Islamic Republic, a developmental project by the state facilitated and provoked the mobilization of new social groups. These developmental pushes, common to middle-income states, generated new expectations among the population for upward mobility, changed livelihoods, and changes in the cultural and political order. Moreover, these modernization drives also changed the balance of power in society.

The two political regimes differed, however, on the scale of elite competition and the role of popular mobilization. In the Pahlavi monarchy, a narrow political elite developed an exclusionary social-welfare compact. Although the monarchy attempted to create loyal state cadres from a small professional class, it did not rely on popular mobilization. Instead, expansions of state-welfare policy in the Pahlavi monarchy recurrently came after repressing or countering the threat of left-wing mobilization by oppositional political organizations.

The Islamic Republic, in contrast, formed during a revolutionary upsurge that toppled the previous state. Political elites relied on popular mobilization to embed state organizations deeper into Iranian society as well as to compete with each other for state power. This created an inclusionary social-welfare compact, which expanded over time. It also, however, meant that elite competition and popular mobilization were intertwined processes. From this perspective, the 2009 Green Movement was not the expression of an awakened civil society set against an ossified, backward-looking state. Instead, it was an outcome of the various and conflicting lineages of state-building efforts by the Islamic Republic of Iran and the response to those efforts by newly empowered social classes.

This account provides a more comprehensive understanding of what actually happened in the Islamic Republic. It also reassesses the long-term consequences of welfare politics in middle-income countries. Welfare politics created new social-policy institutions while also generating new social challenges from below, such as the 2009 Green Movement. These consequences hardly came from a religious or Middle Eastern blueprint. The Islamic Republic, like many middle-income states in the world economy over the past century, attempted to use state capacity in order to "catch up" with the wealthy countries of the world. Because of historical circumstances of revolution, war, and lack of foreign assistance, the Islamic Republic relied on welfare making as a main source of capacity building and state making. In the postwar period, political elites launched a developmental project that in many ways mirrored the Pahlavi monarchy's earlier attempt to "catch up" with wealthy countries. As before, this project did not materialize in a great leap forward in relative wealth levels, but it did create, expand, and empower particular groups in society that mobilized from below.

The book proceeds as follows. Chapter 1 offers an overview of the three main theoretical formulations used to analyze politics in the Islamic Republic: totalitarianism, rentierism, and populism. These perspectives, which focus on top-down assertions of state power, lack a conceptual space for observing the roles that social mobilization—both contentious and institutionalized—have played in constraining and directing state action. Theories of welfare-state formation, in contrast, link together elite conflict, social movements, political economy, class structure, and boundary drawing among status groups. Instead of the common conception that welfare policies in semiauthoritarian states—especially oil-producing "rentier" states—act as a bribe in place of the granting of social citizenship, the history of welfare-state formation in Europe and elsewhere illustrates the more general contradictions that occur when states implement and widen social policies. By expanding welfare, the state may be temporarily fortified against social challenge, but it is eventually constrained by its own social contract and can be challenged again by newly empowered social classes.

Chapter 2 examines the politics of welfare policy under the Pahlavi monarchy. Like many middle-income countries in the 1950 and 1960s, the Iranian state constructed an exclusionary form of corporatism predicated on generous social-insurance provisions for a narrow set of the population in the civil-service and industrial sectors, including oil production. These were watered-down versions of more radical welfare reforms that had been introduced during the contentious periods of state making in the 1905–11 constitutional revolution and the Mossadeq government of 1951–53. The Pahlavi monarchy crushed and then copied successive generations of left and liberal opposition movements. After the 1950s, the Pahlavi monarchy embarked on a developmental project that attempted to expand welfare and educational access to some formerly excluded segments of the population. Yet the bureaucratic form of the project, as well as the modernizing vision of a narrow political elite, limited its implementation and access. The revolutionary coalition of 1977–79 combined together the rebellious and newly empowered cadres of the Pahlavi developmental state and the far larger segment of the population excluded from access to the state-welfare system.

Chapter 3 discusses how the aftermath of the 1979 revolution and the subsequent war with Iraq structured a dual-welfare regime in the newly formed Islamic Republic. A parallel set of organizations that overlapped state activities, including welfare, emerged as a result of the struggle between contenders for state power as well as a consequence of social mobilization from below. The victorious political elite of this postrevolutionary state, once their contenders had been thwarted, soon became internally divided on nearly all major questions of state rule, leading to a wider and more competitive structure of elite politics. This elite competition was exacerbated during the exigencies of making war and created numerous spaces for social demands from below to materialize into expanded access to welfare through new and existing social-policy institutions. Welfare expansion also produced pathways for upward social mobility tied to newly created "martyr" status groups. The end result of this first decade of revolution and war was a warfare-welfare complex that the Islamic Republic heavily relied upon for tools of governance. The chapter focuses on the Imam Khomeini Relief Committee (IKRC), a revolutionary organization that politicized its welfare activities as a legitimation strategy by targeting particular strata of the population that had been excluded under the Pahlavi monarchy such as the rural elderly, female-headed households, and the extremely poor. Partly as a result of this organization, absolute poverty in Iran was drastically lowered over the postwar period. Yet the state also became inextricably beholden to IKRC activities as a foundation for the implementation of government policies, because of the competitive struggle between political elites, which prevented any one faction from consolidating and taking over the state apparatus. The welfare organization thus constrained the government's ability to swiftly shift policies after the war.

Chapter 4 considers the most transformational organization of the Iranian welfare state in the Islamic Republic's first two decades—the Primary Health Care (PHC) network in rural villages. The PHC system in Iran came to resemble a "health-developmental state," as technocrats inside the Health Ministry utilized the new policy space created by the 1979 revolution to implement a vast program of rural health-care expansion. This laid the institutional foundation for a state push for family planning as the war ended, which intertwined with social demands from below by women for increased control over family size. The surprising outcome of this policy was the most rapid decline in birthrates in world history—a demographic transition of immense proportions.

Chapter 5 analyzes the developmental push of the Islamic Republic that began in the 1990s under President Akbar Hashemi-Rafsanjani (1989–97) and continued under Mohammad Khatami (1997–2005). This period saw state attempts for a series of liberalizing political and economic reforms, but their full implementation was blocked by the competitive elite structure and broad social constituencies that had been generated during the war period. Nevertheless, social-welfare expansion did continue as the state expanded and added on to the corporatist organizations of pensions and social insurance inherited from the Pahlavi monarchy. In addition to a massive increase in primary and secondary education since the revolution, these policies fomented the expansion and empowerment of a new middle class by the late 1990s, with raised expectations for standards of consumption as well as social and political change. These grievances were partly shaped by the inherent instability of the dual-welfare regime and the explicit status boundaries embedded in social policies.

Chapter 6 returns to the 2009 Green Movement and situates the unexpected mobilizations of that year in the context of the previous thirty years of welfare politics. I discuss the social composition of the protestors and their grievances, as well as the particular repertoires of action that developed throughout the mobilizational wave. This mobilization combined symbols and strategies of nationalism and citizenship that were embedded in the postrevolutionary order, later contributing to the surprise election in 2013 of Hassan Rouhani. From this still-unsettled political shift, two trajectories of state-society relations in the Islamic Republic are possible—a return to the exclusionary welfare politics of the Pahlavi period or an expansion toward a more universal social citizenship. I conclude the study by considering the contradictions that development and social policy present to middle-income countries in the world economy and the resulting forms of politics that we are likely to experience in the coming decades of the twenty-first century.

METHODS AND MATERIALS

Because of a host of geopolitical and ideological reasons, Iran's welfare system has never been systematically analyzed in depth, including by scholars inside the country. My book relies on research conducted during several field trips to Iran over the period 2006–11, including a twelve-month period of fieldwork during 2009–10. Although I discuss the formation of social policy during the first half of the twentieth century, I focus primarily on the post-1953 period during the Pahlavi monarchy in order to generate a plausible comparison between two successive developmental states within the country's history. Of course, pre- and post-1979 Iran are not two independent cases. Instead, as the sociologist Jeffrey Haydu advocates in the historical analysis of a single country, I use these two successive welfare regimes to examine different state approaches to an analogous set of developmental problems.[17]

Because of the limitations of secondary scholarship, I collected a wide array of primary data in order to construct the historical narrative: interviews with current and former government bureaucrats from labor, welfare, and housing ministries; interviews with social-policy administrators in welfare organizations such as the IKRC, the village health-care network, and the Social Security Organization; archival research in government and university libraries in Iran; interviews with Iranian social scientists; newspaper and journal articles in Persian on issues of welfare and economic policy; hundreds of conversations with individuals in different occupations and social strata about their experiences with the welfare system; participant observation of the 2009 Green Movement; and visits to welfare offices in multiple provinces in both urban and rural areas. For the latter, I spent time outside Tehran for the purpose of identifying patterns and variations in welfare policy in provinces other than the capital. This included a month-long stay in the southwest province of Khuzestan and a month-long stay in the northern province of East Azerbaijan. This provincial fieldwork delivered two insights. First, given that there is little research on contemporary politics and social structure in provinces outside Tehran, I could barely scratch the surface with my visits and explorations. Second, even with this realization, or arguably because of it, I recognized the importance of provincial politics and social structure on the country. This is reflected in the analysis of state-society relations in the book. I hope that this provokes future research to fill the large gaps left from my own efforts.

A note on the use of interviews is warranted. Given the politicization of research and fieldwork that still occurs in Iran, I informed all interviewees that any statements or answers would remain anonymous. It is a limitation on the presentation of data, but without such fieldwork, this book would be impossible. As Ching Kwan Lee wrote in her deeply researched ethnography of worker unrest in China, "either we remain committed to the scholarly project and try the best we can to overcome political and practical hurdles, or we give up on the possibility of research altogether."[18]

CHAPTER I

Can an Oil State Be a Welfare State?

I will consider it a great advantage when we have 700,000 small pensioners drawing their annuities from the State, especially if they belong to those classes who otherwise do not have much to lose by an upheaval and erroneously believe they can actually gain much by it.

—Otto von Bismarck, in a speech to the Reichstag, 1889

Citizens do not give up making demands for representation or for better government simply because they are not taxed.

—Dirk Vandewalle

The Iranian journalist Abbās Abdi once half-joked that if he had religious authority, he would issue a fatwa declaring oil as harmful as alcohol.[1] Abdi expressed a view held well beyond Iranian intellectuals. A large literature in social science focuses on the negative effects of oil extraction for democratization and development. In this view, oil states are not supposed to be welfare states.

Part of the argument lies in the definition of a "welfare" state as contrasted with "rentier" states. Modern welfare states provide social protection through redistributing a portion of the resources procured by taxing the activities of the domestic economy. Conversely, states with external rent revenues, such as the extraction and sale of oil, distribute windfall resources rather than taxes. According to this perspective, people who live in a rentier economy view these distributed resources as gifts or handouts from a ruling elite, rather than a tax on their own labor and production. Individuals perceive social benefits as a capricious reward from their leaders, not a social right linked to citizenship. This has consequences, in turn, for state-society relations. Individuals and groups expend effort struggling over the distribution of rent-derived resources, instead of independently engaging in productive economic activities. This dependence on the state limits the formation of social classes with autonomous power, whether capitalist or working classes. States that accrue sufficient revenue through nontax sources do not need to elicit consent or engage in bargaining with subject-citizens for the purpose of additional revenue extraction. Instead of taxpayers giving up material resources from below in exchange for collective public goods, including social-welfare policy, rentier states allocate material resources from above in exchange for patrimonial allegiance. The absence of taxation results in the absence of a social compact, and a perverse and stabilizing "authoritarian bargain" is installed, whereby social policy acts as a bribe for political obedience. The long-term effects of rentier income thus distort the political economy of a country away from the path of democratization and capitalist development experienced in wealthy regions of the world economy.[2]

This conception of welfare policy is quite common in Iran, not just among journalists but also in decades of scholarship. Welfare policy tends to be presented as a hegemonic project of ideological exhortation coupled with a crass political machine wherein social policy is narrowly targeted at poorer strata to secure support or, at least, compliance. Afsaneh Najmabadi explicitly contrasted the welfare benefits of the Pahlavi monarchy in the 1970s with postwar European welfare states.[3] In Europe, taxation of citizens provided the "supply" while pressure from working-class organizations furnished the "demand" for state-provided social welfare. In Iran, conversely, welfare benefits derived from oil extraction were handed out by a state under little pressure from organized labor. Accordingly, state welfare in Iran was charity, not social contract—more like the poor laws of seventeenth- and eighteenth-century Europe or the court largesse of premodern empires. For the Islamic Republic, the sociologist Ali Rezā Alavi-Tabār argued that the "pathological" characteristics of the state are derived from its "rentier-based" nature.[4] One can hardly open a newspaper in Iran without a mention of rentier-state theory. A 2007 headline in the newspaper *Mardom-Sālāri* (Democracy), for instance, proclaimed "The Rentier-Based Government Is the Reason for Poverty and Inflation."[5] Without much empirical evidence, assessments of contemporary Iran assume that oil rents are the "supply" and the requirements of authoritarian control are the "demand" that produces state-welfare policy.[6] The social and political determinants of these policies and their consequences are either ignored or subsumed under theoretical formulations associated with the rentier state. This argument would make sense if all states formed in similar ways and proceeded along similar paths of development. It would also make sense if the origins of European welfare states were as uniform as the rentier paradigm portrays them. In reality, state formation has varied quite widely over time and place, including the formation of welfare states. As a result, we can use theories of welfare-state formation to reframe state-society relations in a way that more thoroughly accounts for postrevolutionary social change in Iran.

MIXING OIL AND ISLAM

If the 1979 revolution in Iran had one effect on the study of revolutions, it was the reintroduction of the role of ideas in shaping large-scale social change.[7] The manifestation of mass politics mixed with religious symbolism convinced some scholars that revolutions could indeed be "made," as opposed to the prevailing structuralist interpretation of revolutions in the late 1970s.[8] Indeed, the Islamic Republic's leaders claimed their ideals embodied a theoretical and practical rejection of political categories derived from Western history.[9] As a result, the ideological content of Shi'i political Islam is often added on to the rentier-state thesis to explain political and social characteristics of postrevolutionary Iran.

With ideas from political Islam supercharged via revenue from oil rents, some scholars have portrayed state-society relations in Iran as totalitarian. In this view, the state can afford to implement an ideologically coherent program of social engineering to create a revolutionary social order. Totalitarian arguments are highly voluntarist explanations of social change, since they assume that a state can remake society through the will to imagine a new world and whatever means it takes to achieve it. The concept of totalitarianism itself, whether used to explain varieties of fascism or communism, has been repeatedly challenged by historians and social scientists as problematic.[10] As Charles King noted, "the totalitarian model of communist politics was never really much of a model at all. It did not explain (nor, to be fair, did its adherents claim to explain) precisely how the system held together, since it was assumed that brute force was the key variable."[11] Totalitarian states were believed to possess extraordinary state capacities to carry out their utopian visions. Upon examination, however, perceptions of excessive levels of authoritarian power were often based more on propaganda from these states (as well as their enemies) than from an analysis of the actual state-society relations that manifested.[12] As Jan-Werner Müller has pointed out, in the case of the Mussolini regime in Italy, wherein intellectuals originally coined the term *totalitaria* to describe the new state, the Fascist party engaged in "far too many compromises . . . even to come close to achieving 'proper' totalitarianism."[13]

Rather than a totalitarian political order, a more persuasive argument about the Islamic Republic is that the state fosters a mix of Iranian nationalism, Shi'i political Islam, and anti-Western sentiment that forms a core ideology, which resonates with particular social groups. This ideological mix either generates bases of support within active defenders of the state's agenda and representative institutions, or at least creates tacit acceptance of the state as legitimately acting in the majority of the population's interest. Here we tread upon the large arena of social science that links normative ideas and political ideologies with social movements and state rule.[14] In the case of Iran, scholars have devoted substantial attention to the antecedents and components of the ideas, discourses, and slogans of the revolutionary period.[15] The difficulty lies, however, in illustrating how a particular set of ideas not only allowed for the consolidation of a postrevolutionary state but also how that state utilized a coherent set of ideas to maintain and expand its institutional structures over several decades. This is something no scholar has seriously attempted for Iran, perhaps wisely. The ideational mix that has emanated from Iran's ruling elites and their factions over the past three decades is hardly uniform or consistent. Even if it had been, the social translation of ideas into lasting institutions—in Iran's case, the routinization of a revolutionary charismatic authority that supposedly wielded these ideas—is mediated by other intervening factors, such as preexisting social structure, oppositional groups outside the state, position in the world economy, or the struggles for power within the revolutionary elites themselves.[16] As Fred Halliday and Hamza Alavi noted with regard to the Middle East, caution is warranted when assigning historical outcomes to ideological currents: "What specific terms or symbols mean is a contingent matter in the sense that it is decided by specific situations and political forces. Ideologies are not infinitely flexible . . . , [but] they are sufficiently ductile to allow very different interpretations and uses."[17] To be sure, debates over economic and social policy in postrevolutionary Iran partly relied on Islamic jurisprudence. As I show in subsequent chapters, however, these debates were "ductile" to a high degree because of the pressures of elite competition and popular mobilization on state institutions.

RENTIERIST PARADIGMS

Many scholars who disregard ideological or religious explanations tend to prefer a rentier-based argument. When asking the question, "Why are there no Arab democracies?" for example, Larry Diamond dismisses religious-cultural explanations, instead opting for the "structural . . . ways in which oil distorts the state, the market, the class structure, and the entire incentive structure."[18] Diamond's argument recalled the original formulation of the rentier state by Hossein Mahdavy, an Iranian social scientist. Mahdavy resurrected the concept of economic rent from classical political economy in order to analyze the Islamic Republic's predecessor, the Pahlavi monarchy. He argued that the *source* of economic resources affects the potential for economic growth as well as democratization. Specifically, reliance by a state on external rents, as opposed to taxing the "productive" profits and wages of domestic economic activities such as industrial manufacturing or agriculture, distorts the state's investment patterns toward imports and consumption, and away from capital formation and labor-absorbing manufacturing.[19] The rentier state "acquires an independence from the people seldom found in other countries," and the state's ability to distribute these rents without sanction or powerful opposing interest groups increases its authoritarian tendencies.[20] Mahdavy's analysis of Pahlavi Iran spawned a large theoretical enterprise on the negative repercussions of rentier states more generally.

The historian Homa Katouzian also put forth a related argument prior to the 1979 revolution. Modern states garner revenues from taxing an independent productive base of capital and labor. In rentier states, he claimed, social classes are dependent on the state for employment, capital, and welfare.[21] The state expends resources to reproduce its own bureaucratic and military apparatus, co-opt potential opposition groups into submissive clients, and emphasize consumption among a concentrated elite at the expense of investment. As subsequent scholars argued, rentier states were the antithesis of Max Weber's Protestant ethic.[22] These governments extract and allocate instead of produce and accumulate. Not only do political elites in a rentier state feel less beholden to the citizenry because of the ability to obtain windfall revenue from the world market, but citizens, in turn, are also forced into "rent-seeking" behavior in order to improve their livelihoods.[23] This can lead to the development of a rentier "ethics" or "mentality" among the population, a passive set of norms of fealty toward networks of patronage in lieu of a civic ethics of political participation. If the 1776 American Revolution's slogan was "No Taxation without Representation," then the ideal rentier state embodies its antidemocratic opposite: no taxation necessary; therefore, no pressure for political representation follows.[24] The original rentierist paradigm generated an conceptual spectrum that clusters productive, accountable, and efficient states (along with autonomous civil societies) on one end and extractive, allocative, and corrupt states (along with dominated civil societies) on the other.[25]

Influenced by these ideas, it is common to hear Iranians proclaim their nation was "cursed" with oil. The resource curse not only invites foreign meddling but also fosters a corrupt "rent-seeking economy" that generates and reproduces a class who live off of the state. As with the Pahlavi monarchy, accusing the state of fostering a "dependent" citizenry runs throughout the Islamic Republic's own political history. The revolutionary radicals of the 1980s claimed it of the Pahlavis; the technocrats under Akbar Hashemi-Rafsanjani in the 1990s labeled it of the war economy; the liberal reformists around Mohammad Khatami assigned it to the unaccountable institutions of government run by conservative elites; and Mahmoud Ahmadinejad turned the term against his liberal predecessors in the 2000s.[26] Many Iranians repeat the assertion that the government "buys off the poor," or that there is a class of "dependents" on the state who are the sole group benefiting from oil rents. This allegation runs into a substantive problem, common to countries with fragmented welfare systems.[27] No matter the social class or the status group of the individual, most Iranians tend to state that *another* social class or status group is benefiting more from state social policies, and not their own. Moreover, Iranian history stubbornly does not pay heed to rentier-state theory. The two decades in which unprecedented allocation of oil revenues toward social-welfare programs took place in Iran—the 1970s and the 2000s—ended with the two most contentious mobilizational upsurges in the country's modern history: the 1979 revolution and the 2009 postelection Green Movement. If welfare is a bribe by the state, then it is not a very dependable one.

This first generation of rentier-state theory was widely criticized by social scientists.[28] Cross-national studies called into question the statistical associations linking rentier states with weaker economic growth and increased authoritarianism.[29] As economic historians have noted, the presence of state-generated rents can be crucial for fostering economic development.[30] Rent, defined as the income derived from an economic activity that exceeds whatever income that activity would derive in a free market with full competition, is not a throwback or a developmental impediment in the history of capitalism. Indeed, as the economist Joseph Schumpeter contended, rents—the promises of superprofits that draw entrepreneurs from one activity to another—are what make capitalism so spectacularly creative as well as destructive.[31] All successful capitalist states are, in some manner and at some times, rentier states.[32] Rent-seeking practices were not absent for capitalist development before the twentieth century in the United States and Europe. Instead, such states regularly engaged in and promoted rent creation for their domestic industries at the expense of foreign competitors.[33]

Rentier-state theorists counter that "good" sources of rents derive from industrial production, whereas "bad" sources derive from commodity production. Yet, just as there is wide variation in political outcomes between states that draw revenues from industrial production, there is equally wide variation of political outcomes for states that draw revenues from commodity production. If oil rents condition state formation in Nigeria, then they also condition state formation in Norway.[34] As Timothy Mitchell points out, "most of those who write about the question of the 'rentier state' or the 'oil curse' . . . have little to say about the nature of oil and how it is produced, distributed, and used."[35]

More recent appraisals of rentierist theory have consequently opened up the black box of rentier states to examine variations between different elite coalitions and social compacts. In the Middle East, Kiren Chaudhry showed how the oil exporters of Saudi Arabia and Yemen, even while facing similar pressures and opportunities from the world economy, took different strategies of industrialization and liberalization, based on differing lineages of state and class formation.[36] David Waldner argued that Turkey and Syria, even though only the latter was a rentier state in the 1970s, both failed to forge successful developmental states because of high levels of elite conflict, which forced the state to incorporate large cross-class coalitions.[37] Michael Herb examined oil-rich Middle Eastern monarchies and determined that their chances for breakdown or stability rested on internal elite networks, not dependence on oil revenues.[38] Lastly, in the case of Saudi Arabia, Steffan Hertog argued that the supposedly powerful autonomy of rentier states protected from their own societies led to bureaucratic and institutional fragmentation within only two generations of rule.[39] This occurred even while the Saudi state created profitable and well-managed state-owned enterprises resembling "islands of efficiency" that "defy the resource curse."[40] In sum, as Gwenn Okruhlik puts it, rentier theory, as it is usually applied in the Middle East, is a political economy that ignores the politics.[41]

In response to critics, a second generation of rentier theory has produced a more limited set of claims for the resource curse. Oil rents are unfavorable only when received by unaccountably authoritarian institutions and during selected time periods when commodity prices are high.[42] Still, the key problem of rentierist theory remains. State institutions are not endogenous to oil rents. If access to oil rents structures state actions, then changes in oil revenues should correspond with changes in state actions. As Chaudhry noted about the Saudi kingdom, however, "the extent to which the market undercuts or invigorates the political economy of ascription [i.e., how state networks function in the system of rule] depends on the organization and composition of the institutions that govern the economy."[43] In the case of Iran, we cannot explain shifts in economic and social policies of the state by looking to changes in world oil prices. For instance, in the late 1990s, when global oil prices neared an historical low, the Islamic Republic under President Mohammad Khatami increased the budgets for welfare agencies such as the Social Security Organization and the Imam Khomeini Relief Committee. At the same time, the Khatami government cut back on most other state expenditures. Conversely, during record-high oil prices between 2007 and 2011, the government under Mahmoud Ahmadinejad attempted to remove subsidies for energy and basic goods, even while it was increasing expenditures on development projects and infrastructure.

Ever since Mahdavy, the argument at the heart of rentier-state theory has been a model that holds the taxation-based fiscal compact as an essential mechanism of political democratization. As the political scientist Victor Menaldo has argued, however, "it is not axiomatic that the key to democratic government is actually a fiscal compact forged between the ruler and the ruled."[44] Autocratic governments from Bismarck's Germany to Chiang Kai-Shek's Taiwan have successfully taxed elites and masses under a variety of political coalitions. Those groups who are taxed do not always push for democratization, nor can they overcome collective-action problems simply through the mechanism of being taxed by the state. Conversely, Menaldo lists states that have democratized "through mechanisms other than the taxation-representation nexus." In Mexico, with oil as a major state revenue, "rivalry between enfranchised and disenfranchised groups induce[d] democratization from below." In Chile during the nineteenth century, when the state profited mightily from nitrate exports, a split in the economic elite forced each faction to extend suffrage "strategically to advance its interest against rival elites." In Colombia, with both oil and coffee production, "political elites split and agree[d] to democratize in order to avoid violence." In gas-rich Trinidad and Tobago, elites pursued democratization when public goods delivered more value than patronage politics.[45]

These insights are absent from contemporary discussions about Iran. Does oil make the state stronger, or weaker? Does it make Iranian society more passive, or less passive? Does it increase the size of government, and if so, relative to what ideal middle-income country? Rentierist theories of Iran poorly account for social change, including who protests, who does not, and why. As the political scientists David Waldner and Benjamin Smith underscore, there is a need "to embed resource-rich states in broader approaches to state-building." Instead of "focusing on the subset of resource-abundant countries," they argue, we should develop "more encompassing theories of state formation."[46] This applies to Middle Eastern states more generally. As the historian Roger Owen advised, we should move away "from the idea that the societies of the region exhibit a distinctive form of political, social and religious behavior."[47] As I argue below, therefore, a more fruitful course is envisioning Iran as a middle-income country in the former Third World. Iran's experiences have been subject to many of the same historical processes that other non-European states underwent.[48] State formation in Iran over the past century exhibited characteristics of centralized bureaucratic rule as well as personalistic power networks.[49] For a more encompassing view, we need to account for what conditioned the particular forms of political rule as well as the institutions through which state-society relations operate.

BEYOND POPULISM

As an alternative to rentierist accounts, postrevolutionary Iran is often analyzed as a populist state. The portrayal exists in Iranian culture, as for example in the tradition of *luti bāzi*—the exploits of lumpen bandits who are folk heroes and villains in the country's historiography. Along these lines, the sociologist Majid Mohammadi argued that the Islamic Republic was a "thug-ocracy," whereby the state organized "a rootless and obedient class" to protect the clerical elite and their supporters.[50] In more systematic fashion, Hossein Bashiriyeh, perhaps the most influential political scientist in postrevolutionary Iran, argued that the radical clerical faction of the 1979 revolutionary coalition under Khomeini knew, unlike the moderate liberal faction who filled the posts of the provisional government, that "any attempt to establish a stable domination would require the articulation of the pressures of the lower classes."[51] As a result, the elite in the Islamic Republic spend state resources to mobilize lower classes' support against foreign or domestic oppositional groups that challenge the government.

There is a tension, however, in populist accounts of Iran. One group of scholars argues that the core of Iranian politics operates through personalistic networks of patrons and clients, or, more directly, corrupt officials and their cronies in bazaars, banks, industrial conglomerates, nonstate foundations, and military organizations.[52] To its credit, this neopatrimonial account shifts the analytical focus away from the *source* of the state's revenues, such as oil, and attempts to examine what the state *does with* its revenues. Ever since the sociologist Robert Merton studied welfare services provided by large political machines in U.S. cities, this has been a preferable approach over the rentier thesis. As Merton wrote, "it is important to note not only that aid *is* provided but *the manner in which it is provided.*"[53]

The problem with neopatrimonial accounts, however, is the inability to explain changing institutional patterns wherein state resources are distributed. Nor can they explain electoral dynamics in Iran, which repeatedly upended these networks and reordered elite political coalitions within the Islamic Republic. When surprising change happens in Iran, as it often does, the concept of last resort is populism. Since the word is used in a variety of political contexts around the world, however, the concept of populism is nebulous. As Eric Taggart explained, populism has "an essentially chameleonic quality," because "it is *always* partially constituted by aspects of the environment in which it finds itself."[54] There is a rump definition of populism: "The political mobilization of mass constituencies by leaders who challenge established elites."[55] However, this minimalist definition is of little help in understanding the political institutions that emerge from popular challenges.[56]

As Kenneth Roberts mapped out for Latin America, there are four competing conceptualizations of populism: a sociological perspective, which identifies populism as a coalition between an elite fraction and multiple social classes that occurs in early stages of industrialization; an economic perspective that sees populism as fiscal largesse and expansionist or redistributionist policies undertaken to placate social desires for mass consumption; an ideological perspective that links it to a discourse of conflict between "the people" and "the powerful"; and a political-institutional perspective, which associates populism with mechanisms of top-down political mobilization by personalistic leaders that undermine or circumvent existing institutional forms of political mediation.[57] Eric Weyland contended the concept had been stretched to fit too many cases and attempted to narrow the definition to one of strategy: populism is to be seen when leaders base their rule on considerable but fluid and noninstitutionalized support from unorganized masses.[58] In contrast to populist strategy, two other alternatives exist. The first is neopatrimonialism, defined by rulers establishing informal ties with narrow social groups to create a base of support. The second is defined by formal political parties ruling through organized ties to corporate bodies such as labor unions or rural farmer associations. After much conceptual wrangling, however, Weyland and Roberts both come to the same conclusion: populism is not a permanent form of governance at all. It is a method of rule that "tends to be transitory," which "either fails or, if successful, transcends itself . . . into a different type of rule that rests on nonpopulist strategies."[59]

In the Middle East, the concept of populism has a long pedigree. Populism was named as one of the founding principles of Kemalism in Turkey. Arab Republics, from Iraq and Egypt to Syria and Libya, also used the word to distinguish their economic policies as part of an "Arab" socialism distinct from the Soviet model. Scholars portrayed the rule of Middle Eastern states during decades from the 1930s to the 1960s as an "authoritarian populism" homologous to Latin American states in the same era. After all, both regions generated import-substitution strategies of economic development, corporatist bodies for formal workers and peasants, agrarian reforms, and social benefits directed at an expanded public sector. In addition, during the 1970s scholars noticed that these Middle Eastern states, as was also occurring in Latin America, were transforming such populist-authoritarian forms of rule into bureaucratic-authoritarian ones as their bases of support contracted.[60]

In this scholarship, unlike the process-based analysis of the concept of populism applied in Latin American contexts, the main use of populism for Middle Eastern states centers around a specific, fixed social compact between state and society.[61] Populism, as it is generally applied in Middle East studies, reflects an earlier sociological conception whereby populism is defined as a particular "stage" of development in the Third World that becomes untenable in an age of globalized capital flows and post–Cold War politics. Not coincidentally, while the term "populism" had a positive connotation in that earlier era of Middle East state building, it now is used negatively, as a critique of contemporary politics as antidemocratic and illiberal.[62] Middle Eastern states are largely defined by what they are not. Unlike Latin American accounts, then, the generalized use of populism as an explanatory concept for Middle Eastern states, Iran included, is stuck with accounts that rely on an ersatz modernization theory of successive development stages.

Populism may describe a temporal mechanism, then, but it cannot carry the entire theoretical burden of explaining political and social outcomes in postrevolutionary Iran. Populism best characterizes moments of political struggle during which individuals and groups attempt to reorder elite structures and state-society ties. We should not throw out the concept of populism, therefore; but we need to situate it within a broader framework.[63] Although patterns of populist mobilization are "influenced but not determined by underlying structural and institutional conditions," these mobilizational "moments" can realign elite coalitions as shifts in social power force rulers to utilize alternative strategies of governance.[64] By conceiving of populism as a mobilizational moment, instead of a stage of political development or an institutionalized form of governance, we can analyze state-society relations without falling into the trap of modernization theory, which assumes neopatrimonial politics are a traditional and aberrant flip side to efficient and modern bureaucratic states. Jeffrey Winters reframes this social mechanism as "mobilizational power," whereby mass mobilizations sustained by "draining commitments of personal time and energy" through "horizontal and personal networks" can upend established elite networks of power. Mobilizational power, although difficult to sustain and rare in occurrence, can "trump" elite sources of social power. These upsurges can be "unpredictable and devastating to oligarchic and elite interests."[65] In this book, I move away from presenting populism as a stable system of rule. Instead, I examine the particular forms of welfare organizations that emerge from moments of popular mobilization that challenge, constrain, exploit, or overturn elite networks.

THE WELFARE STATE AS SOCIOLOGICAL LENS

Using the term "welfare state" to understand contemporary Iran requires us to ask a prior question. Why do welfare states exist anywhere? In the absence of state-created social-welfare policies, there are often alternatives. These lie in the sphere either of the market or of the household. In addition to state intervention in labor markets, tax policies, insurance funds, and health programs, individuals can attempt to mitigate social risks through wage income, private savings, landholdings, labor sharing, mutual-aid societies, or family assistance. Nonstate forms of welfare are not necessarily traditional in form, since the unraveling of state-welfare compacts can produce new networks of mutual aid and social assistance.[66] Yet the "great transformation" of the nineteenth century was the increasing penetration of market commodification into daily life. This increased the insecurities that individuals experienced as their livelihoods were disembedded from previous social ties. The "double movement" that Karl Polanyi described, whereby the state is compelled to reregulate the market and decommodify the reproduction of society, is not just a theorization of the limits of laissez-faire capitalism.[67] It is also a particular recounting of the origins of the welfare state.

For many early theorists who explained the rise of the welfare state, industrialization itself required governments to more fully intervene in the regulation and protection of social life. Even though the words *Sozialstaat* and *Sozialpolitik* had appeared in Germany by the mid-nineteenth century, the term "welfare state" came into use only in Britain in the late 1930s, partly as a propagandistic contrast to Nazi Germany's "warfare state."[68] Nevertheless, the British welfare state, especially its design under the 1942 Beveridge plan, was assumed to be a natural outcome of the long development of capitalism in the United Kingdom as well as an archetype that other states would eventually emulate as their own economies industrialized. Scholars argued that the welfare state did not simply arise from the need for states to ameliorate the impact of markets. Rather, it was as much an outcome of the process of modernization as was the factory or the wageworker. Changes in demography, urban structure, and technology within a functionally differentiating society, such as Emile Durkheim described in France, were eroding the traditional institutions of self-protection via family and community.[69] In response, the welfare state in modern Europe acted to encourage new communal bonds of solidarity. Moreover, by raising average levels of consumption and limiting the pendulum swings of economic boom and bust, as John Maynard Keynes stressed, the welfare state contributed to the taming of capitalism.

T.H. Marshall theorized the welfare state as the final stage in the extension of citizenship rights as states and capitalism grew in tandem, a process of "gradual addition of new rights to a status that already existed."[70] The classes and conflicts born out of capitalism produced civil rights of property protection and legal contract in the seventeenth and eighteenth centuries, political rights of suffrage and representation in the nineteenth century, and social rights that moved from ameliorating poverty toward addressing the "whole pattern of inequality" in the early twentieth century. Marshall realized that capitalism was in tension with industrial society, since it produces inequality as well as the demand for egalitarianism. Yet he believed that the welfare state could balance the need for social justice with the need for economic growth.[71]

In the aftermath of global unrest during the late 1960s, a subsequent generation of scholars critiqued the focus on industrialization as a general cause of welfare-state formation. Variation in welfare policies between European states and the timing of policy introduction called into question a simple, linear trajectory of welfare-state formation and democratic development. In contrast to Marshall's pattern, for instance, Germany implemented the world's first health-insurance program in 1883, followed by old-age pensions in 1889. Otto von Bismarck's government strategically granted these social rights to undermine and sidestep the demand for political rights in an absolutist state. Furthermore, when scholars looked at the agents who forced the state to put social polices into practice, they found that collective organization and action on the part of different social classes mattered for determining policy outcomes. Labor unions and labor-linked parties pushed for state intervention in employment laws, extending pensions, and fiscal redistribution. Business groups demanded to pay less for social provisions, limit their required coverage of workers, and free up the ability to invest for profit. Uprisings among the rural dispossessed or the urban poor compelled states to consider replacing traditional poorhouse systems of charity with less punitive programs. State policies were not determined by the needs of industrialization and capitalism, scholars argued. Instead, states were forced to enact social policies because of the growing power of social classes and their disruptive forms of popular mobilization.[72]

A Marxist spin on Marshall's noted tension in twentieth-century capitalism emphasized the contradictions emerging within welfare states. James O'Connor argued that capitalist states need to foster both accumulation and legitimization, but pursuit of one goal inevitably undermines the other.[73] Welfare policies in the form of education, health insurance, and pensions socialize the costs of reproduction of the labor force and "pacify and control" the surplus population not in the labor force. But private capitalists, who can use their power to limit their contributions to the state's revenues, appropriate the profits gained under this newly legitimated system. Over time, this creates a "structural gap" between the state's requirements for legitimation and its ability to foster accumulation.

Claus Offe went even further, arguing that while the welfare state had operated as a temporary solution to class conflict, it undermined the basis for the continued profitability of the economy as welfare policies further increased the relative power of workers. However, the removal of the welfare state would be equally disruptive to capitalism, given that reproduction of the labor force was no longer possible along nineteenth-century laissez-faire lines. For Offe, "while capitalism cannot coexist with the welfare state, neither can it exist without the welfare state."[74] The Marxian critique of the welfare state theorized social policy as fundamentally Janus-faced. Welfare policies were an attempt by the state to co-opt working classes and preempt their further mobilization. Yet they also represented a long string of victories for popular movements that had been secured through self-conscious struggle.

Both the "pluralist-industrial" model of this first generation of scholars and the Marxian model, which held that the state acted largely in the long-term interests of capitalist power, entertained certain assumptions about actors and their interests. If we relax these assumptions, as Walter Korpi argued, studying the welfare state becomes a method to analyze the "power resources" held by different actors in society.[75] The processes by which welfare institutions are created, function, and change can reflect this distribution of power. Whereas social class is an important cleavage through which power is differentially distributed, other lines of cleavage, corresponding to market access or status distinction, can equally generate uneven power resources. Institutions do not arise solely because of functional requirements of governance, or needs for capitalist regulation, but are also a result of compromises and settlements between different social groups.

Looking back on Europe itself, the assumed linear relationship between democratic rights and social-welfare expansion needed rethinking. As Gosta Esping-Anderson noted:[76]

> When it holds that welfare states are more likely to develop the more democratic rights are extended, the [democracy] thesis confronts the historical oddity that the first major welfare-state initiatives occurred prior to democracy and were powerfully motivated by the desire to arrest its realization.

This was certainly the case in France under Napoleon III, in Germany under Bismarck, and in Austria under von Taaffe. Conversely, welfare-state development was most retarded where democracy arrived early, such as in the United States, Australia, and Switzerland.

Esping-Anderson focused less on social expenditure or linear paths of development and instead analyzed how welfare states actively shape the social order by decommodifying daily life. This was defined by the "degree to which individuals, or families, can uphold a socially acceptable standard of living independently of market production."[77] Esping-Anderson later complemented this with the concept of defamilialization, which "unburden[s] the household and diminish[es] individuals' welfare dependence on kinship."[78] Altogether, this power-resources paradigm is a conflictual model of welfare-state formation that examines the institutional patterning of social policy as outcomes of "societal bargaining." These outcomes may not necessarily be contradictory, as in a Marxian reading, but they do reflect struggles of power that are subject to change in the future.

Esping-Anderson's historical sociology of the welfare state identified the structure of political coalitions and conflict as the key to understanding welfare-regime formation. A main determinant of the type of emergent welfare state was whether the rural class was part of the ruling coalition that first implemented major social policies. In Scandinavian countries in the early twentieth century, small land-tenure farmers allied with urban labor parties to produce full-employment welfare states that also generated high subsidies for farming. On the European continent, rural capitalists' activities were capital-intensive and thus allied with conservative parties against the rising threat of labor. The social-insurance model of the "Bismarckian" or corporatist welfare state was "explicitly a form of class politics" that sought to consolidate the divisions among the working class through status distinctions via occupational groupings. In the United States, the New Deal contained the promise of universalizing access to social benefits, but the power of Southern rural capitalists blocked its main tenets.[79]

Even with these insights, the power-resources model had some rough edges. State-welfare policy often overlays onto uneven gender-power relations in the workplace and household, and can exacerbate or ameliorate power imbalances. Decommodification of male workers' labor in the factory benefited and relied not only upon state-provided pension and health benefits but also on already-decommodified activities of female labor in the household.[80] States themselves were not uniform entities but complex institutions that could contain internal "veto points," which checked the implementation of welfare policies regard-less of the power of business or labor coalitions.[81] The provision of welfare by nonstate actors continued apace with the rise of welfare states, often acting as third "pillars" and filling in the mix of social policy available in any country.[82] Religious norms proved to be impor-tant not only in laying the ideological tracks for future social policies but also because powerful religious organizations such as the Catholic Church aggressively fought state attempts to usurp their domains of socialization. State-church conflict that cut across lines of denomination were as crucial for shaping welfare policy as capital-labor conflict that cut across lines of class.[83]

One more element was largely left out of the original accounts of wel-fare-state formation in Europe: the influence of war and geopolitics. Unlike social scientists, historians certainly recognized the link between warfare and welfare. As A.J.P. Taylor put it succinctly: "The Luftwaffe was a powerful missionary for the [British] welfare state."[84] Ross McKib-ben noted how the British experience of World War II and the London Blitz shaped social expectations for the state: "People had 'radical' expec-tations of the war: less class distinction, more state control, education reforms, leveling of incomes and increased social services were thought the most likely outcomes."[85] No matter the ideological platform of the party in power, European states mostly adopted social-policy initiatives in waves that coincided with the ends of World War I and World War II.[86]

Wars and geopolitical crises are not solely external shocks that directly cause changes in internal welfare politics. Rather, such events provide openings for internal social agents to push for new and expanded policies.[87] Mass participation in war engenders an egalitarian sense of social justice, whereas the exigencies of war are often a catalyst for institutional change and the creation of new state organizations.[88] In addition, geopolitical threats can create internal cohesion among political elites to carry out developmental projects that incorporate new segments of the population. Government efforts to secure the participation and support of workers and citizens often lead to expan-sions of social-citizenship rights near the conclusion of wars or directly afterward, especially those wars that grind on long beyond the initial bouts of nationalist fervor.[89] Mass conscription is arguably another form of taxation, after all, one that theories of the rentier state never bothered to include in models of state formation. Yet conscription has been a main mechanism of state making as well as an arena of social resistance throughout history. As Charles Tilly pointed out, sociologists who looked solely to taxation as the only pathway to the modern social contract "could effectively strengthen their theories by considering the whole range of state-sustaining resources before closing in on taxation as a special, if very consequential, way of acquiring those resources."[90]

Studying the welfare state involves more than uncovering the sources of state income. As this book shows, it involves the examination of political economy, class groupings, state institutions, and relevant external influences. Even in poorer countries in the global South, more people interact with welfare systems than with most other government institutions. Welfare states, Walter Korpi noted, "are likely to be of relevance for the formation of values, attitudes, and interests among citizens in ways that are of relevance for patterns of collective action." This is because welfare institutions "tend to create templates" that emphasize some lines of cleavage, "while downplaying others."[91] These processes influence the ability of individuals to form coalitions during future collective action. Welfare expansion can politicize the segments of society that it reaches as well as the segments that it does not. An investigation of Iran's welfare system can illustrate patterns of political organization and conflict that earlier analyses have overlooked in focusing solely on the country's supposed rentier characteristics.

WELFARE-STATE THEORY IN THE GLOBAL SOUTH

A stark problem for theories of the welfare state was that most studies concentrated on wealthy Northern states with large social-welfare systems. Scholars have slowly turned their attention to welfare states in the global South. As Robin Blackburn pointed out, for most of nineteenth-century Europe, whether in democracies or absolutist monarchies, "the comforts of a state pension were in practice only extended to functionaries and military men."[92] In Latin America, a region where postcolonial state formation preceded much of the non-European world, a similar pattern took hold. In the early twentieth century, most Latin American states implemented social-insurance programs for narrow groups of workers in important civil-service and industrial sectors. The industrialization of Latin America, unlike that of Europe, never produced a majority proletarian workforce—that is, a mostly urban, wage-earning, and formally employed labor force. Instead, state welfare was expanded for formal workers in government and industry, while the rest of the population entered into what came to be known as the informal sector—the majority not formally employed in wage-labor occupations.[93]

As a result, the welfare mix in most states in Latin America before the 1980s contained social-insurance and employment protection, similarly as in corporatist European states, but accessible only to the small share of workers in formal employment. For those in the informal sector, individuals relied on the household and the labor market as their only precarious insurance against social risk. Even liberal systems of means-tested social assistance, as had developed in the United States with such programs as Aid to Families with Dependent Children, were not made available to informal workers in Latin America. This should not be surprising, as Latin American states in the middle of the twentieth century were also middle- and lower-income countries in the world economy. With few exceptions in the region (Cuba and Costa Rica, for example), they possessed neither the ideological inclination nor the available resources to implement welfare regimes that extended far beyond their small formal labor forces.[94]

Whereas Latin America was often used as negative comparison vis-à-vis European welfare regimes, the rise of East Asia encouraged scholars to turn their attention to the role of social policy in rapid economic growth.[95] Here, expansion of education was implemented by authoritarian states in South Korea, Taiwan, and the city-states of Singapore and Hong Kong. This expansion, however, was not supplemented with generous social-insurance programs for skilled industrial workers. The result was a highly educated labor force that lacked the corporatist protections of formal workers in Latin America. This policy mix formed part of East Asian states' developmental strategy of flexible, export-oriented production, which many countries engaged in by the 1960s. In these "productivist regimes," social progress came via rapid economic growth, not through state programs of income redistribution.[96] Other state interventions, such as postwar land reform conducted in the geopolitical shadow of the Chinese revolution, helped to condition this relatively equal pattern of growth. Scholars initially came to the consensus that, in lieu of the formal welfare organizations of the type developed in European states, East Asian states had developed a paternalistic and "Confucian" welfare system that utilized informal, familial links. Yet after successive rounds of comparative analysis, as well as the democratization of most of these countries through large-scale social movements, scholars began to theorize East Asian state-welfare policies as an outcome of elite fear of rural unrest amidst successful socialist revolution in China and Vietnam.[97] Instead of filial piety, then, it was threat of organized social mobilization against state rule that convinced East Asian authoritarian elites to adopt changes in social policy. The region challenges the notion that welfare programs come in tandem with, or after, democratization. In East Asia, welfare policy came first; democratization, later.

For socialist states in Eastern Europe and the Soviet Union, Janos Kornai argued that midcentury efforts to build up a universal system of education, health care, and pensions within these poorer countries produced a "premature welfare state," the inefficiencies of which mirrored those in the sphere of socialist production.[98] Although there was no labor market in these countries, and full employment was a key goal of state elites, social policy was allocated "to a large extent at the point of production and through managerial discretion, rather than on the basis of individual rights."[99] A fierce critic of socialist inefficiency in distributing services, Kornai did not specify the historical origins of socialist welfare policy. Instead of a premature version of the Western welfare state, Eastern European welfare states had their own trajectory, growing out of a Stalin-era push for full employment layered on top of earlier, Bismarckian systems, built in the 1930s. These policies were even more "productivist" and "paternalistic" than those found in East Asian states, since distribution of benefits was stratified based on an individual's contribution to state-defined goals and conceptions of socialist citizenship through occupation, not on rights qua citizen.

Changes in Eastern European welfare policies after 1989 challenged the conception of socialist welfare states as simply premature versions of European ones. Although market reforms brought about "emergency measures" in economic policy, in many cases these did not lead to a retrenchment of social spending. The post-1989 era forced realignments in social policy as privatization, migration, informal employment, unemployment, and externally led restructuring of these countries' political economies took place. Notably, however, social spending as a share of public expenditures in most Eastern European states exhibited only small declines, especially compared to cutbacks in Latin American welfare programs during the 1990s and 2000s. This surprising outcome in postsocialist Europe was partly due to public protest expressed in a new democratic framework, and partly because universal conceptions of socialist welfare policy were still embedded in citizens' expectations. As a result, contemporary welfare systems in Eastern Europe and the former Soviet Union display a wide range of policy mixes.[100]

Overall, research on welfare and social policy in the global South has led to two important advances. First, it has historicized the process of welfare-state formation, which was previously bound within an overarching paradigm of modernization. This earlier conception led most analysts to regard welfare policies in poorer countries as premature or deviant versions of European welfare policies. Second, the wide divergence of social policies in the global South has challenged the prevailing theoretical models used to explain a narrower set of European welfare-regime types.[101] As Göran Therborn has noted, welfare rights did not develop as a result of taxation-induced democratization nearly anywhere in the world.[102] In order to understand social change in postrevolutionary Iran, we need to move beyond the grand linear models of an ideal welfare state as well as exceptionalist accounts of the Islamic Republic's own institutional makeup.

As Melani Cammett argues, "theories linking the origins and variation of social policies to power resources, developmental strategies, or political regime type cannot adequately explain the diversity of welfare regimes across the Middle East."[103] In the wake of the 2011 Arab uprisings, unexpected unrest from Tunisia and Jordan to Bahrain and Saudi Arabia should have undermined the notion that social policy functioned as a "bribe" that lulled these countries' populations into political complacency. Yet we still read accounts of a welfare bribe in newspapers and media reportage on the region. The specter of the rentier paradigm haunts our ability to make sense of the region even as large segments of these countries' populations revolt against the "authoritarian bargain" that rentier theory insists is stable and operational.

In this book, I adapt theories of welfare-state formation to make a novel argument for the expansion of social policy in Iran after the 1979 revolution. As Stephan Haggard and Robert Kaufman argue for the global South, welfare policies can be examined by looking at the social and political struggles taken part in by coalitions of domestic groups and political contenders. At key historical junctures, competition and struggle can create a "critical realignment" of social policies whereby segments of the population are either included or excluded from the state-provided mix of social welfare. In the Iranian case, the 1979 revolution and the 1980–88 war with Iraq acted as critical realignments in the coalitions of domestic groups relied upon by new postrevolutionary political contenders.

Haggard and Kaufman can be complemented with recent political-science scholarship on social policies in authoritarian states. As Stephen

Haber, Isabel Mares, and Matthew Carnes have argued, elites in autocratic states strategically bargain with politically influential segments of society. States with narrow elite coalitions tend to ignore social policy or provide it solely to privileged social groups. If multiple threats to rule exist within and without society, the elite may pursue a strategy of "organizational multiplication" in order to disperse political threats and contain competition. As Haber identified in Mexico under the Institutional Revolutionary Party: "Regimes premised on this logic of organizational multiplication confer economic rights to broader segments of the population. Although their resulting property rights system is more extensive, it is also more uneven."[104]

In Iran, elite competition and popular mobilization intertwined to expand social policy after the revolution and the war period. The Islamic Republic created or expanded an array of corporatist organizations—often with social-welfare benefits at their center. Yet recurring intra-elite competition produced a dynamic whereby corporatist bodies became sites of bottom-up inclusionary claims from groups such as students, women, villagers, and professionals. As differing elite segments reached out to newly mobilized social groups in order to trump or check their rivals, often by expanding access to parts of the social contract, new political opportunities arose. In this sense, Iran's civil society—celebrated by journalists, intellectuals, and academics—was partly an unruly outcome of state building.[105]

As Dan Slater has argued, political elites in authoritarian regimes tend to form enduring and cohesive compacts because of legitimate threats to rule and not as a result of stable patronage networks.[106] Although Iran's postrevolutionary political elite did not agree on much, they did perceive the external geopolitical order as hostile almost to an existential degree. Though this political elite went through intense periods of interfactional strife, the enduring antisystemic position of the Islamic Republic in the geopolitical order placed the notion of self-sustaining modernization high on everyone's agenda. Oil revenues do not automatically flow into a massive increase of state infrastructural power via welfare expansion for purposes of social leveling, class reshuffling, and balancing the rural-urban divide. These were political decisions motivated in part by the enduring threats of the international system. By virtue of how the postrevolutionary political elite responded to a perceived geopolitical threat, a host of transformations in a purportedly Islamist political order—social, political, aesthetic—ended up looking like postrevolutionary changes from Russia to China to Cuba.

By looking at the case of the Islamic Republic through the lens of historical sociology, we can view Iran's welfare system as an institutional mapping of conflict and compromise between different social strata, status groups, and elite actors inside and outside the state. In this manner, we can identify mechanisms outside the taxation nexus by which expansions in welfare provision can enlarge and empower particular social classes and status groups, who in turn may make new demands on the state. To be sure, social science has shown taxation to be one pathway in the expansion of state capacity and, eventually, democratization. Yet, other pathways to state capacity and social citizenship have existed, and the arrow of causality may point in the opposite direction.

CHAPTER 2

Seeing like a King

Welfare Policy as State-Building Strategy
in the Pahlavi Monarchy

The Enlightenment initially arrived . . . as a centralizing
rather than liberating force. . . . On the one hand, by eroding
and deriding all the old transcendental bases of certainty and
hierarchy, it undermined the authority of the self-appointed
agents of the Higher Order, and the residual legatee of
sovereignty was man himself and his mundane interests. . . .
On the other hand, the rationality it commended required the
authority of experts and the implementation of their plans. In
conditions of backwardness in particular, where *rattrapage*
[catching-up] constituted the first imperative, this technicist-
authoritarian element was likely to predominate (and there
was, and is, danger of chaos if it does not).

—Ernest Gellner

At a midscale restaurant I frequented in eastern Tehran in 2009,[1] one of
the managers often invited me to sit near the front desk for jokes and
gossip with the wait staff. At the end of our conversations, he sometimes extended his hand not to shake mine but to show me his ring. On
its crest was an impression of the last shah of Iran, Mohammad Reza
Pahlavi. The manager liked to kiss the ring, at least when I was standing
there, and then say, "This country needs a king." One can buy such
royal paraphernalia in the Tehran bazaars or antique shops. Given the
tumult in Iran since 1979, such displays of personal nostalgia are understandable. These emotions, sincere as they are, have little to do with
ancient traditions. Their origins largely come from one of the most rad-

ical state-building projects of the twentieth century: the developmental dictatorship of the Pahlavi monarchy.

Pahlavi official histories portrayed the end of the Qājār Dynasty (1785–1925) as mired in political chaos and social disintegration. There was plenty of truth in the claim. Iran's population suffered more famines during the nineteenth century than in any previous century, partly from grain hoarding by local elites and the Russian annexation of northern territories.[2] This story, however, emphasized all political events before the 1925 coronation of Reza Shah as the coherent manifestation of a preexisting Iranian nation-state.[3] Late nineteenth-century protests against British and Russian imperial-commercial designs; the 1905–11 constitutional revolution, which allied urban intellectual, clerical, and pastoral rural elites against the old Qājār state; and the 1921 putsch by the Persian Cossack Brigade and its tough-headed colonel—Reza Khan—were complex events to be later smoothed out by nationalist historians.[4] Though rooted in existing elite structures at the outset, the Pahlavi Dynasty rapidly engaged in mythmaking as a central tenet of state making from the 1930s continuing on through the 1970s.[5] Any consideration of state-society dynamics in the Pahlavi era should begin with the understanding that, by its own intent as well as from the perspective of its critics, the monarchy's reach and vision were exaggerated. The power of the twentieth-century Iranian state, in other words, has been overstated.

This led to two results. First, events in Iran were seen through the prism of the Pahlavi monarchy's modernization project—including subsequent policies enacted in the Islamic Republic. Second, the coherence and cohesiveness of state rule was assumed to be nearly omnipotent.[6] This view portrayed Iranian society as detached from government institutions, while a dynastic nationalism promoted in an age of mass media reinforced the monarchy's image of autonomous power. Consequently, academic studies of twentieth-century Iranian politics as well as popular discussions about the country tend to wield a vocabulary seemingly derived from Baron de Montesquieu's *Persian Letters*. As one of Montesquieu's main sources, Jean Chardin, wrote in his 1711 travelogue: "At present, then, the government of the Persians is a monarchy—despotic and absolute, since it is entirely in the hands of a single man who is the sovereign chief both in spiritual as well as in worldly affairs; the complete master of the life and goods of his subjects. There is certainly no other sovereign in the world who is as absolute as the king of Persia."[7]

Remarkably, little has changed in much contemporary scholarship. No matter the era, terms like "sultanistic," "despotic," or "arbitrary" rule are used to explain social and political patterns in Iran. After the 1979 revolution, this perspective was again raised to stress the continuity between Islamic Republic and monarchy: the "turban for the crown."[8]

To be sure, neither the Pahlavi monarchy or the Islamic Republic of Iran resemble the liberal-democratic ideal state, but this prevailing view of Iran's political development ignores or elides how social forces shaped and pressured these states over time. We still do not possess a "people's history" of modern Iran, but this overarching story of powerful absolutism raises an obvious question. If the Pahlavi state was so powerful, especially after the 1953 ousting of Mohammad Mossadeq up through the 1970s, then how could there have been a popular revolution in 1979? To achieve such a feat, came the subsequent answer from the new elites in the Islamic Republic, the revolutionary leaders surely were divinely inspired.

Analyses of the Pahlavi era, in other words, tend "not to explain the state at all but to explain it away."[9] To rethink the Pahlavi period and make sense of subsequent comparisons with the Islamic Republic, this chapter examines how the implementation of social-welfare measures in Iran were joined to shifts in social power among particular groups. The Pahlavi political elite, like those in many twentieth-century postcolonial states, possessed a high-modernist vision to transform the social order as a means to emulate and catch up with wealthy countries in the world economy.[10] This vision drove the political elite to implement top-down, state-led social-welfare policies. Certain groups were favored over others. This happened, however, not solely by fiat from above, but often as a response to social unrest and policy demands from below. This process repeatedly occurred in Pahlavi Iran, from the provincial rebellions of the 1920s, to the labor strikes of the 1940s and 1950s, and ultimately in the urban student and worker demonstrations of the 1970s. Policy intentions and policy outcomes were never identical. Explaining social change through the opposition of an autonomous modernizing state hovering over an immobile, traditional society minimizes the tensions between state policy as an instrument of the rulers versus an institution taken advantage of and molded by the ruled. As the Venezuelan anthropologist Fernando Coronil argued, the latter conception should not be ignored, because "plans are formulated by the state but are not plans of the state, for they are produced in conjunction with other powerful actors that shape the state and are modified by the ongoing play of politics."[11] Nowhere is this more apparent than in Pahlavi Iran, where a top-down "White revolution" led to an unexpected outcome: a popular bottom-up revolution, which swept away a seemingly all-powerful monarchy and its self-proclaimed "2,500 years" of lineal descent. Welfare policy was part of the Pahlavi state-building strategy, but it did not act as a coherent co-opting political force.

WELFARE IN SERVICE OF THE STATE
UNDER REZA SHAH PAHLAVI

Between 1905 and 1912, a wave of nationalist revolutions swept through the agrarian empires of Russia, China, the Ottomans, Mexico, and Persia. To observers and participants alike, these looked as promising and confusing as the Arab uprisings in West Asia and North Africa one century later. None of the revolutions resulted in a stable democratic state, and the ensuing political coalitions crumbled or were sidelined by authoritarian centralizers. The revolutionary discourses taken up by new political elites masked the structural continuities between the old regimes and their twentieth-century replacements. The common protagonists among these upheavals were homegrown intellectuals on the margins of imperial power.[12] For Iran, such intellectuals served as the conduit for social and economic policies instrumentalized by the Pahlavi monarchy for the purposes of state building.

The term "intellectual"—originally a secular-tinged epithet hurled against the cosmopolitan likes of Émile Zola—had itself only spread in the 1890s during the French Dreyfus Affair. It quickly took root in Persian letters, first with Arabic loan words and then the coining of a Persian neologism *rowshanfekrān* (enlightened thinkers). Secret societies, print media, and private correspondence traveled across a transnational Persianate sphere, from London and Paris to Constantinople, Baku, Bombay, and Cairo.

Through these loosely bound networks, roving merchants, disgruntled Qājār elites, dilettante travelers, and other self-identified intellectuals discovered and reformulated political and social ideas of the day. They sought to mine a usable past from the rich veins of Iranian, Islamic, and European history.[13]

The impetus for such intellectual ferment came from reflections on Iran's late nineteenth-century political impasse and need for national rejuvenation. Discussions did not remain in the abstract for long. The Persian court was not exempt from the surge of assassinations of state leaders across the world.[14] In 1896, Qājār Shah Nāsser al-Din was shot in Tehran's Abdul Azim Mosque by an "itinerant radical" who followed the writings of Istanbul-based intellectual Jamāl al-Din al-Afghāni, a late nineteenth-century Islamist modernist who traversed Ottoman-Persian-Indian networks of political thought.[15] The shah's close advisor feared the public's response to news of the shah's death, and thus arranged for Nāsser Shah's corpse to be driven to the palace seated upright in the royal carriage. Thanks to the efforts of his attendants, the shah's arm waved to the crowds. The spectacle of a dead regent gesturing in the air was bizarre, but it symbolized an important political reality in late nineteenth-century Iran. During the late Qājār period, state legitimation already rested to some degree on cultivating and responding to broader social demands.[16]

Inspired by reforms in the Ottoman Empire, European liberals, Russian social democrats, and German and Japanese industrializers, a series of underground committees formed in Tehran and other Iranian cities that commiserated on the possibilities for political change. A 1905 fiscal crisis and an inflationary spiral led to uprisings and protests against the Qājār government, with participation by bazaar merchants and armed tribal groups. The growing unrest culminated in a 1906 constitutional proclamation by antistate provincial elites and the convening of a national assembly. The more radical participants issued proposals calling for a constitutional monarchy. The new state would be compelled to promote "social justice," including universal suffrage, freedom of speech, free education and health care, land reform, taxation of wealth, an eight-hour workday, national conscription, and a unification of the Persian territories under a single language.[17] Amidst the revolutionary fervor, in April 1908 the new parliament passed the country's first retirement law for deceased civil servants. Half of a civil servant's salary would go to the deceased's family. Borrowing from religious precepts for inheritance, if the benefits were split among family members, female recipients would receive half the share of male recipients.[18] This was a simple form of pension provision, and no other social-insurance legislation would appear until 1922.

The revolutionary-patchwork coalition soon fragmented around geographical and material interests. Russian and British advisors took the opportunity to expand the Great Powers' zones of influence into Persian territory. Aided by foreign munitions, Qājār-loyal forces were able to pursue a divide-and-conquer strategy. By 1914, the country was occupied throughout most of its territory and the constitutional movement rent asunder. Yet the 1917 Russian Revolution provided space for political maneuvering with the retreat of tsarist forces in the north of the country. It was in this environment that Sardār (Colonel) Reza Khan balanced himself among the swirling centrifugal forces and turned the British-supplied Cossack Brigade into a vehicle for reestablishing sovereignty. He quickly implemented one of the constitutionalists' key demands—conscription—and packed the still-existing parliament with supporters. With an expanded army, campaigns to stamp out separatist or resistance movements in the provinces during the years 1920–25 were successful. The campaigns were also popular in the capital among nationalist intellectuals, and parliament voted to depose the Qājārs and crown Reza "Pahlavi" as shah in 1925.[19] One of the few men in the assembly to protest against the measure was a young member of parliament named Mohammad Mossadeq.

Iran set an institutional pattern in the 1930s repeated during subsequent periods. Instead of a sui generis blueprint, most elements of Reza Shah's state-building program originated from reforms demanded by social movements during the constitutional struggles. Yet these policies were selectively implemented by the new state for the purposes of centralization and consolidation as well as appealing to the government's social base of young etatist reformers and large merchant houses. From the late 1920s onward, the Iranian state carried out judicial reform, census registration (and the assignment of fixed surnames to the majority of the population along with it), tribal settlement and "pacification," a civil code, land titling, and the monopolization of commodities such as tobacco and opium for export. A lasting reform was the construction of the Trans-Iranian Railway, long wished for by Iranian intellectuals as a sign of national power and territorial integrity.[20] Territorial centralization allowed new economic linkages to spread within a coalescing internal market. As with most late-developers in the 1930s, domestic production for military use was the first step. Light-weapons and ammunition factories were set up with public funds, as well as textiles and raw-material refinement. Public banking and credit services were soon established for industrial ventures. Nationalist intellectuals joined the project, as Reza Shah "gathered around himself those who saw salvation of the country in speedy economic transformation."[21] The founding of University of Tehran, in 1934, as a public center for knowledge production avowedly emulated late nineteenth-century European disciplinary divisions. Last, and most remembered today in Iran, Jacobin-derived anticlericalism, in combination with the spirit of

catching up to Western states, resulted in a controversial series of sarto-
rial laws requiring men to wear the European bowler hat and women to
remove the veil in 1935.[22] Ali-Akbar Siāsi, minister of education and
Tehran University rector, wrote of the need for such laws in a 1931 dissertation chapter tellingly titled "The Emancipation and Consolidation
of National Sentiment":[23]

> We know that the ten to twelve million Persians, although of the same race
> and, with few exceptions, of the same language and religion, used to form
> groups that were rendered heterogeneous by the large distances that sepa-
> rated them and by the bad state of roads. Every one of them had its own
> mores, customs, and costumes. . . . [T]he main reason of [Reza Shah's dress]
> policy, and main social problem being the Europeanization of the Persian, it
> was felt that the imitation of [the Europeans'] external appearance would
> not fail to facilitate the adoption of [European] ideas; that the Persian, by
> abandoning his long robe, his cloak, his bonnet, all of which seemed to serve
> as a refuge for traditionalism, would definitely capitulate to the advance of
> Western civilization, to which he would thenceforth abandon himself with-
> out shame or constraint. And in fact, dressed in a short jacket and a hat with
> visor, he seems indeed less ill at ease in his march towards modern progress.

As Siāsi saw it, good roads and good clothes went together. The Pahlavi
monarchy did not cast off traditions, however, when it suited building
up nationalist morale. In 1935, Reza Shah issued a decree that the formal name of the country would thereafter be referred to as Iran. The
term derived from ancient and medieval texts which connoted "of the
Aryans."

Kemal Atatürk was certainly a model for Reza Shah. Arguably, however, the Pahlavi state's vision was even more radical, given the lack of
nineteenth-century Ottoman-style reforms, which acted as the foundation for twentieth-century Turkish state building. During the 1930s,
many ideologies of modernization and industrialization were on hand
for new state builders: communism, fascism, and New Deal liberalism.
As the historian Amin Banani described, the sentiment of Reza Shah's
"New Order" was "an inflated glorification of the past; a deprecation
of foreigners that too easily betrays a sense of inferiority; an appetite for
industrialization far beyond the bounds of economic rationale, not for
the sake of efficiency and welfare but as a symbol of prestige and status;
an indiscriminate imitation of the surface gloss of Western societies; and
a burning desire to become a truly sovereign and consequential power."[24]
The content of the Iranian government's policies cannot easily be
explained with recourse to theories of patrimonialism or traditional
rule. Certainly, new networks of power and distribution were estab-

lished; but to what end? These, as Ernest Gellner surmised, were accompanying effects of the imperative by Iranian elites to catch up from the periphery.

The mantra of modernization resulted in an aura of a powerful and autonomous state apparatus in 1930s Iran. Yet, as with state formation anywhere, resistance to the new policies was widespread, especially among middle-strata elites cut out from networks of power than emanated outward from state ministries. Lower-ranking clerics denigrated new secular schools; urban guilds fought against the state's monopolization and taxation of commodity exports, and junior tribal khans evaded the army's attempt to settle and disarm their soldiers. These revolts were far more serious than was presented in nationalist discourse. Conscription and taxation fell onto the poor, leading to major riots in Tabriz, Isfahan, and Shiraz, whereas the wealthier could buy their military exemption.[25] In Max Weber's original formulation, sultanism denoted those (non-European) regimes where despotic power had been so concentrated in the state that all other autonomous sources of social power were extinguished. Repeated unrest under Reza Shah's reign proved that the aura of omnipotence was overstated. So did the impetus for his government's social-welfare policies. These were often pushed onto the monarchy from below and then reformulated as state-building strategy.

The constitutional period saw a variety of left-wing parties emerge in Iran, often with connections to Caucasian and Russian worker organizations that eventually took part in the 1920 Baku First Congress of Peoples of the East. A wave of labor strikes in Iran during the 1920s included mobilizations by printers, teachers, and police. Protestors often occupied government buildings—a traditional tactic of petitioning the state reinvented by nascent unions and spontaneous worker gatherings. The decade ended with a 1929 strike of at least nine thousand oil-refinery workers in Abadan against the unpopular Anglo-Persian Oil Company.[26] Alongside this rising agitation, labor reforms and social-insurance measures were discussed in newspapers and journals. The national assembly passed of a series of labor laws in the 1920s, though they mostly remained unenforced. The real welfare institutions came during the state-building efforts of the Pahlavi monarchy, which selectively implemented legal measures for protecting civil service staff and industrial laborers. These acts set the foundation for social policy in later periods.

The main targets of Reza Shah's social-policy reforms were the growing pools of civil-service professionals and workers in industry and transportation. The 1922 Civil Service Law established pay scales, a retirement age, and a pension fund for state employees. The state bureaucracy grew, reaching ninety thousand employees by 1941. Beginning in 1931, a contributory social-insurance scheme was created for unskilled workers in the Ministry of Roads (responsible for building the Trans-Iranian Railway). In 1933, this law was expanded to all workers in state factories and mines. Teachers in the expanding public-education system were given vacation and sick leave. Middle class social reformers pushed for the 1936 Factory Act, which implemented health and hygienic services in state factories.[27]

The British-owned Anglo-Persian Oil Company, as well as domestic private industry, was exempt from these laws, and enforcement remained weak.[28] Yet the timing of policy implementation was telling. A wave of social-insurance policies also became law in Europe during the early 1920s, after the end of World War I.[29] In Iran, as well, socialist and liberal intellectuals pushed these policies onto the state, with the threat of organized worker unrest in the wings. Reza Shah's ministerial officials chose to implement social insurance for middle-class civil servants first, and public-sector industrial workers second. The industrial working class was not as large as the civil-service sector during this period, as initial legislative decrees predated Iran's industrialization drive of the 1930s, which was spearheaded by German investment and trade.[30] In sum, the first modernization drive of the Pahlavi state fostered the creation of middle-class occupations through educational expansion in professional-technical fields as well as sending Iranians abroad. The establishment of central authority employed these individuals and linked them to the state through welfare measures that rarely reached other segments of the population.[31] The new working classes in industry were included as a secondary measure.

In August 1941, British and Soviet forces invaded Iran, under the excuse of Reza Shah's refusal to expel German citizens from the territory. In truth, the British were interested in securing oil supplies and creating a buffer territory to defend colonial India in case of a Nazi victory over the besieged USSR. Western Asia was rocked with anti-British protests during World War II, and the invasion of Iran was conducted under the assumption that Reza Shah would lean toward the Germans if the war continued. The Soviets saw northern Iran, as did their tsarist predecessors, in the Russian imperial ambit, and decided to go along with the invasion to prevent its loss. The Tehran army gave little resistance to the invasion, as it had mostly been designed for quelling internal unrest. Reza Shah's son, Mohammad Reza, was appointed the new regent after the British approved.[32]

During the period from 1941 to 1953, social protest emanating from below and social policy implemented from above occurred again. Widespread political mobilization pushed new demands onto the state agenda. The main protagonists were new middle classes and a more organized industrial working class. These were also the two main social groups Reza Shah's government had attempted to co-opt through social policy. Emulating other late-developers, the Pahlavi monarchy harnessed a growing bureaucracy to establish power over an unruly territory. Bureaucratization was a key historical mechanism of state formation, as it ensured that economic decisions could be made only by going through state structures.[33] In order to fulfill the visions of modernization held by semiperipheral elites, no matter the ideological climate, state builders assembled together new cadres and workers. These groups, inspired by the postwar intelligentsia, began to make demands and claims on the state once political opportunities arose. These demands were largely framed in nationalist terms. Given the global milieu of national-liberation movements and the dismantling of European empires, this was to be expected. Another source, however, was the recently assembled nationalist discourse on which Reza Shah's project of state modernization relied. With a young king on the throne and the presence of foreign powers close at hand, an opportunity soon presented itself.

NATIONALISM FROM BELOW, IMPERIALISM FROM ABOVE

After 1941, effectively half of Iranian territory was under occupation, including oil-producing provinces in the north and south. As British and Soviet forces commandeered supplies and utilized the country as an overland corridor for conducting the war, social resentment built. The economy deteriorated, bread shortages occurred, and sporadic riots took place over rising prices.[34] Nevertheless, the country retained formal sovereignty. The weak position of Mohammad Reza Shah (hereafter, "the shah") forced him to curry favor with local notables and power brokers. The veil was again permitted to be worn in public, placating the Shi'i clerical establishment. Landed elites, smarting from Reza Shah's taxation policies, filled the parliament, cabinet positions, and the prime minister's office with handpicked candidates. Rural tenant farmers and smallholding peasants were often compelled, via landlord-appointed village representatives, to vote for the choice of their landlords. Out of 148 cabinet ministers who held posts between 1941 and 1953, 81 were sons of titled elites, whereas only 13 were Western-educated technocrats.[35] The rapid turnover of politicians was a product of highly factionalized parliamentary politics—the prime ministers lasted on average eight months during this period.

When landed elites attempted to seize the institutions of the state, powerful new social movements in Iran acted as a countervailing force. Iraj Eskandari, the nephew of a famous constitutionalist, was imprisoned in the 1930s with other socialist intellectuals as the "group of 53." In 1941, he helped establish the Tudeh (Masses) Party, remaining its leader until 1979. The party's main slogans were "Work for All, Education for All, Health for All"—in other words, a radically inclusive welfare state—and "Land to the Tiller." As Ervand Abrahamian noted, the Tudeh in its official program declared itself a socialist party, drawing "most of its support from urban wage earners and from the salaried middle class—especially the intelligentsia."[36] By the end of World War II, the party had a wide membership among formal workers in the transportation, mining, industry, and oil sectors across the country. Tudeh intellectuals framed their appeal in nationalist hues. For example, the party celebrated the eleventh-century epic *Shāhnāmeh* as a radical folk poem.[37] Tudeh leaders often rode, rather than led, the wave of labor unrest that came during the war, including an Abadan general strike in 1946—the largest labor action in the Middle East up to that year.[38] The upsurge forced the (by then renamed) Anglo-Iranian Oil Company to concede the eight-hour day. Tudeh Party members in the parliament then pressured the government to pass the first labor law in the Middle East.

The early years of the Cold War strained this left-leaning nationalist surge. After calling for oil nationalization and concessions from British and American oil companies, Tudeh leaders publicly supported giveaways for Soviet oil extraction in the north—although privately expressing exasperation at Soviet machinations. Two short-lived autonomous movements in Azerbaijan and Kurdistan produced separatist republics in 1946, with Soviet backing. These states briefly introduced far-reaching social reforms in land access and women's suffrage before collapsing after Soviet withdrawals.[39] Nationalist splits from the Tudeh took place, with small parties such as Khalil Maleki's "Third Force" springing up over the next decade—a harbinger of nonaligned politics soon to appear across the Third World.[40] Repression of strikes had increased as early as

1943, but after a failed assassination attempt on the shah in 1949, Iran's government banned the Tudeh Party. Martial law was enforced in Tehran, and the shah convened a constitutional assembly that gave the monarch the right to dissolve parliament.

Even with the state crackdown on labor unrest and leftist mobilization, Iran's parliament passed bills for labor reform and social insurance. The legislative language utilized recommendations of the International Labour Organization for contributory pensions and disability compensation for all workers in transportation, mining, industry, and commerce. Ratified in 1949, the bills were implemented selectively under the newly formed ministries of labor and health.[41] Although unsatisfactory for the organized left, these social-insurance laws were nevertheless the first to cover Iranian formal workers in large firms outside the public sector. In other words, new social reforms outlasted the upsurge in labor unrest and were subsequently expanded during the 1951–53 tenure of Prime Minister Mossadeq. Protests helped to convert demands from below into state policy.

With Reza Shah's abdication and a weakened state, the period 1941–53 witnessed a flourishing of new ideologies and organizations. New publishers and magazines, and the 1940 inauguration of Tehran Radio, signaled a burgeoning literary and music scene. A group of intellectuals formed the National Party, hyping Persian nationalism and the pre-Islamic past. The Toilers' Party, with many artists and writers in its ranks, broke with the Tudeh over the 1946 Azerbaijan crisis. The Iran Party was an additional middle-class organization of engineers and lawyers with a nationalist agenda. Lastly, as with the Muslim Brotherhood in Egypt, new Islamist political groups appeared in Iran.[42] The most famous organization, Fedāyin-e Islām, and its young lay leader, Navvāb Safavi, carried out several assassinations among the political and cultural intelligentsia. The name Savafi was the nom de guerre chosen by a former graduate of the German Technical School in Tehran, an employee of the Anglo-Iranian Oil Company, Mojtabā Mirlāhi. Though never more than a few hundred members, the call by Fedāyin-e Islām for the "purification" of the social order, use of propaganda of the deed, support for oil nationalization, and criticism of pro-Pahlavi clerics led to an outsized importance in Iranian politics.[43]

Mohammad Mossadeq, the member of parliament remembered for his vocal opposition to Reza Shah's government, reemerged during the 1940s as a strict constitutionalist again attempting to set limits on the shah's powers. In 1949, Mossadeq created the National Front to link together the growing list of nationalist parties, middle-class associations, left-leaning intellectuals, and sympathetic clergy. The main issue of the postwar era was the highly unpopular concession of the vast majority of oil revenues to foreign oil firms. The shah guaranteed low royalty rates for over fifty years as the state's concession to the Anglo-Iranian Oil Company (AIOC)—that is, until 1993. In 1951, Mossadeq introduced a bill in the parliament to nationalize the oil industry, which the sitting prime minister, Ali Razmara, opposed. Razmara's assassination by the Islamist Fedāyin opened up the slot, and Mossadeq entered the running. The seventy-year-old Mossadeq then used the National Front to help mobilize a mass movement, including street demonstrations and Tudeh-led strikes, to induce the parliament to pass the nationalization law and appoint him as prime minister to implement it.

Mossadeq corralled together the diverse nationalist upsurge of the post–Reza Shah era to enter the prime minister's office. Mossadeq's newly formed government created the National Iranian Oil Company (NIOC) and asked the British to transfer control of AIOC. Once the British refused, NIOC took over AIOC operations, an action that promptly resulted in a U.K. blockade of oil exports. The ensuing 1951–53 crisis pitted a nation-state barely free from semicolonial occupation against the greatest imperial power of the modern era. Mossadeq attempted to reclaim executive control from the shah through clever utilization of parliamentary and electoral provisions. When the shah refused to turn over control of the army, Mossadeq resigned, only to return to power through a July 1952 popular uprising. The Mossadeq period left a lasting impact on the Iranian political repertoire. Throughout 1951–53, Mossadeq utilized social mobilization as a weapon against the state. After 1979, the same political tactic reappeared in the Islamic Republic.

The details of the 1953 coup d'état have been recounted many times over. At least two points are uncontested. First, the United Kingdom attempted to convince the new U.S. Eisenhower administration that, as a British cable put it, "the security of the free world is dependent on large quantities of oil from Middle Eastern sources. If the attitude in Iran spreads to Saudi Arabia or Iraq, the whole structure may break down, along with our ability to defend ourselves."[44] Second, royal and landed elites in Iran were able to fracture the nationalist coalition that underpinned Mossadeq's power base. By 1953, Islamist groups portrayed the prime minister as a godless communist whereas Tudeh members saw him as a bourgeois stooge. Nevertheless, it took thirty-two

Sherman tanks entering Tehran, between fifty and three hundred casualties, and the threat of shelling Mossadeq's house to finally succeed in toppling the government. In unsubtle fashion, the United Kingdom and the United States named the plan after the *Iliad* hero who fought the Trojans on Asian soil: Operation Ajax.[45]

Just as in the late 1920s, the social movements and political mobilization of 1941–1953 failed in institutionalizing democratic rule but succeeded in institutionalizing new social-policy regulations and expanded welfare organizations. Following the nationalization of the oil industry and the economic crisis brought on by the Western blockade, the period 1951–53 witnessed even more labor unrest than in the 1940s. The National Front sought to keep popular support through the enactment of a broad reform program, including new welfare guarantees. In the final year of Mossadeq's premiership, the parliament passed a series of welfare laws, including a Workers' Social Insurance Bill, that expanded on the previous act of 1949. The new law created a prototype version of the Social Security Organization (SSO), later dismantled after the 1953 coup but resurrected by the shah in the 1970s. The SSO was to supervise all social-insurance funds and extend coverage to workers in large and midsized establishments. The organization also was given the right to force employers to hand over documentation about hiring and pay. Successive governments under the shah never rescinded the social-insurance law, although the organization was defanged.[46]

Even with the repressive aftermath of the 1953 coup, then, a decade of mobilization had been imprinted onto state institutions. These new social policies partly reflected the demands of organizations and their social bases that placed the most pressure on the state. Such programs did not merely emerge from top-down autocratic strategies of control. On the contrary, new social policies came after contested moments of social mobilization and political response. The shah was more securely in power after 1953. The Pahlavi monarchy, however, did not possess a tabula rasa on which to construct the vision of a modern Iran. The Iranian government was constrained by the social mobilizations of the past while its technocrats attempted to engineer the social and economic transformations that they thought would ensure the longevity of the state. Nearly fifty years later, I visited the Social Security Organization's Tehran headquarters and discussed the institution's history with midlevel officials. Rather than attributing it to the subsequent modernization drive of the shah, they quickly pointed out that the institution's pedigree originated in the Mossadeq period.[47]

ALL GOING ACCORDING TO PLAN

The Pahlavi state enacted a series of development plans after 1953 that continued into the 1970s. As with most Third World planning efforts, the initial pushes for modernization in Iran involved large-scale infrastructure projects and capital-intensive investments in industry. Social welfare was low on the list of priorities until the 1960s, when the shah's technocrats took the upper hand in state policy. In that decade, the government proposed a "White Revolution" to create and expand a variety of welfare organizations for urban and rural areas.[48] The narrow elite groups at the top of planning institutions, however, were ill prepared for how events on the ground might not go according to plan. As a result, the welfare institutions of the Pahlavi state empowered certain social groups but excluded others.

The Plan Organization (PO) was founded in 1949, expanding a government economic council from the final years of Reza Shah's reign. With American consultation, the PO formulated a seven-year plan. The funding was to come partly through President Truman's Point Four program, but the tumult of the early 1950s prevented most of its implementation. After the 1953 coup, Abol-Hassan Ebtehāj—a young economist under Reza Shah who worked for the International Monetary Fund (IMF) during the Mossadeq period—was appointed head of the PO. Ebtehāj, often remembered as Iran's "first technocrat," scuttled the old plan and crafted a new seven-year plan in 1955 with American technical assistance. Large, visible projects were the theme, including the construction of enormous dams in central and southern Iran.[49] Because of a new royalty agreement granted by the United States and the United Kingdom after the ouster of Mossadeq, oil revenue began to accrue to the state at higher levels. The planning apparatus was meager, however, and funds tended to be directed at large projects without much spillover to rural regions.[50] As economic growth resumed, private-sector imports increased during the late 1950s, along with higher inflation. The state's spending promises began to outpace cash flows. By 1960, Iran's government needed foreign financing, which was supplied by the IMF in exchange for a reduction in the state budget and a cut in imports. Private-sector activity stagnated, and austerity on the public purse—an early version of structural adjustment—led to a recession from 1960 to 1964.

The economic slowdown was coupled with new social mobilizations. Manufacturing wages largely stagnated during the entire decade, whereas prices ticked upward. In 1957, a wave of labor unrest took place across the country, which unsettled state elites. Aside from wage increases, however, implementation of Mossadeq-era social-insurance laws was also a key demand. One Isfahan textile factory reportedly went on strike fifty-two times between 1957 and 1961. Tehran taxi drivers went on strike, as did printing and construction workers.[51] Tehran's brick factories—nestled in the dense southern neighborhoods of the capital—experienced wildcat strikes in 1957, as did oil complexes in Khuzestan.[52] In response, the organization SAVAK—a Persian acronym for Organization of Intelligence and National Security—was created in 1957, partly in order to undermine independent labor organizing. SAVAK officials reportedly stopped a delegation of American labor officials from showing a training film, because it contained images of a labor strike. As David Levintow, a consultant to Iran for the United States Agency for International Development (USAID), wrote to his superiors: "Even a cursory examination of the present condition of most Iranian workers suggests that they now constitute a potential, albeit presently controlled, threat to the stability and the continued tenure of the regime."[53]

During the 1960s, then, it was not too surprising that the Pahlavi monarchy promoted new welfare measures. The Ministry of Labor, however, was barely funded for the expansion of formal labor-welfare policies. Instead, the state focused on establishing corporate unions, through which labor politics could be hopefully channeled. Absentee elite landowners often owned manufacturing enterprises in urban areas and refused to pay any contribution to social-insurance schemes. Few employers would hand over accurate records, and the state lacked regulatory power to determine the eligibility of workers for social insurance. The Civil Service Retirement Office had only fifty staff members to run a fund for one hundred and twenty thousand state workers. From 1954 to 1960, the number of workers insured under various public social-insurance programs remained unchanged at around a hundred and eighty thousand, which meant about seven hundred thousand to eight hundred thousand people including dependents. This amounted to 4 percent of the population in 1960.[54] As in most postwar countries in the Third World, social insurance was a privilege for a small minority of the Iranian labor force.

A student movement centered in the most prestigious public universities of the country began to mobilize alongside the new wave of labor unrest. Between 1946 and 1950, universities had been founded in Shiraz, Tabriz, Mashhad, and Isfahan. The 1958 toppling of the Iraqi Hashemite monarch and the 1960 coup in Turkey—both of which had emerged out of protest waves—led the shah's government to switch prime ministers and relax its tight hold on public debate. Opposition intellectuals soon declared the creation of a Second National Front. This linked together leftist and nationalist groups, whose "most active and militant elements were university and high-school students in Tehran."[55] The prime minister in 1960, Jafar Sharif-Emāmi, made a hollow promise to conduct free elections. Though only twelve thousand students were registered in Iran's universities by 1959, student organizations led a series of protests in 1961 against the new government, calling for constitutional freedoms and the release of political prisoners. Eventually, a teacher was killed at a demonstration outside the parliament. The shah appointed another prime minister, Ali Amini, to placate the protestors.[56]

Amini was associated with the National Front before the Mossadeq period and subsequently joined the liberal wing of the Pahlavi elite. In 1954, Amini helped to negotiate the new oil-consortium agreement with the United States and United Kingdom. As Iran's ambassador to the United States in the late 1950s, Amini was also known to be favored for prime minister by the new U.S. president, John F. Kennedy. The National Front was unimpressed, however, and called for Amini to step down. It was demanded that Mossadeq, under house arrest since 1953, be released. Student demonstrations escalated to major clashes with police on Tehran University's campus in January 1962. As a result, the university chancellor resigned, and several National Front leaders were arrested. The shah dismissed Amini as a conciliatory measure, but the growing unrest convinced many in the government that a more radical response was necessary. The new 1963 development plan, now on a five-year scale, announced a much-touted strategy for industrial growth and socioeconomic modernization. In the wake of the Cuban Revolution and a crop of self-proclaimed revolutionary republics in Egypt, Iraq, and Turkey, Iran could gain legitimacy by catching up to wealthy countries through a revolution of its own—a White Revolution. This would outflank perceived threats of leftist movements from outside as well as nationalist officers commandeering the state from the inside. As the historian Nikki Keddie pointed out, the Pahlavi state-building project owed as much to Nasser as it did to Atatürk.[57]

IRAN'S COLORED REVOLUTION

A year before entering the Nixon administration, Henry Kissinger wrote an essay for *Daedalus* about Otto von Bismarck entitled "The White

Revolutionary." This was not a reference to the shah's developmental push of that same decade, at least not overtly. Instead, Kissinger wished to illustrate the manner in which, "in the guise of conservatism," the German chancellor "swept away the dilemmas that had baffled the German quest for unity."[58] As he saw it, Bismarck was able to balance the antagonisms of his age and, through political acumen, transcend them. The term came from an 1868 poem, *Monsieur de Bismarck,* by Ludwig Bamberger, a liberal politician and economist who had taken part in the 1848 revolutions. Bamberger was exiled to France, returned later to Germany to work for Bismarck in the Reichstag, and eventually helped to found Deutsche Bank:[59]

> We cannot for one moment doubt that he was a born revolutionary. For revolutionaries are born just as legitimists are born, with a particular cast of mind, whereas chance alone determines whether the circumstances of his life make of the same person a White or a Red.

More recent assessments argue that the German chancellor was less perspicacious than his reputation suggests.[60] Nevertheless, Bamberger's ode to Bismarck was the equivalent of Mohammad Mossadeq's writing a laudatory poem about Mohammad Reza Shah.

Kissinger's paean to the German "revolution from above" in 1968 is fitting. That same year, Samuel Huntington's *Political Order in Changing Societies* was published. The two works by the two Harvard colleagues are both theorizations of authoritarian modernization. The strong hand of a centralizing state was needed to first initiate and then control an otherwise unruly process of rapid social change. Huntington's book reportedly circulated among pro-Pahlavi intellectuals in the 1970s. The argument jibed with the times, as it was the underlying sentiment of the Pahlavi Monarchy's White Revolution.

Iran's policy shift in the 1960s was a response to the unrest of the previous decade. Neither the small but growing middle class that had supported the National Front nor a sizable portion of the student population gave full legitimacy to the Pahlavi monarchy after the 1953 coup. Landed elites—some quite wealthy; others, smallholders—dragged their feet on state-proposed economic reforms. The Shi'i clergy were largely quiet on economic issues, but then again, many local clerics were also landholders, with autonomous sources of income. The first mention of a White Revolution reportedly came from the shah's close aide Asadollāh Alam, who suggested it in 1958 after the Iraqi monarchy's overthrow.[61] The notion signified a bloodless replacement of the old elite with a new technocratic-professional stratum at the state's commanding heights. The term took on a life of its own, however, as state elites, including the shah, sensed it to imply different outcomes. It eventually resulted in a manifesto of sorts, attributed to the shah and published in English and Persian. The text promised land reform, nationalization of forests and pastures, a literacy corps, sale of public factories, enfranchisement of women, and worker profit-sharing. Land reform was by far the most sweeping element. Prior to the 1960s, landholding in Iran fell into four broad categories: royal holdings (3.8% of all villages), state holdings (5.8%), endowment holdings or *awqāf*, a form of trust sanctioned in religious law (11.5%), and the remaining forty thousand villages privately owned by large landowners of an estimated thirty-seven extended families (36.5%), medium-sized landowners (13.4%), and small peasant holders (29%).[62]

The state's push for a new modernization drive occurred in a particularly turbulent international environment. After Nasser's coup in Egypt and the toppling of Menderes in Turkey, the United States became preoccupied with Iran's susceptibility to revolution from below or, perhaps equally as bad, neutrality in the Cold War. In 1961, amidst protests against the shah in Iran as well as in Europe, a U.S.-government Iran Task Force encouraged Prime Minster Ali Amini to counter his government's domestic unpopularity with new policies. As Robert Komer, a loyal "New Frontiersman" in the National Security Council under the Kennedy administration, warned, "if we are treading on the edge of potential disaster in Iran (for which Khrushchev sits patiently waiting), we must . . . take crisis measures."[63]

The shah's Bismarckian strategy for a White Revolution took shape between 1961 and 1963. Amini and his minister of agriculture, the former agrarian specialist and left-leaning journalist Hasan Arsanjāni, wanted to create a class of small rural landholders, a state-induced reform they believed was occurring throughout the Third World. Implementation began in 1962, even though Amini was soon dismissed. In its ideal form, the White Revolution overcame the backwardness represented by "feudal" elements in the countryside—whether or not this European term was applicable to Iran's rural social structure. It was a highly nationalistic venture that attempted to outmaneuver the National Front and leftist parties. Both had been calling for land reform for decades and using terms like "feudalism" to describe blockages to Iranian development and social progress. The color white was juxtaposed against the forces of black reaction—that is, the clergy and the "feudal" landlords—as well as the specter of Red communism.[64]

Over subsequent years, land-reform policies redistributed between 50 and 65 percent of existing agricultural plots. Even in tempered form, the effect was still radical. As Ervand Abrahamian explained,[65]

Amini's initial plan limited landlords to one village. Excess land was to be transferred to sharecroppers with tenancy rights. The watered-down version allowed landlords to pass villages to close relatives as well as to keep for themselves orchards, woodlands, plantations, mechanized farms, and agrobusinesses [sic]. Religious foundations were also allowed to keep their long-standing endowments [awqāfs]. Despite these dilutions, land reform accomplished what it was designed to do, undercut the notables, even though some large landowners, including the Pahlavi family, managed to transform themselves into successful commercial farmers.

The plan was based on a particular vision of modernity, whereby the shah would transcend the antagonisms of perceived backwardness in a semiperipheral country through political dictum. The land-reform measures were less attuned to providing a better livelihood to the country's peasants. There were no cadastral surveys conducted before parcel redistribution took place. As a result, between 1962 and 1972, most peasant stakeholders received less than the minimum parcel required for subsistence production. Landless sharecroppers did not receive any parcels at all, further commodifying the labor force and increasing migration to urban areas. The concentrated landed wealth of the (mostly absentee) landlord class was disbursed, however. Those who stayed in the countryside were encouraged to begin large-scale capitalist agricultural concerns.[66]

The outcome was neither a self-sufficient rural class nor a highly productive agricultural sector. Instead, the real beneficiary of land reform was the state itself, since power became further centralized in Tehran as the autonomy of provincial elites was removed. Ultimately, "inefficient" peasants failed to live up to the expectations of state technocrats. Government officials spent the late 1960s and 1970s applying various schemes of mechanization and relocation that disenchanted and dislocated many village households.[67] As wage differentials between city and country increased, along with a lack of stable support for agricultural production, migration greatly increased to urban areas. This derural-ization was the opposite effect of what land reform was supposed to accomplish. As the most radical element of the White Revolution, land reform was the "biggest push" of the Iranian state during the 1970s. It was not, however, a response to broad social demands by peasants. Instead, it emerged from the developmentalist vision of state elites, one that was shared by their intellectual critics.[68]

Before the 1960s, the Pahlavi state relied on the military, the landed elites, and the upper stratum of clergy as sources of social power. The White Revolution unsettled this mix. As nationalist intellectuals and supporters of the shah squared off about who was best suited to modernize Iran in an authentic fashion, such rapid and visible social change provided an opportunity for Islamist politics to stake out a related position. As 1979 revolutionaries would later argue, the White Revolution was often interpreted as a deviant version of development, a case of "pseudomodernization." To label this critique as particularly Islamist, however, ignores the fact that nearly all the country's public intellectuals, from the 1960s onward, relied on tropes of authenticity, indigenous development, anti-Western essentialism, and "Iranian–Islamic romanticism." As Ali Mirsepassi noted, "It was even popular for the intellectuals who participated in the government to make anti-Western . . . remarks."[69]

Ruhollah Khomeini, a Qom-based Grand Ayatollah—the highest classification of religious scholar—began to speak out against the shah during the early 1960s. Notably, Khomeini did not stress land reform or women's suffrage in his critiques. He preferred to denounce corruption of the state, media censorship, enrichment of government clients, neglect of the livelihoods of workers and peasants, selling oil to Israel, and the granting of "capitulations" such as extraterritorial rights for U.S. personnel.[70] For instance, in a 2 December 1962 speech in Qom, Khomeini accused the Pahlavi state of "dependent development" or pseudomodernization:[71]

> Foreigners must come even to build a road. Do international obligations demand this? If you have doctors and engineers [then] you have education. If you say you have education, you have wealth, you have students, and you have doctors and engineers: Why do you hire them from outside the country? Why do you pay foreigners a hundred thousand *tuman*s a month? Answer this! If you have no answer, then pity this country! For a hundred years it has had universities, but it has no doctors.

Khomeini did not yet call for an end to the monarchy, but his speeches were enough to warrant his arrest, which quickly led seminary students and supporters to mount protests in 1963. The shah exiled him to Najaf, in Iraq. Outside Iran's territory, Khomeini would continue his critiques, emulating lay intellectuals such as Jalal al-e Ahmad and Ali Shariati. Such inventions of tradition were hardly limited to Islamists. The combination of Third Worldism, a discourse of authenticity, and the sacralization of nationalist tropes was not unique to Iran, or even the Middle East. It was common stance throughout the postcolonial world, one the Caboverdian writer Amilcar Cabral described as "a return to the source."[72]

UPWARDLY MOBILE RADICALS

The vision of Iran's state technocrats for social transformation was on par with modernization programs around the Third World for a "New Order," from Indonesia and Korea to Brazil and Mexico. To carry it out, ministries under the shah sought out functionaries who had been educated in the United States and Europe. The strategy of the Pahlavi government was "to pursue economic growth as rapidly as possible."[73] Early attention to agriculture soon fell to the wayside as the state poured oil revenues into capital-intensive industry and construction. State-granted monopolies and trade restrictions allowed for regulation of imports, while rising oil income cushioned the budget. In addition to the monarchy's private holdings in industry (which helped to fund the large Pahlavi Foundation charity), a domestic industrial bourgeoisie emerged thanks to easy access to credit, high tariff barriers, and exclusive production licenses. Of the 473 large industrial concerns in the private sector, 370 were owned by just ten families. Family capitalism took shape through the rise of new conglomerates and business groups. Some of them had roots in the landed elite or wealthy mercantile classes, but others were nouveau riche.[74] GNP per capita grew around 8 percent per annum during the 1960s. As with most big pushes in states that used import substitution as a strategy for ramping up domestic production, however, continued efforts along the same investment paths tended to decrease productivity growth over time.[75]

The technocrats at the Ministry of the Economy believed they had discovered the secret to growth through planning. After high growth rates for the 1960s and oil-price booms in the early 1970s, the shah's ministers targeted growth rates at a staggering 15 percent per year for the fifth development plan (1973–78). Instead of the expected economic takeoff, the growth momentum began slowing by 1972. By 1975, it was apparent than investment bottlenecks were a serious constraint. Budgets were annually doubled or even tripled over the course of the mid-1970s. State funds were directed mostly at defense and capital-intensive industry rather than more widespread investments in health and education. The latter could have served as long-term inputs for growth in case oil prices collapsed. Many development projects went unfinished, as rising demand for goods and services could not be supplied by domestic sources. In short, "big-push" development was suitable for a country where capital was in limited supply, not one where capital was overly abundant and lacked profitable outlets for investment.

Retrospectively, it is tempting to see the developmental vision of the Pahlavi monarchy as hubris and nothing more. However, many Iranians today still believe that, if not for the 1979 revolution, the country would have entered the club of wealthy nations. After all, this is exactly what the shah promised. For example, in a 1963 speech in Isfahan, he said,[76]

> With respect to farming, industry, social activities, good works, the effect of this move in the future will be so great that I think the necessity of this order will be obvious to everyone. . . . The next generations will live in an environment which I hope will be equal and comparable to the highest social standards anywhere on the planet. . . . Your income should be such that you and your family are full. That you will have smart clothes. That you will have a nice house.

Echoing Juscelino Kubitschek's promise that Brazil would achieve "fifty years of progress in five," Mohammad Reza Shah also pledged, "what has taken others centuries to perform or has been accompanied by bloody revolution, which in itself can cause problems, we are performing in a short period."[77] The technocrat king saw no contradiction between a tradition-clad monarchy and a developmental state. If anything, he believed the two were interlinked. Given the political resilience into the twenty-first century of other Gulf monarchies to Iran's south— Saudi Arabia, Kuwait, the sheikhdoms of the United Arab Emirates— the shah was not wrong in this regard. The key political difference was that the Pahlavi monarchy never developed the dispersed kinship networks of Gulf Arab monarchies that allowed them to withstand crises of succession.[78] Instead, the Pahlavi monarchy rationalized the armed forces and state ministries toward bureaucratic institutions. When the revolutionary upsurge came in 1978, these institutions proved to be unreliable sources of power for the shah.

Though unplanned by the state, people who ended up as revolutionaries in 1979 were also linked to the new social-policy initiatives of the White Revolution. These individuals were not part of the state elite, but their upward social trajectories were rooted in transformations spurred by Pahlavi state building. In fact, the welfare system of the Pahlavi monarchy sheds light on the social forces that took part in the 1979 revolution as well as on popular mobilization in the postrevolutionary period.

The pillars of the shah's welfare policies in the 1960s and 1970s were social-insurance benefits for formal wage-workers and civil servants, educational expansion in urban areas, and literacy and public-health campaigns in rural areas. Worker profit sharing, a policy of the White Revolution, was extended to nearly three hundred thousand workers by the mid-1970s. This amounted to around 14 percent of industrial laborers.[79] State-linked trade unions were established in the 1960s and coordinated annual wage increases. These corporatist bodies came in response to the labor unrest of the late 1950s and channeled demands for material improvements into negotiated gains.[80] By 1960, social-insurance coverage for the expanding formal labor force was still minimal. In that year, a Workers Welfare Bank was established to provide low-interest loans for housing and large family expenses. Funds were provided from the Social Insurance Organization (SIO), created by the 1949 Insurance Act. The shah, symbolically, opened the very first account in the bank.[81]

Over the 1960s, the number of individuals enrolled by the SIO tripled from fewer than two hundred thousand to over six hundred thousand workers. Including dependents, between two and a half to three million individuals were covered, amounting to around 8 to 12 percent of the population. In 1974, social-insurance laws for manual workers were changed to centralize social-insurance funds under a single organization—a proposal that dated back to the Mossadeq era. As a result, the Social Security Organization (SSO) was created under the Ministry of Welfare, also founded in 1974. Coverage was extended to urban salaried workers in the private sector, and voluntary insurance was offered to the self-employed. Civil servants were insured through a separate fund, the Civil Servants Retirement Organization. Rural social insurance, although legislated in 1969, never materialized. In 1976, the government announced a plan for a comprehensive welfare system to be implemented under a newly merged Ministry of Health and Welfare.[82] On the cusp of the 1979 revolution, then, a framework existed for a social-insurance and health-care system that covered formal wage labor in large enterprises and workers in the civil service, the military, the oil and gas industries, and other government sectors. However, the large rural sector—around 50 percent of the country's population—was de facto excluded, as was the growing pool of informal workers who had been migrating to urban areas since the 1950s.[83] Access to state welfare came, as in most countries, through the workplace. The model was unequal by design.

As a result, many Iranians relied on welfare networks outside the state, often through mutual-aid societies or kinship networks. In cities, most individuals lived within walking distance of local mosques or private halls that housed neighborhood associations. These councils (*hayāt*), often sponsored by merchant notables in urban bazaars, funded charity measures, health care, and education for the poor. In Tehran alone, there were reportedly twelve thousand of these councils operating outside state-welfare networks, mostly formed from the late 1960s onward.[84] In other words, formal corporatist welfare measures looked generous from the perspective of state ministries, but many individuals were excluded from concretely visible links to the "Great Civilization" that the monarchy was building.

In the educational sphere, public expansion occurred at all levels during the 1960s and 1970s. Kindergartens were introduced, elementary- and high-school enrollment doubled, college attendance tripled, and the number of students in universities abroad reached eighty thousand.[85] The shift was similar to Nasser's Egypt, where university enrollments tripled from 1954 to 1970. In both countries, newly acquired professional and technical credentials were a key mechanism of status distinction, which could be converted into higher incomes and stable employment. Both regimes also believed in education as a political strategy. In Nasser's case, school and university expansion helped to ameliorate class privileges in Egyptian society. Educational institutions provided upward mobility for the low- and middle-income youth who tended to support his brand of Arab socialism.[86] In Iran, new cadres for the Pahlavi developmental push could be generated in order to replace hostile nationalists in the middle class who continued to scorn the monarchy.

Educational expansion resulted in two main consequences. First, as sons and daughters of the upper class often went abroad for their education, elite universities increasingly allowed in students from lower-income households. These individuals were more disposed toward hard sciences, medicine, and engineering than previous generations of students had been. The historian David Menashri, for example, observed firsthand in the late 1970s that Tehran's engineering students were usually first-generation university goers who took the bus to campus and spoke with working-class accents. Cultural and artistic departments, conversely, were filled with the sons and daughters of the preexisting Iranian literati elite who arrived via chauffeur.[87] These newly arriving students became the constituency of the radical-left opposition in the 1970s, such as the Marxist Fedāyān-e Khalq (no relation to the 1950s group of similar name) and left-Islamist Mojāhedin.[88] Such groups had underground campus presences and heroic oppositional discourses. Tens of thousands of students and graduates were also connected to organizations outside the country and their umbrella institution, the National Union of the Confederation of Iranian Students.[89] During the 1979 revolution, then, universities became nodal points for organizing street demonstrations, because students were some of the most militant members of the opposition.

Second, even with institutional expansion, Iran's educational system maintained a centralized status hierarchy. Resources and people tended to flow toward Tehran and a few other cities. A study of Shiraz's Pahlavi University Medical School, conducted just before 1979, estimated that the chance of enrollment was three hundred times greater for children of military households and one hundred times greater for professional households than for those of working-class and rural families.[90] Furthermore, because state social policy poorly targeted lower-income households, many students tended to drop out after the first few years of primary education. This was especially the case for girls, often pulled from school by families before the age of puberty. By the revolution, Iran still had one of the lowest percentages of higher-education enrollment, doctor-patient ratios, and primary-school completion rates in the Middle East.[91]

The last pillar of the Pahlavi welfare system, also announced as part of the White Revolution, was the Literacy and Health Corps for rural areas. These programs borrowed from postrevolutionary Cuban models, which had become popularized internationally in the Third World during the 1960s. From 1962 to 1979, the Literacy Corps trained about two hundred thousand high-school graduates, with incentives of a monthly wage and exemption from military service.[92] Literacy Corps volunteers taught rudimentary Persian language literary skills to over two million children and one million adults. This was part welfare project and part state-building project, as many members of Iran's ethnic minorities used Persian as a second language, if at all.

Mobile Health Corps stations were also sent into the field, and the state claimed that four hundred units served twenty thousand out of a total fifty-five thousand villages. This seems to be an exaggeration, as the number of health workers was limited by the system of recruitment. Iran's circumscribed medical-education system was geared to produce highly specialized doctors, not primary-health workers. After 1964, medical graduates eligible for the army were drafted into the Health Corps rather than into regular military service, but this put a cap on the number of doctors available. In addition, the primary-health care delivered by Health Corps doctors was unconnected to local hospitals. As two community doctors observed of the Health Corps stations in *The Lancet* in 1973, "While these are a potential resource, their numbers are few, and the interest they have in rural areas remains questionable."[93] As mentioned later, in chapter four, pilot projects for a more comprehensive "barefoot-doctor" program began in 1974 with WHO assistance, but they did not receive much support from the state.

These programs were followed up with a Development Corps, which used military equipment to install basic sanitation and potable water in villages. A main impediment to the White Revolution's welfare push into the countryside was the top-down organization of these programs. In some cases, peasants and rural inhabitants perceived little difference between the previous impositions of the landlords and the new impositions of the state.[94] In other cases, villagers preferred local customary elites to newly appointed state officials, who tended to reside off-site, in nearby cities.[95] Women teaching in the Literacy Corps were required to wear a military skirt and not allowed to wear the veil—the main form of dress among women in rural Iran. Men who spoke only Persian had to communicate with villagers whose primary language was sometimes Kurdish or Turkish. As Asghar Schirazi described it,[96]

> This regime's penetration of rural life began with the way land reform was decided on and carried out (i.e., from the top), which perforce turned the peasants, who until then had been subjects of the landlord, into subjects of the state. . . . The Soldier of Knowledge did his military service by attempting to teach the peasants to read and write. He usually did so reluctantly, being constrained to fulfill his state-imposed obligation in an unfamiliar environment and to use teaching material having little to do with rural life. Then there was the Army of Health, also composed of secondary school graduates who had to do a sort of paramilitary service in rural regions. The third military force of this sort was the Army of Counseling and Construction, whose troops were supposed to teach the rural population agriculture—after acquiring the knowledge they were required to impart themselves in a two-month course in town.

In sum, a main constraint of the rural-welfare component of the White Revolution was the limited capacity of central state institutions to link into everyday life in the countryside. This would dramatically change after the 1979 revolution. Certainly, during the last two decades of the Pahlavi era, literacy did increase in both urban and rural Iran. Yet the urban-rural literacy gap remained, as table 4 shows.

TABLE 4   LITERACY LEVELS IN IRAN BY SEX AND SECTOR, 1956–76

Year	Population Total (x 10³)	Rural (%)	Male literacy Urban (%)	Rural (%)	Female literacy Urban (%)	Rural (%)
1956	18,955	69	45	11	21	1
1966	25,789	62	61	25	38	4
1976	33,709	53	74	44	56	17

SOURCE: Statistical Center of Iran.

NOTE: Literacy rates are calculated as a percentage of total individuals over reading age (6 years).

The effect of the various welfare corps on rural life was decidedly mixed. As Eric Hooglund noted, "Since the opinions of the peasants were not sought in either the formulation or the implementation of projects, it was difficult to enlist their active support for programs supposedly intended for their benefit."[97]

The effect on many of the men and women working in corps projects, however, was more profound. Many members were enthusiastic middle-class individuals, with romantic notions of peasant life, who became radicalized by destitute conditions in rural areas.[98] As men and women traveled around Iran in these programs (or became conscripted in the military more generally) they helped to foster a "revolutionary counter-culture" after returning to city life. As the historian Mohammad Tavakoli-Targhi recalled of his brother, who served in the Literacy Corps: "His understanding of the problems of village life politicized his consciousness and spurred the formation of a new revolutionary identity in him and many others. His subsequent involvement with leftist groups was the direct and unintended consequence of the state's programs of development."[99] After the revolution, many literacy and health corpsmen returned to villages for new rural-development projects under the Islamic Republic. Just as with university expansion in cities, then, rural welfare programs functioned as vehicles for upward mobility by the country's expanding middle classes. Yet during the 1979 revolution, many of these individuals used the new social power obtained through such organizations to mobilize against the very state that created them.

In sum, a main consequence of the developmental push and the expansion of state welfare in the 1960s and 1970s was the relative and absolute growth in size of the professional salaried and urban working classes. Historically, these two social groups had made the most public demands on the state from below during the Pahlavi era. The welfare expansions of this period were directly targeted at these classes, yet their loyalty was not secured. Instead, the White Revolution, the oil boom of the 1970s, and the promises of catching up through developmental state building contributed to a heightening of social expectations among these individuals. Many resented the limited access to political power that their newfound cultural and economic status would have implied. Furthermore, as national wealth and status increased, inequality in access to various welfare and educational institutions became even more apparent. Sporadic protests had been growing during the 1970s over such issues as urban slum clearances, bazaar regulations, and labor demands. Yet when the mobilizational wave of 1977–78 began, it was these two social groups—not Islamist-linked ones—that spearheaded the first set of demonstrations and protests.[100]

THE AMBIVALENCE OF MODERNIZATION

The revisionist historian of the French Revolution François Furet wrote: "For almost 200 years, the history of the Revolution has never been other than an account of causation, thus a discourse about identity."[101] Accounting for the 1979 Iranian revolution is contentious for the same reasons. Explanations inevitably contain assumptions and expectations about widespread political processes of the twentieth century. Theorists implicitly or explicitly view Iranian history in comparison with other states and regions. One of the best explanations is by the social historian Ervand Abrahamian. Abrahamian argued that the 1979 revolution occurred because of what may be called a "modernization gap." Economic modernization was occurring, but not a concomitant political modernization that was necessary to release "the mounting tensions" produced by economic change. This led to a form of "uneven development and lopsided modernization."[102]

The shah's supporters believed that state modernization would carry the country upward for a few more decades, perhaps long enough to reach the club of wealthy nations promised by the shah. According to Abrahamian, however, an inflation-driven economic crisis and a foreign-induced institutional crisis—the latter spurred by Jimmy Carter's admonition on human rights—created a set of political opportunities. With these openings, social mobilization by various groups increased. Each group came to believe in Ayatollah Khomeini's leadership of the opposition as the most obvious solution. Bazaar-based workshop proprietors saw him as a defender of private property and an intractable foe of the monarchy. The intelligentsia saw him as an anti-imperialist

Mossadeq in clerical regalia. Workers saw him as a populist redistributor of status and wealth. Rural households saw him as someone who could fulfill the White Revolution's failed promises.[103] Lastly, and perhaps contrary to the idea of a modernization gap, the bureaucratization of the state allowed civil servants and public-sector workers to see themselves "not as cogs in the state machinery but as members of the discontented middle classes."[104] Was this a gap between different forms of modernization, however, or a gap in theories of modernization?

As modernization is not an actual process that can be either undertaken or deviated away from, but rather is a metaphor about a wide variety of historical changes, the term is not always useful for understanding such changes. As Frederick Cooper pointed out, "twenty years from now everything will still be modern, but it could possibly be quite different. Trying to escape from the false dichotomy of modern and traditional, we find ourselves with a concept whose main value is to correct past misuses of the same word."[105] If the economic growth and industrialization that occurred during Iran in the 1960s and 1970s could be called modernization, then why not the development of a strong state apparatus with a monarch at the top of it? Kingship and patrimonial structures of rule continue to exist into the twentieth and twenty-first centuries. Intertwined with bureaucratic organizations in most semiperipheral countries, such patrimonial networks are as modern as other types of state formation.[106] Abrahamian could retrospectively look back and posit that a growing economic segment of Pahlavi Iran was modern whereas the political apparatus was not, but this was more the making of a claim than the explanation of a cause.[107]

Theories aside, Abrahamian crucially showed that the form of modernization undertaken by the Pahlavi state fostered the monarchy's own oppositional coalition. This is why the political scientist Tim McDaniel identified the Pahlavi monarchy as an autocratic modernizer akin to late-nineteenth-century Russia. Through rapid modernization, the state undermined "the formation of strong and legitimate social elites and inhibits the maturation of hierarchical relations among classes."[108] State-led economic planning prevented the formation of coherent elite bases that could support the shah, such as a business or professional class. Although true, such an account does not need to be flattened into a modern/traditional dichotomy. Merchants and clerical elites who opposed the shah did not do so because of a residual traditionalism.[109]

An alternative theorization, one that was popular among many Iranian social scientists themselves, was that the revolution and its outcome stemmed from "dependent capitalist development" experienced under Pahlavi state rule. Theories of dependent development were a reworking of 1960s dependency theory as semiperipheral states underwent rapid industrialization. Relations of dependency, formulated from experiences of the nineteenth-century world economy, had been associated with manufacturing in the metropole and primary-commodity production in the periphery. Once manufacturing spread to the Third World in the postwar era, a new conceptualization of unequal global development was formulated.[110] In Iran, as in many middle-income countries, the local industrial capitalist class was "dependent" on the state to provide protected markets. It also relied on foreign capital to provide high-tech inputs and managerial skills. Iranian social scientists tended to attribute this dependence to the predominance of oil in the economy, which prevented the emergence of an "independent" bourgeoisie with their own, autonomous sources of power.[111] This line of thought followed Karl Marx, as well as Barrington Moore, in attributing the march of modernity to an independent bourgeoisie in Western Europe and North America. Iran, however, carried the burden of "Asiatic patrimonial" production relations for centuries, with "total power" embodied in the state.[112] This image of state-society relations was Marxian-Weberian in origin, and "overstated" the Iranian state.[113] As in modernization theory, dependency theorists also attributed the rise of the Shi'i clergy to a developmental hangover. Unlike landlords and nomadic tribal elites, the Shi'i establishment was the last autonomous bastion of "traditional" power that the shah had not undermined. Once the opportunity arose amidst the mobilizations of 1977–78, this social group allied with "traditional" mercantile bazaar merchants. By dint of the peculiar dependent nature of Iranian development, these classes were able to establish political hegemony over less-developed capitalist and "modern" working classes.[114]

This interpretation tends to reify political orientations within classes that were, at the time, quite in flux.[115] As Maurice Zeitlin noted on similar debates concerning the Chilean elite during the 1960s, theoretical assumptions of dualism by intellectuals resulted in seeing societies "transmogrified entirely into an opposition between disembodied forms of traditionality vs. modernity."[116] If Iran's landlord families easily slid into the role of industrial capitalists in the 1960s, then what does that imply about the traditionalism of any social group in Iran before the revolution? Bazaar merchants, for instance, crafted new, autonomous organizations and strategies in response to attempts by the Pahlavi state to impose commercial regulations. For many of these merchants, the

1970s was a time of capital accumulation and associational expansion, not one of retrenchment into traditional networks. As Arang Keshavarzian critically noted, "the bazaar-as-tradition perspective uniformly presents the bazaar as untouched by state policies, agencies, and agendas. The only moment when the state enters these accounts is when bazaars react negatively to it."[117] Even today, the teleological assumptions in this type of interpretation continue to blind explanations of postrevolutionary Iranian society. The social role and ideological orientation of Iran's clerical establishment have changed over the past four decades, often because of internal political struggles and external social pressure. Clerical attitudes and actions are, however, inevitably depicted as traditionalist. Such a view reveals little about what happened in Iran during the postrevolutionary decades.

A final explanation of the revolution relies on contingent, process-based accounts of the political mobilization that occurred between 1977 and 1979. These analyses generally stress the cross-class nature of the revolutionary coalition and the various ideologies that combined into a syncretic source for mass protest.[118] Amidst an underdetermined revolutionary situation, Khomeinist cadres acted as the Bonapartist force that managed to take over the state.[119] Process-based theories can be taken to an ultimate endpoint, wherein the making of the 1979 revolution was totally and radically contingent.[120] These accounts are useful for understanding how the actual events played out. The revolution was not a single event but a long chain of mobilized upsurges. Instead of seeing the process as inevitable, we should use the thought experiment that the biologist Stephen Jay Gould asks for the study of evolutionary life. If we rewound history to the summer of 1977, would the revolution have proceeded the same way, or occurred at all? There is no logical reason to think so, but as Gould remarked, "our strong desire to identify trends often leads us to detect a directionality that doesn't exist, or to infer causes that cannot be sustained."[121]

Even with a radically contingent account whereby a situation is labeled only retroactively as "revolutionary," the changing sources of social power in Iran should be examined. These were utilized by millions of individuals in various ways during the mobilizational upheaval, and influenced the postrevolutionary period as well. This is not the place for a full accounting of the revolution, which has been analyzed far more than any other aspect of twentieth-century Iran. There is insight to be gained, however, in relaxing assumptions about the direction of history embedded in earlier notions of modernity and tradition or Iran versus the West. Such theories are not entirely wrong, but they can be reformulated without teleological baggage.

The Pahlavi state was neither a neopatrimonial regime that failed to modernize nor a state engaged in a deviant or false modernization. Instead, the Pahlavi state was in fact a modernizing state, inasmuch as its own elites saw their task as modernization, however they defined it. The struggle to catch up generated imperatives to *do something*. What that meant, however, was not given. Elites' perception of modernization is crucial here, since they are the ones who determine state policies on social welfare and economic investment. Pahlavi-state technocrats, the shah included, believed in a particular path of action. If pursued vigorously enough, they thought, this would bring Iran toward the levels of wealth, status, and power possessed by Western countries.

As Ernest Gellner noted, the "struggle to catch up" in the world economy was the critical imperative. For Iran, this involved the expansion of particular social classes and groups—professional state cadres and industrial working classes—that were supposed to aid in the state-building project. To do this, the state worked to create social-welfare institutions that buttressed and empowered those classes. In the Pahlavi era, the result was a corporatist welfare regime that included some of these social classes and groups but excluded many others. Once linked up to the state, new middle and working classes did not simply receive state-welfare benefits and accept them silently. Rather, social welfare was used as a foundation with which to make additional demands on the state. This process repeated during much of Iran's twentieth century from the constitutional revolution onwards—from the rebellions of the 1920s, to the strikes of the 1940s and 1950s, and ultimately to the student and worker mass demonstrations of the late 1970s. Threats against the government, real or perceived, were a driving force for state expansion of social policy. Only a blind reading of history could insist that welfare expansion in Iran ultimately acted as a co-opting force.

The revolution did not pit a modernizing society against a traditional state, nor did it pit a traditional society against a modernizing state. Instead, as the historian Steven Pincus argued, based on his rereading of the 1688 English revolution, "revolutions only occur when states have embarked on ambitious state modernization programs." For Pincus, modernization is a "self-conscious effort" to transform the state. These efforts include bureaucratic centralization, a strengthened military, an increase in economic growth, and the gathering of cultural and technical information about the people within the particular state's territory. During these periods, "the political nation is convinced of the need for political modernization but there are profound disagreements on the proper course of state innovation."[122] Obviously, a great deal of historical distance separates England in 1688 and Iran in 1979. Such disagreements over the future path of Iran were not simply profound; they were vehemently impassioned. Nevertheless, the insight here is that none of the social groups that participated in the revolution entered from a static position, whether "traditional" clergy, urban bazaaris, or rural peasants.

As the next two chapters show, these groups also underwent transformations in organization, ideology, and orientation in the decades before the revolution. Peasants, once believed to be absent from the revolution, given fewer protests in the countryside, were involved in urban revolt. As anthropologists observed, the post-1960s generation of rural youth were highly politicized and traversed easily between city and country.[123] The bazaar is characterized as an unchanging, even medieval, economic social structure, but the term explains little about changing social activities within the dense commercial networks of city centers. In reality, bazaar merchants innovated organizational forms and entrepreneurial practices amidst the economic environment of Pahlavi import substitution industrialization.[124] Lastly, segments of the Shi'i clergy were arguably one of the most transformed social groups in Iran. The proof is easy to see. Ayatollah Khomeini left Iran in 1963 with an orthodox notion of Shi'i political jurisprudence. He returned in February 1979 with an idea new to the history of Shi'i political thought: an Islamic Republic. Those two terms had never been put together before. It was a vision of an alternative modernization for Iran.[125] As Pincus states, "it is precisely the modernizing state's actions to extend its authority more deeply into society that politicize and mobilize people on the periphery."[126] The 1979 revolution was eminently about modernization, but not as an abstract yardstick to be achieved or an inevitable force against which bastions of tradition were destined to react. Instead, the revolution set different groups of modernizers in fervent struggle against one another.

CHAPTER 3

Creating a Martyrs' Welfare State

*1979, War, and the Survival
of the Islamic Republic*

"In 1981, we had small stations all over Tehran for war
volunteers to sign up."

"Yes, but how did you get volunteers for the war in the
first place?"

"We made a lot of promises."

—Interview with former city official, Tehran, June 2008

That a revolution happens at all is remarkable. That the state it produces
lasts longer than a few years is even more remarkable. The Pahlavi monarchy crafted social policy with a particular vision of modernization in
mind. The newly formed Islamic Republic, however, possessed no blueprint. Ayatollah Khomeini held forth on the just order and egalitarian
society to be produced by a revolutionary state following Islamic principles. He did not elaborate this social order in much detail. Calling on
state officials to concentrate their efforts on the downtrodden, Khomeini
"left the clerics and technocrats in the government an area of activity
where policy questions could be made relatively free from his influence."[1]

Among historians and social scientists, this area of activity is mostly
unexamined. The mix of social policies that emerged under the Islamic
Republic is usually explained away as a residual effect of other political
processes. Delivered from the state on high to select segments of the population, social welfare is attributed to a combination of ideological decree,
oil-bloated largesse, and loyalty-securing patronage.[2] Welfare is to function as a soft tool of control that barely masks an underlying set of coercive mechanisms. Untethered by any need for revenue extraction, the
state hovers over society in a rentierist dirigible. Given this common

portrayal of shaky foundations, it is understandable why the Islamic Republic's collapse has been predicted every few years since its inception.

This caricature of social policy portrays a complex set of policies and institutions as a mechanistic state contrivance. It elides attention to social pressures from below, political competition from above, or the incorporation of external ideological and organizational influences. The assumptions underlying this caricature have consequences for those who study contemporary politics. If social policy is a matter of controlling and disciplining the masses, then the social forces of political change must lie elsewhere. There is no need to examine the "black box" of welfare politics.

In this book I argue the opposite. Social policies of the postrevolutionary state played a central role in the consolidation and legitimation of the Islamic Republic as a nation-state. At the same time, social welfare was a crucial arena of popular contestation and constraint on state elites themselves. Moreover, the state's capacities and limits in other economic and political spheres are difficult to understand without grasping the intended and unintended effects of social policies over the past three decades. As visitors over the years have attested, Iran's sociocultural transformations during this period of time are stark and surprising.[3] This is not a result of the dichotomous separation of state and society. It is the outcome of the links through which new social forces and new elite factions transformed each other. To see these links, we need to open the black box of welfare politics in the Islamic Republic of Iran.

The sections in this chapter examine the political and ideological environment of the first postrevolutionary decade. First, I show how the welfare system of the state's initial decade became dual in structure and overlapping in function. As soon as the revolution culminated in victory, it turned vicious. A bloody struggle between factions and camps occurred within a broad revolutionary coalition. At the same time, widespread popular mobilizations pushed their social demands onto the agenda. These two processes occurred as the country rapidly experienced civil war, externally imposed autarky, and then interstate war with Iraq from 1980 to 1988.

A chief outcome was the formation and fortification of a set of parallel state institutions, including ones charged with the provision of social welfare. These parallel organizations served to mobilize assent from below, absorbing social demands but also constraining and directing state capacity toward particular ends. Even with the ascension of forces loyal to Khomeini, parallel institutionalism became a defining characteristic of the Islamic Republic. It also provided a widening space for intra-elite factionalism and popular contestation beyond the war's end and Khomeini's death.

Second, whether in the 1979 constitutional debates or in subsequent struggles between Parliament and the Guardian Council, the codification of social and economic policies was not preordained by a sanctified plan. Instead, factional politicking and ad hoc responses to pressing social demands took leading roles. The combination of elite competition and popular mobilization forced state officials to pursue both guns and butter while the war with Iraq unexpectedly dragged on. As a result, the government multiplied the incentives for war participation on and off the front. The expansion of social policy through parallel welfare institutions reordered the distribution of material and symbolic resources within the population at large. Revolutionary institutions created pathways for newly valued status groups. In turn, a sacred concept of *martyrdom* became profanely instrumentalized to the service of the state, albeit with unintended consequences.

The Islamic Republic inherited the corporatist welfare organizations of the Pahlavi monarchy but also created a second set of postrevolutionary welfare organizations that directly targeted those segments of the population excluded from the previous system—a "martyrs' welfare state." This dual welfare regime was more inclusionary than the Pahlavi system, but it also was more varied in institutional form. Parallel organizations overlapped each other's welfare activities. Instead of merging various welfare organizations into a single social-policy apparatus, the state repeatedly proliferated new organizations to compete with old ones and new activities for existing organizations.

I highlight two of these social-policy extensions during the war period (1980–88). The first is the Imam Khomeini Relief Committee, an antipoverty organization that became vital to war efforts. The second is Iran's "G.I. Bill," the creation of pathways for war volunteers into higher education after the reopening of the country's university system. These are principal examples of the connections between warfare and welfare in the Islamic Republic. The legacies of both social policies long outlasted the war's end.

Last, I highlight the growth of intra-elite conflict as state officials peered out onto a postwar vista. Though they had already survived assassination attempts, internal purges, and battlefield tragedies, the first postrevolutionary decade did not unify Khomeinist cadres. Even with intractable antagonisms, however, the war did force agreement among revolutionary elites on one matter. To survive, the Islamic

Republic needed to compete with the rest of the world on external criteria of modernization, not their own.

FROM DUAL POWER TO DISTRUSTFUL PARALLELISM

On 1 February 1979, after more than a decade in exile, Ayatollah Khomeini stepped off an Air France 747 jet onto a Tehran airstrip. Ten days later, the revolution triumphed. Journalists rushed to snap photographs of Khomeini's homecoming. In pictures of the event, at least six fellow revolutionaries also emerged from the plane. By 1989, three of them were dead (Motahhari, Lāhouti, Ghotbzādeh), and one was in exile (Bani-Sadr).[4] Ebrahim Yazdi, also on the plane, would become the deputy prime minister of the provisional government four days later, rise to foreign minister in April, resign in November in response to the occupation of the U.S. Embassy, and become relegated to the political margins for two decades. Mohsen Rafiqdust, a former political prisoner who drove Khomeini that day from the airport to the city center, would become the first minister of the Islamic Revolutionary Guards in 1982 and head of the welfare body and economic conglomerate Foundation of the Dispossessed in 1989. Even among those who professed allegiance to Khomeini, the political fortunes of these revolutionaries were uncertain.

The revolutionary coalition winnowed down over the next four years. The occupation of the U.S. Embassy in November 1979 precipitated a crisis that drove liberal-nationalist moderates out of leadership positions. From 1980 to 1982, internecine violence decimated leftist and Islamist factions struggling against groups closely united under Khomeini's leadership. Yet in 1983, with all competitors sidelined and war with Iraq afoot, internal conflict between Khomeini-aligned elites continued. This should not be too surprising. Nearly all postrevolutionary states, even one-party authoritarian regimes, exhibit factional competition. In Iran's case, however, intra-elite conflict never became institutionalized within a well-organized political structure, as occurred with Mexico's Institutional Revolutionary Party (whose name itself tells the story) or the Chinese Communist Party.[5] On the contrary, intra-elite conflict contributed to an unwieldy proliferation of parallel institutions of governance. A central source of this conflict was struggle over social welfare and economic policy.

On the day of Khomeini's arrival to Tehran's Mehrābād airport, three million people reportedly lined the streets to his final destination of

Behesht-e Zahrā Cemetery, on the road to the seminary-filled city of Qom. This is likely an exaggerated number, but it still suggests a key feature of the 1979 revolution. The population of Iran in that year was 35 million. If we include demonstrations in all other cities, towns, and villages in 1978–79, it would not be an exaggeration to estimate that popular mobilization leading up to the fall of the shah likely involved more than 10 percent of the country's citizens. If we exclude some 45 percent of the population under fifteen years of age, the figure reaches far higher, as do opposition claims of six to nine million total participants in the revolution. No matter the exact number, it was a mass phenomenon that dwarfed participation levels in the French and Russian revolutions, as well as the 1989–91 collapse of the Soviet Union, by an order of magnitude.[6]

This upsurge of mobilization did not end on 12 February 1979. Educated Iranians studying and working abroad came back home expecting to shape postrevolutionary society. Young migrants in urban areas returned to their villages with new hopes for better livelihoods and higher prestige. Workers kept their bosses locked inside offices. Peasants rushed to occupy unsupervised land. Armed with emotional energy garnered from street demonstrations and heightened senses of empowerment against authority, many people pushed to upend the status quo felt in everyday experience. In offices, factories, seminaries, universities, high schools, villages, and households, many believed the new order was up for grabs. After the revolution, authority could be delegitimized. "Everywhere we looked," a man in Ahvaz reminisced, "we saw little versions of the shah."[7]

During the Islamic Republic's first decade, much of this popular upsurge was repressed or contained. However, much of it was also absorbed and channeled into parallel institutions of governance. Reinhard Bendix called the latter "mobilizing assent from below," a process common in those remarkable revolutions that survive their initial paroxysms.[8] It is one means by which revolutionary situations end and the task of building a government begins.[9] Even as the Islamic Republic's leaders projected a victorious front of national unity to the outside world, competition within the revolutionary coalition and mobilizational upsurges from below weaved and heaved together. These two political processes shaped the state's parallel structure and expanded social policies to new segments of the population.

When the shah finally departed, on 16 January 1979, his newly appointed prime minister, Shāpur Bakhtiār, attempted for several weeks to placate popular demands. Still in Paris, Khomeini had already approved the formation of a revolutionary council of close aides and opposition figures to coordinate protests inside Iran. In front of the crowd at Tehran's Behesht-e Zahrā on 1 February, he refused to recognize Bakhtiār's government as legitimate. Four days later, he authorized Mehdi Bāzargān, the liberal head of the Liberation Movement, as acting prime minister for a provisional government. The country entered a revolutionary situation of dual power, where "two or more political blocs . . . *claim* to be the legitimate state."[10] Over the previous month, increasing cycles of protest had accompanied the breakdown in public legitimacy. Government workers were often on strike, including the police. As a result, neighborhood committees took over public functions such as traffic, food provisioning, fuel distribution, sanitation, and self-defense. Popular committees formed in hospitals, factories, and schools.[11] When Khomeini arrived at the airport on 1 February, these committees, not the police or army, provided the security.[12]

In the final week of the revolution, defections splintered the armed forces. Large caches of weapons began to be handed over to protestors.[13] Many of these popular committees suddenly became armed. There were weapons everywhere. A man described how, in the Caspian coastal city of Rasht, "[his] sister transported Kalashnikovs across town under her chador."[14] A boastful tale of youthful militancy, perhaps, but most Iranian men who served for conscription in the shah's army had small-weapons training. On the whole, the 1979 revolution was nonviolent. Many people slept in the streets of Tehran to prevent tanks from amassing in columns.[15] In the last days, however, skirmishes with guns and Molotov cocktails flared between an array of opposition groups—most notably the Marxist Fedāyān and the Islamic Mojāhedin-e Khalq—and elite sections of the imperial army. Just a year previously, such leftist organizations were in retreat because of losses in Che Guevara–styled guerilla campaigns against the Pahlavi monarchy. In the last six months of the revolution, however, such opposition groups gained thousands of acolytes. As the manager of a large company awkwardly admitted to me, during the height of the revolution he "belonged to the Albanian faction of the Fedāyān." Why would an Iranian student choose to side with Albania—associated at the time with the Stalinist holdout Enver Hoxha? It had little to do with Albania and more with the competition between oppositional groups for radical bona fides: "Because it broke off from the Maoist faction, which someone told us was reactionary."[16] In sum, at the cusp of the shah's fall Iran contained a large but disorganized left, a small assembly of liberal religious nationalists, and Islamist groups drawn or pulled under the umbrella of Khomeini's leadership.

The sheer variety of organizations, ideologies, and political expectations that made up the revolutionary coalition should not be underestimated. As long as the Pahlavi monarchy had remained in place, this coalition stood largely united. This mobilizational antiregime glue, as James Jasper phrases it, revealed "the power of negative thinking."[17] Just under the large splash in *Keyhān* newspaper of 16 January 1979, THE SHAH HAS GONE, a smaller headline read, IMAM KHOMEINI: IF THERE IS NO CONSPIRACY, MARXISTS ARE FREE TO EXPRESS THEIR OPINIONS.[18] Once the shah was no longer around to blame, however, the most difficult day of the revolution arrived: the day after.

On 11 February, the armed forces declared their neutrality, Bakhtiār fled, and the revolution was declared victorious. As with any revolution, the subsequent consolidation of a new state was far less straightforward. In the case of Iran, however, integration of already-mobilized committees, networks, and other revolutionary groups under the full control of a unified state apparatus was never thoroughly achieved. For example, most people can remember the occupation of the U.S. Embassy on 4 November 1979. Student followers of Khomeini made the decision to enter the embassy gates without his foreknowledge. Yet on 14 February 1979—a mere three days after the revolution's success— Fedāyān supporters had tried the same act, also unbeknownst to the group's own leadership. Committees claiming adherence to Khomeini prevented them from succeeding.[19] Beginning from the first days, postrevolutionary power was consolidated by forming or commandeering parallel groups to outflank contenders.

There is a long list of such bodies formed just in 1979 alone. Nearly all functions of government had at least one parallel organization. The thirteen-member Revolutionary Council, led by Morteza Motahhari, shared several members with the Bāzargān provisional government even as it competed with it. The council introduced its own legislation and proposed a draft of the new constitution. It also supervised an ad-hoc system of courts organized under a revolutionary tribunal system, which clashed in jurisprudence with existing civil courts. A Khomeini confidant, Ayatollah Mohammad Beheshti, set up the Islamic Republic Party (IRP) within a month of the revolution. The party published a newspaper, *Jomhuri-ye Eslāmi,* and quickly moved to cultivate a mass base in order to challenge leftist parties. Beheshti's son reminisced that the main function of the IRP was the making of cadres, and he claimed that eighty thousand people signed up on the first day (29 March 1979), even members of the Mojāhedin-e Khalq. In June, a Tehran committee organized a Khomeinist militia known as the Islamic Revolutionary Guards. In Napoleonic fashion, its members refused the hierarchical ranking system of the armed forces' officer corps. The 1979 constitution, approved in a December referendum, combined the Fifth Republic–inspired structures of Parliament and president with separate bodies of Islamic guidance overseen by an unorthodox advent in Shi'i political thought, the Guardianship of Jurisprudence.[20] In sum, a leading dynamic of the postrevolutionary period was the proliferation of public and semipublic organizations that overlapped in functions and duties. This parallelism had an enormous impact in the realm of social and economic policy.

A wide range of revolutionary welfare organizations was created or recognized ex post facto and given authority. Alongside the Planning and Budget Organization (PBO), which housed the technocrats of the shah's era, an economic mobilization force was devised to handle rationing and distribution of goods. Instead of utilizing the Ministry of Agriculture, a newly formed organization, Construction *Jihād,* dispatched thousands of young revolutionaries to villages for work on rural-development projects. Private charity organizations linked to bazaars, which had supported families of militants while the latter were in prison, were absorbed into the Imam Khomeini Relief Committee (IKRC). The lands and assets of the shah's Pahlavi Foundation were converted into the Foundation for the Dispossessed, the first of many semipublic conglomerates created during the initial decade of the Islamic Republic. These welfare bodies operated independently of the Social Welfare Organization, which had been created under the Ministry of Health and Welfare before the revolution.

Table 5 gives a sense of this parallel institutionalism. The creation of Pahlavi state organizations over time is displayed in the left column. Revolutionary parallel organizations are displayed in the right column. After the end of the Iran-Iraq war, some organizations eventually merged, designated in the table in boldface type. Where none is listed in bold, these parallel organizations have remained independent until the present—as can be seen for the many welfare organizations listed in the bottom rows of table 5.

This book discusses many of these parallel institutions. Yet the phenomenon itself—both the emergence and the persistence of parallel institutions—needs to be explained. What shaped the state in such a fashion?

TABLE 5   CHRONOLOGY OF STATE INSTITUTIONS AND REVOLUTIONARY PARALLELS IN IRAN, 1890–2011

State institution	Parallel revolutionary institution
Planning Organization (1949)	Economic Mobilization Force (1979)
→ Planning and Budget Organization (1973)	
→ Ministry of Planning and Budget (1983)	
→ Planning and Budget Organization (1989)	
→ Management and Planning Organization (2000)	
Ministry of Agriculture, Trade, and Industry (1932)	Construction *Jihād* (1979)
→ Ministry of Agriculture and Rural Development (1975)	→ Ministry of Construction *Jihād* (1982)
→ **Ministry of Agriculture and Construction *Jihād*** (1989)	→ **Ministry of Agriculture and Construction *Jihād*** (1989)
Ministry of War (1890)	Islamic Revolutionary Guards Corps Organization (1979)
→ **Ministry of Defense** (1951)	→ **Ministry of the Islamic Revolutionary Guards Corps** (1982)
→ **Ministry of Defense and Armed Forces** (1989)	→ **Ministry of Defense and Armed Forces** (1989)
Ministry of Health (1941)	Imam Khomeini Relief Committee (1979)
→ Ministry of Health and Social Welfare (1975)	
→ Ministry of Health and Medical Education (1986)	Foundation for the Dispossessed (1979)
	→ Foundation for the Dispossessed and Veterans (1988)
	→ Foundation for the Dispossessed (2004)
Social Security Organization (1975)	Martyrs Foundation (1979)
→ Ministry of Welfare and Social Security (2003)	→ Martyrs and Veterans Foundation (2004)
→ Ministry of Cooperatives, Labor, and Social Welfare (2011)	Fifteenth of *Khordād* Foundation (1981)
	Foundation for War Refugees (1981)

NOTE: Year in parentheses indicates date of institutional creation or of title change; arrow indicates organizational title change. Merging, if it occurred, is noted in **boldface** in both columns.

First, although many revolutionaries distrusted anyone associated with the previous government, the collapse of the Pahlavi monarchy occurred far more quickly than had been expected. In 1979, the provisional government under Bāzargān appointed caretakers, chosen from the liberal-nationalist opposition, of the existing ministerial and military forces. Their attempts to centralize control under the old apparatus quickly failed. As an alternative, new organizations could be formed, quickly staffed with loyalists, and directed to specific tasks without worry of counter-revolutionary sabotage. Islamic associations appeared within government ministries, the Central Bank, and the Plan and Budget Organization. Islamic association members tasked themselves with ferreting out managers uncommitted to the new government. As Prime Minister Mir-Hossein Mousavi stated in 1986, with a dash of revolutionary paranoia, "before our intelligence services and forces of order become aware of some particular deviation, the pure heart and the political sensitivities of the Islamic Associations sound the alarm and draw attention to the signs of danger."[21] Along the way, parallel organizations outside the old bureaucratic institutions, as well as Islamic associations inside them, turned into rapid promotion vehicles for selected individuals into the top echelons of the postrevolutionary government.[22]

Second, Khomeini-aligned revolutionaries used parallel institutions to attack, silence, or absorb competing groups within the 1979 coalition. Some of the contenders, like the socialist Tudeh Party, enjoyed little organizational clout, and professed loyalty to Khomeini's anti-imperialist credentials soon enough. Those with larger social bases, however, were not so easily cowed. Supporters of other grand ayatollahs such as Ayatollah Shariatmadāri protested the creation of a supreme jurist at the pinnacle of the state. The Marxist Fedāyān and Islamist Mojāhedin, with newly minted followers among the educated children of the middle class, demanded full nationalization of private property. Armed organizations of Kurds in western Iran, Arabs in southwest Khuzestan, Baluchis in southeastern provinces, and Turkomans in northern Khorasan claimed territory and challenged centralized rule from Tehran. Already by 1979, uneasy tensions within the coalition were clear. During 1980, these struggles turned into a rolling civil war across multiple fronts. Parallel institutions formed the Khomeinist vanguard for countering these centrifugal pressures.[23] Once a full-fledged war with Iraq commenced, in September 1980, parallel mobilization was forced to the front of Khomeinist strategy for state consolidation.

FIGURE 3. Cartoon from *Bohlul*, a satirical magazine named after a companion of the seventh imam, who survived under the Abbasid Caliphate by acting insane (*Bohlul* 90 [June 1981]: 3). The caption reads: "In the new system, the teacher is in the service of the student, and the principal is in the service of the teacher."

Finally, the creation of parallel organizations became an unplanned tool, which harnessed popular mobilizations. The 1979 revolution challenged not just the monarchy's political center but also its local representatives around the country. As Eugen Weber pointed out for France, historiographical terms used to describe the initial years of the Islamic Republic such as "centrifugal" and "centripetal" assume a preordained national unity.[24] In fact, Iran could have broken up along some variety of ethnic or provincial cleavages after 1979. Political unity and center-periphery relations had to be reconstructed through a combination of force and consent. As Kaveh Ehsani noted, "the postrevolutionary power structure that consolidated during a civil war against domestic oppositions (1979–1982) and the Iran-Iraq War (1980–1988) was Khomeinist in ideology, but it was based on networks of local activists and institutions."[25]

An example can be seen in the cartoon from the satirical 1981 magazine *Bohlul* reproduced here as figure 3. At the time, universities in Iran were closed while the overall educational system was being reconstructed and the qualifications of teachers and professors were scrutinized. As Mohammad Javād Bāhonar, IRP member and prime minister, stated in a 1981 interview several months before his assassination, a new generation of students took part in a revolution not just against the state, but also "against the previous educational system."[26] The *Bohlul* cartoon shows a student seated and smugly smoking. The teacher anxiously bows while eyeing the young man's finger near a Kalashnikov. The caption reads: "In the new system, the teacher is in the service of the student, and the principal is in the service of the teacher."

As discussed in chapter 2, these networks owed much to social change fostered during the Pahlavi era, which broke down the urban-rural divides of the nineteenth-century agrarian social order. The last two decades of state building under Pahlavi rule deepened internal markets, created a generation of new provincial elites, and linked rural livelihoods with urban economic networks to an unsurpassed degree. Parallel organizations, often backed by a piece of paper signed by an IRP delegate in Tehran, transformed into avenues for aspirational revolutionaries, clerical and lay alike, to push aside this establishment.[27]

These parallel bodies organized and channeled the social activities that political scientist Jeffrey Winters describes as "mobilizational power." For Winters, in opportune times such as revolutionary upheavals, the use of personal, face-to-face horizontal networks can undermine existing authorities and their power resources. As most observers of Iran noted at the time, seemingly charismatic individuals during the revolution possessed mobilizational power to sway minds and provoke others to act. The term also applies, however, to the "sharp change" in the power of actors who are "in a state of mobilization for a given period." This is the power that derives from mass disruption of institutions through social upsurges. Such mobilization cannot be sustained indefinitely, because of the normalization of politics and the exhaustion of emotional energy experienced in revolutions and social movements.[28] Yet in postrevolutionary Iran, mobilizational power stamped itself onto the state. This dynamic tended subsequently to be ascribed solely to the charismatic qualities of a revolutionary leader: Khomeini. This attribution overlooks the manifest interests, motivations, and actions of millions of participants in the postrevolutionary period.

This may seem counterintuitive. Did not Khomeini dictate the terms by which the postrevolutionary order proceeded? Not necessarily. Consider the story of a Health Ministry official, Amir Mehryār, about state policy on contraceptives. English-language accounts of Iran tell a story that Khomeini decided to ban birth control after the revolution. This is incorrect. As early as mid-1979, ministry officials raised the issue of contraception with Khomeini. They stressed the toll of a rising population on the state's ability to provide welfare for the masses. Given his knowledge of preexisting favorable rulings by ayatollahs Mahallati and

Beheshti, Khomeini issued a written response in September 1979, the year of the revolution, which sanctioned modern contraceptives. It was soon delivered to all Ministry of Health offices. Even a missive from the Imam, however, was not enough to stem the revolutionary tide of skepticism associating birth control with the machinations of the ancien régime. Clerks, nurses, technicians, and local clergy in many health offices refused to believe the order. Ministry of Health officials obtained at least five more written endorsements of birth control from Khomeini and other grand ayatollahs over the next several years. Yet the issue remained highly contentious among newly hired local staff, some of which worked in the offices' Islamic associations.[29] As discussed in chapter 4, it took a vast effort of health officials, clerics, and state leaders in the late 1980s to finally implement the policy.

In sum, institutional parallelism in postrevolutionary Iran stemmed from the rapid emergence of a political vacuum, the attempt by Khomeinist forces to fully seize power while impeding challengers, and the mobilizational upsurge of broad segments of population. As the sociologist Asef Bayat described of this period, "the rhetoric used by the Islamist authorities reflected the intense competition between them and secular leftist forces over who could mobilize the poor politically. The poor took advantage of this discursive opportunity to advance their claims—without, however, lending much allegiance to either side."[30] Parallel institutions in the Islamic Republic permitted state officials to placate and channel contradictory pressures from different segments of the population as well as competing elements of the new political elite. These dynamics can be seen in the social-welfare and economic-policy framework that emerged during the Islamic Republic's first decade.

CONTRADICTORY CONSTITUTIONALISM AND THE SOCIAL CONTRACT

During the early postrevolutionary years, a heady mix of ideological influences fed into debates over what policies and outcomes would befit an Islamic economy. However, the precise contours of an Islamic approach toward a modern world economy, aside from general prescriptions against usury, were an open question. By 1980, President Abolhassan Bani-Sadr had been elected to replace Mehdi Bāzargān. A Sorbonne-trained economist from a Hamadan religious family, Bani-Sadr published the book *Monotheistic Economics* in the open intellectual climate of 1979. Influenced by *Our Economics,* a 1968 text by the

Iraqi thinker Mohammad Baqir al-Sadr, Bani-Sadr argued that Islamic economics transcended the equally vexed problems of actually existing capitalism and socialism. In his own book, more talked about than read, Bani-Sadr proposed a diffused Islamic state, which would set limits on property and wealth accumulation. In this system, all citizens could become "*mujtaheds* [Islamic jurists], and no one will need to ask his duty from another."[31]

As president, Bani-Sadr quickly set about taking a route opposite to what he had proposed in his own book. He attempted to centralize the country's many parallel institutions under executive control and mobilized followers to back his efforts. His move raised the ire of leftist parties and Khomeinist cadres alike. To placate the latter, President Bani-Sadr promoted IRP member Ali Rajāi from education minister to prime minister. Both Bani-Sadr and the IRP believed that Iran's top universities were swarming with leftist counter-revolutionaries. The president and the party jointly organized mass rallies and assaults on elite campuses in August 1980, inaugurating a self-described cultural revolution that shut down Iran's higher-education system for three years. This did little to stop leftist activism, though it arguably led to a more polarized militancy on all sides. Rajāi and his clerical comrades pushed back against Bani-Sadr's Bonapartism with mass rallies of their own during the summer. When Iraqi forces invaded, in November 1980, Bani-Sadr headed to the war front in order to coordinate military strategy while criticizing his opponents' attempts to usurp executive authority. As he turned to the Mojāhedin-e Khalq for organizational support, IRP members in Tehran worked toward his impeachment.

What sort of economic policy came from this struggle? In 2009, I discussed these early policy debates with a former official from Iran's Central Bank. It was 1980, he recalled, because he "was still able to wear a tie to work." Amidst the tumult, the former official told me, the new cabinet gathered to discuss foreign-exchange reserves held by the government. Central Bank representatives informed everyone that these reserves were mostly invested in banks in New York, London, Germany, or Japan. One of the meeting's participants, the scruffily bearded Behzād Nabavi, asked why the money was held in the banks of imperialist countries. Could it be shifted to friendlier states, such as Libya, Syria, or Algeria? Nabavi was informed that all these countries had negative balance sheets. The danger loomed that any money sent to them would likely disappear. Nabavi insisted on pursuing another course: What about the Soviet bloc? Why not Poland? How about

Czechoslovakia?[32] The conundrum had no ready-made answer, but the options that Nabavi offered were nevertheless telling. Instead of a doctrinal blueprint, the bank official reminisced, the more important determinant of social and economic policy after 1979 was the intellectual milieu of the Third World after 1968.

In Iran, concepts of self-sufficiency, anti-imperialism, dependent capitalism, comprador classes, and sub-imperial states were the main currency of revolutionaries' interpretations of the Pahlavi monarchy's development policy as well as the world economy as a whole. Attempts to indigenize political economy—before 1979 in theory, afterwards in practice—occurred in competition with abstract credos of liberal and Marxist thought. As the Tehran University political scientist Hamid Enāyat noted in a 1979 study of Islamic political thought, "one of the urgent tasks of Islamic modernists has been to demolish what they see as the presumed theological and canonical foundations of stagnation, and, by derivation, of Muslim submissiveness and quietism."[33] Various permutations of Islamic economics presented answers to this predicament that, it was hoped, could resonate in Muslim-majority countries. As the historians Sami Zubaida and Charles Tripp have detailed, Islamic economics, though never self-coherent, was a prime example of intellectual responses to self-perceived backwardness. The ambiguity between source texts and modern questions of political economy, however, guaranteed in practice that "many different and even contradictory interests, ideas, sentiments and aspirations" would be expressed in the "dominant idiom" of political Islam.[34]

A key outcome of these disputes is Iran's 1979 constitution. The constitutional language itself shows the competition between ideological and political camps, and highlights the reshaping of relationships between state elites and social groups in the postrevolutionary era. Subsequent policy struggles during the war years over the correct balance of state and market continued to reveal the limitations of religious jurisprudence for deciding matters of state. Debates during and after the constitutional assembly over welfare and economic policy opened up avenues for challenging government authority that would be seized by reform-minded political elites and democratic social movements in the postwar era.

The 1979 constitution was debated and codified by a seventy-two-member assembly in the fall of that year. The process reflected both a rapid attempt to legitimize the new order and as well a compromise between extant revolutionary groups and their sociopolitical agendas. The assembly members were elected in August 1979, fifty of them backed by the IRP. Forty-one members were seminarians, and forty-four had not earned a high-school diploma.[35] From August to November, the assembly extensively retooled preexisting drafts of the constitution.[36] The final document is heavy with contradictions, whether in matters of governance, delegation of powers, or civil liberties. The language calls for "the planning of a correct and just economic system, in accordance with Islamic criteria, to create welfare, eliminate poverty, and abolish all forms of deprivation with respect to food, housing, work, health care, and the provision of social insurance for all" (Article 3). The economy's structure should "consist of three sectors: state, cooperative, and private" (Article 44). Legitimate and legally acquired private property is allowed (Article 47), but the government must make land available, especially for rural households and laborers, for "each individual and family to possess housing commensurate with . . . needs" (Article 31). The longest section on social welfare, Article 43, contains a constitutional amalgam of liberal, religious, nationalist, and *marxisant* positions. Under the government's purview are included:[37]

[Provision of] basic necessities to all citizens: housing, food, clothing, hygiene, medical treatment, education, and the necessary facilities for the establishment of a family.

Ensuring conditions and opportunities of employment for everyone, with a view to attaining full employment, placing the means of work at the disposal of everyone who is able to work but lacks the means, in the form of cooperatives, through granting interest-free loans or recourse to any other legitimate means that neither results in the concentration or circulation of wealth in the hands of a few individuals or groups, nor turns the government into a major absolute employer.

Preventing the exploitation of another's labor.

Prohibition of infliction of harm and loss upon others, monopoly, hoarding, usury, and other illegitimate and evil practices.

Prevention of foreign economic domination over the country's economy.

Emphasis on the increase of agricultural, livestock, and industrial production in order to satisfy public needs and to make the country self-sufficient and free from dependence.

The recorded minutes of the constitutional assembly meetings display those issues on which debate did or did not take place. The shorter articles concerning welfare, social security, and housing were approved quickly. Article 29, which ensures the availability of social insurance and health care for elderly, unemployed, and disabled individuals, was passed without any opposition. In fact, this article in the constitution repeats the technocratic language of the prerevolutionary Social Security Organization's mandate: social insurance as a citizenship right, with premium costs to be jointly shared by state, employer, and employee. No assembly member objected to carrying over this Pahlavi-era welfare organization into an Islamic Republic.[38]

For the lengthier Article 43, however, two full meetings in October 1979 were required to hammer out the language. The debate was a harbinger of political struggles over social and economic policy during the first decade of the Islamic Republic and involved many of its chief architects. Even with the dominating presence of religious jurists and Khomeinist allies, no consensus was reached on the appropriate social policies for a new revolutionary order. Ayatollah Beheshti chaired the meetings and attempted to outline the key characteristic of an Islamic economy: a country without poverty or stark income inequality.[39] Grand Ayatollah Nāser Makārem Shirāzi worried aloud about the reach of the state and the nature of the social contract. Should the constitution guarantee welfare for society on the whole, or for each specific individual? Mohsen Nurbakhsh, future head of the Central Bank, stated that though he did not want Iran to resemble Maoist China, an economy freed from foreign dependence must utilize state planning to achieve self-sufficiency. Bani-Sadr requested that language on combatting economic corruption be added. Ayatollah Musavi-Tabrizi demanded clarification for any stipulated relationship between economic independence and public ownership of production. Ayatollah Hossein-Ali Montazeri used an analogy from hadith to argue that the state should act as "father" to the nation. The constitution should therefore require the government to promote the "establishment of family for all." In response, Beheshti joked to Montazeri, asking whether this meant that "the government itself should arrange marriages [*khāstegāri beravad*]?"[40]

As the debate went on, the article's subsections lengthened. Housing, health, education, and employment were discussed, with Beheshti occasionally exalting the proceedings by reminding the members that this was "an Islamic revolution, not a Marxist one, and not a capitalist and bourgeois one."[41] Ali Khamenei responded that, this being the case, not all economic affairs belonged under the state.[42] After hedging the language, the assembly approved each subsection by a wide majority. In the article's final form, however, the distribution of responsibilities for social-welfare policy between public, semipublic, and private entities was not spelled out. Instead, the assembled delegates put more than enough on paper so that differing factions could justify various agendas for decades to come.

The indeterminate nature of the text resembled the uncertain direction of the revolution itself. As Prime Minster Mehdi Bāzargān stated on public television in May 1979, Iran had become a nation of "hundreds of chiefs."[43] The sheer number of organizational competitors, some no larger than twenty or thirty members, led to violent propaganda by the deed—ferocious attempts by various groups to push the new coalescing power bloc in one direction or another.[44] In May 1979, the small religious but anticlerical group Forqān assassinated Ayatollah Motahhari and failed in an attempt to kill Akbar Hashemi-Rafsanjani. That same month, the southern city of Khorramshahr erupted in Arab-led protests, and in July oil pipelines were bombed in Abadan. Kurdish *peshmerga* occupied cities in the northeast, leading to major clashes with government troops during revolts in Mahabad and Sardasht. Early on 4 November, with Bāzargān and Foreign Minister Yazdi in Algiers, a student group calling themselves the Student Followers of the Line of the Imam [Khomeini] cut the U.S. Embassy gates, using tools hidden under their female comrades' garb. The students mostly hailed from Tehran's elite universities. Unconsulted and taken by surprise, Khomeini and close aides realized that the event could help push aside the pesky moderate factions of the revolutionary coalition.[45] Complaining that "they put a knife in my hands . . . [but] others are holding the blade," Bāzargān resigned two days after the embassy occupation. The Revolutionary Council took charge of the government until the subsequent election of President Abolhassan Bani-Sadr. A popular referendum approving the 1979 constitution, held in December, took advantage of the high emotional tenor of the moment.[46]

The problem of dual power lingered. The yearlong embassy crisis divided leftist groups on whether the new Islamic Republic was sufficiently anti-imperialist. Their standoff halted possibilities of a broader left coalition to impede the brutal curtailing of social and political rights during the consolidation of the state in 1980–83. By the end of 1980, President Bani-Sadr was subsequently suspected by IRP members of using the Iran-Iraq War to wrench control of the state away from their own hands. In mid-1981, Bani-Sadr was impeached. His new allies in the Mojāhedin-e Khalq, whose members had gone underground, attempted to overthrow the government with a wave of assassinations.

Ayatollah Beheshti, President Ali Rajāi, and more than a hundred other high-ranking officials were killed. The Jacobinic response by the IRP, which included thousands of executions, effectively destroyed the non-Khomeinist left and silenced the religious-liberal organizations linked with Bāzargān.[47]

Even the socialist Tudeh, which publicly supported Khomeini, fell victim to cloak-and-dagger absurdities. The 444-day occupation of the U.S. Embassy convinced Soviet diplomats that they needed to better protect their remaining political brokers in the revolutionary coalition. A microfiche containing the names of Tudeh members was reportedly hidden in a wall of the Soviet Embassy, known to only two agents. When one of these agents defected to the British in 1982, he allegedly took the list with him. The British government, eager to curry favor with Khomeini and prevent Soviet influence in postrevolutionary Iran subsequent to the invasion of Afghanistan, apparently handed the list over to the Islamic Republic. In turn, the revolutionary government arrested all Tudeh leaders and accused them of collaboration with the Soviets.[48]

The Islamic Republic Party, when united against liberals, Marxists, or the Islamist left, proved remarkably adept at maneuvering to control the new organs of government. Ayatollah Beheshti founded the IRP as a mobilizational vehicle of state consolidation—as he stated, "the party is my temple [ma'bad]." As Bani-Sadr later wrote from exile, the party "intended to attract a large social spectrum, including intellectuals of the left, conservative clerics, capitalists, workers, peasants, progressives and reactionaries."[49] Beheshti needed to sell the concept to Khomeini himself, who held the common position that political parties caused the failure of both the 1906–11 revolution and the 1951–53 nationalization campaigns.[50] Beheshti's son later clarified: "Mr. Beheshti said the party is my temple, not my idol [ma'bud]."[51] Of the 216 deputies elected to the first parliament in 1980, 131 were IRP-affiliated. Of these, 40 percent were nonclerics.[52] The parliament swiftly chose Akbar Hashemi-Rafsanjani as speaker, who moved with characteristic pragmatism to resolve the hostage crisis. According to Hassan Ghafuri-Fard, a Kansas-trained physicist, Khorasan governor (1980–82), and energy minister (1982–86), IRP membership rolls eventually reached two million.[53]

Beheshti was keenly aware of the pliability of political Islam. He advocated for birth control, the right of women to run for president, and, like Montazeri, the necessity of a supreme jurist as a novel political institution. Islamic jurisprudence, the IRP pamphlet *Our Positions* stated, "provided new solutions for new occurrences and pondered issues in society." State officials must reassess popular demands only "in cases where the wishes of the people run counter to Islamic values."[54] The Beheshti-penned publication emerged after the first and only IRP Congress, where core members of the party had already taken to calling themselves *maktabis*— followers of the school of Islam. Although the term originally distinguished followers of Khomeini from other groups in the revolutionary coalition, it soon became a symbol of internal schism.[55]

After Beheshti's death, Ali Khamenei became the IRP chief. Khamenei lacked Beheshti's ability to join together the diverse ideological strands among Khomeini loyalists. By 1982–83, with the Iran-Iraq War reaching a tacit stalemate and IRP leaders in command of the state apparatus, differences among Khomeini's supporters became apparent. Contained within the party was a core faction of Jacobinic *ulema* (Islamic clergy) who saw no contradictions in using the state to pursue a radical transformation of both the domestic and the international order. Advocating for "export" of the revolution and redistribution of social resources, they portrayed capitalism as an inherently exploitative system. Activist *ulema* were to be the center of a morally competent vanguard to implement this political vision. Yet the IRP also housed more established, conservative members of the *ulema*. Unlike the middle-ranked clerical upstarts who resented the historically quietist stance of Qom, these conservatives advocated a much stricter adherence to perceived limits of Islamic jurisprudence. They also tended to advocate for the economic inclinations of their commercial supporters in urban bazaars, who feared the consequences of etatism and nationalization projects.

At first, both sides took to calling themselves *maktabi,* but the term jibed better with the radical core. The seniority of conservative IRP members in the Shi'i hierarchy, however, provided them with opportunities to occupy high judicial positions in the government. This included the supervisory twelve-member Guardian Council of jurists, mandated by the 1979 constitution to advise and consent on the religious suitability of any legislation by the parliament. The radicals tended to reside in the second and third parliaments (1984–88, 1988–92) with Mehdi Karroubi as speaker, as well as in the cabinet of Prime Minister Mir-Hossein Mousavi's government. With Beheshti gone, and Khomeini unwilling to sanction the purging of either side, the IRP could not contain its own members' mounting schisms. Radical factions included sympathizers of the late Ali Shariati; the Muslim Students' Association, some of whom had occupied the U.S. Embassy; the Mojāhedin of the Islamic Revolution; the *Khāneh Kārgar* (House of Workers) trade unions, which had replaced autonomous workers' unions after the suppression of the latter; and the Association of Militant Clerics, which included later reformers such as Mohammad Khatami and Mehdi Karroubi. The conservatives were represented by the Society of the Militant Clergy, the mercantilist Motalefeh Party, and the Society of Lecturers of the Qom Seminaries. Social and economic policy rested at the heart of the differences inside the IRP. In 1987, Khomeini gave permission to dismantle the party for good, but not before party schisms exposed the limits of religious jurisprudence for coordinating a wartime economy.[56]

THE MAKESHIFT ECONOMY

In the first decade after the 1979 revolution, the ambiguity of what constituted a proper Islamic response to questions of labor, industry, consumption, and welfare meant that these two factions could justify a wide variety of prescriptions on religious grounds. Even during 1979–80, when Bāzargān's or Bani-Sadr's government proposed economic and social policy, doctrines gleaned from "Islamic economics" apparently were barely used at all.[57] Early 1980s planning documents exhibited a similar lack of related terminology.[58] In early 1985, the Plan and Budget Organization (PBO) head Mohammad Taghi Bānki told the press that an Islamic economy should strive to "free the country from the single-product economy and lay the foundation on the export of manufacture products." In the welfare arena, it should "provide social security and public health care for the people." Bānki claimed these policies as part of a revolutionary social contract: "the Islamic revolution was materialized by the oppressed people and, therefore, facilities should be provided for them."[59]

Bānki's policy outlines could have been easily transposed to any developmental state. Such policy dilemmas had occurred before. The Bolsheviks in postrevolutionary Russia, for instance, emulated the experience of Wilhelmine Germany more than the tenets of Marxist scripture. The USSR's combination of "messianic zeal with ferocious pragmatism" is equally apparent in 1980s Iran.[60] Revolutionary elites formulated economic and social policy according to exigency, not plan. Mohsen Nurbakhsh, appointed Central Bank head at the young age of 30, put it this way: "No one predicted the speed of the revolution's victory. So we were not looking for an economic theory or ways to use it . . . to build the country."[61] Just as Lenin had described the situation during the USSR's own civil war, the Islamic Republic erected a "makeshift" economy amidst internal challenge and external conflict.[62]

As the 1979 constitution stated, self-sufficiency in industrial and agricultural production was a long-term goal of revolutionary elites. The upside would be a reduction on oil dependence as a main source of state revenue. Almost immediately, however, tradeoffs between investment and consumption confronted the revolutionaries. The political field after 1979, with its wide range of competitors and uncertain rules of the game, awarded legitimacy to radical measures and immediate results. Bāzargān's provisional government raised wages and social spending, doubled credit to farmers, and nationalized the banking sector. The Revolutionary Council established and transferred assets to the Foundation of the Dispossessed and selectively confiscated industries and lands belonging to individuals suspected of being corrupt. These were mostly people who had been close to the shah as well as those who could not defend themselves against the accusation.

The impulse to expand the public sector, however, did not only stem from an economic vision held by Khomeini's close supporters. In 1980, the PBO delivered a modest ten-year plan with targeted steady industrial growth and basic social-welfare improvements for the population. The Revolutionary Council, before being replaced in July by the first elected parliament, rejected the PBO plan as inadequate. Though Beheshti and his allies did not want to be seen as drawing their ideas from the *marxisant* left, their response to mass mobilization and competing popular demands was to intervene economically via the state and its parallel institutions.[63]

During the war years, government intervention was repeatedly resisted by the Guardian Council's establishment clerics. Whether on the issue of land redistribution, housing, rent control, trade nationalization, or labor contracts, Prime Minister Mousavi and his radical parliamentary allies tended to demand more state control. The Guardian Council almost always opposed the moves, claiming that the proposed legislation was in violation of Islamic law. Amidst appeals to tradition, the battle to steer the state in turbulent and uncharted waters led to an unconventional form of religious-legal justification: rule by emergency. With Khomeini's encouragement, lawmakers proceeded as early as 1981 to argue that necessity (Pers. *zarurat*; Ar. *darura*) permitted the bypassing of first-order *sharia* principles on questions of private property. This Quranic prescription for the supersession of primary religious commandments by secondary ordinances is part of the Islamic tradition, but it had rarely been invoked by Middle Eastern states—even in Saudi Arabia or Kuwait, where religious jurists are the main legal custodians.[64] The rule of necessity tends to be interpreted as applicable in those circumstances where acts usually forbidden, such as the consumption by individuals or communities of meat that is not *halal,* are temporarily allowed in a time of emergency such as famine. For most of the radicals, "the explosion of social problems" constituted such an exigency.[65] As the Mashhad MP Hadi Khamenei, younger brother of then-President Ali Khamenei, stated, "Those of us who are in parliament must know where our duty lies. Is our duty to uphold Islam and the undisputed formulations of *feqh* [jurisprudence], or to protect the weak and do what is best for them?"[66] Notably, however, the radicals never bothered to use such justifications until the opposition of Guardian Council became apparent. The disagreements were deeper than mere technicalities. Both factions applied the primary principles of *sharia* toward vastly different approaches to state rule.

The situation thus tended toward institutional deadlock while the war burned on. The result was ad hoc governance. After months, or even years, of legislative shuffling, laws were approved with built-in time limits of three to five years written in emergency clauses. By the time of approval, however, many of these policies were already implemented de facto as well as being contested by those with an interest in the matter. For instance, well before the parliament received approval, the state had nationalized all foreign trade and large segments of domestic trade. Land occupations by peasants or former landlords, if disputed, were already tied up in court claims. As the head of the Guardian Council complained to Khomeini in 1985, the parliament's actions implied "in the name of necessity that every commandment was a prohibition and every prohibition was a commandment."[67] Governmental deadlock ensured the continued usefulness of parallel institutions to bypass parts of the state in the realms of social and economic policy. This often involved relying on Pahlavi-era organizations and proposals.

In matters of taxation, the Revolutionary Council faced such a question as early as 1979. Should taxation be conducted solely within the jurisdiction of religious, nonstate organizations? Senior *ulema* had spent the preceding decades arguing against the legitimacy of state taxation under the Qājār and Pahlavi dynasties. They believed that such actions reduced the authority of the religious establishment. After the revolution, however, Beheshti and Rafsanjani countered, averring that "establishing an equitable taxation system to respond to the needs of the Islamic Republic's programmes is in perfect harmony with the principles of Islamic order."[68] Religious organizations could be folded into the state if needed. A 1967 law on state taxation policy was reaffirmed by the Revolutionary Council, in spite of grumbling by other *ulema*. Yet most foundations and clerical organizations in Qom and elsewhere were allowed to continue collecting the *khums* tithe from their followers. The result was fiscal parallelism.

Government technocrats in planning bodies, who admitted for the role of the state in a time of emergency, soon forged an uneasy compromise with radical politicians. As the war consumed resources, decisions tended to be over far more mundane matters. Mohsen Nurbakhsh remarked that economic discussions at the time were rarely about laissez-faire or etatist models in the abstract. The survival of the economy, including securing the population's basic needs and protecting infrastructure from attack, was the guiding principle.[69] As a researcher in the Ministry of Welfare and Social Security described to me, welfare policy during this period authorized "paying attention to the lowest social strata."[70] The system of rations and subsidies in place under the Pahlavi monarchy were restructured and expanded. So-called luxury subsidies, for example on red meat or confectionary sugar, were abandoned and replaced with a program for essential items like milk, sugar, rice, kerosene, and cooking oil. Government prices were held at low levels. Goods were distributed via an economic mobilization booklet that every family received. The organization set up for this coupon program, *Basij-e Eqtesādi* [Economic Mobilization], preceded the volunteer military brigades known as *basij* that exist in Iran today. According to Ezzatollāh Sahābi, the latter group's origins partly stem from the government's effort, even before the war began, to deal with the international blockade imposed during the hostage crisis.[71]

Distribution of basic goods was administratively regulated both through the PBO and the parallel Economic Mobilization Organization. Along with coupon rations, vouchers were created for purchase of consumer and producer products in cooperatives and special stores. Quotas existed for these goods, but the government also sensibly allowed black and gray markets to proliferate in the bazaar. Utilized mostly by the middle class, entrepreneurs in this so-called free sector took advantage of arbitrage opportunities engendered by clunky state regulation. Even state newspapers contained advertisements in their classified sections for resale of import and export licenses, which were technically illegal.[72] As in many war economies, a researcher at the Ministry of Welfare and Social Security recalled, the result was a tiered system of distribution and consumption:[73]

> If I wanted a refrigerator, the "free" price was five to six times more than the government price, but I would have to wait one year for the government-priced good. The government gave preferential quota allowances for employees in the public sector, but you could get the same good in the bazaar at the free price. . . . Up until 1989, we supported the minimum needs of society with two methods: price controls and quotas. We could not improve the goods, but at least we could control and ration them.

The rationing policies effectively raised the consumption floor for the poorest classes, especially in urban areas. The coupon booklets were, for the most part, distributed to all families regardless of affiliation with the new government. The booklet identified place of residence in order to force citizens to remain in their hometowns and prevent migration to urban centers. This failed spectacularly. Migration to cities compelled the government to provide impromptu permits for informal housing and commercial trades such as street peddling.[74]

Another response was the expansion of public employment, which more than doubled from 1.7 million in 1976 to 3.5 million in 1986. Economists inside Iran tend to attribute the size of the public sector to the state's oil dependence and an environment of rent-seeking practices. Yet in most low- and middle-income countries, there is a social-insurance motive for expanding government jobs. Public employment is not necessarily the most efficient way of providing social insurance. For states with low capacity, however, it is the most direct method of reaching a significant portion of the population. As the economist Dani Rodrik puts it, "creating additional jobs is administratively a much simpler task than running an unemployment scheme or figuring out how to subsidize job security in the private sector."[75] By 1983, a majority of Iran's workers were employed by public enterprises. This increased access to social welfare for millions of individuals who had been excluded from social-insurance networks before 1979.

Under embargo, difficulties in procuring sufficient foreign exchange from oil exports led to heavy government borrowing from the Central Bank. Functionaries at the PBO were aware of the consequences of printing money to pay for the war as well as to subsidize basic consumption, but they reasoned there was no other choice. By 1983, many items were "four to seven times more expensive than at the time of the revolution."[76] Consequently, after initial pay raises during the first years, the salaries of public-sector workers were inflated away as the war economy took priority. With a basic safety net of rationed goods at the bottom and price inflation at the top, income and expenditures were compressed more nearly equally. As a woman in Tabriz reminisced, "we all got poorer together."[77]

Not all policies targeted the poorest strata, however. The state subsidized prices for building materials such as cement and stone. Nationalized state banks provided cheap loans at a nominal interest rate, around 4 percent from 1980 to 1990. The private sector was reluctant to invest in manufacturing, and profitable activities in licit and illicit trading were largely available to politically connected individuals. As a result of high inflation combined with fixed low-interest credit, anyone with capital tended to invest in housing. A construction boom took off during the first half of the decade. According to economist Kamal Athāri, "the real home of the private sector in Iran has always been in construction and housing, and this was most true in the 1980s."[78] It was during the war decade that landed estates of the shah's senators and aides were parceled out and the foundations laid for the postwar boom in apartment high-rise construction in Tehran and other cities.

Given the array of economic strictures, allowing parallel institutions to carry out state functions often presented the least bad option to both sides of the political elite. Revolutionary institutions could be justified as nonstate entities, satisfying conservative qualms about the zealous nationalization drive of the radicals. They also could be promoted to radicals as transformational organizations counterpoised against the symbolic and institutional apparatus of the ancien régime. In sum, wartime politics channeled state building further into the parallel institutional sector.

The Imam Khomeini Relief Committee was the first of these parallel welfare organizations, and arguably the most important. It engaged in reorganizing social life for those most affected by war on the front lines as well as in the cities and the countryside. Through this organization, the state targeted formerly marginalized social groups. It is a useful lens onto one of the key social transformations of postrevolutionary Iran. Through organizations such as the Imam Khomeini Relief Committee, the protection of livelihoods through self-organized kinship networks were replaced with state-linked welfare networks to an extent previously not experienced in Iran.

THE IMAM'S BLUE BOXES

The sprawling and lavish headquarters of the Imam Khomeini Relief Committee sits in northeastern Tehran next to an amusement park. As the largest paragovernmental welfare institution of the Islamic

FIGURE 4. Imam Khomeini Relief Committee donation tent with iconic motif of hands. Tabriz, February 2010. (Photo: author.)

Republic, the IKRC provides a range of services to a selection of target populations. These services include financial aid and health insurance to low-income families, interest-free loans for housing, scholarships for young Iranians, and stipends for the elderly poor in rural areas. Although it solicits donations from the public, the organization relies on the Iranian government for the majority of its revenue. It is colloquially known in Iran as *Komiteh-ye Emdād* (Relief Committee), and its blue octagonal collection boxes are spread out among the country's cities and towns.

For all countries, a major aspect of welfare politics involves the drawing of symbolic boundaries between the deserving and undeserving poor.[79] In Iran, the demarcation of deserving individuals was recurrently contested over the course of the revolution, the Iran-Iraq War, and the postwar period. When I visited the IKRC's Tehran headquarters, the organizational habitus of this large institution was clearly visible. Managers wear the oversized suit, visible beard, and accoutrements of the religious-revolutionary counterculture that grew up in the public sector after 1979. The IKRC's journal features in-house religious scholars writing on the moral ills of poverty and social scientists discussing the issue in developmental terms. One article quotes Imam Ali, for instance: "It is very likely that poverty turns into blasphemy."[80] Poverty alleviation is presented as pious, something any Islamic state is beholden to undertake. At the same time, poverty reduction is extolled as congruent with the Millennium Development Goals promulgated by the United Nations.

In Muslim-majority countries, religious-aid organizations are often located outside the networks of the state. As governments in Asia and Africa retrenched their social compacts because of economic and political crises, these organizations often replace state-provided welfare.[81] The IKRC, however, was linked with the expansion of the social contract through Iranian state formation. It predates the fall of the Pahlavi monarchy and has a revolutionary pedigree. The original IKRC governing council, formed twenty-two days after the February 1979 collapse of the Pahlavi monarchy, contained Khomeini loyalists who had long participated in underground opposition to the state. Men such as Mehdi Karroubi and Habibollah Asgarowlādi coordinated relief for families of political prisoners during the shah's rule. The IKRC subsumed together these nonstate aid networks, previously centered in urban bazaars. Amidst the 1979 revolution, as multiple factions contended for influence in the new government, Khomeini proposed that the IKRC should be viewed as a symbolic manifestation of state support for those who had demonstrated in the streets: the "deprived and excluded." Its structure and duties considerably expanded, however, during the long war with Iraq between 1980 and 1988.[82]

Khomeini insisted on the state's role in social protection: "Those who have been deprived their whole life should not be so in an Islamic Republic."[83] Earlier relationships of charity could not suffice, however. The active participation of the masses in the creation of the new state meant, at least rhetorically, that bottom-up participation was to be stressed. Ali Khamenei outlined the IKRC's position within Iranian state-society relations: "With the formation of the IKRC in the early phase of the revolution, the Imam [Khomeini] conveyed the importance of the dispossessed for the opinions of government officials and *institutionalized* it."[84] The IKRC was born amidst revolutionary strife. It absorbed that period's conflict-forged categories into its operational rubric. Its organizational identity, including the habitus of its staff and volunteers, is bound up with these origins.

By the time the war began, in late 1980, IKRC offices had spread to most Iranian provinces in both urban and rural areas. When Iraqi forces bombarded the southwestern port city of Khorramshahr in initial surprise raids, one of the buildings reportedly shelled was the local IKRC office.[85] The state's initial response to the war was to rely on provincial networks that had sprung up after the revolution. Friday prayer leaders, for instance, became major coordinators and political brokers of provincial life. They also assumed chief roles in coordinating IKRC activities in their areas.

The IKRC itself became a principal avenue for upward social mobility, along with other new parallel institutions such as the Islamic Revolutionary Guard Corps, the volunteer *basij* militia, and the Construction *Jihād*. Individuals who expressed commitment to the new state were quickly registered, this enrollment bestowing on them the social prestige that came with cadre status. Some of the initial casualties of the war in southwestern and western Iran were, in fact, IKRC workers who aided Iranian armed forces in the evacuation of civilians from areas under attack. These individuals were quickly awarded the category of martyr by the state.[86]

The IKRC became a logistical support body as much as a social-welfare institution. Along with its initial mandate of supporting the deprived and needy, the organization took over the centralization of volunteer aid efforts in the war. IKRC collection caravans would roll through towns and villages across Iran soliciting aid. Three hundred fifty charity stations for soldiers operated behind front lines, coordinated through four main IKRC centers in southwestern and western Iran. In the main war theater of the Fao Peninsula, some three thousand to six thousand soldiers reportedly used the IKRC station daily.

The organization paid compensation to war injured and dead. Debts of soldiers were wiped clean in some cases, and fees for therapy care were also covered. Cash and IKRC aid also went to families whose property and livelihoods were damaged by shelling and fires near the war front, or, as the war progressed, by missiles fired from Iraq into Iranian cities, including Tehran. In 1987, during what was called the War of the Cities, the IKRC compensated nearly one hundred fifty thousand families around the country for damages resulting from war or natural disaster. Families of war dead were certified with martyr status and received aid from IKRC until the establishment of the Martyrs Foundation, which took over this welfare function.

Lastly, the IKRC supported the large number of war refugees who fled the front or lost homes to bombardments. It set up tent camps, arranged shared housing in cities away from the front lines, and provided food and medicine to the most indigent of the refugee population. This did not include only Iranians from war-affected areas. Afghans fleeing their own country's civil war as well as Shi'i Iraqis expelled by the Ba'athist state ended up in IKRC camps. A reported thirty-four thousand refugees were covered by the IKRC by 1986, rising to seventy-six thousand in 1987. Subsequently, the Refugee Foundation was established separate from the IKRC to handle the needs of refugees, though these individuals continued to utilize IKRC services in tandem after the war.[87]

In sum, the IKRC became indispensable to the state's conduct of the war. In 1990, marking the eleventh anniversary of the welfare body's founding, Parliament Speaker Mehdi Karroubi announced, "Today we realize that if [the IKRC and other welfare organizations] did not exist, there is no knowing what would have happened to the . . . revolution and the country."[88] The effect of war on welfare policy went deeper, however. By constructing and expanding the categories of martyrs and devotees of the revolution as deserving targets of social protection, the state created a framework through which political mobilization and the making of claims could take place from below.

Data on IKRC beneficiaries show how the organization expanded the reach of social protection in Iran. The two main IKRC funds are the Martyr Rajāi Program and the Continual Assistance Program. The Martyr Rajāi fund originated independent of the IKRC in 1980, when the new government introduced a bill to extend pension benefits to elderly poor in rural areas. As a status group, this segment of the population had never been included in Pahlavi-era welfare policy. Named after the assassinated president Ali Rajāi, the program was originally carried out by the State Welfare Organization, an umbrella body of numerous Pahlavi rehabilitation and aid organizations merged under the Ministry of Health after the revolution. In 1985, the Martyr Rajāi Program was transferred to the IKRC, and it continues today for rural inhabitants over sixty years of age. A monthly grant of cash or in-kind goods is given, depending on household size. During the war, beneficiaries of the Martyr Rajāi Program and their dependents grew to number more than one million people.

The second main IKRC fund, the Continual Assistance Program, reached another one million recipients during the war years. The fund delivered aid to both rural and urban areas. At the same time, the IKRC initiated a variety of ad-hoc programs based on determined needs. In some cases, as with a soldiers' fund and a war-refugee fund, the activities were later transferred to other welfare organizations. Nevertheless, after the war the reach of IKRC programs continued to grow. No matter their ideological orientations, subsequent governments relied on

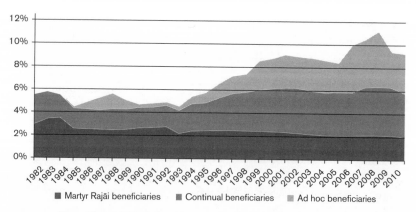

FIGURE 5. Imam Khomeini Relief Committee beneficiaries, 1982–2010 (percentage of total population). (Source: Statistical Indices of Iran, various years.)

IKRC programs as part of their own policy initiatives. As figure 5 shows, the IKRC hardly withered away after the war. Even as the population roughly doubled in size over three decades, the relative coverage of the population by the IKRC increased.

As the data in figure 5 indicate, major beneficiary expansions occurred after 1993, 1997, and 2005. Not coincidentally, these were presidential-election years—even though those elections produced quite different presidents.

As the largest revolutionary-welfare organization, the IKRC's trajectory over the past thirty years illustrates how warfare and popular mobilization became entrenched in welfare politics.[89] It was not the only way, however, through which the Islamic Republic multiplied the incentives for war participation on and off the front lines. As the state reordered the distribution of material and symbolic resources, revolutionary institutions created pathways for newly valued status groups. In doing so, the state profanely instrumentalized the sacred concept of martyr in service of its goals. The emergence of this martyrs' welfare state, however, produced a new set of unintended consequences in the postwar period.

THE G.I. BILL OF THE ISLAMIC REPUBLIC

There are two war generations in Iran. One is the generation that fought in it, and the other was born and grew up during its long slog. Social policy was forced to address both of them. As Farideh Farhi points out,

"The Iran-Iraq War became the basis of a new political milieu that has remained even after the war, despite the rise of other ways of thinking about and conceiving politics."[90] Unfortunately, a social history of the war in Iran does not exist in Western-language scholarship. For Iranians, however, the war saturates contemporary arts and letters in the Islamic Republic. During the 1980s and early 1990s, films and novels were produced about the "sacred defense," children's stories of famous martyrs and their deeds were published, TV specials and documentaries were beamed in directly from the front lines, and war satires and lampoons eventually emerged.[91]

In the early years, the war effort remained largely defensive and confined to the southwest. As Iran's armed forces increasingly became successful at repelling attacks and retaking territory, volunteers for the infantry were not hard to procure.[92] The war dragged on, however, and expanded to multiple fronts. Eventually, major Iranian cities were subjected to Iraqi missile and bombing raids—the so-called War of the Cities. In tandem, the Islamic Republic's nationalist-religious appeals grew in volume. State media emphasized propagandistic tales of martyr glorification and selfless sacrifice. Cultural production alone, however, was far from effective in securing loyalty and legitimation from the population.

Instead, as Sheila Fitzpatrick described the Stakhanovite workers of the Stalin-era USSR, the more resonant cultural trope of state-sanctioned martyrdom in Iran was one of "everyday heroes."[93] The word "hero" was ubiquitous in 1930s Russia, used for polar explorers, border guards, and aviators with their own films, poems, and novels. The martyr occupied a homologous position in the Iranian cultural field in the 1980s. Just as the Soviet hero drew from earlier Russian folk themes, the martyr is a trope in Iranian popular entertainment as well as high culture that long predates the modern era. It was certainly a mobilizational frame. But the increased volume, so to speak, of official exhortations as the 1980s wore on was a sign of the weakened ability to recruit through such entreaties alone, not a sign of strength. The cultural sphere portrayed the popular effort as one of collective unity, even as material realities widely differed.[94]

In reality, incentives proffered by the state mounted as the war years went on. The notion that most volunteer soldiers came from unemployed and illiterate youth, for example, is inaccurate. Both public and private sectors kept employed volunteers on their books. They continued to receive wages by government order as they fought, sometimes at overtime rates. In 1985, the state mandated that workers should get a 5 percent raise for every six months of military service. One factory with three thousand workers reported that 541 of them had been to the front for a period of over six and a half years, placing a high burden on the company's finances. In 1988, the Minister of Education stated that one-fifth of the male teachers in the country had fought in the war.[95] From one government tally of 217,489 war martyrs—a category that included deaths on and off the war front, as noted above—115,080 were classified as public-sector workers, and 39,001 were classified as workers in the private sector. The third largest category consisted of 36,898 pre-university students, many of whom were young volunteers.[96]

The status shift toward rewarding war participation had an effect on life chances as stratified by social class. According to changes in urban household expenditure between 1976 and 1986, "the illiterate had a better chance of being in the top fifth of the distribution, and the more educated had a greater likelihood of being in the bottom 40 percent."[97] To some extent, this represented a delinking of educational attainment and income during the 1980s. Yet this status shift also occurred alongside an expansion of educational opportunities for war participants and their families. In fact, the state desperately needed educated cadres. An estimated seven thousand physicians, for example, emigrated during the early postrevolutionary years.[98] This represented 40 percent of Iran's doctors, forcing the state to recruit physicians from countries such as Bangladesh to work in public hospitals.

In 1982, the nationwide test (*konkur*) for university entry was finally given. After three years of cultural revolution, the Islamic Republic would reopen higher education in 1983. University slots were allocated to new groups linked to the status categories of martyr: war participants, families of war casualties, and members of revolutionary organizations such as the Construction *Jihād* or IKRC. The slots were called the "revolutionary quota," and included many people not fighting at the war front. The quota for revolutionary-status groups kept expanding in scope and numbers as the war continued. The 1983 quota gave slots to martyr families (5%), handicapped veterans (2%), and members of revolutionary organizations (23%). In 1984, members of nomadic groups were allowed to apply. In 1985, a slot was added for volunteer veterans who had served for more than six months. In 1987, a new slot for the families of disabled veterans was introduced.[99] The percentage of positions for public universities is charted in figure 6. As enrollment in higher education increased from 160,000 in 1977 to 200,000 in 1988, this rising quota linked university access to war participation.

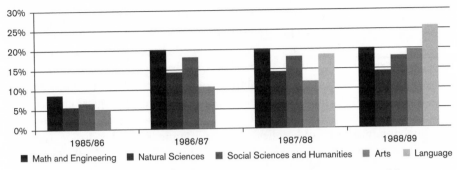

FIGURE 6. Percentage of total positions in selected educational fields among public universities reserved for revolutionary-status groups in late-1980s Iran. (Adapted from Habibi 1989: 32–33.)

In 1989, the government affixed this new education policy as a crucial segment of the martyrs' welfare state. The parliament approved a law to facilitate handicapped and volunteer veterans to enter universities and higher educational institutions. It prescribed that up to 40 percent of public-university slots that year would be reserved, if possible, for veterans and their families. The "G.I. Bill" of the Islamic Republic had come into effect. In creating it, the political elite of the Islamic Republic hoped to foster a newly educated group of loyal cadres and technically trained professionals for the needs of the postwar era.

A POSTWAR VISTA

The war ended in 1988 amidst public shock that Khomeini had finally agreed to a United Nations–backed cease-fire after years of claiming impending victory. An oil price crash in 1986 made it impossible for the government to further sustain both "guns and butter"—war mobilization and social policy. Iran's belated moves toward accepting cessation of hostilities with Iraq, as stipulated in UN Resolution 598, came after the Management and Planning Organization (renamed from the PBO) concluded in early 1988 that, because of low oil revenues, social expenditure would be cut by 25 percent if the war continued. Even with the end of the war, however, the remaking of status categories by war mobilization had an influence. When Khomeini discussed postwar guidelines for reconstruction shortly before his death, he demanded that veterans and martyr families be given priority in "all social, economic and cultural privileges."[100]

The system of basic-goods rationing, consumer subsidies, cheap credit for middle classes, public-sector expansion, and the granting of status privileges to war veterans and members of parallel institutions formed one half of a sui generis revolutionary welfare regime. The other half, consisting of primary health care and family planning for the rural countryside, is detailed in chapter 4. As this chapter has argued, though, rather than charismatic leadership or religious maxims, the Iran-Iraq War provided the bulk of the unifying direction and ideological glue for the development of Iran's economic and political institutions after 1979. The organizations and policies of the Islamic Republic during this period were not developed as narrow, co-opting networks of patronage. Instead, they emerged as contingent responses to the interaction between factional competition within the political elite and popular mobilization from different social strata and status groups: that is, in response to pressures from above and below.

The divides of the political elite during the 1980s produced deadlock within the state apparatus. The continued standoff convinced a segment of the revolutionaries that this factional tussle needed to be shifted toward an apolitical rule of experts. Before leaving office in 1989, Prime Minister Mir-Hossein Mousavi expressed this view in a speech to the entire parliament:[101]

> For ten years this nation has lived for God. . . . The world is blind to our achievements. Is this our problem, or the world's? . . . Whether we want it or not, we are in strong competition with the outside world. *Our ideology is based on humanitarian grounds, and the world asks how much steel we produce. The world asks about our scientific, economic, and cultural progress and gauges our ideology on that basis.* . . . This country's financial progress has been assigned to us. Even if there were no competition, it would still be our duty to make this country the most prosperous in the world. . . . It would be a grave mistake to think that the righteousness of our ideology frees us from the need for the tools in our task. What are the tools? *Besides the nation's faith and resolve, our biggest assets, management and research, should be utilized.* . . . Of course, social justice is not enough to utilize these assets, but it is necessary. The way to achieve social justice is not necessarily through left-wing militant tendencies, or by catering for the greedy rich. To achieve social justice does not require the shutdown of the private sector. The rights of the deprived must not be observed at the cost of violating the rights of others.

Coming from one of the radicals at the heart of the Islamic Republic's political elite, Mousavi's remarks are revealing. Many revolutionaries, especially the Khomeinist core, were cognizant of and even fretful about the country's relative levels of wealth and status in the world economy. Iran was in competition with "the world," and the legacies of the 1979 revolution would be judged by the world's criteria, not by the revolutionaries'.

Mousavi went even further in the speech. He laid out a path for squaring the revolution's goals of social justice with the world's demands of material success. He spoke of how the "science of management" was being used by capitalist Western countries to increase levels of economic production. Moreover, "laws pertaining to a minimum wage, maximum working hours, medical and unemployment insurance, social security, free education, et cetera, are implemented more strictly in those countries than anywhere else." Iran's revolutionaries, Mousavi recalled, once believed the aim of Western social policies was to "silence communists and prevent left-wing social movements." Yet, he asked, "today, when communism has reached a dead end, why are those policies being pursued?" Mousavi answered that the "science of management" had been more important than the threat of the left for the creation of these welfare policies in wealthy countries. The policies were not simply an issue of moral obligation to the people. To Iran's revolutionaries, Western countries could hardly be characterized as moral. Instead, Mousavi argued, the welfare state was fashioned in the West in order to increase levels of production.

This remarkable admission by Mousavi was, of course, a political move directed at both comrades and competitors. By 1989, conservatives had been railing against state intervention in economic and social policy for nearly a decade, claiming that religion did not sanction breaches of the private sphere and its hallowed contracts. Mousavi, however, did not couch his justification for state-welfare policies solely in terms of the 1979 revolution's spiritual superiority over Western powers. Instead, he used the technocratic discourse of the developmental state. Certainly, this language was always tied in with the postrevolutionary order, especially among those in the political elite who saw their task as transforming the country through state power. By the end of the war, however, the justifications for state intervention had shifted. This ideological change was gradual, but over the next two decades, it enveloped the entire political elite. Revolutionary etatism had produced an existential realization. The Islamic Republic would modernize, or it would perish.

CHAPTER 4

The Revolution Embedded

Rural Transformations and the Demographic Miracle

If by "society" we mean a group of people who have learned to work together, French society was limited indeed. . . . The people of whole regions felt little identity with the state or with people of other regions. Before this changed, before the inhabitants of France could come to feel a significant community, they had to share significant experiences with each other. Roads, railroads, schools, markets, military service, and the circulation of money, goods, and printed matter provided those experiences, swept away old commitments, instilled a national view of things in regional minds, and confirmed the power of that view by offering advancement to those who adopted it.

—Eugen Weber

Unlike other countries in the Middle East, especially those on the Persian Gulf, there are few full-time domestic servants in contemporary Iran.[1] Live-in maids, nannies and butlers still exist, but in trifling proportions in comparison with other Gulf countries. One rarely sees maids or nannies accompanying Iranian families to a park, a mall, or a bazaar. This was not the case before the 1979 revolution. When attending the odd dinner party in Tehran or Tabriz, I often asked people about the extent of servant labor in the prerevolutionary period. Many people remembered a widespread presence of domestic-service labor. Most, however, answered that today "servants are just too expensive." Instead, as dramatized in Asghar Farhādi's 2011 film, *A Separation,* wealthier families tend to hire domestic labor at hourly rates for special gatherings and occasional housekeeping.

What happened to Iran's labor market? One could argue that the wealthiest Iranian families left the country during the 1979 revolution. New wealthy households, though, replaced these families soon enough. One could also argue that, before the revolution, foreign migrant labor was more available for household-service work, as in the rest of the Gulf region today.[2] Foreign labor is still present, however, in contemporary Iran. It is commonly used in the construction and transport sectors. In the domestic-service sector, overall wage costs reflect the general price in the labor market, Iranian and foreign workers combined. Something must have happened to the supply of female labor, since women are more commonly hired for domestic work in Iran, as elsewhere.

This shortage of permanent, live-in servant labor is the case even though *more* women entered the Iranian labor market for most of the postwar period. In 1990, the female labor-force participation rate stood at 9.7 percent—just over 1.4 million women. By 2005, the rate increased to 17 percent—with 4 million women in the formal labor force. Although female labor participation in agriculture and industry has declined from 2005 onward, partly because of the increasingly harsh effects of international sanctions, female labor participation in service sectors continues to grow.[3] The increased female presence in the service sector makes the nonexistence of full-time domestic labor even more puzzling. With even more females competing in the labor market, one would expect the price of household-service labor to go further down. The puzzle largely disappears, however, if we examine the relationship between social policy, demographic change, and female livelihoods.

Underlying women's decisions to transfer their labor from household to market activities, and from reproductive to productive activities (including having fewer children), were broad shifts in access to state welfare. Welfare can help to *decommodify* households—that is, lessen the need to participate full-time in the labor market—by subsidizing the reproduction costs of food, health, education, and housing. Welfare can also help, however, to foster labor-market participation by providing market-remunerated skills and credentials, improving infrastructure that expands markets, and reducing the time needed to spend in the unpaid labor of household reproduction.[4] Among scholars of the welfare state, this is sometimes termed the *defamilization* of households. As feminist writers have long noted, state welfare systems help to structure the gender division of labor within households as well as in the formal labor market.[5] The story of increasing labor participation by women in Iran, often represented as an individualized symbol of autonomous empowerment, is also a symbol of how social policy in the Islamic Republic transformed opportunities and incentives for women's labor over three decades. Even for women who do not participate in the formal labor market, these changes still greatly matter, via expanded access to education and shifts in marriage patterns. Though many women remain outside the formal labor market, the transformations are still visible, particularly in Iran's rural areas. As the political scientist Eric Hooglund remarked of his conversations with educated young women in a rural town in Fars province: "Women are arguing not about whether [they] should work but rather about what kind of work is appropriate for women."[6]

In this chapter, I show how the revolution became socially embedded in the Iranian countryside. In rural Iran, the most transformative welfare measure implemented by the Islamic Republic was the creation of primary health-care clinics. Just as in the previous chapter, these changes were linked to revolution and war. Primary clinics, access to prenatal health care, and family-planning initiatives contributed to Iran's rapid demographic changes in the postrevolutionary era. Though there are complex reasons for the shifts in birthrates from the late 1970s to the 2000s, as in any country, population change in Iran cannot be explained without detailed attention to social-welfare policies. Rather than an illustration of top-down control by the state, or an autonomous society rebelling against it, the social processes linked with Iran's rapid decline in average family size reveal how the revolution and its aftereffects became deeply embedded in everyday life. As a result, thirty years of Iranian welfare policy in rural areas have leveled life chances between town and country and fused together a nation-state far more intertwined than under the previous regime. To adapt a phrase from the historian Eugen Weber, the Islamic Republic turned peasants into Iranians.

A HEALTH-DEVELOPMENTAL STATE

The Imam Khomeini Relief Committee (IKRC), discussed in the last chapter, is hardly a model of bureaucratic efficiency or accountability. Another Iranian institution, however, is closer to such an organizational ideal. Whereas public attention is focused on Iran's quota-based aid organizations attached to martyr- and veteran-status groups, there is a remarkable silence on the most successful social-policy effort since the 1979 revolution. Given the contentious nature of Iran's political field, where accusations of corruption and populism are commonplace, this silence may be evidence of its success. This is Iran's Primary Health Care (PHC) system, especially its network of rural health houses, which extended health-care access to the countryside.

As an "island of efficiency" in Iran's postrevolutionary planning apparatus, the Ministry of Health's institutional achievements resemble nothing less than a "health-developmental state."[7] As the sociologist Peter Evans has noted, developmental states in the twentieth century tended to be preoccupied with industrial transformation. Many planners saw improved welfare or health measures as either a side effect of rapid growth or a costly impediment to it. More recent development theories, however, stress that improved welfare is not just an end in itself—an expansion of human capabilities—but also a fundamental input into economic growth.[8] As Patrick Heller showed in the case of India, like industrial policy, organization building is central to creating the capacity to reach down into parts of society that had not previously been linked to state-provided social policy. Just as the nexus between economic planners and business elites was crucial to South Korea's manufacturing growth, successful expansions in social policy can be carried out by state organizations with analogous forms of "embedded autonomy."[9] These organizations needed to be internally cohesive, with commonly shared norms, and externally rooted through broader social groups. In Iran, the rural PHC network was such an organization. Rarely discussed in the clamor of elite political debates, it bolstered the tremendous changes in everyday life that altered Iran's social and political horizons.

LOW TECH, HIGH RESULTS

The backbone of the rural PHC system is a countrywide network of village health houses. Each health house is staffed by two trained health workers and is located no more than an hour away from any village. In these clinics, all services are free, and health workers attend to nearby households under their purview. Doctors visit each health house at least one day a week and usually are in residence at nearby health centers serving multiple health houses. Referrals for advanced treatment in major cities can be obtained from these doctors. By 2010, this network provided health services for more than 95 percent of the rural population—more than 20 million people.

Figure 7 charts health-house construction over time in rural Iran as well as the resultant coverage of the rural population. Even though a pilot group of health houses was tried out under the Pahlavi monarchy,

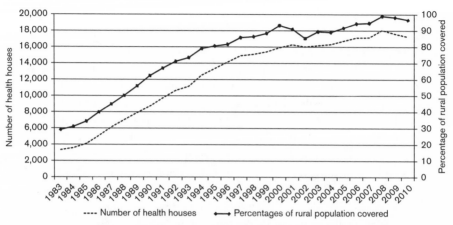

FIGURE 7. Health house construction and rural population coverage in Iran. (Source: Statistical Indices of Iran, various years; rural population estimates from World Bank.)

as I discuss below, the main health care available to rural Iranians before the 1979 revolution were the mobile clinics of the Health Corps. The expansion of health houses occurred after the revolution, as figure 7 shows. Indeed, the fastest rate of health-house construction and the greatest rise in health-care coverage occurred during the war and the reconstruction period: roughly 1985–95. As Welfare Ministry officials told me in Tehran, state-welfare policy in the 1980s prioritized health services, especially in rural areas. In order to observe clinic activities and understand the PHC network, I visited five village health houses in three separate provinces during 2009 and 2010. I interviewed patients, health workers, pharmacists, and doctors about their experiences, memories, and opinions of the program as it developed over the post-revolutionary period.

The core site for primary care was the village health house. During the 1980s and 1990s, access to hospitals was made easier via the distribution of rural insurance cards, which individuals could take to specific public hospitals in urban areas if they needed inpatient care. Yet these cards were also distributed through the rural PHC networks until the rural health system was more fully integrated with urban hospitals, in the 2000s. As one can observe during visits, the infrastructure of health houses is simple, often with a lobby or waiting room, one or two examination rooms, and offices for the health workers. Given their rapid construction around the country, health houses tend to look the same across provinces. Lobbies are plastered with posters showing how

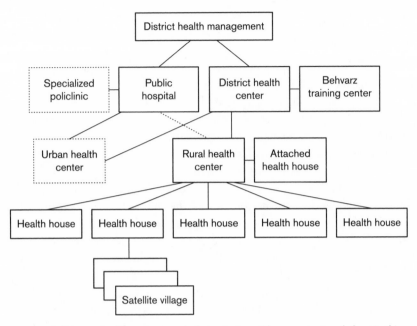

FIGURE 8. Primary health-care network design in Iran. The organizational chart in this figure illustrates how the primary-care system scales health services up from local health houses to district levels.

health campaigns promoted by the government changed over time as the epidemiological transition—the shift in prevalence from communicable to noncommunicable diseases—took hold. Old, faded posters discussed tuberculosis, for instance, whereas newer posters focused on child care, cancer, breastfeeding, AIDS, and youth mental health. Health workers' offices contained large medicine cabinets, which, though not bursting with the latest European brand-name pharmaceuticals, were well stocked with generics usually produced inside Iran. Doctors also regularly brought in medicines from local supply centers. In every health house, I saw a large box of condoms in the medicine cabinet, always on a bottom shelf.

The organizational chart in figure 8 illustrates how the primary-care system scales health services up from local health houses to district levels. A clinic's health workers are usually from that same village or a nearby area and are required to maintain residence in the village for at least one year. They are trained for two years, in exchange for serving two years after their training. This seems like a short time requirement, but it did not reflect the experience of those health workers whom

I interviewed. All had been in their posts for far longer periods than what was strictly required. As they recalled, only about 10 to 20 percent of newly trained health workers did not stay on. Turnover is so low that many health workers whom I met were about to retire after fifteen to twenty years of service in the same village.

"It is a steady job, and I grew up here," was a common explanation. Many started their positions unmarried but later married on the job, with the result that husband and wife paired up as clinicians. One facet of the system is crucial to its success. Every health house is required to have at least one of its health workers to be female. The local knowledge of clinic workers gained through village residence comes in handy. They are practically on call all the time, in addition to making regular checkups during house calls. One health worker told me that the night before I visited, someone showed up at her house door at 11 P.M. needing medical attention after a fall. Local presence was characterized as an advantage: "They already know us and are not ashamed or suspicious about our services and medical advice."[10] Once a month, all health workers go to district health centers for Ministry of Health briefings. Once or twice a year, they travel to the provincial capital for sessions on the latest health rollout campaigns, techniques, testing, and retraining.

One level up, in a rural health center much larger than a village clinic, I spent an afternoon with pharmacists as they filled prescriptions for elderly women. I asked them about drug prices and availability. As domestic pharmaceuticals are highly subsidized by the government, each prescription filled usually cost less than a dollar.[11] Each rural health center covers around nine thousand people, contains a separate maternity center, and provides outpatient care. In contrast to most state offices in Iran, the atmosphere of both centers and clinics appeared unusually calm and relaxed. Village life usually seems slower to those from the outside, of course, but something else was going on. I asked more-experienced health workers and doctors, who had attended to the same villages for the past fifteen to twenty years, during which period the system had been best managed. By this, I meant management in the Weberian sense of bureaucratic rationality. Were health services and administration best organized under President Rafsanjani, Khatami, or under Ahmadinejad? Here was a typical exchange:[12]

> Was it easier to get supplies for this health house twenty years ago, ten years ago, or is it easier now? Was the central administration better organized before or did it get better later?

Health Worker: There was not really that much difference. In the last few years there is less emphasis on family planning and more on the newer diseases we are supposed to help treat.

—What are the new diseases you see today that you did not see earlier?

HW: High blood pressure, diabetes, arthritis, depression.

—Why do people in this village get depressed?

HW: Everyone has televisions and radios now. Their sons are not always around. They know what is going on elsewhere, and this can lead to depression.

As noted by the health worker, and as international health organizations have also reported, Iran's disease portfolio has been transformed under the Islamic Republic. Chronic disease has replaced infectious disease, or, as one worker colorfully put it, "we moved from diarrhea to diabetes." According to WHO/UNICEF estimates, Iran's most rapid expansions in child immunization levels for tuberculosis, polio, diphtheria, and measles occurred between 1984 and 1990.[13] This period corresponds with the years of fastest health-house expansion in figure 7.[14] According to a 1990 study, residence in rural areas and use of clinic prenatal care were two factors associated with higher immunization rates.[15]

The health worker's comments are striking, because it is difficult in Iran to find a government bureaucracy that is not affected by the vagaries of political factionalism. Often I would hear in other agencies—such as housing, education, or planning—that moving from Rafsanjani to Khatami was not that bad, but the coming of Ahmadinejad took off the top layer of staff or put the ax to important technocratic programs. Each new administration brought new directives and shifted resources around the state as a result. Contrastingly, the Ministry of Health seemed an island of bureaucratic efficiency in a turbulent political sea.

This large bureaucracy, moreover, was embedded within the local knowledge accumulated by health workers. For example, state-funded rural insurance pays for anyone who lives in the village and is not employed by the government or nearby factories; in those cases, insurance comes through other funds. Today, however, many Iranian villages are populated by the very young and the very old. Sons and daughters are studying in city schools, or working in provincial towns and capitals, or migrating from job to job when they can find one. The PHC system is set up so that these "absent" village residents do not fall through the cracks. They can return to the village and receive health care provided that their names have been recorded in the annual village census. This occurs at the Persian New Year, when most migrants return to their villages, ensuring that the census is taken when village populations are greatest. In addition, as of the mid-2000s, absent village residents can utilize rural insurance in urban hospitals and clinics. In this way, at least, the rural-welfare system subsidizes the welfare costs of urban labor markets. During the New Year holiday period, in late March, a health worker goes to each household and collects insurance information, checks national IDs, registers all the eligible members, and sends the data to district centers.

Remarkably, these health services could extend to noncitizens also. In one village I visited, two Afghan families who had moved in several years ago also received free care from the health house. This may have been an exceptional case, but in a study of Afghan communities surrounding the eastern city of Mashhad, many migrants stated that they utilized their neighborhood health and education services—none of which were available in their home country. Citizenship was not a criterion for receiving welfare services. According to public-health officials, this was likely a response by the state to the fact that over a million Afghan refugees had moved to Iran since the 1980s Soviet invasion, with a new influx in the 1990s after the Afghan civil war began. The state lacked regulatory capacity to register all Afghan refugees, but public-health concerns motivated state policymakers to permit them access to basic services.[16]

Monitoring through health houses is low-tech but successful. Data on village deaths, child and maternal mortality, births, age and sex ratios, and contraception usage are collected on an information wheel shown in figure 9. The data collection is a simple and effective way to measure a wide variety of indicators, which are then aggregated at the national level. Health Ministry officials can determine new problems or lagging regions and can direct resources accordingly. For example, even as infant mortality declined rapidly during the 1980s and 1990s, maternal mortality rates were decreasing at a slower rate. In 1979, maternal mortality rate stood at 250 deaths per 100,000 live births; by 1996, it had decreased to 37 deaths per 100,000 childbirths. The decline was impressive, but health officials were subsequently tasked with getting the figure under 25 by the year 2015, in accordance with U.N. Millennium Development goals. As a result, a new surveillance system for maternal deaths was implemented, whereby every incident of maternal mortality was documented for preventable cause. This led to new policies regarding midwives and hospital procedures across the system in

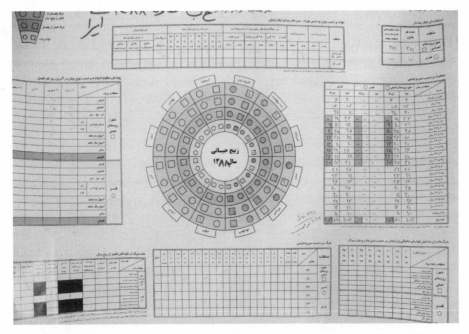

FIGURE 9. Information wheel covering 1,062 Iranian citizens over several villages. (No personal information is displayed. Photo: author.)

2001. By 2009, maternal mortality had reduced to 22 deaths per 100,000 childbirths.[17]

By the late 2000s, most Iranians took this PHC system for granted as a part of the social contract, if they even knew about it. In large cities such as Tehran, I was sometimes asked by young, cosmopolitan urbanites why I was traveling around to dusty villages. I replied that I was researching the welfare system in rural areas, especially the health-house network. On several occasions, these well-educated citizens flatly told me that they had never heard of such a thing.[18] When that happened, I asked if they had heard of Dr. Ali Rezā Marandi, Minister of Health under both the Mousavi and the Rafsanjani administrations. Young Iranians usually read the name of Marandi in primary or secondary school. He had received numerous international awards for efforts in child-vaccination campaigns and increasing family-planning services, including the United Nations Population Award. These awards, like nearly any positive international recognition of Iranians, are proudly discussed in the country across the political spectrum. By carving out a financially secure and organizationally efficient primary-care system, Marandi and other officials at the Ministry of Health were instrumental in the creation of Iran's health-developmental state.[19] This somewhat insulated bureaucracy contributed not only to increased human-development indicators but also to the most rapid decline in birthrates recorded during the twentieth century. The politics of this extraordinary process—overlooked in most accounts of postrevolutionary Iran—reveals much about the social transformations that intertwined welfare with the tumult of revolution and war.

A SOCIOLOGY OF IRAN'S DEMOGRAPHIC TRANSITION

Most families in Iran have naturalized the shift from having around six or seven children in 1979 to fewer than two today. Over the duration of my fieldwork, I often asked people, in various settings, why this shift happened. Some attributed it to poverty and difficult economic conditions after the revolution. I followed up this question by asking another: If the economy were better, would they want a larger family? No, they said. They liked small families. Other people said that previous generations were less modern, less educated, or, as it was frequently put, less cultured. No person, unless he or she was in the public-health field, ever said to me that the shift could be attributed to any government directive.

Iranians have accepted the idea of small family size so much as to perceive and describe it as part of their contemporary culture. Non-Iranians, on the other hand, have tended to attribute the decline in family size as culturally determined in a different sense. Within popular journalistic accounts, as well as in most Western scholarship, there is a misconception that the early years of the postrevolutionary era were formally and authoritatively pronatalist. It is true that the birthrate went up slightly after 1979, only to decline after 1985–86. The common story goes like this. The revolutionary leaders of the Islamic Republic were against contraception. They told families to have more children as their Islamic duty, and the population dutifully complied. This story attributes nearly all power to shape ideas, norms, and motivations to the state. People in Iran have little agency to make decisions, especially poorer ones who may be beneficiaries of state-welfare institutions. This is the type of explanation common in many accounts of Iran, but it is rarely if ever investigated. The actual story, however, is far more surprising and revealing.

The best available estimates of population growth for Iran have been compiled by a team of demographers at the University of Tehran. They annually interpolated total fertility rates—that is, birthrates—from 1972

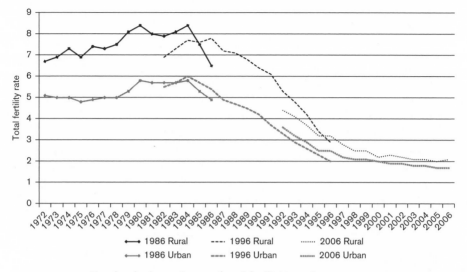

FIGURE 10. Rural and urban estimates of total fertility rates, Iran, 1972–2006.
This figure presents total fertility-rate estimates at urban and rural levels. (Source:
Abbasi-Shavasi et al., 2009: 49.)

onward by using decennial censuses and other coordinating surveys.[20]
Figure 10 presents total fertility-rate estimates at urban and rural levels.

Three observations from these birthrate estimates must be highlighted. First, in urban areas after 1972, the birthrate decreased slightly
but then flattened out until the 1979 revolution. In rural areas after
1972, birthrates, already high, were *increasing* before the 1979 revolution. Arguably, Pahlavi-era family-planning initiatives begun in 1966
were not effective in the medium term. Instead, the health system during
the Pahlavi period contributed to the first half of the demographic transition: low mortality with high fertility, with a consequent boost in
population growth.

Second, urban and rural birthrates both increased just after the revolution. By the mid-1980s, still during the war years, birthrates began to
decline. This drop occurred *before* the government commenced its official family-planning program, in 1989. Given the timing, *other* factors
must have contributed to this segment of the decline.

Third, the most rapid birthrate decline corresponds with the years
1989–2000, when fertility trends dropped to the population-replacement
rate (roughly 2.2 children per woman). During this period, the rural-
urban gap in birthrates shrank to near parity. Ever since this period,
demographers around the world have been fascinated with Iran. The

only country with a more rapid fertility transition in the fourth quarter of the twentieth century was the Maldives (current population 328,000). During the 2000s, continued low birthrates across Iran reflected how decisions regarding family size became nationalized—there was little difference between households in urban or rural areas.

The steep rate of decline in Iran's birthrate was neither expected by its planners nor initially believed by outside organizations. The first Five-Year Plan (1989–94) assumed that the birthrate would decline as a consequence of new family-planning initiatives. Yet the 1989 document still projected Iran's population to be 100 million in 2010. This projection was 25 million *more* people than the country's actual population in 2010. Similarly, the United Nations Population Division (UNPD) continually overestimated Iran's total fertility rate during the 1990s. Here are the UNPD estimates from biennial reports: 1990, 4.30; 1992, 5.40; 1994, 4.52; 1996, 4.77; 1998, 2.80.[21] Only after Iran's 1996 census results had been made public did international and state agencies realize that they had overshot their estimates. Caricatures of Iran as autarkic and traditional led to a misreading of the country's internal dynamics.[22]

Several questions can be asked about variations in fertility trends as well as the overall postrevolutionary decline. First, why was there a lack of decline before the revolution? Second, why was there a rise after the revolution? Third, why was there a small decline during the war years? Fourth, why did a large decline take place after official family-planning programs commenced?

Addressing these questions can help in understanding the overall trend as well as point to particular social mechanisms occurring at different points or simultaneously. In addition, breaking up this complex question can help determine what part of the decline might have come from the supply side of state policy or the demand side of social attitudes and opportunities for individual action. For our purposes, two concepts derived from fertility transitions elsewhere are useful. In South Korea, rapid declines in fertility were associated with rising age at first marriage. *Marriage delay* reduces fertility by shortening the time that women have available for producing children, even if they are spaced at the same intervals as before. In Indonesia, fertility decline mostly occurred within marriage. There, *lowered marital fertility* was achieved by a combination of contraception use and wider spacing of births.[23] In Iran, these two mechanisms both played a role but likely were temporally staggered.

It is misleading to claim that without the 1979 revolution there would have been a more rapid fertility decline in Iran, and therefore less population growth over time. Although the Pahlavi government used an official discourse of family planning during the 1970s, that decade's rapid economic growth may have led to expectations of higher living standards in the country, which exacerbated population growth. The Pahlavi government's 1966 family-planning program emphasized the supply side, providing contraception. Family-protection laws were passed from the 1960s onward, ensuring key de jure rights for women's access to health care. Eventually, Health Corps medical staff were trained in the use of contraception and relied on mobile clinics to bypass poor infrastructure. But the overall focus remained on urban areas, relying on distribution of birth-control pills as the preferred mode of contraception. This method was biased toward younger urban women. Rural older women tended to limit contraception use until they had approached or exceeded their desired family size. Birth-control pills often were difficult to obtain regularly, and women would discontinue their use.[24] Moreover, public-health professionals with suitable expertise in rural development did not supervise the family-planning program. Instead, the program was "overmedicalized," as a World Bank practitioner later described it.[25]

This attitude was not peculiar to Iran. In the post–World War II era, American foundations and international bodies placed a high priority on population control in the development agenda for the newly independent Third World. Aid for other programs was often tied to population-control campaigns. Advice for Iran from the United States–based Population Council was almost verbatim with advice given to Kenya or Pakistan. Like other development assistance, the model tended to be one-sized and was supposed to fit all countries. By the end of the 1970s, the reputation of this "population establishment," as described by the historian Matthew Connolly, was greatly tarnished. Sterilization campaigns in India, for example, where mobile teams bribed or coerced millions of women into accepting IUDs, had been made public in the international media.[26] Discussions regarding population became tied to the rebellious politics of the Third World during the 1970s. During the 1974 World Population Conference, held in Bucharest, Romania, even the World Bank's representative told the assembly that he was "appalled" by the "patronizing attitude of the mostly white Anglo-Saxon representatives" from northern organizations and the United Nations. The shah did not register this growing sentiment, at least not in public. His twin sister, Ashraf Pahlavi, represented the monarchy at the Bucharest conference to tout new birth-control programs in Iran.[27]

As a result of the growing Third World criticisms of these policies, calls for a "new international health order" appeared in tandem with other proposals for restructuring relations between the global North and South.[28] During the 1970s, the international consensus on public health shifted away from unilateral disease treatment and high-technology transfer toward more comprehensive primary health-care that addressed the socioeconomic needs of poorer countries.[29] Iran was no exception. In 1972, a WHO-supported pilot project on health houses began in the province of West Azerbaijan. Indeed, this was the first time the term "health house" [khāneh behdāsht] was reportedly used in Persian.[30] In addition, Shiraz University, in Fars province, began a "middle-level auxiliary-health-worker" training project in the small town of Marvdasht.[31] Yet by 1978, the New York-based Population Council estimated that Iran was unlikely to achieve significant reductions in the birthrate by the year 2000, placing the country in the same category as Afghanistan, Nepal, Nigeria, and Sudan. This was the case, it noted, *despite* the disproportionately large expenditures by the Pahlavi government on family planning.[32]

The problem partly stemmed from the overall structure of Iran's health system. In 1973, only fourteen thousand physicians existed for all of Iran, with half of them living in Tehran. PHC-based pilot projects reported their findings to the government as well as to international agencies, but the domestic medical establishment of medical-school deans and high-status physicians opposed recommendations for a universal PHC. Instead, without infrastructural support mass campaigns from above wilted. Rural Iran lacked usable roads, water supplies, and immunization for communicable diseases. As the medical sociologist Carol Underwood assessed: "There was little attempt to acquaint physician-trainees with the health problems of rural Iran; . . . even health bureaucrats avoided trips to rural areas." As a result, rural health care was less a system than a fragmented collection of organizations and multiple delivery outlets.[33]

In other words, family planning under the shah suffered from the same handicaps that much of Pahlavi-era social policy did—an emphasis on so-called modern methods and high-technology solutions ill suited for the social realities of a middle-income country.[34] This contributed to the limited effects that the Pahlavi family-planning program exerted on the birthrate in the 1970s, with even a slight increase in rural birthrates in the later years of the decade. It is myopic to state that the birthrate decline in Iran would have been the same or would have occurred sooner if the revolution had not intervened. Instead, Iran might have resembled wealthy Gulf Arab neighbors to the south or poorer Pakistan to the east, where birthrates remained higher in both cases.

The 1970s global march to demand "health for all" culminated in the September 1978 Alma-Ata Conference on Primary Health. Iranian health officials, even as their government faced growing unrest at home, attended this major conference in Kazakhstan. All 134 attending delegations endorsed the declaration, calling for the international health community to reprioritize health resources toward comprehensive primary care in the Third World.[35] The revolution occurred shortly thereafter, and both urban and rural birthrates rose in Iran. From afar, this seemed an example of the early charismatic power of the Islamic Republic to sway masses. Here was a new government opposing the modernizing direction of the Third World and initiatives such as the Alma-Ata Declaration. Upon closer examination, this oft-repeated narrative unravels.

In reality, a consensus on birth-control policies among Shi'i religious jurists did not exist before the 1979 revolution at all. The Pahlavi government rarely bothered to seek the opinion of the top clerics in the Shi'i establishment. According to the anthropologist Michael Fischer, clinics supported by local seminaries were set up in cities such as Shiraz and Qom, and some attempted to offer family-planning services. These were closed by the Pahlavi monarchy "at government request in an effort to systematize and not duplicate."[36] During the 1960s, Khomeini opposed the shah's White Revolution initiatives but did not mention family planning by name. In 1964, a Shiraz University gynecologist sought out a ruling (*fatwa*) on contraception from Grand Ayatollah Bahauddin Mahallati—a Shi'i jurist of the highest rank. Mahallati ruled that birth control was not prohibited by religion if the effects were temporary and did not make women permanently sterile. This, in fact, was the only *fatwa* issued before the revolution by an Iranian top cleric on the matter at all.[37]

In 1971, the Lebanese sheikh Mohammad Mahdi Shamsuddin and the Iranian ayatollah Mohammad Hosseini Beheshti both spoke at length at a conference on Islam and family planning in Rabat, Morocco. Each of them supported—with recourse to religious jurisprudence—modern methods of birth control as well as sterilization.[38] Shamsuddin later came to be known as one of the spiritual leaders of Lebanese Hezbollah, and Beheshti was a key revolutionary allied to Khomeini. Given that both men were enmeshed in Khomeini's exile networks in Najaf, Iraq, during the 1970s, it would have been surprising for either of them to have taken a position opposing Khomeini's opinion on the matter. Instead, as they became more politicized from the 1960s onward, some segments of the Shi'i clergy close to Khomeini came to believe that older clerics were reactionary, backward, and subservient to the heights of political power. Beheshti's arguments concerning contraception, made before the revolution, revolved around an idea that the emerging and changing needs of the community made it paramount that the representatives of Islam adjust their dogmas according to the exigencies of the present. This was the same argument that radical clerics in the Islamic Republic, faced with the same conservative clerical establishment, would make during the 1980s.

Of course, the shah's family-planning program was associated with the government that carried it out. Along with a general distaste for population control expressed by both radicals and conservatives around the Third World, the link with the former regime provided cause for many Iranians to view any birth-control measures with suspicion.[39] Revolutionary cadres tended to distrust technical expertise, including the lower-level staff working at the Ministry of Health. In this case, the mobilization from below against the upper technocrats on the issue of population control was a key rallying cry. As mentioned previously, ministry staff formed coalitions with other employees such as janitors, gardeners, and kitchen workers to agitate for a leveling of the bureaucratic-status order and pay scales. As with other ministries, these energies were absorbed and directed into an Islamic association within the ministry. The association's leaders were junior provincial clerics, who largely opposed contraception and family planning.[40]

However, in this case, there was also a countermobilization from above. The revolution had cut off the top bureaucratic layer of all the ministries, as government officials fled or were purged. Some of these men were the very medical professionals of high international repute who had quarreled with widespread rural primary health-care in the first place. Mid-level ministry technocrats thus saw room to implement the radical measures endorsed at Alma-Ata, modeled on Chinese and Cuban primary health-care systems developed in the 1950s and 1960s, after those countries' respective revolutions. They began a decade-long campaign to ensure religious endorsement of family-planning measures. Starting as early as mid-1979, Health Ministry officials raised the issue of birth control with Ayatollah Khomeini, stressing the toll of a rising population on the state's ability to provide welfare for the masses. Khomeini issued a written response to a report in September of that year essentially sanctioning modern contraceptives. It was delivered to all

Ministry of Health offices as an official *fatwa*. Yet even a missive from the Imam was not enough to stem the revolutionary tide of skepticism against the ancien régime's machinations. Ministry of Health officials obtained at least *five more* written endorsements of birth control from Khomeini and other grand ayatollahs over the next several years.[41] Contrary to popular assumption, Iran's family-planning program was never suspended at all; it just remained passive within the state. Families continued to receive contraception if they requested it—5.6 million families did so in 1981.[42] Rather than a religious commandment from on high to produce children, therefore, much of the resistance to birth control was due to politics from below.

Apart from any ideological incitement, the Iran-Iraq War is usually given as the reason for increased birthrates. Certainly, the wartime rationing system of food and consumer goods provided a set of incentives for larger family size. Ration booklets were given out based on household head counts, including infants and small children. Yet according to demographic data it appears that the birthrate actually peaked around 1980–81; the war did not start until near the end of 1980. The war's role has probably been exaggerated as the main causal factor, although it did have an impact, since it diverted available resources away from the family-planning program.

What appears to have been more important was that, just after the revolution, hundreds of thousands of people decided to get married. The crude marriage rate from 1976 to 1978 was around 5 per 1,000 individuals per annum. In 1979, it shot up to 8.1, and went even higher, to 8.8, in 1980.[43] It is well known that the Islamic Republic lowered the legal age of marriage from 15 to 13 for girls and from 18 to 15 for boys. Yet the average female age at first marriage stayed the same as before the revolution—from 19.7 years in the 1976 census to 19.8 in the 1986 census. The state's exhortation to marry younger—in order to keep sexual relations within marriage, they argued—was not the key factor. Rather, it was the revolutionary milieu itself that likely led to the rapid increase in marriages. Young couples believed that their economic horizons would be better after the fall of the old regime. A similar change occurred after the 1917 Bolshevik revolution in Russia, even though the USSR passed progressive laws that made it easier for women to divorce their husbands. In 1926, the marriage rate in the European areas of the USSR stood at 11 marriages per thousand people per annum. In 1911–13, before World War I began, the rate stood at 8.2. In other words the marriage rate jumped nearly 35 percent in the first decade of the USSR's existence.[44]

Iranian revolutionaries of all persuasions promised that the distribution of wealth would change from what it had been in the past. Iran was a wealthy country, as the 1970s boom indicated, but the people had not received their just share. Increased marriage rates were, essentially, a vote for the new regime's promises that life would get better. The government even established a Marriage Foundation to provide financial assistance for new couples. After marriage, birth patterns stayed within the same cultural expectations as during the 1970s. Women were encouraged by extended families and kin groups to marry at a young age and then have their first child soon afterward. Yet because the marriage rate went up, the fertility rate did also. In other words, the Iranian revolution raised expectations, as revolutions tend to do in their initial years no matter where they happen. This contributed to an increase in the birthrate.[45]

Revolutions may heighten expectations, but wars can quickly reduce them. Discontent with the war hit new levels in 1985–86. State revenue from oil sales collapsed, war expenses ran higher, and inflation ramped upward. The results of the 1986 census alerted Health Ministry officials that population growth had been 3.9 percent per annum since 1976. Over the next three years, Ministry of Health officials and Planning and Budget Organization (PBO) technocrats stepped up a campaign to move the state toward a major family-planning initiative. State elites were clearly divided on the issue, sometimes because of principle but also because of fear of being tainted with the aura of the old regime.

The PBO head Masud Roghani-Zanjāni discussed the 1986 census results with Prime Minister Mir-Hossein Mousavi. He related the message that public-health professionals and PBO technocrats believed Iran's high birthrate would make increasing income per capita nearly impossible in the postwar economy. Out-of-control population growth would lower overall health rates, damage agricultural production, and produce a generation of unemployed youth. All this, Roghani-Zanjāni stated, would create "conflict with the [political] system." Health Ministry members strategized how to use revolutionary terminology to their advantage. Instead of the term "population control," with all its negative connotations, the public-health phrase "child spacing" was promoted. Crucially, Khomeini's missives were available to use against skeptical clerical resistance in expanding family planning. With Khomeini's support, "none of the clergy could resist this policy," Roghani-Zanjāni later recalled, "and only God knows if he had not done this what situation we would have been in."[46] Mousavi's cabinet

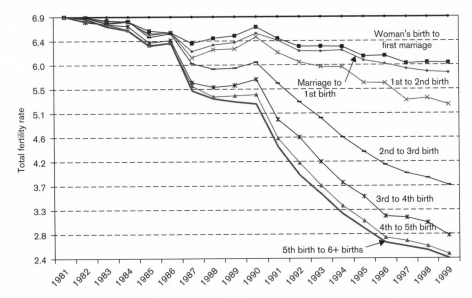

FIGURE 11. Decomposition of fertility rates in Iran by age at first marriage and child spacing, 1981–99. (Reproduced with permission from Abbasi-Shavazi, McDonald, and Hosseini-Chavoshi 2009: 79.)

took a vote on whether to begin a family-planning campaign. It narrowly passed—by a single affirmative vote.[47]

Just as state elites were divided, pressure from below pushed in different directions. The eventual reinstatement of active family planning in 1989 was not just a technocratic fix from above. Women's organizations in the 1980s heavily lobbied the state to create more access to contraception. They used revolutionary discourse against the very clerics who interpreted religious scripture for purposes of castigating birth control. Tools of population control, women's groups proclaimed in public media and in newspapers, should be in the hands of the people and involve their active participation.[48] As long as these activists could present their aims as piously nationalist, then the mobilizational legacies of the revolution would open a place in the public sphere to struggle for amending family laws and other state measures that had codified gender inequality early in the revolution.[49]

Yet birthrates had already been declining in the 1980s, from a total fertility rate around 6.9 in 1980 and 6.3 in 1986 to 5.3 by 1988. To differentiate this segment of the decline from its rapid descent during the 1990s, figure 11 decomposes changes in the birthrate via changes in the marriage age as well as length of time between births. In other words, figure 11 allows us to separate out marriage delay from birth spacing. The bottom trend line in figure 11 shows the total fertility rate as it decreased over two decades. The lines above this show what portion of each year's decline can be attributed to the different segments of fertility change.

In this decomposition graph, from 1981 to 1986, we can see that most of the decline in the overall fertility rate came from women delaying their age of first marriage. From 1987 to 1990, women reversed course, marrying at earlier ages again—a mini-boom in marriage at the end of the war—yet the birthrate continued to decline, mostly because women were increasing the length of time between the births of children after their firstborn.

In other words, *marriage delay* was the main factor in the early 1980s, whereas *lowered marital fertility* was the main factor in the late 1980s. Subsequently, during the years 1991–99, both marriage delay *and* lowered marital fertility contributed to the decline in birthrates, with the largest segment being due to women limiting their fertility after two children.

During the late 1980s, the decline within marital fertility seen in figure 11 came likely stemmed from a complex interaction between state and society. As shown in chapter 3, income levels were stagnating or deteriorating for much of the population by 1986. Even though the distribution for basic needs had been brought to a more nearly equal level by wartime rationing, perceptions of deprivation ran high. Because of both the war and expectations of revolutionary upward mobility, migration to urban areas continued even while economic conditions deteriorated. Most recollections of the late 1980s by Iranians today are of hardship in procuring goods and housing. Getting married earlier may have been one form of coping with this reality, as the mini-boom in marriage suggests.

Upward mobility during these years of stagnation was possible, but it often had to be achieved through the acquisition of status, not of economic capital, given the limits on entrepreneurial activity at the time. For women, with even stricter limits on formal labor-market participation, the economic route must have seemed even more tightly closed off. Instead, the main route to status attainment in Iran was through the education of one's children to diploma level and then toward professional fields such as engineering and medicine. Before the revolution, this route was mostly limited to only the upper social strata. With the revolution and war, more of the population began to pursue this path, taking advantage of new welfare- and social-policy organizations, some of which were linked to martyr-status groups. These opportunities included expanded education for adults and children, rural health-care programs, pension payments for the elderly poor, and the passive but still existing family-planning program, which provided contraception. New interactions with the state intertwined with aspirations for status mobility and likely contributed to lowering the ideal family size for many women even *before* the active family-planning program began in 1989. Recall that child-immunization rates expanded to near-universal levels during the later years of the war. This meant that Iranian women were taking advantage of the services offered by the new health-developmental state. When the state shifted course in 1989 and altered the supply side of family-planning resources, the demand side from individuals had already been changing due to shifting social norms and new expectations for the life course.

As mentioned above, the demographic transition in South Korea occurred mostly through marriage delay, whereas Indonesian birthrates declined because of birth spacing and decreased marriage fertility. In Iran's case, there was a slight marriage delay between 1981 and 1985, a decrease in marital fertility from 1986 to 1989, and then a combination of both from 1990 onward. The government's policy shift rapidly accelerated these preexisting trends. In 1986, with Ali Rezā Marandi at its head, the Ministry of Health took over the education of medical students from the Ministry of Education. It was renamed the Ministry of Health and Medical Education (MOHME). This ministry and the PBO organized the conference "Population and Development" in Mashhad in 1988, inviting public-health professionals from other countries to attend. At the end of the conference, Marandi repeated Khomeini's *fatwa* allowing the use of contraception. Prime Minister Mousavi, who only two years previously had celebrated a high national population as a God-given gift, declared after the conference that birth control was in Iran's destiny and that Iranian women could prevent unwanted pregnancies by utilizing government clinics and health houses. Two more conferences specifically addressing the religious precepts for contraception and sterilization were held in Mashhad and Isfahan in 1989. The state also used the bully pulpit to declare lowered family size a national priority, with radio and television discussions. Over one hundred articles in the three major Iranian newspapers reportedly covered the subject during the year between 1989 and 1990.[50] Critics of the program were still quite vocal, even in these same papers. Echoing the 1970s, some articles attempted to connect offers of aid by United Nations population agencies with the imperialist agenda of Western powers. The state, nevertheless, pushed forward. Prime Minister Mousavi, nearing the end of his term, argued: "None of the government's development and welfare programs is likely to succeed without a serious family-planning program."[51]

As a result, MOHME was mandated to provide free family-planning services to all married couples and encourage small family size. The ministry was given wide leeway in flexibility for implementation and resources to carry out the program. This was a key reason why MOHME developed the "embedded autonomy" of a developmental state agency as compared with other government organizations. As health officials recalled,[52]

> The Government looked at family planning as an emergency measure, and because of that we never failed to secure our budget. Indeed, we were allocated a separate and independent budget in the ministry, which made it possible for us to be very efficient in the timing of our projects, because we did not share our money with any partners, and there were much less of the usual complications.

Economic incentives in the welfare system were amended so that social security, health insurance, maternity leave, and cash allowances would not be extended beyond three children. The parliament attempted to pass the family-planning bill in 1989, but the prospect of conservative resistance led PBO technocrats to simply move the language into the first Five-Year Development Plan (1989–94), under the control of the executive branch, soon to be run by President Hashemi-Rafsanjani. This way, the government bypassed a possible veto by the Guardian Council and their traditionalist allies in Qom, even as Health Ministry officials attempted to legitimize family planning in the public sphere with reference to religious duties.

Moreover, it was easier to roll out the program because of the preexisting infrastructure built into the welfare system developed during the war. Indeed, the government's own mandate to MOHME reiterated the concepts at the heart of the Alma-Ata PHC declaration. Family planning was more than just population control; it also meant reducing infant mortality, increasing women's education and employment levels, and extending health and retirement insurance to the entire population, in order that parents could replace kinship-based old-age security with state support.[53] The slogans used by the Iranian state during this period attempted to interweave family size, children's educational prospects, parents' quality of life, and national economic development:[54]

- Fewer Children, Better Education
- Less Population, More Opportunities, Prosperous Future
- Better Life with Fewer Children
- Girl or Boy, Two Are Enough

This was vastly different than the coercive aspects of family-planning programs in countries like Indonesia. There, the Suharto government attempted to compete with Islamist political parties outside the state that deployed the issue of birth control to attack the government. Iran's campaign relied far more on persuasion and welfare incentives situated within a framework of religiously sanctioned marriage legitimized by the government. MOHME began to require all newly married couples to attend counseling sessions to obtain their marriage certificates. Here, women and men were separated by sex into classrooms and instructed on options for birth control, on effects of family size, on sexual health, on parental responsibilities for children's health, and on the religious principles underlying these recommendations. In other words, in the realm of sexual and reproductive norms, the Islamic Republic actively engaged in the creative invention of religious tradition for purposes of modernization.

The program contributed to rapid changes in birth patterns. Partly as a result of the health-house system with its embedded female workers, modern contraceptive use quickly rose in rural areas. As educational levels among young women rose, the marriage age rose in tandem. Women bore their first child later in life. Many older women, no matter how many children they had, decided to stop having more children at existing family sizes. As shown above in figure 11, the idea of stopping at two became the main norm underpinning a rapid fertility decline in the 1990s. Iranian women still get married, and still have one child rather soon afterwards. But according to demographers, then they stop, use contraception to control fertility, and delay the second child longer than mothers in many other middle-income countries. This social pattern began before 1989, but the family-planning program quickly accelerated it in the 1990s. The total fertility rate went from nearly 5.6 in 1987 to 2.8 in 1996: that is, estimated birthrates were roughly *halved* in only ten years.

One final aspect of this family-planning program warrants discussion. The contraception program funded by the government was very flexible. According to public-health surveys in the early 1990s, rural women mostly opted for the pill or, once it became available, a

FIGURE 12. Sign from family-planning campaign, Ahvaz, Khuzestan. The sign sat outside a school and a nearby sports complex. Most likely it is from the early 1990s. In the Persian slogan, the connotation is clear that the readers—the parents—will have happier lives with fewer children. The slogan thus appeals to the quality of life of the postwar generation. (Photo: author.)

progestogen injection every three months. Older rural women opted for sterilizations, as did many of their husbands. These surveys also showed, however, that as educational levels rose, women were more likely to use condoms or the traditional method of withdrawal (coitus interruptus) rather than the modern methods given free by the government or also cheaply available in the private sector in urban areas.[55] In other words, even though free birth control became universally available for the Iranian population, more educated women in urban areas still opted for the withdrawal method.[56] This is contrary to the patterns observed in many other middle-income countries.

Two intertwined factors may account for this reversal. First, educated women have easier access to abortion in Iran, although estimated abortion levels in Iran are still low as compared with other middle-income countries.[57] Second, women in Iran express concern about unwanted effects of the hormonal therapies in modern methods of birth control and likely choose the withdrawal method as an alternative if needed.[58] Beneath these choices, however, lie the gender relations of power in the household. Withdrawal is a successful method of birth control if trust exists between partners in the marriage relationship, and if the woman can draw on any one source of personal autonomy, or more than one. For example, even though women have limited access to the formal labor market in Iran, higher educational levels and increased social status can contribute to an equalization of gender-power relations within the family structure. For less-educated or illiterate women, conversely, modern birth control can act as a method to control fertility even if highly unequal power relations persist in the household. Trust of the husband is not required. So, although more qualitative research is needed on the subject, the demographic survey findings may suggest that poorer women in rural areas use the Islamic Republic's welfare state to combat their own husbands' traditionalist, patriarchal disposition toward larger family sizes.

FROM PEASANTS TO IRANIANS

"Roads, more roads, and always roads," wrote a regional governor in late-nineteenth-century France; "this sums up the political economy of the countryside."[59] In Iran before the revolution, only eight thousand kilometers of paved roads existed in rural areas. Between 1979 and 1999, this total expanded eightfold, to more than sixty-seven thousand kilometers of gravel and asphalt roads. As a result of the state's rural-development activities, more than 60 percent of the rural population was linked into the national road network before the first Five Year Plan was even implemented, in 1989.[60] Above, this chapter has focused on another such transformation: the primary health-care networks of rural health houses. These organizations formed the core of the rural-welfare system in postrevolutionary Iran. The result was not only a transformation of the rural sector but also an Iranianization of the disparate provinces, communities, and livelihoods within the territory of Iran. In other words, as compared with the Pahlavi monarchy, these forms of welfare were both socially and spatially inclusive.

Rural-development policies contributed to at least two outcomes by the late 1990s: a gradual reduction in absolute poverty levels and a rapid reduction in the average family size of the population. These changes are often taken for granted. Grievances over access to public services, over employment, and over income inequality are the issues of the day in twenty-first-century Iran. And it is true: the Islamic Republic's postrevolutionary welfare system did not solve the problems associated with inequality—key targets of the upheavals of 1979. But the consequence of these welfare activities, nevertheless, was a state more embedded in society than the previous regime had been. Another consequence, however, was that millions of people raised their expectations in accordance with a growing understanding of upward status-achievement across the entire nation.

This postrevolutionary welfare system repeatedly appears in state interactions with individuals, often as a safety net of last resort. For instance, in a study of poverty clusters in Khuzestan during the early 2000s, communities of war refugees were visited by Iranian social scientists. These were people who could not access old lands for purposes of agriculture or husbandry, and their economic prospects were dim. In the rural areas studied, infrastructure badly needed to be upgraded. In the periurban areas of Ahvaz, migrant families built up illegal housing, with few connections to the water, electricity, and sewage systems of the city. The absence of renewed land reform after the 1980s, or even of a rationalized accounting of land claims, exacerbated the plight of those who were landless. These migrants formed a rural proletariat.[61] Nevertheless, even in these poor Khuzestan communities, this 2004 study documented both the presence of PHC clinics and the IKRC.[62] In other words, welfare organizations were at the very edge of the state in these people's lives.

Another example of the likely effects of rural-welfare organizations in Iran can be seen in the large, sparsely populated southeastern region of Baluchistan in the province of Sistan and Baluchistan, which neighbors the Pakistani province also called Baluchistan. Although they speak the same language, the Baluchis inhabiting these two provinces have a political boundary running through their imagined community. Extended families are often connected across the border between Iran and Pakistan. Yet this political boundary highlights the social changes discussed in this chapter. Even Baluchistan, which most Iranians have never visited, was not immune to the Iranianization of social life. In the early 1980s, demographers observed fertility rates in Iranian Baluchistan as high as 9.5 children per family. In 2006, the province's fertility rate had declined to 3.7. In neighboring Pakistani Baluchistan, the rate still stood at 5.4 in 2006, although down from 7.3 in 2001.[63] As a bureaucratically efficient "health-developmental state" embedded in the countryside, the rural health-care system equalized access from east to west across the far reaches of the Persian steppe.

Through the expansion of education and welfare, both the rural-urban gap and the center-provincial gap narrowed to an extent never experienced before in Iran. This process nationalized Iranian society, equalizing the aspirations across the country for upward mobility and a higher standard of living. Millions of people went to school for the first time, sent their children for annual checkups for the first time, read newspapers for the first time, and moved to cities for the first time. The egalitarian spirit of the revolution and the mobilizational spirit of the war opened pathways for this transformation, as did the bottom-up participation of both women and men. This process, though not without its own struggles, setbacks, and clashes, fed back into the factional elite politics at the commanding heights of the postrevolutionary state. How could any of these elite groups lead this younger, literate, and more politicized population toward its own revolutionary vision? The answer, for some, was ambitious: Iran needed to be a developmental state.

CHAPTER 5

Development and Distinction

*Welfare-State Expansion and the Politics
of the New Middle Class*

No government can now expect to be permanent unless it
guarantees progress as well as order; nor can it continue
really to secure order, unless it promotes progress.

—John Stuart Mill

Whatever the strength of the army and the ubiquitousness of
the secret police which such a government may have at its
disposal, it would be naive to believe that those instruments
of physical oppression can suffice. Such a government can
maintain itself in power only if it succeeds in making people
believe that it performs an important social function which
could not be discharged in its absence. Industrialization
provided such a function for the Soviet government.

—Alexander Gerschenkron

Only a handful of middle-income countries have caught up over the
past half-century to levels of wealth enjoyed by European and North
American countries.[1] This was not for lack of effort, however. No country went untransformed in the wake of rapid modernization drives of
the post–World War II era. Yet as failure and retrenchment set in for
most middle-income countries during the 1980s and 1990s, earlier
developmental models were cast aside. These models were blamed even
for the woes experienced in subsequent "lost decades." Amid the disil-
lusionment, new models were found, new ideas touted, and new states
held as the ideal to emulate.

As Iran exited a decade of war, the political elite of the Islamic Republic also debated how to reenter the developmental race. They did so, however, at a time when the term "developmental state" was an unclear concept. During the Cold War, with its binaries of market and capitalism versus planning and socialism, the phrase was narrowly applied toward only a few countries, and often only after the fact: Japan, South Korea, and select East Asian city-states.[2] In retrospect, a variety of developmental states existed in the twentieth century. Perhaps the least appreciated strain was the Soviet Union.[3] Ideological polemics stood in the way of recognizing common properties of developmental states. No matter the region, all shared one characteristic. Nationalist elites in middle-income countries across the globe attempted to use state power to catch up with the wealthy core of the world economy. As noted in this book's introduction, after the volatile and crisis-prone decades of the 1970s and 1980s, however, most of them ended up in the same economic position relative to wealthy countries. In development studies, it is called the Red Queen effect, after Lewis Carroll's character from *Alice through the Looking Glass*. Through rapid state-led modernization programs, countries were running faster and faster just to stay in the same place.[4] Subsequently, and especially after the 1989 collapse of Eastern European socialist states, many of the same nationalist elites changed their tune. The state was out; the market was in.

Iran was no exception. Just as Pahlavi-era bureaucrats extolled the sureties of modernization theory in the 1960s armed with the latest American social science, a new set of technocrats under President Akbar Hashemi-Rafsanjani claimed that the consensus of expert opinion—supposedly devoid of ideology and political bias—revealed one true path for the Islamic Republic's success. They called this the pragmatist, moderate, modern path. They cited economists and political scientists who, up until that point, were largely unheard of in the postrevolutionary public sphere. In the pages of *Political-Economic Information*, for example, the longest continuously running journal in the Islamic Republic (1986–present), the transformation was readily apparent. The first years of the journal devoted its cramped and inky pages to Third Worldist perspectives on neocolonialism and the exploitation of poorer countries by Western powers. After the Soviet collapse and the death of Khomeini, the journal was translating Samuel Huntington and Francis Fukuyama as its lead articles, with commentary by Iranian elites on how to adjust to the new world order proclaimed by U.S. president George H. W. Bush. Eventually, "globalization" and its associated buzzwords began to appear in the journal alongside the usual hard-nosed realpolitik. Other political elites in Iran soon reacted to the new position. In print media such the newspaper *Salām* and the journal *Bayān*, radicals associated with former prime minister Mousavi labeled the new economic proposals of Rafsanjani's circle as capitalist, Western-dependent, and antirevolutionary.

As often is the case, ideological polemics hid the actual processes at work. The Rafsanjani government attempted to inject market incentives into many of the economic activities that had been taken over by the state after the revolution. What it could not accomplish subsequently became the economic priorities for the Khatami administration. Yet the Islamic Republic hardly became a night-watchman state during the 1990s and 2000s. Liberalization was far more gradual and piecemeal. Even with its highly touted five-year development plans, the political elite of the Islamic Republic never created the autonomous state apparatus to carry these efforts out to the letter. Intraelite conflict continued under a variety of reinvented factional designations and epithets, depending on whom one asked: left and right, pragmatists and conservatives, or reformists and principlists. This conflict slowed down or blocked policy shifts. Ideology aside, however, the Islamic Republic's five-year plans, which finally commenced in 1989, looked remarkably like a to-do list of Pahlavi-era projects. Plan designs included the tendency to be overly ambitious about the transformative power of the state. The political elite wanted Iran to become, in an echo of earlier postrevolutionary states such as the USSR, an antisystemic developmental state. Catching up to wealthy countries in the world economy would prove that the 1979 revolution could deliver material gains in addition to symbolic ones.

The implementation of development plans never went smoothly. In some areas, the failures of Pahlavi-era big-push projects were repeated. In other areas, the plans did achieve considerable success in developmental gains. Some success was evident in key segments of welfare policy. The technocratic elites in the Islamic Republic dreamed of a universal, productivity-enhancing welfare system. Welfare gains would both contribute to a diversified export economy and produce an educated population who loyally supported the postrevolutionary state. Models of the East Asian economic miracles danced in their heads. To achieve this goal, the Iranian government repurposed Pahlavi-era welfare agencies. The most important was the Social Security Organization (SSO) and the fragmented medical system to which it was attached. The formal, corporatist half of the postrevolutionary dual-welfare regime was awakened in the new developmental drive of the Islamic Republic.

The government tasked these organizations with the responsibility of protecting the population against social dislocation while market-led liberalization proceeded. The Rafsanjani government also copied a not-so-hidden version of China's Deng-style sloganeering. Getting rich in the Islamic Republic was not only permissible; it was glorious under God. Some of the new market entrants were those who had risen through welfare pathways forged during wartime. Others felt excluded from the new market-friendly era, however, and resented the changes in status and power that Rafsanjani's reforms prioritized.

Through the 1990s and into the 2000s, the five-year-plan predictions of East Asian–styled economic growth and industrial transformation did not materialize. Iran remained reliant on oil revenue for a main source of wealth creation. The welfare system expanded, but it also ran up against the constraints of a combative, fractured political elite as well as the constraints of a middle-income country with a large, informal labor force. Yet lackluster growth rates did not mean the country was stagnant. The developmental push in the Islamic Republic created and expanded a new domestic middle class. This included newly educated professionals, technicians, business managers, petty entrepreneurs, as well as millions more people who aspired to emulate them. In turn, this new middle class changed the way that Iran's political elites talked about their own country and took positions against each other in factional battles. Though all sides spoke of fulfilling the revolutionary promises of 1979, it was the legacy of the Iran-Iraq War that laid the foundations for a set of surprising and unintended shifts during the 1990s and 2000s. Along the way, the Islamic Republic's technocratic crusade helped to create the grievances that Green Movement protestors would later express against the government itself.

This chapter proceeds as follows. First, I describe the new developmental vision of postwar Iran and the elites who attempted to carry it out. Next, I show how these plans intertwined with the individuals who had been incorporated into Iran's welfare system during the war. The welfare state born from the war, it turned out, extracted heavy costs on the government that became apparent only well into Iran's developmental push. Last, I discuss the political and economic constraints that arose within the Social Security Organization and related medical and health sectors as new middle classes began to exert social power. The two decades after the war in Iran illustrate that the politics of social policy are never solely about poverty, but are also about social inequality and mobility. Looking only at oil revenues, or the ideological debates of the 1990s, we miss the social transformations in Iran that later surprised the world.

FROM PROMISES TO SOCIAL PACT

The end of the war compelled the Iranian government, first under Prime Minister Mousavi and then under President Rafsanjani, to codify and expand many of the promises made during the revolution and the war years into a new, postrevolutionary social compact.[5] On paper, the various laws and regulations passed during the early 1990s amounted to a generous set of social protections and benefits for formal workers and newly trained professionals. These provisions were partly the result of a decade of revolutionary and wartime mobilization that pushed the state to deliver on its promises. It was also partly the result of factional competition that saw multiple segments of the political elite accusing each other of not paying attention to matters of social justice and popular needs. The contours of this social compact illustrate the politics at the center of postrevolutionary societal bargaining.

The 1990 Labor Law (enacted in 1993) was particularly employee-friendly, albeit confined within corporatist structures. The 1979–82 battles between Khomeinists and other radical-religious and secular-left groups over control of the state were also fought in factories and offices, as workers attempted to maintain and expand the autonomous power grabbed during the revolutionary vacuum. Instead, Islamic Workers' Councils and the state-created Worker's House were used to channel the revolutionary labor movement, often coercively, into state-supporting efforts.[6] In addition, more radical members of the political elite attempted to address labor concerns soon after the Khomeinists solidified their control over the state. A Labor Law was introduced by Mousavi's administration in order to placate threats of insurgent labor during the war, though the conservative Guardian Council continued to block various versions until 1990. The Law, finally ratified, stipulated that employees could be fired only upon approval by an Islamic Workers' Council or Discretionary Board. Businesses with more than five employees could not fire a formal worker after the individual had been employed for one month for unskilled or three months for skilled workers. Reasons for dismissal were limited to disability, retirement, resignation, death, or if the employee was initially hired under a short-term contract. All formal workers in the private sector were required by law to be enrolled in the Social Security Organization's social-insurance plan, which created additional contributory costs for employers. Minimum wages for each sector and occupation were set by a Supreme Labor Council and were usually raised each year to keep up with inflation costs.[7] Workers were ostensibly given the right to organize through state-sanctioned councils or guilds, and employment under age 15 was outlawed. Workers could be reinstated after firing if they appealed to labor councils that their dismissal was illegal. The Labor Law stipulated that workers could not be dismissed because of military conscription and allowed for maternity leave and workplace nursing of female employees' infants.[8]

In reality, the law was vastly limited in application. Both the private and the public sector, including government ministries and the Tehran municipality, often used temporary contracts via labor cooperatives or subcontractors in order to maintain flexible, low-cost hiring practices.[9] During the 1990s, new private businesses and their supporters in the political elite pushed for a relaxation of the law. At the same time, worker unrest grew over delayed wage and benefit payments. Many labor activists derided the corporatist unions as mere tools of state control. Yet over the postwar era, some of the main defenders of the Labor Law's provisions, as well as workers' wages and benefits in general, have been representatives from the state-created labor union itself: the Islamic Workers' Council.[10] These corporatist workers' organizations, therefore, engendered constraints on independent action but also created inducements for formal worker participation.[11]

The loophole for contract labor was subsequently expanded. The Khatami administration passed legislation in 2000 that exempted firms with fewer than five employees from the law. In 2003, firms with fewer than ten employees were exempted if they engaged in a tripartite negotiation with their employees and state representatives.[12] About 95 percent of Iran's enterprises employed fewer than ten workers by 2002, or about 49 percent of the urban labor force.[13] Market-friendly business representatives and economists argued that such moves were necessary in order to prevent bankruptcies among small enterprises. The approved exemptions contributed to segmented hiring and wage levels that varied across sectors. The law, for example, does not directly regulate the informal labor force, even though some informal workers may indirectly benefit from minimum-wage pacts. Furthermore, while large manufacturing firms in Iran are still regulated under the Labor Law, nearly the entire construction sector remained untouched because of reliance on temporary labor contracts.[14] The Ahmadinejad administration and the post-2004 conservative-dominated parliaments further debated revisions to the law, including expanding the exemption to firms with up to fifteen employees. No changes were made, however. Pressure on the state from private business continues to be felt through the various Chambers of Commerce that operate as negotiating houses between state and capital. It is notable that, while the labor law was being watered down over the 2000s, independent workers' organizations sprang up in the transportation, agricultural, and manufacturing sectors. The corporate pacts of formal labor regulation that emerged from postrevolutionary societal bargaining, in other words, have been slowly breaking down.

Another segment of the postwar compact was the expansion of social insurance, which included health-care coverage and pension eligibility. The Social Security Organization (SSO), created in 1975 to take over the Pahlavi-era Social Security Fund, had been previously managed within the prerevolutionary Ministry of Social Welfare. The 1979 Revolutionary Council placed the SSO and the Civil Service Insurance Organization under the Ministry of Health's purview, but the Iranian government separated them out again in 1989. In 1986, the Ministry of Health was expanded to take over medical schools and was renamed the Ministry of Health and Medical Education (MOHME). These changes led to a considerably more fragmented social-insurance system than in the Pahlavi era, but one that allowed each institution to pursue socially inclusionary policies at its own initiative.[15]

Access to health-care insurance was expanded through this process. In 1994, the Comprehensive Welfare and Social Security Law was passed (also called the Basic Insurance Act). The law obliged the government to make social insurance and health care universally available to the population according to the articles of the 1979 constitution and the framework of the 1975 prerevolutionary Social Security Law. In 1995, the Public Medical Service Insurance Coverage Act was passed, creating the Medical Service Insurance Organization (MSIO) to provide health insurance to individuals from an assortment of different occupational, income, and status groups. In 2000, parliament began the Urban Inpatient Insurance Scheme, subsidizing inpatient hospital care for the roughly 10 percent of urban residents who did not possess health insurance coverage if and when they entered inpatient care. In 2005, the Rural Health Insurance Scheme was passed, subsidizing secondary health care for rural households that needed services or medical products from urban hospitals or specialist clinics. In 2011, several different health-insurance funds were merged into the Basic Insurance Fund, in an attempt to universalize access to the welfare system. Any individual can enroll in this fund, and the government will pay 50 percent of the insurance premium. Low-income individuals can have much of the remainder paid for by the Imam Khomeini Relief Committee.[16]

In sum, the state approached social insurance using two linked administrative methods. First, the corporatist welfare organizations of the prerevolutionary period were revamped. Second, these organizations attempted to extend benefits to the broader population outside occupational and residential status. Organizations like the SSO borrowed from, and then attempted to move beyond, the Pahlavi-era blueprint of the welfare state. As an official in the Ministry of Welfare and Social Security told me:[17]

> The most effective improvements came at the end of the Khatami administration. There were efforts to consolidate the insurance organizations, and add in various special groups [carpet weavers, nomads, seminary students, etc.]. But at the time [efforts at extension] remained limited. Only in the Ahmadinejad administration did it spread further to those groups without insurance. . . . So the plan changed, from just expanding the existing insurance system to spreading coverage to poorer groups.

The expansionary enrollments under the SSO can be seen in the share of the labor force covered over time, graphed in figure 13.

The figure shows two waves of social-insurance expansion after the 1979 revolution. The first expansion occurs with the end of the war and the Rafsanjani era of market-led liberalization (1988–96). The second expansion happened during the Ahmadinejad years, when the government merged insurance funds and opened up the social-insurance system to the entire workforce (2006–14).

One should remember that, even when SSO coverage levels appeared flat, this was in the context of a growing labor force. In other words, over the course of the postrevolutionary period, a higher relative and absolute share of the labor force came under the social-insurance umbrella of the Iranian welfare system. It went from a narrow core of formal labor protection in a few key economic sectors to a broad swath of the working population. Enrollment of an individual also meant that their families were covered, as well. And from the perspective of the state, expansion of enrollment was not cheap. As the beneficiary pool grew toward universal access, the government needed to pay increasing amounts into a variety of SSO funds to keep them solvent. The financial pressure on the SSO is not simply a product of absolute numbers but also of the benefit structure itself.

When scholars rely on indicators such as industrial output, investments in oil and gas, or employment levels as proxies for economic

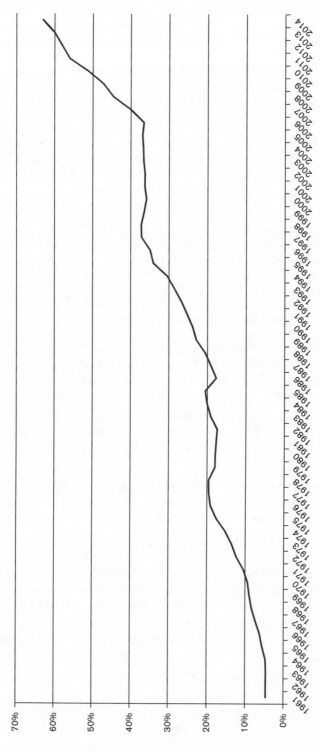

FIGURE 13. Percentage of employed labor force covered by Social Security Organization over five decades (1961–2014). (Source: SSO Statistical Annuals, various years.)

TABLE 6   SOCIAL-SECURITY PROGRAM COVERAGE IN IRAN IN COMPARISON WITH OTHER MIDDLE-INCOME COUNTRIES

Country	Number of ILO categories covered by statute (of 8)	Sickness	Maternity	Old age	Invalidity	Survivors	Family allowances	Employment injury	Unemployment
Algeria	8	x	x	x	x	x	x	x	x
Argentina	8	x	x	x	x	x	x	x	x
Brazil	8	x	x	x	x	x	x	x	x
China	7	x	x	x	x	x		x	x
Egypt	7	x	x	x	x	x		x	x
India	7	x	x	x	x	x		x	x
Indonesia	4	—		x	x	x		x	
Jordan	4	—		x	x	x		x	
Mexico	7	x	x	x	x	x	x	x	—
Saudi Arabia	4	—	—	x	x	x	x		
South Africa	7	x	x	x	x		x	x	x
South Korea	5	—		x	x	x		x	x
Syria	4			x	x	x		x	
Taiwan	7	x	x	x	x	x		x	x
Tunisia	8	x	x	x	x	x	x	x	x
Iran	8	x	x	x	x	x	x	x	x

SOURCE: ILO 2010: Statistical Annex B.

NOTE: x = ILO sufficient; — = present in some form but insufficient for ILO guidelines.

development, they often overlook expansions in social-welfare access. While Iran's GDP per capita places it roughly in the middle-income levels of the world economy, along with countries such as South Africa, Iran has a de jure social-insurance system equal to or better than in many other middle-income countries. In table 6, ILO data on social-security programs throughout the global South are compared.[18]

Iranian social-insurance policies are more comprehensive than neighbors' in Western Asia and the Persian Gulf, such as Saudi Arabia or Jordan. In fact, Iran's social-insurance system, by the late 2000s, more closely resembled large Latin American countries such as Brazil and Argentina and smaller North African countries such as Tunisia and Algeria. Not everyone benefits from these policies, of course. A household member has to be enrolled in the SSO or an equivalent social-insurance program. Nevertheless, the framework for universal social insurance exists in Iran because of the legal expansions of the postwar social compact over successive administrations.

Like many of its neighbors, Iran did implement a universal social policy of a different type, one that reached the entire population in some form. This was the basic system of price subsidies for cooking fuel, bread, rice, electricity, and gasoline. These subsidies were a reform of the price-control and rationing system implemented during the war years. After the war ended, the Rafsanjani government subjected most consumer goods to market pricing, a controversial move resented by many people. Yet the state kept many staple goods at low prices and paid the cost difference in their production. The price of bread in the early 1990s, in real terms, stood at nearly 20 percent of the price at the time of the revolution. The price of petrol was halved over that period. Electricity and other public utilities were so cheap that many households let their bills run up for months.[19] This remained the case for the next two decades. Universal subsidies at the point of production and consumption were a simple way for a state unsure of its own regulatory capacity to provide access to these goods for low-income households. Such subsidies are not progressive in structure, since wealthier households consume more than poorer households in absolute amounts. Yet since poorer households spend a higher relative share of their expenditures on consumption, the policy was justified as pro-poor. Therefore it was politically impossible to remove subsidies throughout the 1990s and 2000s, even though economists in Iran warned that these price levels distorted the investment decisions of domestic businesses and household consumption patterns.[20] The policy benefited both poor and rich alike, and the subsidies came to be both popular and expected. As a result, the subsidies were kept in place until 2011, when the Ahmadinejad government started to liberalize these remaining goods' prices and replaced the subsidies with a bimonthly income grant.

In sum, for two decades after the Iran-Iraq War, the country experienced an unsteady but gradual codification of a social-welfare compact. This was partly an expansion of the corporatist organs of the Pahlavi period and partly a modification of the welfare system built up during the war itself. By the end of these two decades, however, Iran's welfare regime was under pressure at multiple points. This pressure came from two sources: factional conflict within the political elite and social mobilizations from below.

THE RETURN OF THE EXPERTS

Mohammad-Hossein Ādeli was a young California-trained economist who became Iran's ambassador to Japan in the late 1980s. While there, he learned about the country's reconstruction experiences after World War II. Upon his return in 1989, Ādeli was appointed head of the Central Bank of Iran. He helped to implement the first five-year plan with the Japanese experience in mind.[21] In choosing a name, Ādeli described the policy package as a structural adjustment. The term, even in Persian, was crafted with an eye to the prevailing consensus in development at the time. The term may have been in vogue among economists, but it soon became a sore spot. During Rafsanjani's first presidential administration (1989–94), radicals accused the government of copying the plan wholesale from the World Bank and the International Monetary Fund. Instead of the example of Japan, some pointed to Egypt's economic opening under Anwar Sadat, widely seen in Iran as a capitulation to Western powers.[22] Yet the 1989 five-year plan, with its overly ambitious goals for growth, investment, and economic diversification, was not market fundamentalism. Instead, it was technocratic fundamentalism. The ideological change was gradual, but over the next two decades it enveloped nearly the entire political elite. By the late 2000s, every politician in the Islamic Republic framed his or her position in terms of technocratic, expert governance against an opposing side that was ideologically biased and managerially incompetent.

This shift intertwined with the dispositions of Iran's growing middle classes. During hundreds of conversations I had with educated Iranians around the country, people generally expressed their opinions on economic and social matters freely. After the standard pleasantries, often in comparison with wealthy countries in Europe or North America, many individuals began to lament the squandering of Iran's potential greatness. This is a common complaint in any large middle-income country with a keen sense of nationalism. The target of blame, however, was not so common. By a substantial margin, the number one complaint by Iranians was this simple statement: this country has "bad management." Many people in Iran used some variety of management-speak to make claims about politics and society. This was not a main form of claims-making in the early revolutionary years.

Mousavi's long speech to the parliament about modernization at the end of the war, discussed earlier in this book, anticipated the Rafsanjani government's political strategy. Even as political elites believed themselves to be acting in opposition to the international system, the Islamic

Republic had to do what it took to become a developmental state. Rafsanjani's gambit irrevocably shifted the discourse of elite conflict in the Islamic Republic. It is not an exaggeration to state that the political struggles during the next two decades in the Islamic Republic were, in essence, born in these early postwar years. In November 1990, the new president (and, lest we forget, Shi'i cleric) Rafsanjani gave a Friday sermon that was later described by the journalist Mohammad Quchāni as the manifesto of the white-collar *hezbollāhi*s.[23] To a crowd of elite politicians, loyal state cadres, and bureaucrats from across the government, Rafsanjani proclaimed the superiority of consumerism over asceticism, the benefits of work over idleness, and the goal of overcoming individual vulnerabilities as opposed to harnessing the collective power of the oppressed. "There is nothing un-Islamic about the accumulation of wealth," he stated. "Worship and piety are not enough. . . . The deterministic and fatalistic idea that God will take care of everything in its time is a wrong thought that the nation [*ommat*] is afflicted with."[24] It was a speech that owed as much to the aphorisms of Deng Xiaoping as to the recently departed Khomeini. Rafsanjani's sermon included a few low political blows. He attacked the mode of dress and personal comportment of revolutionary counterculture developed at the outset of the Iran-Iraq War:[25]

> We suffer from a culture in which the style of living and the appearance of priests and *hezbollāhi*s [revolutionary supporters] should be unpleasant and ugly. If it becomes a cultural phenomenon that being a *hezbollāhi* means looking unbearable, this is a sin and Islam has fought this. . . . We have religious decrees that you must wear perfume, comb your hair, comb your beard, and wear a clean outfit. The Prophet himself looked at his reflection in water to make sure that he was presentable before his guests.

Moreover, Rafsanjani insisted, this ethos of revolutionary and war mobilization should be harnessed toward development: "While keeping their belligerent spirits, the *basiji*s should be engaged in the phase of economic reconstruction in Iran." Rafsanjani then engaged in a historical volte-face. He declared that technocracy—rule by experts—had always been the true path of the revolution: "The Imam's [Khomeini's] guidance was to relegate the task of reconstruction to the skilled experts without fear of the religiously narrow-minded and the pseudo-revolutionaries . . . and attend to the families of martyrs with attention to foreign policy and the material well-being of the people within the confines of Islamic teachings."[26] One decade after the beginning of the Iran-Iraq war, the fervor of mobilization had been turned on its head by one of its main adherents.

The rise of this self-proclaimed third-way faction in the elite had far-reaching consequences. Most outwardly, it altered the political field by reorienting the available lines of ideological conflict. Other factions of the elite changed their popular strategies in response. One group capitalized during the 1990s on the sense of betrayal felt by many war veterans. Both the state as well as the younger postwar generation seemed uninterested and unappreciative of their sacrifices. Several films captured this sentiment, including *Crimson Gold* by Jafar Panāhi. In this 2003 film, a poor war veteran works as a low-status pizza deliveryman in order to save up money for marriage. Fast food and pizza in Iran, as in most of the global South, are symbols of conspicuous consumption by the middle class. The film's protagonist drives his motorcycle around the wealthy neighborhoods of Tehran delivering pizza, and he observes the lives of the wealthy with awe and, the viewer suspects, quiet disdain. In poor health, one night he fills an order at a luxury apartment, and his former commander from the famous battle of Shalamcheh opens the door. The commander does not recognize the ex-soldier, partly because, as the deliveryman explains, the latter needs to take cortisone injections (assumedly as a treatment from war injuries since some Shalamcheh soldiers were attacked by Iraqi chemical weapons).

Panāhi is a renowned director who, in 2009, supported the election of Mir-Hossein Mousavi and the post-election Green Movement. Yet his cinematic attention to class and social inequality connects with deeply held feelings in a wide swath of Iranian society. A socially conservative 1990s group called the Supporters of Hezbollāhis, which would often show up and harass reformist male and female politicians at public events, titled their glossy in-house magazine *Shalamcheh*—the town in Khuzestan near where Iranian volunteer troops repelled Iraqi forces and thousands of soldiers perished. In 1998, the conservative filmmaker Masud Dehnamaki, a spokesperson for the group, stated: "Supporters of Hezbollāh did not exist before 1989; the group came together around that time to defend the values [of the revolution] and fight those who betrayed it."[27]

This discourse was eventually tagged with the Persian neologism *osulgarāi*, a word that can be translated into English as "fundamentalist," since *osul* means "doctrine," "root," or "tenet." According to several Iranian journalists, state-funded media were aware of the negative connotation of this particular word in Western countries. Preferring not to be lumped in with Sunni salafism, the English-language media in Iran opted to use the term "principlist," which caught on more generally. Political mobilization by supporters of this principlist strand of thought eventually culminated in the 2005 candidacy of Mahmoud Ahmadinejad for president of the Islamic Republic. Ahmadinejad's followers declared themselves the true principlists—meaning those who adhered to the revolution's tenets. They accused not only reformists but also old-guard conservatives of standing in their way. As elsewhere, elite struggles in Iran have a way of changing the use of language. Once Ahmadinejad became president, and especially after the post-2009 intensification of elite conflict within the right itself, other conservatives began to call themselves the bona fide principlists and deemed Ahmadinejad's circle as "deviationists." This tussle notwithstanding, the lineage of Iran's "new right" and the second generation of conservative politicians can be traced back to the politics of the 1990s and the aftereffects of the war years.[28]

The other response to Rafsanjani's gambit came from the Jacobin-styled radicals of the Khomeinist left. These individuals underscored republicanism and political pluralism as the core of the 1979 revolution. Economic modernization was criticized by these radicals as useless, and even impossible, without political modernization, tolerance in the public sphere, and a state religiosity that allowed for social change and new ideas. Much of this radical, left-leaning segment of the elite was essentially kicked out of government in 1992, when the Guardian Council ruled that many former members of parliament could not stand for parliamentary elections in that year. Rafsanjani did nothing to prevent this while president. Instead, he took full advantage of the purge in order to push the remaining policies of the first five-year developmental plan through the new parliament after 1992. This expulsion temporarily relegated the soul-searching religious left to the political wilderness. In 1996, when many of these same revolutionaries again stood for parliamentary elections, they did so as *eslāh-talebān*, meaning "seekers of correction," "of modification," "of amendment," or as they became known, "reformists." The 1996 film *Leili Is with Me* by Kamāl Tabrizi, a black comedy about a man volunteering for war to get a housing loan, captures the sentiment of this "new left." The movie cynically portrays how religious discourse was corrupted during the war years and implies that the abuse of religion by the state in turn led to everyday corruption in society. One year after the film's huge success in Iranian cinemas—a blasphemous scandal to the conservative right and a cathartic revelation to a growing middle class—this reformist current culminated in the election of Mohammad Khatami as president.[29]

In sum, throughout the postwar period the political elite reoriented and reshaped itself. These new elite divisions were heavily debated, and pored over in Iranian media, and were often set in amber by Western journalists as binding ideological divisions. Yet underneath the acrimonious elite conflict, which only intensified over the 1990s and 2000s, the turn toward a developmentalist, technocratic perspective among the elite as a whole was overlooked. The struggle between elites over the next two decades became a battle over who would control Iran's anticipated developmental state, not a debate over the purpose of development. In their appeals to the public, all sides proclaimed themselves the experts, and their expertise as the path to modernization, a decent life, and global status befitting the Iranian nation-state.

THE UPWARDLY MOBILE IN THE NEW STATUS ORDER

Technocratic rule was supposed to be the recipe for securing economic growth unimpeded by politics. Politics, however, immediately intervened from the outside. The halving in oil prices after the 1991 United States–Iraq Gulf War sent Iran's balance of payments into a free fall. When the Rafsanjani government attempted to reschedule its foreign loans with Japan, Germany, and other states via the International Monetary Fund, the recently inaugurated Clinton administration blocked that path. Mohsen Nurbakhsh, then the minister for finance and economic affairs, later recalled that while Iran struggled to obtain foreign financing, Turkey was experiencing its own debt crisis. The "whole of the world's resources" went to the latter's aid in the form of an International Monetary Fund loan package.[30] Iran, conversely, had to reintroduce capital controls and tiered currency rates while facing an inflationary spiral once it lifted price controls. Contrary to the radicals' accusations, the architects of the first five-year development plan had limited relations with either the World Bank or the International Monetary Fund. Instead, they were influenced by the pro-market turn in the United Kingdom and Europe as well as the collapse of the USSR. It was easy, with these other experiences in mind, to associate the woes of the economy with state intervention. Buzzwords of the Rafsanjani period, which resonated well after his administration, included the shrinking of government and the self-sufficiency of public-sector enterprises that could not be privatized. All government agencies were told to reduce their workforce and costs as well as to pursue revenue-generating activities. Subsequent World Bank recommendations mostly affirmed what these technocrats already believed.[31]

Only four of the twenty-two ministerial positions in Rafsanjani's first cabinet went to clerics. Just as in the early years of the revolution, ideas mattered. But this time the ideas were about the power of markets to bypass the disorder of the state. Planning and Budget Organization (PBO) head Masud Roghani-Zanjāni later admitted that these cabinet ministers had little practical experience. Social and political responses to their policies were not realistically considered. They did not perceive, he said, the "latent barriers" that soon appeared as the development plans were being implemented.[32] This may have been the case, but it is more likely that, as in all big-development pushes, the state's vision of society was a simplified reduction of reality that could not easily take into account the cross-cutting political interests of local actors or the variety of social responses to state policies. Two examples illustrate the unintended consequences of these social barriers.

First, mimicking the East Asian Tigers, Iran created three free trade–industrial zones on the country's southern shores during the years 1988–91. These islands and industrial parks were supposed to bring in foreign exchange through tourism, direct investment, and the export of domestic nonoil goods. Instead, these trade zones and the creation of sixteen more special economic zones over the next decade mostly operated as import platforms that bypassed tariffs and customs duties. Pent-up demand for consumer goods among Iranians became the main driver of trade-zone activities, which had been strategically placed along Iran's borders in order to reduce commercial bottlenecks.[33] The Rafsanjani government also built zones in deprived regions, allowed 100-percent foreign ownership of any subsidiaries, promised a fifteen-year tax holiday, and reduced labor regulations.[34] The goal was to lure in foreign investment. The result, however, was the rise of new domestic business elites through import arbitrage rather than foreign-funded manufacturing, as later described by Roghani-Zanjāni:[35]

> There was a political trend [in the 1980s] whereby traditional bazaaris and their allied clerics believed that religion dictated the state could not control price rates. . . . Yet we see that, near the end of the war and afterwards, the businessmen, industrialists, and commercial men who were involved in the process of imports got rich. They did this even while they thought they were not dependent on the political system. In reality, price controls and import licenses caused the rise of these classes. The new businessmen and upstarts were the product of this [postwar] era. And it is this group who later opposed the Khatami government, claiming that only they were adhering to Islam and tradition.

These new business groups were not just limited to bazaaris, however. The push for government self-sufficiency and shrinking the public sector created numerous opportunities for those with political and cultural capital built up during the first decade of the postrevolutionary era to convert these accumulated experiences into economic capital proper. For example, oil and gas ministries began to subcontract out their upstream and downstream activities to companies that had lower labor costs through the use of temporary contracts. These companies were founded and operated by a combination of Pahlavi-era industrialists, state managers, and nouveaux riches who had accumulated capital from housing and construction projects in the 1980s.[36] This was an all-too-common experience of how market liberalization actually proceeded across the global South.

In addition, as Rafsanjani had envisioned, *basiji*s and Revolutionary Guard corpsmen were encouraged to go into business, either within their own organizations or outside them. This was the beginning of a process of military-linked subcontractors building up business conglomerates in Iran. Again, this was hardly unique to the Islamic Republic. It is not accurate to describe the process as a creeping militarization of the economy. What actually occurred was the commodification of bureaucratic privileges gained through military channels. Roughly 70 percent of war veterans had been aged between 16 and 25 at the time of the war. Many of these veterans were volunteers, unmarried, and generally came from working-class or lower-middle-class households.[37] The government mandated that a percentage of jobs in public-sector companies go to war veterans. It also gave favored status to veterans for business loans and licenses. In 1989, the parliament voted to preferentially give such licenses to "veterans and released POWs, [the] head of a family with a male child who has been martyred, [or] a primary dependent of a martyr who must assist the family financially."[38] It should not be surprising what subsequently ensued. A journalist who had covered the 1979 revolution and the Iran-Iraq War remembered one manifestation of this commodified privilege:[39]

> A crop of luxury auto dealerships popped up around Tehran after the war. Who were selling these BMW and Mercedes cars? I talked to the dealership owners, who still looked like they were on the front. These were all Revolutionary Guards.

Not everyone who fought in the war could get a leg up through the state, however. The government saw the public sector as bloated, over-staffed, and full of redundancies. In turn, soldiers and families of war veterans attempted to take advantage of the developmental drive of the state. The status accorded to educational credentials, for example, which briefly had been devalued during the postrevolutionary war years, quickly reverted to normal in the new technocratic zeitgeist. Revolutionary organizations reintroduced meritocratic hierarchies in their own ranks, bureaucratized their management, and sent off their cadres to university slots available as a result of the quota system.[40] The state's emphasis on higher education created many options for families. Āzād (Open) University, established in 1983, formed a private network of colleges that gradually opened up hundreds of campuses in areas that had no previous tertiary education. The public-university system was expanded and given more resources, so that each provincial capital had its own flagship faculty. A distance-learning university system was also set up in 1988, eventually turning into an important arena for credentialing military careerists.[41] Tens of thousands of Iranians could finally obtain the coveted credentials of postgraduate education, highly valued before the revolution but far less accessible. No appellation was more desired than the professional title of engineer (*mohandes*), which arguably operates today as an honorific more useful than any religious credential in Iran, not to mention the rest of the Middle East and South Asia.[42]

This process led to an overproduction of credentials among people who had been raised and educated with the expectation that their livelihoods would reflect their credentialed status. The Islamic Republic's technocratic turn gradually engendered the grievances that members of the Green Movement would later express against the government itself. This blowback certainly was not the intent of the developmental push of the state. Yet it was the result of people in society taking advantage of a broad array of new opportunities of the postwar era for upward mobility.

PENSION CAPITALISM IN THE ISLAMIC REPUBLIC;
OR, THE PERILS OF EARLY RETIREMENT

At the same time when the Islamic Republic was attempting to liberalize its economy, it was also attempting to expand its welfare system. This was not a contradiction in terms. On the contrary, the creation of a universalizing legal-institutional framework for health care, educational access, and social insurance was part of a productivist vision for welfare policy. The World Bank recommended to Iran that strengthening the social safety net would ameliorate the social dislocations brought on by the country's market turn. Rafsanjani's aides also saw welfare policy through the productivist angle. The state's economic shift was not laissez-faire, as critics argued, but directed toward developmental aspirations very similar to the Pahlavi-era technocracy. The vision was for a diversified manufacture-based economy, a flexible and educated workforce, and a steady growth path that would propel Iran closer to the levels of wealth and status observed in Europe and North America. Nevertheless, a large gap existed between universal welfare aspirations and actual institutional outcomes. Pahlavi-era organizations such as the Social Security Organization found it difficult to reach into informal sectors. With their flexible cadre-styled approach, revolutionary welfare organizations such as the Imam Khomeini Relief Committee and the rural Primary Health Care network were more successful.

The politics of social policy after the Iran-Iraq War illustrate the difference between basic-needs welfare organizations, which are mostly engaged in antipoverty and primary health-care initiatives, and welfare organizations such as the SSO that provide the more robust forms of social insurance that are important *after* the general satisfaction of basic needs. The state's top-down welfare organizations proved less effective in the medium term. Nevertheless, SSO policies were the basis for the eventual expansion of social insurance to the majority of the population over the next two decades. Anyone who became an employee of the public or large private-enterprise sector in Iran was usually enrolled in one of two main insurance funds. Government workers mostly entered the Civil Service Retirement Organization (CSRO), whereas workers in the public sector as well as large private-sector enterprises were enrolled in the SSO. In addition to providing retirement pensions, both of these social-insurance funds also covered unemployment insurance, disability compensation, and health-care coverage for the employee's family up to three children (an incentive to limit family size linked to the 1990s family planning initiative). A few state sectors operated their own separate social-insurance funds—oil, gas, TV, and film, as well as the Armed Forces and the Revolutionary Guards Corps. Yet the SSO has always been the largest insurance fund in the country. The Plan and Budget Organization head Roghani-Zanjāni stated in 1989 that 3.9 million workers were enrolled in these multiple insurance funds, and the goal of the first five-year development plan was to double that number.[43]

Because of its obligations to pay health, pension, and disability costs, the government was already in debt to the SSO by the early 1990s. Since the SSO was a state organization, the government was in debt to itself, which meant it could hold back full payment even as it insisted all state agencies should be moving toward self-sufficient revenue streams. For private employers, the contribution share of the insurance premium was quite high: 20 percent of the gross wage by the employer (later raised to 23 percent), 3 percent by the government, and 7 percent by the employee. If the worker was in the public sector or a state-owned enterprise, however, the government was responsible for paying the employer's share.[44] By 1995, more than four thousand public-sector workplaces owed debt to the SSO.[45] In 2000, around 1.6 million employees contributed to the CSRO and 6.1 million employees to the SSO (totaling around 43 percent of the labor force). As a result of higher public-sector enrollments and pools of beneficiaries, both these organizations increasingly experienced fiscal trouble.[46]

The government's underfunding of the SSO was compounded by the retirement regulations of the Islamic Republic, which can arguably be described as extraordinarily generous in comparison with other countries. After the 1979 revolution, the retirement age was favorably lowered. Women aged 42 with twenty years of employment were eligible for a reduced pension, women aged 45 and men aged 50 could retire with thirty years of employment at full pension, and women aged 55 and men aged 60 could retire with only sixteen years of employment. The CSRO has slightly lower retirement payments, but it is more generous on vesting and age requirements: women can retire after twenty years of contributions no matter the age, whereas men need thirty years of contributions. For the SSO, the pension is calculated using the employee's last two years of earnings, when she or he is close to peak earning capacity, not the average earnings of the entire work period. The minimum pension as well as the ceiling is also set at very high levels.[47]

Even compared with other countries in Western Asia and North Africa, which all have generous public-sector retirement packages, the Islamic Republic of Iran's high benefit rates stand out for several reasons. The Islamic Republic partly inherited these policies from the Pahlavi monarchy, which had passed the Social Security Act in 1975 at a time of peak government revenues. After the revolution, the new government did not reduce the benefits but instead made them even more generous for state and industrial workers. At the same time, during the first several years of the postrevolutionary period, women in management-level positions within the state sector were, in essence, bought out to retire early. In some cases, revolutionary courts ruled that women were banned from particular administrative positions. This was the case for judge and subsequent Nobel Peace Prize recipient Shirin Ebādi, who was forced off the judicial bench after the revolution. In other cases, women were told they were eligible to retire early, yet they would still receive a full pension. As the workplace environment in state offices became increasingly regulated in terms of dress and comportment, many educated middle-class women who had entered the public sector before the revolution opted to take the offer.[48] Subtle or overt pressure on women to leave employment did reduce female participation in high-status positions within the state sector. Nevertheless, this pressure, which was surely insulting to women who had acquired the professional and technical credentials to enter these positions, was coupled with material incentives to leave the labor force. As the war commenced, women entered the public labor force again, but in low-level clerical and administrative positions. These women could seek out formal work as a consequence of new public regulations regarding the workplace. As Farideh Farhi points out:

> The Islamic [government], throughout its postrevolutionary evolution, has incorporated developmentalist and culturalist postures vis-à-vis women. These two postures have by no means been in opposition to each other all the time. For instance, the strict application of the Islamic dress code has been used as a mechanism to break cultural barriers against women's presence in the public domain—a license, so to speak, [that] women have so far used very effectively to enter the public space as wage earners or in any other capacity. At the same time, the requirements of a development-oriented liberalisation policy invariably come into conflict with interests that justifiably worry about cultural liberalisation as an intended consequence of economic liberalisation.

After the war, the encouragement of early retirement occurred once again. This time, instead of a gender-oriented policy, it emerged from the government's belief that shrinking public-employment rolls was a requirement of economic growth. Public-sector workers hired during the war years were told to take a buyout.[50] One consequence was that the government kept the benefits package of social-insurance funds generous during the 1990s to induce retirement.[51]

As long as younger workers were entering the formal labor force, as initially occurred because of Iran's 1980s war–baby boom, the state could afford these benefits through new SSO enrollments. Yet, once family size began to rapidly decline over the 1990s, SSO officials realized that a cost inflection point was looming on the horizon where revenues would be surpassed by expenditures to beneficiaries. The United Nations predicts that Iran's population size will level off by 2025 and then begin to decline.

In 2011, only 7.6 percent of the country's population (some 75 million) was over 60 years of age. By 2050, this is estimated to jump to 33.1 percent of a population of an expected 85 million—only 5 million higher than the population size in 2015. The Social Security Organization will be the key organization responsible for maintaining the retirement and health insurance for this elderly cohort.

As a result, the SSO gradually shifted to a riskier strategy through its in-house investment company, SHASTA. As one of the largest management conglomerates in Iran, SHASTA has mirrored global trends in pension-fund privatization and speculation, which Robin Blackburn has labeled gray capitalism. The process is gray "not only because it refers to provision for the old, but also because the property rights of the policyholders are weak and unclear."[52] Iran may seem an unlikely place for the novel financial techniques of a globalized era, but gray capitalism has planted firm roots in the Islamic Republic as a result of the unintended consequences of its developmental push. Until 1976, the SSO simply held workers' pension contributions in fixed long-term deposits. SHASTA was created in 1986, after the revolution, to manage a portion of these investments. In 1989, around 80 percent of SSO's investment portfolio was still held in the form of risk-free bank deposits. Yet by 2000, this share had decreased to 10 percent, while 71 percent of the SSO's total portfolio was composed of direct and indirect investments in riskier assets.

As of 2011, SHASTA reportedly controlled around two hundred companies. This is partly because the government legislated, in the mid-2000s, that handing over firms privatized from the public sector could pay for state debts to the SSO.[53] Consequently, the large state debt accumulated over the past three decades to the SSO has turned the central social-insurance organization of the Islamic Republic into one of the largest manufacturing and investment conglomerates in the country. There are signs that this process has produced less than stellar results. Over the past few years, inflation has eaten away the value of pension checks sent out to retirees, dependents, and the disabled. Nonpayment of these benefits is a main grievance of workers, who had contributed to the SSO in both the public sector and newly privatized companies in Iran. The SSO remained heavily underfunded by the state, reportedly to the amount of over $20 billion (US) in 2011 (roughly 5 percent of GDP).[54]

In sum, the Islamic Republic expanded the social-insurance system even as it maintained a generous benefit structure. As more than a majority of the labor force is now covered by the SSO, these fiscal constraints have created a serious structural impediment to the state's technocratic visions of development. This process has also, however, raised the expectations of the population far beyond the alleviation of basic needs. The latter goal was easier for the state to implement, cheaper to provide, and less socially divisive. Social insurance, however, is far more expensive for a state to maintain, since it requires adequate capacity as well as resources in order to mitigate a variety of social risks. The struggle in Iran is no longer over lowering poverty levels and increasing basic nonincome welfare indicators but rather the politics of inequality. Social insurance, if it is selectively available only to the upper strata of a population, will exacerbate rather than ameliorate these inequalities. Yet a social-insurance system extended to the entire population, as Iran attempted to do, pushes up the economic and the political costs of such an endeavor. In responding to these constraints, the SSO pursued a strategy of gray capitalism. This places the decommodifying role of social insurance on shaky ground. To date, the main beneficiaries of Iran's social-insurance system have not been the poorest strata in the informal sector, although segments are slowly being covered by the SSO. Instead, the main beneficiaries are the middle- and upper-income strata of the population in the formal labor force. The new middle class, not the poor, sits at the center of Iran's postwar welfare state.

MIDDLE-CLASS SHORTCUTS IN A FRAGMENTED HEALTH-CARE SYSTEM

In the case of an increasingly expensive pension system, social mobility through educational credentials and labor markets encouraged by the Islamic Republic's developmental push resulted in unintended consequences for the state. This outcome can also been seen in the politics of health care. The primary health-care system was built up through the Ministry of Health and Medical Education starting in the early 1980s. Yet secondary care (attention by specialists) and tertiary care (advanced inpatient treatment) remained highly fragmented in a mix of public and private hospitals, offices, and clinics. As a growing middle class increasingly consumed health care above the primary health-care level, the government was again confronted with a set of constraints largely of the state's own making.

The health system in Iran is subsidized to a high degree by the government, both through insurance funds and through price controls of medical services and pharmaceuticals. The Mousavi administration reorganized the system of medical training after the revolution and moved the supervision of medical schools in 1985 from the purview of the Ministry of Education to the Ministry of Health. This allowed for a policy shift away from the Pahlavi era's emphasis on specialists and high-technology care, which had previously produced world-quality physicians, but very few of them. One result of the prerevolutionary system was a high rate of professional emigration to Europe and the United States, not greatly resisted by the Pahlavi monarchy. After the revolution, however, medical education was integrated into the primary health-care system, which was expanding across the country. Between 1979 and 1994, the number of medical schools rose from seven to thirty-four, dentistry schools from three to thirteen, and pharmacy schools from three to nine.[55] This shift from elite to mass medical education had long-term effects. One was that Iran started to produce doctors, and a lot of them.

In 1979, the ratio of physicians to the general population was 1 in 2,800. Outside Tehran, it was 1 in 4,000. As the 1980s Health Minister Ali Rezā Marandi recalled of the prerevolutionary training system: "Unfortunately, at that time the road to the United States and a few Western European countries was a one-way road, and almost none of our graduates returned. Due to the fact that medical students were being trained mainly in sophisticated university hospitals, they were not capable of responding to the everyday needs of the community."[56] In contrast, by 2008, the physician-to-population ratio stood at 1 in 690.[57] In 2007, seventeen thousand students were admitted to the universities controlled by the Ministry of Health and Medical Education (MOHME). Sixty percent of these students were female.[58] This was a shift from elite to mass health care. One of the main proponents of Iran's technocratic push, economist Mohammad Tabibiān, defended the effort. In 1995, he grumbled how Iranians' status competition and nationalist self-regard were a structural impediment to the public-health system: [59]

> We might think that we are enlightened people and have PhDs in mathematics, physics, and other sciences in our country, and are a people with an ancient culture and literature, and have one of the oldest cultures in the world, but we must note that in our collective thinking, on the economic scene, we still do not employ logic. . . . We do not pay attention to the shortage of the economic sources and resources of the country. . . . The solution is that, instead of some organization building a very *chic* hospital with CT scanners, etc., we should build ten ordinary hospitals to treat dysentery and other illnesses. As a result, two patients who suffer from complicated heart and brain diseases might die, but instead, 100 ordinary patients and children will be spared death, and this is a logical action. . . . With the amount that is

supposed to be spent on treating a heart or brain patient or severe illnesses, we can import tetanus, rabies, and polio vaccines and save a large number of people.

The emphasis on primary health care meant that doctors became rapidly available for most Iranians. The primary health-care plan, however, lacked a key element. There was no referral system that might have functioned as a cost-efficient gatekeeping mechanism for individual health needs. As a result, once there were plenty of doctors, one could get service from any of them. This was possible because the Islamic Republic greatly subsidized the cost of medical services. As an Iranian health-policy analyst told me in an interview:[60]

> There is no one insurance fund that pools the health costs in Iran. For instance, with a 75 million population, there are almost 85, or some figures say, 90 million insurance booklets, which means that there are some people with two or even three insurance schemes, which is absolutely a waste of resources. If your dad is a public servant, you are entitled to insurance from the MSIO; if your mom is a factory laborer, you are also entitled to insurance from the SSO, and if your brother is in the military, you can have insurance from the Armed Forces Insurance, and if your sister works in the mayor's office, you are entitled to a type of private insurance for some special services. This is the story, more or less, across the country.

While it is estimated that between 6 and 8 percent of the population is still without insurance, many households are thus linked to multiple insurance options. If an individual has access to multiple schemes, he or she can easily use them to bypass the primary health-care system and go straight to specialists for care. Each fund owns and operates its own hospitals and clinics but also contracts out services to a variety of private-sector clinics and health centers. Of the various social-insurance organizations in Iran, the largest funds are the SSO and the Medical Services Insurance Organization (MSIO, created in 1995). The latter covers civil servants, rural households, the self-employed, and an urban inpatient fund, which is offered to people who are already in hospital and found to be uninsured. The Imam Khomeini Relief Committee also pays insurance costs for around two million people.

This overlap was partly a result of political competition. For example, in 2001 during the Khatami administration, the Ministry of Health decided to finally implement a referral process for specialist care, which had been missing from the primary health-care system since the 1980s. This was particularly important in urban areas, where people were falling through the institutional cracks. Several pilot programs were implemented, but existing stakeholders in hospitals and specialist clinics blocked the expansion of the program by not accepting referrals. In 2004, with a conservative parliament back in power following the disqualification of many reformist members of parliament from running in the 2002 parliamentary elections, the members of parliament voted to extend insurance access, but for *rural* areas instead. Although rural-household members had health care in their villages through the primary health-care system, their insurance was not transferrable to most urban centers. The parliament took the action without any consultation with the Ministry of Health, and appropriated the funds to give 25 million people an insurance logbook similar to the ones used by SSO-insured individuals in the formal labor force. Though the Health Minister had lobbied to create a referral system in urban areas, he decided to take the funding and implement it for a rural-referral system. The reason was that a presidential election loomed in 2005, and the cabinet would likely be changed. The political compromise—rural insurance with a general practitioner-styled referral system—was rushed through before the transition to the Ahmadinejad administration. In other words, the competitive political process among the elite fostered an expansion in the social-insurance system.[61]

The absence of general practitioner linkages between secondary and primary health care had important consequences. Throughout the 1990s, the pool of doctors kept expanding in Iran. Consequently, there was a large incentive to become a specialist or subspecialist. These doctors could charge informal fees on top of their subsidized rates, and individuals would pay them. As a result, even though more doctors were produced, particular private clinics became more popular, and individuals paid out of pocket to use their services. This produced an odd paradox. There were more doctors, more insurance, low-priced pharmaceuticals and services, and universal primary care at low or no fees with general practitioners available. Yet out-of-pocket costs went upward from the 1990s onward. At first glance, the problems of the health system in Iran resembled the problems of the Pahlavi era: inequality in health-care access and a prioritization of specialists at the expense of basic health needs. This inequality did not come from lack of investment in the health-care system, although that is how it was perceived by many Iranians. Instead, new problems emerged from the lasting characteristics of state solutions to the old problems. Here is a fascinating passage from an interview with a health-policy analyst who worked several years in the Ministry of Health:[62]

Rural households certainly still use the primary health-care system in the countryside. Yet there was a primary health-care system built in urban clinics, but it is not used. Why not?

It is a long story, but this is one of the reasons why the Ministry of Health wanted to establish a referral system. This is more than a health issue, however; it is about sociocultural issues in cities. Before the revolution, 35 percent of the population was urban, and 65 percent was rural, and the whole population in 1979 was 35 million. After the revolution, the population has doubled, and the rural-urban ratio has reversed. During the war with Iraq, and I remember because I was 15 at the time, there weren't enough GPs, even in Tehran. When I went to the hospital in a rich neighborhood in Tehran, there were GPs from Bangladesh or India. The government decided to establish primary health care in rural and urban areas, because they wanted to rationalize services as well as improve the public-health figures like vaccination rates, infant mortality, maternal mortality, etc., which were horrible at the time. They said, because it was a war, they thought if they rationalized the services they could more easily combat the foreign sanctions, lack of medicines, etc.

The primary health-care system was started in 1981 by Minster of Health Marandi and continued after the war. At the beginning, it was also used in cities. But after the war, urban areas became more affluent, and the socioeconomic practices of the cities changed a lot. As you know, in Iran we have *kesh-ma-kesh* [struggling, conflict]; if my cousin has something of status, then I want something of equal or higher status. This extends to everything, including visiting doctors. Visiting doctors became a fashion. For instance, if I have cancer, and I go to Doctor X instead of Doctor Y, this adds something positive to my character. Nowadays, this is a mania in Iran. As this developed more broadly, people wanted to have access to specialists. And because medical education was transferred to the Ministry of Health, the number of doctors had doubled just during the war years alone, as well as nurses, midwives, and so on.

So there wasn't a shortage of doctors in the workforce at all. During this time, the general practitioner's role faded as more specialists came on the market. In 1981, I was quite lucky if I could visit a Bangladeshi general practitioner in hospital. By 1990, I could choose from three Iranian doctors: a general practitioner, a specialist, and a subspecialist, and the cost for visiting each of them was not too different. Even now [in 2011], for the most famous specialists in Tehran, you pay about $15 [US]. People can afford that, so you would rather not visit a general practitioner, and if you have to, you are reluctant to do so.

The culture [of health-care consumption] changed because the supply changed. There was no cap for it, so, like many things in Iran, we started to mass-produce doctors without any consideration of population-growth rates, social change, etc. Access to specialists became very cheap and oversupplied. The general practitioner usage faded, because the services could be gotten from a specialist, and the primary health-care function was also fading, because basic public-health outcomes like vaccinations were going up, as today this is almost 100 percent even in rural areas.

Of course, even rural areas vary on primary health-care usage. In very deprived areas, like Bandar Abbas, primary health care is still very fundamental. If you are in [wealthier] Mazandaran, you can choose between family doctors. Even in a village of 1,000 households, there are about 20 general practitioners, and the cost is much the same, so what's the point of primary health care when you can go to private doctors?

In other words, doctors in Iran or, more accurately, their public reputations, are being conspicuously consumed by middle-class families as they would be also with cars or clothing items. The presence, as sociologists might note, of Bourdieusian distinction through health-care consumption is corroborated by other studies on medical education in Iran.[63] The overproduction of specialists has contributed to the increase in the so-called brain drain of doctors to wealthier countries. Doctors who obtained their degrees in lower-tier universities "cannot secure a job in their profession unless they are willing to serve in outlying 'deprived' regions."[64] Many doctors (and engineers) in Iran therefore decide to emigrate to wealthier countries.[65]

While the number of doctors and services has gone up, however, the price has not gone down. Because of the fragmentation of the system, every transaction involves a fee, which is mostly paid by insurance funds. While these fees and copays are generally quite small, Iranians become frustrated with the health system because of the time and travel involved, the inability to receive desired diagnoses, and the expectation that the specialists are holding back information. As a medical anthropologist noted:[66]

> Part of Iranians' disgruntlement about medical expenses stems from their expectation that the entire cost of medical care ought to be paid by the government. This is what they had been led to expect from their pre- and postrevolutionary governments' propaganda, along with free education, free water, free gas and electricity, and free bread. Complaints about the cost of health care, especially by members of the middle and upper classes, are expressions of dissatisfaction with the nonfulfillment of these promises.

The observation is arguably a bit unfair in the assumption that the entire country has expected free health care for the past fifty years. For the upper-income strata of the population, this may indeed be the case. Yet health access was poor during the war years, as it was for many during the Pahlavi era. It is more likely that these changing attitudes toward health consumption were tied to the social changes driven by the Islamic Republic's developmental push in the 1990s. The fact that, to a certain extent, these expectations mirror sentiments produced in the latter part of the Pahlavi era is telling, but the historical context is quite different. Instead of a lack of access to some form of public health care—an issue of absolute deprivation—this form of health-care consumption is linked to the status competition produced by the inequality of households in society.

The problems of the health-care system, just as with the social-insurance system, are a product of earlier welfare *successes* in Iran. As the basic needs of the population were addressed through expansion of the war-era welfare state, the epidemiological portfolio of the population shifted from communicable diseases such as tuberculosis to noncommunicable diseases such as hypertension and diabetes. These diseases are harder to treat without long-term medical supervision. They are difficult to pay for without a comprehensive health system that efficiently allocates resources above individual consumption decisions. The state, in turn, needs a higher administrative and political capacity in order to construct and fund such a system. Failure to do so has increased grievances among much of the population. Yet, if the state did manage to equalize health access and treatment, it would likely come at the expense of the middle- and upper-income strata, which currently enjoy the better part of the deal. This contradiction characterizes a dilemma of middle-income countries in general. Such problems are an outcome of successful developmental drives, wherein the politics of inequality outstrip the institutions created for basic-needs provisions.

In sum, examining the social-insurance and health-care systems during the postwar period generates a set of observations about both state and society in Iran that are often overlooked in other accounts. First, competitive conflict among elites in the Islamic Republic tended to add new welfare programs onto existing ones. Differing factions may have labeled their opponents as antirevolutionary or antimodern along the way, but they all agreed on the unspoken developmental role of the state. Second, new, upwardly mobile social classes took advantage of the expanding welfare policies of the government in order to acquire status credentials and occupations that allowed for increased consumption and incomes. This behavior was, of course, encouraged by the state itself as evidence of developmental progress. However, the increasing size and breadth of these middle classes led to an accumulation of social power. New social, political, and cultural movements in Iran mobilized powerful constituencies out of these individuals, including for elections that put reformist politicians in government. The structure of elite politics in the Islamic Republic, with its many veto points, blocked the reformists from fully taking control of the levers of the state. With the presidential election campaigns in 2009 and their controversial outcome, this social power burst out into the open. This mobilization was directed squarely at a state that, for the past two decades, had unintentionally stoked it.

CHAPTER 6

Lineages of the Iranian Welfare State

The reformists rode the demographic wave. In 1997, when Khatami was first elected, their constituents were in their late teens or early twenties, and [strove] for a more open, liberalized society. To some extent, they achieved it. Now they are in their mid- to late twenties. Social liberalization under Khatami helped them get the girl. Now they want to marry. But they lack the tools to do so: money, employment, or housing.

—Amir Mohebiān, conservative newspaper columnist

In Iran, there are two groups of people with connections to the government: those who ideologically believe in the system and those who receive benefits and monetary compensation. The former group, who [are] either brainwashed or supporter[s] through family ties, would not join the Green Movement even if they were dissatisfied with the government. They would rather opt for political apathy and inaction. The latter group, however, will join the movement if their funding is cut.

—Ahmad Bātebi, former student activist

The presidential campaigns of Mohammad Khatami in 1997 and Mahmoud Ahmadinejad in 2005 both used "social justice" and "participation" as mobilizing slogans.[1] These two politicians, opposite on most ideological spectrums, were each attempting to corral together an electoral coalition by responding to popular demands. As social life transformed for many individuals in the postwar years, new frustrations appeared in tandem. The egalitarian society promised in the revolutionary era had not materialized. Intellectual critics of the status quo arose on both left and right. After the hard years of austerity, some argued, individuals soon turned to self-interest, consumerism, and the raw accumulation of wealth. Capitalists were unleashed, and the private sector was rehabilitated. Public evocations of the power of oppressed people had been sidelined. The nation's sovereignty seemed under threat by the exercise of Western state power both through the global economy as well as through international governance bodies. All forms of social relations were increasingly commodified. In sum, every sector of society, including clerics and revolutionaries, was seemingly engaging in a naked competition for money and power.[2] During the 1990s and 2000s, journalists traveling to Iran remarked both on the discontent of many individuals and as well on their vocal expression of it in public.[3] Were these twin phenomena, of rising frustration and rising social power, a paradox? In fact, the two processes were interrelated. They came together in summer 2009, in the form of the Green Movement.

The developmentalist efforts of the Islamic Republic were linked, in large part, to a continued attempt to appease, channel, and utilize the social aspirations of the postwar generation. In doing so, the political elite hoped, the revolutionary project of the Islamic Republic could be relegitimized.[4] The expansion of the welfare system during the 1990s and 2000s attempted to meet the rising demand for health care, education, and social insurance among the population. It also helped to defer entry of some of Iran's 1980s baby-boom generation into the labor force while many pursued professional or technical credentials. All sides of the political elite regarded this new generation as a potential engine of crisis. This is one reason why Khatami and Ahmadinejad both emphasized, each in his own terminology, themes of social justice and popular participation. As with much in politics, these terms could be quite vague, more akin to a Rorschach test. For some, "social justice" meant that the state should mitigate the paternalistic practices that interfered in individuals' daily lives and routines. For others, it meant the state should become even more involved in social protection against the threats brought on by urbanization and market society. At the intersection of these two views was the legacy of the revolution itself. Even for those born long after, the recurring presence of the 1979 revolution in public life reminded individuals of their own ability to shape the fate of the country and the promise of a better social order.

By one measure, at least, the Islamic Republic did deliver. After the economic crises of the Rafsanjani years subsided, absolute poverty levels began to decline at a steady rate. This was partly due to a modicum of growth in the 1990s and 2000s. In addition, the presence of welfare organizations contributed to a more nearly equal distribution of growth through state policy by expanding public health, infrastructure, and education. Even during increasingly harsh economic sanctions from 2011 to 2014, absolute poverty stayed low. Inequality, however, remained high for most of the 1990s and 2000s. As a result, the contemporary politics of the Islamic Republic are linked less to the starkness of absolute poverty than to the dynamics of relative inequality—among individuals, households, cities, provinces, as well as comparisons between Iran and wealthier countries.

In figure 14 below, inequality and poverty trends in Iran between 1984 and 2014 are displayed. The poverty rate used here is the share of the population with consumption expenditures under $5 (US) per day, adjusted for purchasing power (the poverty scale is on the right axis). This is a higher poverty line than the oft-used measure of $2 (US) per day, found in international-development scholarship and journalist reports. Individuals under the $5-per-day line are sometimes described by economists as "near poor," though the terminology is widely debated. Income inequality is measured by the Gini index (left axis), which scales from low to high inequality. An additional measure of inequality, the indicator of general entropy GE(2), is graphed and discussed below. The data are based on reliable household surveys conducted by the Statistical Center of Iran.

Using a rate of $5 (US) a day (noted in the figure by a solid line), absolute poverty increased during the latter years of the Iran-Iraq war. While slightly declining in the first few years of the Rafsanjani government's liberalization efforts, the 1993–94 crisis led to a devaluation of the rial and an inflation shock to the economy. Poverty levels ticked back upwards. Afterwards, however, the poverty rate moved downward throughout the entire Khatami administration (1997–2005).[5] This decline in poverty is remarkable, as oil prices floated between a barrel price of $10 and $30 from 1997 to 2001, hitting a nadir of $10 in 1999. Although oil prices are usually associated with welfare outcomes, in theory, through the spoils of rentier-state distribution, poverty trends in Iran do not neatly follow the oil markets.[6] During the Ahmadinejad administration, the share of the population under the $5-per-day poverty line continued to fall.

However, as shown by the wide dashed line hovering in the middle of the graph from 1984 onward, income inequality remained around 0.45 (as measured by the Gini index) throughout most of the postwar period.

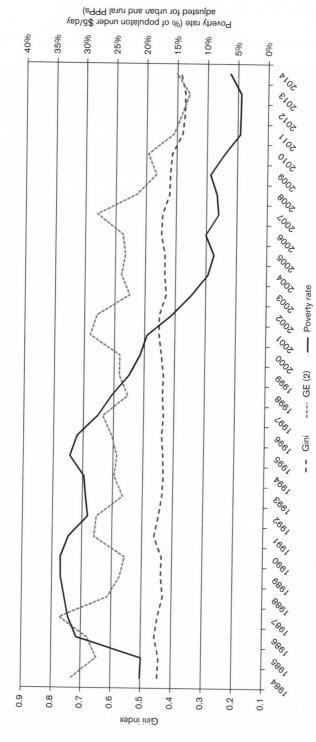

FIGURE 14. Inequality and poverty in Iran (1984–2014). (Source: Salehi-Isfahani 2016, updated by author.)

This is lower than inequality levels for middle-income countries in regions such as Latin America or Sub-Saharan Africa.[7] Yet it is higher than many Middle Eastern states over the same period, such as Egypt and Tunisia. One reservation with solely relying on the Gini index, however, is that the indicator is most sensitive to changes in the middle of the income distribution. To view inequality patterns with a different perspective, figure 14 includes an indicator of general entropy, GE (2), which is more sensitive to income distribution changes at upper income levels. As the graph shows, the GE (2) index is more volatile, fluctuating between 0.77 (in 1987) and 0.36 (in 2013). Distributional changes are likely occurring in the upper stratum of the income distribution that the standard Gini measurement is not capturing.

One interpretation of these inequality trends is that, during the late years of the Iran-Iraq War, inequality was reduced because of compression of higher incomes. In other words, inequality went down because income levels at the top of the distribution were squeezed, not because lower strata saw their incomes rise in relative terms. As most accounts of the Iran-Iraq War attest, this is not a surprising observation. Yet in the postwar years of liberalization and expanding welfare access, the volatility of the GE (2) index indicates that top income shares continued to swing up and down relative to middle- and lower-income households. In this environment, a general perception of social inequality and a widening of the class divide could become palpable, even though inequality on the whole remained stable and absolute poverty declined over time.

Figure 14 also challenges common assumptions regarding the relationship between poverty and politics in Iran. Absolute poverty had been *decreasing* over the Khatami administration's entire tenure, yet the 2005 election of Mahmoud Ahmadinejad was widely interpreted as a victory for populist politics. If this was an instance of populism, it was not the sort that emerges from increasing levels of absolute poverty. Instead, a common theme in both elections was inequality of access to new opportunities and livelihoods. Discontent with the status quo led many to choose Khatami in 1997 *as well as* Ahmadinejad in 2005. Discontent again manifested in the 2009 Green Movement demonstrations over that summer's election results. Electoral politics and street politics were linked. The epigraphs at the beginning of this chapter provide some signposts to explain the shifting political orientations of the period. As the conservative columnist Amir Mohebiān noted, although many in the postrevolutionary generation experienced new chances for upward mobility, the social compact of the postwar era came under severe strain. Most individuals were connected in some fashion to Iran's welfare system. Amid decreasing family sizes and increasing expectations, many hoped for an upgrading of this system through new social policies addressed to new needs. Conversely, Ahmad Bātebi, a student who took part in 1999 protests near the University of Tehran, expressed a sentiment commonly heard among Green Movement activists. The government used social-welfare policy only to buy support from a small slice of the population, to the exclusion of all others. These two perspectives are contradictory. In one version, contentious politics was driven by individuals connected to state social policies demanding an upgraded social contract. In the other version, individuals connected to state social policies became depoliticized and loyal to the status quo.

If protest is any measure, it is hard to claim that the postwar generation was duped by the state. There was a high degree of social contention in Iran even before the 2009 Green Movement. Neither was this same generation, however, disconnected from state-welfare policies. Instead, the generation that voted overwhelmingly for Khatami during the late 1990s partly came from families often connected to state social policies in wartime and educated through state social policies in the postwar period. Rather than securing political sentiments, major shifts in political orientations were rooted in the social transformations of these years as younger Iranians took advantage of these new opportunities. The unexpected election of Khatami in 1997 was partly an outcome of these changes.

Another trend counters the common perception that the state in Iran easily buys the loyalty of the population. State-welfare efforts during the 1990s and 2000s were not targeted just at the poor. Instead, the largest expenses were directed at expanding the social insurance, healthcare, and retirement systems of the country. These measures tended to benefit the middle and upper strata of the country, with households linked in some fashion to formal labor markets. Welfare expansion was part of a state-developmentalist push for higher growth rates, a skilled labor force, and diversified production away from reliance on oil. These goals, in turn, had a political rationale: justifying the postrevolutionary state and its place in the world economy. Poverty declined during this period, but the perceptions of social inequality did not go away. Instead, new and old forms of status were used to create and reproduce social inequalities. These status cleavages generated resentment among many people on either end of the political spectrum. Political elites in the Islamic Republic were not only aware of this growing resentment. They actively tailored their message to strategically curry favor with the population. Ahmadinejad's unexpected election in 2005 was partly an outcome of these changes.

In sum, state welfare did not purchase mass loyalty over the long run. This chapter examines the socioeconomic shifts of postwar Iran in order to assess the surprising electoral dynamics inside the country. Elite conflict among differing political factions contributed to a universalizing push for welfare policy. These policies helped to buttress the expansion of new middle classes over the 1990s and 2000s. Aside from material benefits, aspirations for middle-class lifestyles expanded, whether in the country's growing cities or in the increasingly connected countryside. Though linked to another electoral cycle, the demonstrations of summer 2009 showed how social demands from below pushed beyond the dynamics of elite competition. In addition to recounting my own observations from Green Movement protests, this chapter situates these rallies and marches within the larger postrevolutionary trajectory of the Islamic Republic of Iran. In this sense, Green Movement demands for political inclusion and the forcefulness of the protests were a symbol and an expression of the postwar *empowerment* of Iran's new middle classes.

THE KHATAMI YEARS: PROMISE AND FAILURE

Iran's 1997 presidential election pitted a relatively unknown former Minister of Culture, Mohammad Khatami, against a hand-picked candidate of the conservative elite, parliament speaker Ali-Akbar Nāteq-Nuri. Rafsanjani-linked technocrats (such as Tehran mayor Gholāmhossein Karbāschi), who had coalesced into a formal association known as the Servants of Construction, threw their resources behind Khatami's campaign. Yet the new professional-technical stratum of Iranian society was not the only group that voted for the reformist side. Khatami received nearly 70 percent of the vote in 1997, representing a wide swath of industrial workers, self-employed individuals, ethnic minorities, housewives, and a sizable portion of the armed forces. University students, organized on campuses through the state-sanctioned Office for Strengthening Unity, were important in introducing Khatami to young voters in the provinces. As the political scientist Fātemeh Sādeghi recalled, everyone voted without any idea that others existed like themselves. The magnitude of the Khatami landslide shocked them into recognizing that participation could again be a powerful political force for change.[8]

The unexpectedly high voter turnout revealed the mobilizational power that could be utilized via the participatory republican institutions of the postrevolutionary state. The unexpected loss by conservatives, however, led them over the next eight years to claw their way back into power through nonelected government bodies. It was through these bodies—the Guardian Council, the office of the leader, the revolutionary judicial system, and other parallel organizations—that Khatami's policy efforts were impeded or slowed. Cabinet members were ousted from their positions, and Khatami associates were harassed out of various posts. Tehran mayor Karbāschi was put on trial for corruption, for instance. In response, as with previous governments, Khatami would usually reappoint these individuals in new posts under the executive branch. Soviet analogies from the 1980s were widely discussed. While his predecessor, Hashemi-Rafsanjani, had pursued an economic perestroika and failed, Khatami and his reformist allies believed that a political glasnost would create space for a surging social mobilization to compel the state onto the path of change. Khatami's close advisor, former U.S. Embassy occupier and Intelligence Ministry official Said Hajjāriān, characterized this strategy as "pressure from below, negotiation at the top."[9]

The strategy of this new left or, as they often described themselves, the modern left, was to harness popular mobilization in order to realize, as Hajjāriān wrote, "the hidden capacity" of Iran's constitution.[10] Instead of a solidification of the 1997 electoral coalition, however, the strategy led to its fracturing. Conservative elites were willing to go beyond the confines of existing state organizations in order to block reformist initiatives, yet Khatami's government was largely unwilling to use the same tactics. In the more permissive cultural and social climate of the late 1990s, the slowness of political change was increasingly criticized. Newspapers and journals, some published by secular liberals and other long-suppressed members of the 1979 revolutionary coalition, had been increasing in number throughout the decade.[11] Many of these new media had been critical of Rafsanjani government reforms and the publicized corruption associated with his policies. The media subsequently turned attention toward exposing the shibboleths of the postrevolutionary order to scrutiny. Formerly taboo topics were fair game: the grueling length of the Iran-Iraq War, the execution of thousands of political prisoners near the conflict's end, the sidelining of Grand Ayatollah Montazeri and other religious scholars who disagreed with state-sanctioned orthodoxy, the domestic assassination of dissidents, and the accumulation of wealth by state cronies.[12] Rafsanjani's reputation underwent a series of broadsides by a new generation of muckrakers-*cum*-intellectuals, contributing to an embarrassingly low vote total when he ran for parliament in 2000. When the state judiciary closed down many of these newspapers in July 1999, students in the University of Tehran and surrounding campuses protested. In response, state forces attacked student dormitories at nightfall, with one reported death. The next few days in Tehran witnessed student-led riots that shocked reformists and conservatives alike. The 1997 coalition front was fraying.

The Khatami administration followed up the campaign slogan of participation with the implementation of local municipality elections in 1999. The promise was to both decentralize the state as well as increase political accountability. City and village councils, authorized in the 1979 constitution but never previously put on the ballot, were opened up with 190,000 positions to be chosen by the electorate. This was arguably the high point of reformist mobilization in the Khatami period. Individuals enthusiastically took part in the 1999 municipal elections. Once elected, however councilors "spent the majority of their first term laying down the foundations for the newly created institution as opposed to managing local affairs."[13] In 2003, local council elections were held again. Turnout declined, because of a lack of interest among those who had previously voted reformist. The low participation led to a slate of conservative candidates, associated with a new group calling themselves the Alliance of Developers of Islamic Iran, elected to the Tehran city council. Out of this group, a relatively unknown professor of civil engineering and former governor of the northern province of Ardabil in the mid-1990s (and subsequently removed by Khatami) was chosen as the new mayor of Tehran: Mahmoud Ahmadinejad.

The reputation of Khatami among many was a well-intentioned but ineffectual politician. He was still reelected in 2001 by a high margin. His main opponent was former Labor Minister Ahmad Tavakoli, known for hostile opposition to the reformist cause. The office of president itself, however, seemed to have been disempowered. This outcome was a stark contrast to the constitutional amendments put in place in 1989, which Rafsanjani had instigated in order to strengthen the executive branch.[14] In 2002, leftist economist Fariborz Rais-Dānā, who ran for parliament in 2000 but was disqualified by the Guardian Council, described Khatami's performance in harsh terms:[15]

> Mr. Khatami . . . announced that he believes [in the] constitution. And in my opinion, this constitution cannot present real democracy in Iran. If you look to this constitution, you are inside a loop, a vicious circle. Democracy means

that the power should come from people. . . . But in this constitution, you are inside a loop, and you can never give the real power to people.

For many, the final symbol of reformist capitulation to conservatives came in the 2004 parliamentary elections. Guardian Council members, observing the low turnout of the 2003 local council elections, gambled that reformist politicians could be eliminated from the legislative branch. The council ruled that that 24 percent of the candidates for parliamentary seats—nearly 2,000 people—were unfit to run. This total included eighty sitting members of parliament who belonged to the two main reformist political associations: the Participation Front (led by Khatami's brother) and the Organization of the Mojāhedin of the Islamic Revolution (led by Behzād Nabavi). The disqualification rate stood at three times that of the 2000 parliamentary elections. The most cited excuse was a vague "lack of respect for Islam." Reformist members of parliament and colleagues staged a sit-in at the parliament offices for twenty-two days to protest the decision and, perhaps, force a constitutional crisis.

Reformist politicians put out calls for mass support. These went largely unheeded by formerly mobilized bases of the 1997 election coalition. As the writer and political analyst Morad Saghafi explained: "Over the preceding seven years, every time the government or parliamentarians had issued warnings about imminent conservative threats to the reform movement, their supporters had rallied, only to witness the struggle abandoned and a deal struck at the top. This time they responded with a weary shrug—even the students, who had always been at the forefront of the struggle."[16] Khatami appealed the disqualifications to leader and supreme jurist Ali Khamenei. After consultation with various sides, Khamenei pressed the Guardian Council to revise its stance and at least allow incumbent members of parliament to stand for reelection. The Guardian Council ignored the leader's advice. Hesitant for fear of the consequences of a head-on confrontation, Khatami announced that the elections would go ahead with the approved candidate slates. To many, it was pure naiveté on Khatami's part. The president believed in the constitutional principles that assigned the highest responsibility of conflict resolution between elites to the position of the leader. The conservatives, on the other hand, disregarded the constitution when it pleased them to do so. The power move by the conservatives was compared to the U.S. Supreme Court's arbitrary decision on *Bush v. Gore*.[17] Reformist groups split on whether to boycott the elections, and conservatives swept the parliamentary vote. The outcome effectively ended the reformist agenda. There was no longer any legislative support to push for political change.

Under pressure from below, however, elite antagonisms in the Khatami era drove state politicians to expand social-welfare access. Though vague, social justice was the other buzzword of the 1997 election. Khatami's cabinet contained a spectrum of left-liberal thought on economic policy. At the Planning and Budget Organization (PBO), the new head, Mohammad-Ali Najafi, pushed for a continuation of the policies recommended by Rafsanjani confidant Mohsen Nurbakhsh. The extant liberalization of the economy needed to be completed. The PBO economist Masud Nili, for instance, argued that if the state's role was limited to "a functioning market and greater interaction with the outside world," then political and social development could follow.[18] However, the Minister of Economic and Financial Affairs, Hossein Namāzi, held firm to a leftist view, remaining skeptical of private-sector approaches. The conflicts in the cabinet over the proper role of state and market continued throughout Khatami's tenure. Compared with the previous administration, however, there was one key difference in welfare policy. Rafsanjani's development plans placed low a priority on welfare policy as an objective in itself. The Khatami administration increased social spending for welfare organizations such as the Imam Khomeini Relief Committee (IKRC) and health and educational agencies. With an eye toward fiscal discipline and political control, however, the administration also attempted to streamline the existing parallel welfare system in the Third Development Plan (2000–2004). The Ministry of Welfare was to be merged with extant pension and health-insurance bodies under the Social Security Organization and the Civil Service Pension Fund.[19] In addition, the welfare duties of the IKRC and other semi-public foundations [bonyāds] would be folded into a unified social-insurance and aid system. Once conservative parliament members reacted to the plan, new social-insurance programs for urban inpatients and rural households were introduced.[20]

There were two main impediments to the reformists' vision of a universal welfare state along the technocratic lines adopted from the Rafsanjani period. One was related to politics. The other was tied to the structure of Iranian society. Politically, conservative elites perceived the attempt to merge and centralize parallel institutions into single organizations of governance as an avenue for shifting power away from unelected organs of rule and toward the executive branch. Reformist buzzwords of "good governance" did little to win them over. Khatami's agenda was blocked accordingly. Finally, in 2003, the main pension bodies of the Social Security Organization and the Civil Service Pension Fund were centralized under a newly renamed Ministry of Welfare and Social Security. The Khatami administration was unable to include the IKRC or any of the *bonyāds* under the Ministry's bureaucratic umbrella.[21] As in the 1980s, parallel organizations were used by competing factions to obstruct large-scale policy shifts.

The second impediment, making obstruction by conservatives easier, was that welfare policy in a middle-income country such as Iran could not effectively emulate social policies from wealthy European countries. Social insurance in rich countries is tied to a formalized pool of workers who make up the vast majority of the labor force. Formal salaried or wage-labor positions, with long-term contracts, have access to pensions, health insurance, and other benefits. At the center of most European welfare systems, in other words, is a labor force that is largely employed in formal positions. The expectation of Iranian technocrats was that as the economy grew, the rural sector would shrink, and its migrant urban populations would be similarly absorbed into a formalizing labor force.[22] Once this occurred, new workers would automatically be enrolled into welfare institutions that the Islamic Republic had inherited from the Pahlavi monarchy. Institutions such as the Social Security Organization were set up for occupations in the formal labor force, not for enrolling informal labor and other hard-to-target workers. Certainly, as public-sector employment grew in the 1980s, so did the size of this formal labor force. The Rafsanjani administration believed that development would grow an accompanying formal private sector housed in modern-styled businesses. If that materialized, most of the remaining population would be integrated into large, formal insurance pools. The vision was not far from the Pahlavi monarchy's view of welfare policy. Although the Khatami administration extended SSO insurance to new employment groups, the passivity of this effort belied that it too adhered to a similar vision of development. Reality did not conform to the visions of development held by Iran's liberalizing political elite. Even with the economic growth of the 1990s and 2000s, the informal labor force did not shrink.

A strategy of welfare expansion through the formal labor force encountered structural dilemmas of social policy common to poorer countries. There is no middle-income country in the world that has been able to shift most of its labor force into formal occupations. Instead, after half a century of attempts to achieve these goals, the growth of so-called informal or precarious work continues. This includes self-employed workers, family labor, piecework in small enterprises, and craft manufacturing in rural areas. These can no longer be seen as traditional occupations that fade away with economic development. This informal sector and the households contained within it are the majority of the world's population, making up around 40 to 50 percent of Iran's labor force as well.[23] These households rarely hold occupations that provide long-term, stable wage employment. This sector is more difficult to tax, regulate, and therefore to enroll in welfare programs. The corporatist, Pahlavi-era welfare organizations in Iran were disadvantaged in targeting the informal sector. They were based on a different model of social policy. Here, revolutionary welfare organizations such as the IKRC or the bonyāds, for all their inefficiencies, had an advantage. These bodies actively administer benefits on the basis of status and location, not on employment.[24] As a result, different segments of Iran's parallel welfare system targeted different groups of individuals.

Even with increased welfare funding and expanded access to multiple programs during the Khatami era, the government performed rather poorly in advertising these activities. This was partly due to schizophrenic debates within the reformist movement itself over prioritizing political over economic development. By the late 1990s, welfare organizations in revolutionary bodies such as the IKRC had become associated with the conservative-religious establishment. Liberal critics saw these beneficiaries in negative terms. The targets of poverty alleviation were no longer the dispossessed, to be mobilized by a revolutionary state. Instead, echoing critiques of welfare states elsewhere, poor beneficiaries were often deemed, in the media as well as by politicians, state-dependent individuals who acted as a drag on economic growth and social progress.

Khatami's relative passivity in explaining and promoting his government's welfare policies—not to mention refraining from using the policies as a political weapon—was arguably one of the reasons that the 1997 coalition fractured. A disconnect between state-welfare policies and social perceptions took hold. For example, most young urban Iranians whom I met had little or no knowledge of the country's rural health-care system. They believed that rural households had no welfare access before the rise of Ahmadinejad, and this is why rural areas supported his 2005 candidacy. At the same time, many middle-class Iranians expected their health care to be freely provided through employers or the educational system. Iranians' unfamiliarity with the social-welfare system is not unique to the Islamic Republic. In states with fragmented welfare systems, people tend to view programs that target the middle- and upper-income strata in a different light. The United States is a key example. As the political scientist Suzanne Mettler has shown, American citizens tend to be largely unaware of the relatively pro–middle class social-policy system in their country that is subsidized by the state but delivered through private organizations. The very citizens who benefit from state policies, for instance, rarely recognize health-care and housing subsidies as part of the American welfare system. Unawareness of this "submerged state," as Suzanne Mettler labels it, leads individuals to believe that government favors the "undeserving poor" instead of the "deserving majority."[25] In the Islamic Republic of Iran, the new middle classes that took part in the 1997 and 2001 elections often held similar perceptions of state social policies. Others benefited from state largesse while they rose through sacrifice and hard labor. Khatami did not attempt to address this growing disconnect in the population. His opponents learned from the mistake, especially a group of new upstarts on the right that made both the reformists and old-guard conservatives uneasy.

THE RISE OF AHMADINEJAD AND THE NEW CLASS

Few expected the 2005 presidential election of Mahmoud Ahmadinejad. He was largely unknown even when appointed in 2003 as mayor of Tehran. Ahmadinejad's rapid rise once again illustrated the mutability of politics in Iran. The election outcome also suggested that a large segment of the population had become frustrated with the inadequate performance of the political elite and state promises of a developmental leap forward. Alongside Rafsanjani, who ran again for president in 2005, the reformists put forward Mostafa Moin as their candidate: a noncleric medical doctor, former president of the prestigious Shiraz University, and Khatami's Minister of Science, Research and Technology. Long embedded in the university system, Moin had accrued symbolic capital in technocratic institutions with high social status in the Islamic Republic. Yet among seven candidates in the 2005 election's first round, Moin placed a disappointing fifth, below former Revolutionary Guards commander and police force head Mohammad-Bāqer Qālibāf, parliament speaker and breakaway reformist Mehdi Karroubi, former president Rafsanjani, and then-mayor of Tehran Mahmoud Ahmadinejad. The latter two, as the top vote getters, squared off in the second round. In a 28-million-voter turnout, around 60 percent of the voting population, Ahmadinejad won 61 percent of the vote. Rafsanjani had tried to appeal to young Iranians, with flashy campaign ads and colorful posters. Many reformists held their nose and supported him after Moin and Karroubi lost out. It was not enough.

In July 2006, Morad Saghafi was interviewed by a prominent reformist daily, *Shargh,* about the implication of the election results. He noted that Ahmadinejad had rose up through the state itself. He represented one segment of a new class of politician:[26]

> From the third year of the revolution on, the political scene of the country was under the control of a small number of individuals who identified themselves in terms of two different factions: the left and the right. I am not saying that these two groups did not have rivals; they did. But the political game in our country was between these two groups. There was also a serious effort to keep the game in the hands of these groups and prevent another force from entering this game. But neither of these two forces realized that it was possible for a third force to emerge from among them. They thought that this third force could only be shaped from outsiders; therefore, by blocking the way to the outsiders entering the regime, they overlooked the birth of a third group within the circle of the regime and from among the two ruling factions in the country.

As Saghafi pointed out, the social force that swept Ahmadinejad into office was neither a class movement nor a novel idea. Ahmadinejad's slogans were quite general, "in which every individual could see his ideals and wishes." The candidate's most famous slogan was a promise to bring the nation's oil wealth "to the table of people." Yet reformist candidates and even Rafsanjani all "spoke in terms of the masses." Why did they not generate wider appeal? Saghafi explained that many Iranians were frustrated with a technocratic elite that had been, by 2005, in charge for sixteen years:

> When, for sixteen years, the society faces a series of problems, and the individuals who should be attending to these problems do not take any steps in this connection, without a doubt we will face a decline in the status of these political forces. . . . Had an individual come from the outside, perhaps the story would have been different. If, other than these 500 or 1,000 attorneys, general managers, directors, and deputy directors who were administering the country during the sixteen years after the war—and they were continually circulating within the limited circle of the elite—an individual had come and these gentlemen had agreed to go and sit on the second row and have another hundred people sit on the front row, perhaps the result would have been different.

A key problem, Saghafi continued, was that Khatami's government had never presented a well-defined vision of economic change:

The problem of a segment of reformists is that they consider paying attention to the economy equal to and synonymous with populism. As if one cannot go along with the intellectuals and also understand the economic problems of the people in the southern part of the city. Unfortunately, our political forces do not think about political economy, and the failure of the reformists was not because of the economy, but because of the political economy. Those who did not pay attention to the political economy lost the game. Do the political forces in European countries, whether on the right, on the left, or in the middle, not speak about the economy? Does speaking about the economy mean that they are populists?

Saghafi argued that an increasing market dislocation of the 1990s had created a sense of unease among the middle class. Confronted with the narrowness of the political elite on the reformist side, its would-be supporters grew frustrated with the lack of attention to everyday problems which had grown acute by the late 1990s. Khatami and his allies "made frequent mention of organizations and civil society," Saghafi critiqued, but "we did not witness any serious activity by them in this regard." The lack of mass organizations in the Iranian political sphere hampered the ability for reformists to maintain the electoral mobilizations of 1997. They assumed that something called "civil society" existed as an automatic social force, rather than a set of like-minded individuals which needed to be galvanized through recurrent political action.[27] As intellectuals well read in social theory and political philosophy, invoking civil society was the mantra of the reformists. However, it was not their method.

Supporters of Ahmadinejad, conversely, were linked to actual organizations. These new conservative elites did not come from outside the political establishment. Instead, they were produced within it. Ahmadinejad and many of his aides were a "new class" of functionaries that occupied mid-level administrative positions in revolutionary and government organizations for most of the 1990s. These men and women were not clerics, but lay engineers and managers, often posted in provincial bureaucracies—such as Ahmadinejad's tenure as governor of Ardebil. Their cultural capital came from within the postrevolutionary system, and was predicated upon the maintenance of political institutions within which they had learned to navigate and move upward.[28] Ahmadinejad's campaign in the first electoral round stressed his Spartan lifestyle in opposition to well-known elites. He targeted issues of unemployment and inflation, while the abstract rhetoric of reformists discussed human rights and social freedoms.[29] A few days before the first round election, *basij* members and individuals in other conservative cultural and political groups were encouraged to spread the word and vote for this new principlist candidate.[30] These were organizations rooted in communities usually outside the reach of reformist mobilization. In the second round, holdout conservative elites threw their institutional networks and mass media behind Ahmadinejad. Of course, pro-state conservatives alone could not have elected him with over 60 percent of the vote. Most who voted for Khatami in 1997 also voted for Ahmadinejad in 2005. The reformists had a hard time making a case for voting for Rafsanjani—a man they had spent years pillorying in the press. As Mohammad Quchāni wrote in *Shargh,* "Some of Ahmadinejad's criticisms against Hashemi [Rafsanjani] were similar to those levied by the reformists against him five years ago. . . . We could not justify in just three days why people should vote for the target of our past attacks."[31]

In other words, Ahmadinejad did *not* win by appealing to the poorest of the poor. As noted above, absolute poverty had been declining in Iran, so this would have been a losing strategy. On the contrary, poverty reduction had created a new base for political mobilization, among those voters looking for a more equal distribution of social opportunities for upward mobility and the material resources with which to pursue them. Themes of corruption and elite privilege did not resonate among the destitute as much as among the lower middle class. The election in 2005 was not a rejection of the developmentalist project of the Islamic Republic, but a reaction to its failure to live up to its promise.

The 2005 film *Poet of the Wastes,* written by radical-turned-reformist Mohsen Makhmalbāf and directed by Mohammad Ahmadi, contains a witty scene expressing the sentiment of the time. The protagonist is an amateur poet who is looking for a job—any job. He applies for a government post as a garbageman. In his job interview, he is asked about his political viewpoint:[32]

Job Interviewer: Are you an adherent of the right or the left?

Middle, sir.

Middle? What's that?

I'm an adherent of work. I want to live. Whichever side is good, I like.

[Annoyed] *Left or Right?*

Well, I don't know. Left and right keep changing sides. Yesterday they were left, today they are right, tomorrow again they are left. Sir, I don't know . . . [guessing] Right? No, Left! Sir, for God's sake I don't know which is correct.

Ahmadinejad was expected to toe the line of the old conservatives, but he had his own agenda. He jockeyed to get his aides into cabinet and advisory positions during his first year in office. He brusquely ignored established conservative elites in the parliament who had backed his second round campaign. While the new president reaped international media attention for provocative comments at the United Nations and other venues, at home he resembled a would-be technocrat in revolutionary garb. Unlike the Rafsanjani administration's negative balance of payments and shrinking budgets, Ahmadinejad had the luxury of rising commodity prices and a global asset bubble to pad revenues. He proceeded to scatter money around the country in thousands of small and large infrastructure projects, often visiting remote provinces and alerting the local residents of his endeavors. His policies looked more statist than previous governments' efforts, but there was plenty of money available to put to use.

While the Rafsanjani and Khatami administrations were repeatedly accused of catering to international financial institutions such as the IMF and World Bank, they never had significant relations with either body. Disdain for the World Bank and the IMF had thrown a spanner in late 1980s and 1990s attempts to formulate economic policy. Under Ahmadinejad, however, conservatives began to covet the status of associating with these agencies. By the mid-2000s, every elite faction wielded statistics from Transparency International, *The Economist,* or World Development Reports. Numbers were thrown against each other in blaming the opposite side for poor economic performance. Positions and policy red lines quickly changed. Entry into the World Trade Organization was a key goal of the reformists during the late 1990s, and so was then opposed by conservatives. Yet once Ahmadinejad came into office, and various strands of the conservative elite had finally pushed out the reformists from any governing body, there was nothing left to oppose. World Trade Organization accession soon became a goal among conservative parliament members. After 2005, much of the government as well as other conservative politicians publicly stated similar goals. Conservatives began to sound more and more like their reformist opponents.

This did not dampen the conflict within the political elite. One year after the 2005 election, the conservative coalition which had elected Ahmadinejad began to fracture even quicker than the 1997 reformist coalition. Ahmadinejad's polarizing effrontery in public made the widening fissure apparent. The core belief of the conservative elite by the early 2000s was that anyone who questioned the office and position of the leader—as the more adventurous reformists had been doing by the 1990s—was anti-revolutionary and needed to be expelled from the political elite. Once this had largely been accomplished after 2005, allegiances to the leader did not matter in the political field since all claimed fealty. Instead, conservative elites attacked *each other* over issues of governance and corruption.[33] The criticisms mounted against the president were largely of a technocratic nature, as were his responses and counterattacks. Management-speak and appeals to expertise had become part of the conservative political toolkit.

Ahmadinejad attempted to appear as a stalwart manager of the state. His proposed economic policies quietly borrowed many of the previous two governments' unfinished plans. These included privatization of public sector companies with dividend shares going to the poorest households; housing construction outside of major cities for newlywed couples through subsidization of private contractors; banking expansion and reform of non-performing loans; the creation of a value-added tax; and the removal of price subsidies for fuel, electricity, and basic staples. Ahmadinejad pursued these endeavors vigorously and through his own channels. He stripped the older bureaucracies of independent power. The Management and Planning Organization—formerly the Planning and Budget Organization—was brought in under the president's office.[34] Ahmadinejad's attacks against the civil service bureaucracy—which had been painstakingly rebuilt during the 1990s—were even perceived as a threat by many conservatives in the parliament. The rule of experts had become so dominant among the elite that the only paths to power seemed to run through the harnessing of one's own expert clique. By removing some of the alternatives, Ahmadinejad was securing his own circle's edge in steering the state apparatus.

Along the way, the president frequently enraged reformists as well as these old-guard conservatives by presenting himself as the true agent of reform and renewal. In hundreds of speeches to provincial audiences, Ahmadinejad usually stressed at least two points: his own advisors' expertise in local affairs and his ability to accomplish the projects that were left unfinished by previous governments. The president's resonance among crowds did not come from repeating the ideological slogans of the 1979 revolution. It came from grasping the long-term transformation in Iranian politics after three decades. Expertise had become the most valuable marker of status within the elite, competing with and supplanting declarations of revolutionary commitment. It was an inversion of the status order which had been flipped over during the tumult of the revolution and war years. In figures 15 and 16, this inversion of status is illustrated through the changing composition of parliament

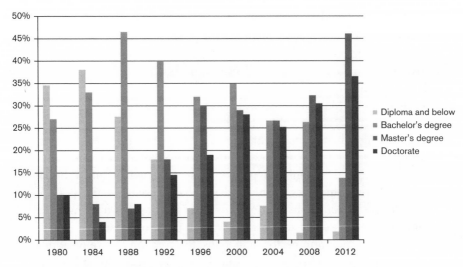

FIGURE 15. Educational level of members of parliament (percentage of total), 1980–2012. (Source: Alem 2011: 42; updated by author.)

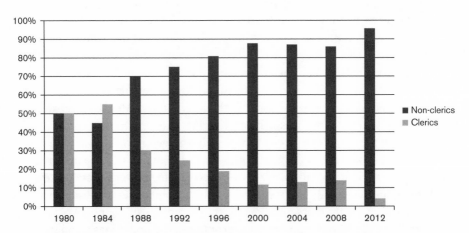

FIGURE 16. Percentage cleric vs. noncleric members of Iranian parliament, 1980–2012. (Source: Alem 2011: 42; updated by author.)

members over the postrevolutionary era. The Islamic Republic had slowly displaced its own clerical class.

After 2005, the entire Iranian political elite, across the ideological spectrum, proclaimed technocratic bona fides of various origins (sometimes dubious ones).[35] One pattern from previous eras of elite conflict reappeared. As conservatives battled over managerial priorities and expert credentials, social policies continued to expand beyond earlier targets. Samadollāh Firuzi, Social Affairs director of the Ministry of Welfare and Social Security, stated the intentions of the Ahmadinejad government were to fully execute the outlines of the 1990s Basic Social Insurance Plan.[36] SSO officials noted that the Ahmadinejad government was attempting to implement a long promised extension of social insurance to informal workers in construction, transportation, and village manufacturing sectors, which had barely begun in the Khatami period.[37] This was not just populist hype. In discussions with construction managers, I was told that developers of new buildings were being forced to hire more expensive domestic labor—often Turkoman-Iranians—instead of employing Afghan workers who resided in the country illegally. The reason was that the state was finally regulating construction firms to require workers to be enrolled in the SSO.

Moreover, the Imam Khomeini Relief Committee was being used as a coordinating body for a planned liberalization of subsidies, even while it continued to cover health insurance premiums for poor households. This latter move was a stark example of the dynamics of factional repositioning that led to expansions in the welfare system. The IKRC, a revolutionary organization from the 1980s, and the removal of subsidies, a policy promoted by reformists in the 1990s, were both being used by Ahmadinejad to reap the legitimacy of performance execution. In the process, various segments of the old conservative faction supported the initiative. This slow but unmistakable policy convergence occurred partly because the conservative elites believed they had sufficiently pushed the reformists out of power. Consequently, conservative success in the political short-term led to emulation of reformist-era developmentalist strategy in the long-term.

In sum, after three decades of elite conflict, a general ideological consensus existed in the Islamic Republic for a mixed public/private social-insurance model with poverty alleviation programs for the poorest Iranians. It was a dual-welfare regime, comparable to the social-policy systems in Brazil, Turkey, or Malaysia. With the rise of new elites out of conservative factions, but with continued intra-elite competition, the result was a trend towards convergence on an expansion of social policy after more than two decades of elite disagreement on the substance of these policies.

The biggest surprises were still to come. Even with an economic boom from 2007 to 2008, an apolitical air of malaise among was palpable among the middle class. No one predicted that much mobilization would occur in the 2009 presidential elections. The electoral surge in the summer of 2009 and the post-election Green Movement once again proved many wrong. Subsequently, while Ahmadinejad claimed victory in the political battle over the 2009 election, he soon implemented the most market-friendly reform of the entire postwar era of the Islamic Republic. Ahmadinejad pushed through a removal of subsidies for fuel and basic staple foods, something his predecessors had never accomplished. In place of subsidies, his government proposed to pay out income grants to poorer households. Such targeted cash transfers were a well-known International Monetary Fund recommendation for most Middle Eastern countries. The forceful mobilization of the Green protests, however, shook the conservative elite. What was supposed to be a small, exclusionary welfare policy was converted into a universalizing and inclusive policy—a population-wide bimonthly cash transfer. These events—the Green Movement and the process of subsidy reform—revealed the fractures and possibilities of Iran's dual-welfare regime.

THE SPIRIT AND SUBSTANCE OF GREEN MOBILIZATION

On the morning of 13 June 2009, the day after Iran's tenth presidential election, I was at a conference in nearby Yerevan, Armenia. I recognized an Iranian professor and asked if he had any news of the preliminary results. "Fraud," he said. "They stole it." One day later, I flew into Tehran and witnessed the largest street protests in Iran since the 1979 revolution. The Green Movement surprised not just outside onlookers but also many Iranians themselves. The Islamic Republic's 2009 presidential election campaign, though predicted to be scripted and formulaic, mobilized new networks of activists and created a carnivalesque atmosphere of public participation in the weeks leading up to the vote. Early election returns by the Mir-Hossein Mousavi campaign showed the former prime minister to be in the lead with at least a runoff vote expected. News quickly shifted on election night, however, to the Interior Ministry's declaration of a landslide for the incumbent Ahmadinejad. Shock and dismay among Mousavi supporters turned into small protest gatherings of hundreds that night in Tehran, some violent. The next night, the unrest involved thousands. If fraud did occur, as many believed, vote rigging on that scale was unprecedented in postrevolutionary Iran. Two days later, on 15 June, over a million people marched in Tehran's Freedom Square, with nonviolent rallies continuing each day for the next week.

The state's coercive efforts to contain the protests were not the only challenge to the Green Movement. Organizational disarray within oppositional forces was an even greater impediment. Almost all the contention occurred in the capital, Tehran, though smaller protests occurred in other cities for one or two days. Eventually, the protest numbers dwindled. Ahmadinejad was sworn in as president on 30 July 2009, and the recognized leaders of the Green Movement—Mousavi and former speaker of parliament Mehdi Karroubi—began to call for public rallies on holidays with symbolic revolutionary and religious significance. These rallies kept the movement in the news, but did little to convince fence-sitters to participate. Eventually, with the exception of a massive December rally in Qom for the funeral of Grand Ayatollah Montazeri, an oppositional icon for many in Iran, self-identified Green activism moved almost wholly to the online sphere by spring 2010.

In sum, the Green Movement rose unexpectedly, but protest mobilization did not last long. In figure 17, I combine newspaper reports, my own estimates of crowd sizes, and interviews with movement participants to graph out the mobilization wave (in logarithmic scale so that the 15 June protests do not crowd out the Y-axis). A box in the figure's upper-right corner lists protest events and estimated sizes from late July 2009 to February 2010, which are excluded from the graph's time frame.

Although these are rough estimates, the trend in figure 17 is clear enough. The postelection uprisings quickly spread beyond initial protest participants, peaked only a few days after the election, and then narrowed to a generally consistent size that continued to sporadically punctuate the postelection order. If a period during the Green Movement most exhibited the broad cross-class mobilizational power that can force political reform onto a state with divided elites, it was early on in the protest wave.[38] Analyzing the 2009 protests in Iran, then, must take into account quieter processes of demobilization as much as the dramatic and unexpected outbreak of protest that briefly captured world attention. How did this movement take shape and surge so quickly, and why did it dissipate?

During my previous visits to Iran from 2006 to 2008, the popular climate among former reformist sympathizers was apathetic, almost Brezhnevian in tone. Many Iranians took up Ahmadinejad as a symbol of boorishness and incompetence. Their critiques were sometimes tinged with a class element: distaste for the parvenu. Others did not mind the

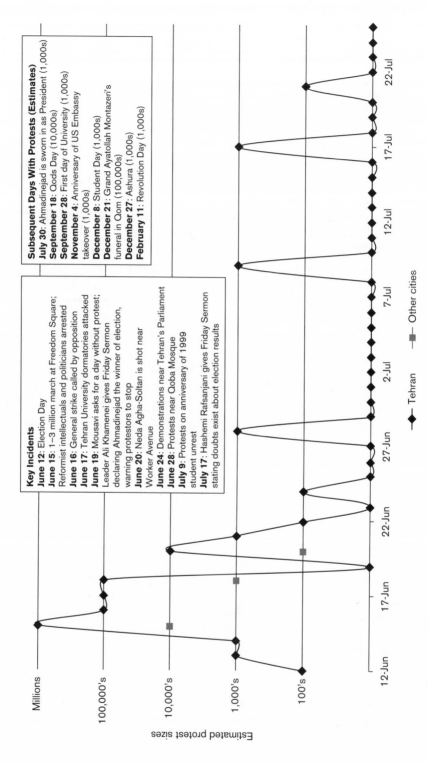

Key Incidents

June 12: Election Day

June 15: 1–3 million march at Freedom Square; Reformist intellectuals and politicians arrested

June 16: General strike called by opposition

June 17: Tehran University dormatories attacked

June 19: Mousavi asks for a day without protest; Leader Ali Khamenei gives Friday Sermon declaring Ahmadinejad the winner of election, warning protestors to stop

June 20: Neda Agha-Soltan is shot near Worker Avenue

June 24: Demonstrations near Tehran's Parliament

June 28: Protests near Qoba Mosque

July 9: Protests on anniversary of 1999 student unrest

July 17: Hashemi Rafsanjani gives Friday Sermon stating doubts exist about election results

Subsequent Days With Protests (Estimates)

July 30: Ahmadinejad is sworn in as President (1,000s)

September 18: Qods Day (10,000s)

September 28: First day of University (1,000s)

November 4: Anniversary of US Embassy takeover (1,000s)

December 8: Student Day (1,000s)

December 21: Grand Ayatollah Montazeri's funeral in Qom (100,000s)

December 27: Ashura (1,000s)

February 11: Revolution Day (1,000s)

Estimated protest sizes

Millions
100,000's
10,000's
1,000's
100's

12-Jun 17-Jun 22-Jun 27-Jun 2-Jul 7-Jul 12-Jul 17-Jul 22-Jul

◆ Tehran   ■ Other cities

FIGURE 17. Green Movement postelection protest incidents, June–July 2009. (Source: Harris 2012b: 437.)

president's grand boasts, since here was a noncleric who clearly sounded like an Iranian nationalist. In fact, Ahmadinejad blended an assortment of nationalist myths—lay and religious, pre-Islamic imperial and pan-Muslim spiritual—into a potent discourse. His paternalistic tone, however, embarrassed and angered many in the newly educated strata who saw themselves as independent of the state.

Among these people, the Khatami years were nostalgically remembered as halcyon days, though in many public and private arenas the hard-won relaxations of social regulations were still in place. A well-publicized but highly ineffective state effort at policing dress among women and men in Tehran's main squares during the hot summers generated mild grumbling but was easily evaded. Religious head coverings continued to creep revealingly upward among women, and hairstyle and dress carried on operating as main sites of status and class distinction for both sexes. Those who could afford luxury clothing brands displayed them, while innovations existed for conspicuous consumption by those less wealthy. With a short visit to any of Tehran's bazaars or malls, one could obtain a metal Gucci emblem to be subsequently fastened onto a pair of Chinese blue jeans. Furthermore, the commodity-linked economic boom from 2006 to 2007 set off a speculative binge by the aspirant middle classes in land, housing, or any other activity with which one could arbitrage social connections. The import of expensive European cars—100-percent tariff included—was a notable topic of interest at cafes. Outside Iran, scholars looked desperately for signs of resistance—teenage hedonism, rap music, and brain drain were posited as weapons of the weak. Inside the country, intellectuals and social scientists lamented the public's lack of "social capital."[39] Philosophers maintained in newspaper op-eds that Iranians were anomic and materialist, yet still trapped "between tradition and modernity" because of exceptional circumstances of history and culture. Or so it seemed.

According to an Iranian reporter who had covered several domestic elections, the truncated length of the country's political campaigns, which usually begin one to two months before the election date, tends to "make for compressed excitement." In Mashhad in 2001, he told me, during the reelection campaign of former President Mohammad Khatami, most people proclaimed their abstinence from voting but then showed up in a remarkably high turnout.[40] One individual said that he had returned to the country twenty-five days before the 2009 election but felt no sense that any popular mobilization was happening until around ten days before the voting. Another reporter from state-run

Press TV, who had traveled widely with the campaigns of Mousavi and Karroubi, told me that, outside Tehran, their events generally were routine and rested on appeals to revolutionary status groups: war martyrs, university-student associations, local clerics and their mosque networks. The reporter noted that, whether cheered or heckled, the events did not go beyond the standard frames of Iranian political discourse. The divisive incumbent president was labeled as incompetent, and reformists promised to be better stewards of the state. The president was also being challenged on similar grounds by a fourth candidate, Mohsen Rezāi—a man impeccably credentialed as former Commander of the Revolutionary Guards during the 1980s war.

It seemed, therefore, that the electorate might be too apathetic to allow the reformists an opportunity to take back the presidency. The first week of June 2009 changed the stakes of the coming election for many Iranians. One-on-one debates between each of the four candidates on live television, beginning with a heated debate between Ahmadinejad and Mousavi over the incumbent's record in office as compared with his predecessors', broke through a slate of political taboos. Mousavi was remembered as a rather skinny lay Islamist revolutionary who steered the country through the Iran-Iraq War but then retired to a mostly apolitical existence of painting, poetry, and architectural design. He had declined to run in 2005 and announced his 2009 candidacy only after other candidates, including Khatami, abstained. Suddenly he was reborn as a symbol of challenge to the status quo and the best chance for toppling the polarizing incumbent. A young woman told me that a group of her friends had attended an exhibition of Mousavi's collected paintings a week before the election in one of the dozens of art galleries that pepper Tehran's north-central neighborhoods. Instead of grandfatherly and jejune, the sexagenarian's abstract pen work and calligraphy was considered sexy.

This libidinal resonance was related to an increasing mobilization of everyday fun that emerged during the week of the televised debates. Some debates were projected onto large screens in public parks, generating peaceful but competitive sloganeering among candidates' supporters on streets and highways. While Ahmadinejad's campaign events were slickly organized and well funded, they utilized existing institutional networks of state supporters, such as the locals of the *basij* corps. At several of these large pro-Ahmadinejad events, the president would arrive late to the podium and move through his prepared talking points. Mousavi and Karroubi events, conversely, could either fall apart before they even began—one Karroubi rally in Vali Asr Square had the electricity pulled on it—or they could be intense and galvanizing, surprising many of their own participants. Mousavi's campaign was backed by wealthy supporters and reformist organizations, including think tank–styled meetings that created slogans and slick posters. Yet according to Mousavi campaign volunteers, individuals with no ties to the campaign also improvised slogans and signs that were picked up by the campaign.

After each night's televised debate, small and medium-sized groups, mostly of young people, would congregate in Tehran's main streets and squares. Opposing candidates' supporters would move among the crowds and hand out signs, chant slogans, and engage in teasing and catcalling to their opponents' side. Spontaneous political gatherings of this size are rare in contemporary Iran, and a "carnivalesque egalitarianism," as the sociologist Javier Auyero described for Argentinian movements, drew in thousands.[41] Police presence grew throughout the week, but mostly to keep the opposing campaign supporters apart. The peak of this preelection mobilization was likely a pro-Mousavi human chain that formed along one of Tehran's longest streets on 8 June, four days before the election. On the same day, a large Ahmadinejad rally was held at the enormous Mosalla Mosque, in Tehran.

In effect, the apathy toward political participation was gone and belief in a sort of rump democracy emerged. Civil society, at least in the usual definition of nonstate associational member organizations, had little to do with this process. To an extent, for the Iranian milieu, public gatherings sanctioned as election-related events reduced the costs of individual participation. Yet the mobilizational forms that emerged did not fall within a dichotomous conception of state and civil society, although this is how scholars and participants alike reified the outcomes after the fact. Instead, the preelectoral mobilization resembled the "boundary-spanning contention" that the political scientist Kevin O'Brien observed in Chinese village elections, where the demarcation between institutionalized and unconventional political behavior is fluid.[42]

Still, how did anyone actually know that participation costs in preelection rallies would be lowered and risks minimized? Up until that week, impromptu rallies in Tehran had been rarely seen for years. It was hardly the state-sanctioned events that generated the most momentum, but rather the informal spillover of mobilization into new arenas of public interaction. There were very few preexisting activist networks that could reduce the free-rider problem of participation through reciprocal understandings of social trust. Instead, as blog posts of preelection rally participants attest, it was the very act of attending that gave rise to the collective solidarity and emotional effervescence that generated the *perception* of low participation costs.[43] The sociologist Randall Collins characterizes it well: social movements are a mass type of interaction ritual.[44] Initially skeptical attendants of rallies stood outside the main crowd, were handed a placard or a ribbon, and then later remarked surprisingly in online testimonials at their own feelings of exhilaration and optimism.

The slogans, banners, and clothing items utilized by Iranians in these interaction rituals (such as green ribbons, headbands, hand signals, face paint) went through a period of creative improvisation and then, as Erving Goffman would have predicted, a subsequent homogenization. As certain symbolic forms of social solidarity become more acceptable than others, a shared repertoire of action emerged. These became important during subsequent protests as markers of trust, mechanisms of cohesion, and indicators of political orientation. Furthermore, the countermobilization of Ahmadinejad supporters, with routines of catcalling and teasing between small groups in streets and squares each night, was not simply the expression of authoritarian clients squaring off against lifelong democrats. Rather, it was a simultaneous escalation of emotional effervescence on both sides. This escalation produced an unexpected mobilizational momentum before the elections had even taken place. Many people shifted from caring much about the race to intensely awaiting election day. On that day, voter turnout, according to both state and opposition accounts, was 80 to 85 percent of the eligible population.

Once postelection unrest erupted, preelectoral symbols reemerged with an even greater resonance, though hardly planned in advance. For example, the use of a long green string during the "human chain" event on 8 June, before the election, symbolizing the connectedness and breadth of Mousavi supporters, showed up in the repertoire of a rally that I attended on 16 June. I watched hundreds of people wearily hold up a green string for a march of nearly three hours. It was through these tiny, cumulative symbolic actions, face-to-face, that the unexpectedly large protest sizes quickly materialized after the election. There was nothing automatic about the Green Movement, in other words. It was a conjuncture of the rapid emergence of an oppositional culture in the preelection period, the last straw of an election perceived as stolen and triggering deeper sets of accumulated grievances against the state, and a quick upsurge in public protest that joined together a weak-tied but broad coalition of actors in a more or less unified emotional space of high ritual density. This momentum peaked very early in the protest wave, as figure 17 displays. The remaining protests over the next several months, occurring mostly on symbolic revolutionary holidays, were attempts to rekindle the earlier emotional energy of the postelection weeks.

Who protested? There are no survey polling data to parcel out the social characteristics of Green Movement participants and their frequency of protest. According to opposition accounts, 107 individuals died as a result of repression in postelection protests from June 2009 to March 2010, whether on the street, in jail, or in hospital. Of this total, 13 percent were women, and at least 22 percent were active university students. A smaller, perhaps less representative, sample of twenty victims from another source revealed 52 percent students, 14 percent white-collar employees, 19 percent shopkeepers, and 14 percent workers.[45] In either accounting, this is certainly a broader coalition of social actors than in previous protests in postrevolutionary Iran. Although the Green protest wave arose for conjunctural reasons, therefore, its movement dynamics arguably illustrated broader processes of class formation and the possibility of cross-class coalitions in social protest.

For Iran, the class composition of the protests was not a speculative question. During and after the movement, activists and journalists heatedly debated the class basis of the demonstrations. If the Green protestors were mostly in the "middle class," then did these individuals represent broader social dissatisfaction with the postrevolutionary state? Were they constitutive of Iranian civil society, or, even more nebulously, the Iranian nation? Or were protest participants a narrow segment of society that loudly proclaimed its opposition to the election outcome, while a silent majority had voted in favor of the government? In response to commentators who dismissed Iran's protestors as part of a slim bourgeoisie, for instance, Hamid Dabashi argued that the widely observed participation of people who were both educated and unemployed meant that these protestors could not be grouped in the middle class.[46] The debate itself tended to confuse the issue further, since Iran is a middle-income country in the world economy and its class structure differs from wealthy countries in North America and Europe. How class was analytically pinned down for a social movement had broader implications for the representation of political claims and international appeal of self-identified Green activists. One's position on the matter often determined the definition of class that was used, not vice versa.

Perhaps the household locations of people who may have protested could provide some clues. Tehran's geography, with northern high-rise apartments at the feet of the Alborz Mountains and a sloping south-ward tilt, is often used as a proxy for social class. Before the 1979 revolution, it was widely known that "uptown" and "downtown" were shorthand for wealthy and poor. To some degree, even though the city and its greater environs have nearly trebled in population over the past three decades, this is still the case in popular terminology as well as neighborhood layout. After the Green protests in June 2009, Iran's Interior Ministry eventually released a full list of polling stations in the country, with the official vote counts at each station tabulated for the four presidential candidates. For reasons not made clear, the Ministry never provided a corollary list of the specific locations of these 45,692 stations. In other words, one can see the vote totals for all the polling stations in Tehran and other provinces, but *cannot identify the neighborhood* each polling station was located in, limiting the ability to investigate voting patterns by income or any other variable. Nevertheless, a few polling-station numbers were listed in newspapers and blogs during the election period. From these, select stations can be identified in districts with different income levels. These results are presented in table 7 as a very rough proxy for voting patterns by income level.

Although the data should be treated with caution given accusations of fraud by the opposition, the voting trends in table 7 do associate income level with candidate preference. Lower-income Tehran neighborhoods voted for Ahmadinejad, while middle- and upper-income neighborhoods voted for Mousavi. From this perspective, it seems that an income-based definition of class neatly resolves the question of who participated in postelection protests. Indeed, table 7 hides the fact that votes for Ahmadinejad may have been even more skewed toward low-income households, since individuals in Iran can vote anywhere they like and are not registered at particular polling stations. Therefore, it is possible that poorer individuals who work in wealthier districts such as Niavaran could have voted for Ahmadinejad there. Furthermore, Tehran is far wealthier than the rest of Iran, and so a "middle-income" neighborhood in the country's capital likely possessed higher-income households than in other provincial cities and towns such as Yazd or Abadan, where middle-income neighborhoods may have voted for Ahmadinejad. Even Tehran's low-income neighborhoods listed in the table are wealthier than the poor neighborhoods of most other cities.

Yet a static snapshot of urban voting preferences hides the complex roles of class and geography in movement participation. As Asef Bayat noted of Tehran, this "paradox city" developed multiple sites of cross-class

TABLE 7   REPORTED 2009 VOTING RETURNS IN SELECTED TEHRAN NEIGHBORHOODS

Neighborhood	Ahmadinejad	Mousavi	Karroubi[a]	Rezāi[a]	Spoiled[a]
High-Income					
Mirdamad [3, 249]	116 (7.4%)	1359 (87.1%)	35	45	6
Niavaran [1, 66]	276 (14.4)	1502 (78.4)	83	43	13
Shahrak-e Gharb [2, 112]	352 (13.7)	2072 (80.5)	59	78	13
Middle-Income					
Kerman St. [4, 317]	538 (29.3)	1204 (65.5)	13	57	25
Khosh St. [10, 116]	733 (35.8)	1197 (58.5)	31	46	39
Mehrabad [9, 1086–87]	921 (41.8)	1172 (53.2)	16	54	41
Low-Income					
Javadieh [16, 2190]	568 (54.4)	439 (42.0)	1	11	26
Javadieh [16, 2191]	618 (65.9)	283 (30.2)	3	14	20
Meydan Fallah [17, 2399]	1350 (77.9)	327 (18.9)	5	19	31

SOURCE: My thanks to Ali Reza Eshraghi for identifying locations of specific polling stations from newspaper and online reports. Ballot results from identified polling stations were obtained from Iran Ministry of Interior's Web site (www.moi.ir).

NOTE: Numerals within square brackets designate district number and polling-station numbers.

[a]Vote returns under 5 percent for candidates reported only in absolute numbers.

interaction since the 1979 revolution.[47] These processes undoubtedly played a part in broadening the protest dynamics of the Green Movement. Let me relate two ethnographic observations to illustrate. The Tehran Metro connects the far-flung neighborhoods of the city along a set of north-south and east-west subway lines. East and West Tehran contain wealthy and poor neighborhoods alike, most of which popped up after the revolution through government housing policies, informal land grabs, and illegal license procurement.[48] On protest days, I took the metro from distant East Tehran into the city center along with thousands of other individuals who hopped on at various stations. These easy-access paths were important before the election during the campaign mobilizations, but became crucial for the postelection demonstrations, since road traffic would often be blocked or simply jammed to a standstill on days of protest. On the train we mingled with others who, through tiny and silent symbolic cues, displayed the appearance of a protestor just under the surface. However, it was difficult, though not always impossible, to tell where anyone was from or what their background was. The protests drew not only the politically militant but also the socially curious, misfit teenagers, and large families with children. I often saw odd sorts jumbled similarly together in Tehran's large public parks on Thursday evenings.

A few weeks after the election, I attended a welcome-home party for a man who had been caught by police near a protest that he was not even attending and held in jail for more than two weeks. He had stayed in a large cell with nearly twenty other detainees. Since the arrest seemed quite random, I figured this jail cell's population might represent a more randomly selected sample of the protest crowd who were haphazardly thrown into trucks and police cars. I asked the man if he had befriended any of his cellmates during these two weeks, and if so did he know where they lived in Tehran. "Of course," he replied, "we are all friends now, and I am going to see some of them next week." Four or five of the cellmates were from southern Tehran and had taken the Metro train up to the protests where they were subsequently arrested. Urban space, in other words, facilitated the cross-class mobilizational surge of the Green Movement.

As sociologists like to point out, class is not a static grouping that automatically bestows identities onto people. Instead, people can identify, at times, with others who have experienced similar class trajectories. As with any middle-income country, Iran's occupational structure looks different than it would in a wealthy country. Yet shifts in Iran's occupational structure through time show the rapid changes that have occurred over the past three decades. These changes also help us partially understand the collective identities and grievances observed during the Green protests. In table 8, I condense and adapt occupational classification data from Iranian censuses collected by two economists, Sohrab Behdad and Farhad Nomani.[49]

Table 8 shows changes in the *relative* size of occupational classes during the postrevolutionary period. Several notable trends stand out. First, formal wage workers shrank as a percentage of the labor force after the 1979 revolution. The relative share of formal wage earners has not recovered to prerevolutionary levels, even though many more individuals are in the formal labor force because of absolute growth. The relative decline in formal wage positions was partly produced by capital flight from the import-substitution sections of the Pahlavi monarchy's industrial base. The Islamic Republic did return to industrial planning during its five-year development plans beginning in the late 1980s, but the process of formal wage labor proletarianization, at least in the form understood by classical political economy, stagnated in relation to other segments of the labor force. Second, as the inverse of this process, the informal sector, consisting mostly of self-employed workers or workshop owners, has persisted over the past four decades as a substantial

TABLE 8 OCCUPATIONAL STRUCTURE OF THE IRANIAN LABOR FORCE, 1976–2006
(PERCENTAGE OF TOTAL LABOR FORCE)

Classification	1976	1986	1996	2006
Capitalists	2.1	3.1	3.6	7.5
Modern	*12.8*	*6.5*	*14.1*	*17.3*
Traditional	*87.2*	*93.5*	*85.9*	*82.7*
Professional-Technical	5.4	7.0	10.2	12.3
Private Sector	*21.3*	*8.3*	*14.6*	*30.3*
Public Sector	*78.7*	*91.7*	*85.4*	*69.7*
Informal and Self-Employed	43.5	44.3	41.2	39.3
Unpaid Family Workers	*26.7*	*9.9*	*13.3*	*8.4*
Formal Wage Workers	40.2	24.6	30.7	30.4
Private Sector	*84*	*67*	*69.5*	*76*
Public Sector	*16*	*33*	*30.5*	*24*
Political Functionaries	8.3	16.8	11.1	8.7
TOTAL LABOR FORCE (thousands)	8,799	11,002	14,572	20,476

SOURCE: Behdad and Nomani 2009, 89.

NOTE: Column percentages do not add up to 100 percent since unspecified workers are not included. Italicized percentages refer to percentages of the occupational category, not of the total labor force.

Classifications: **Capitalists** are owners of physical and financial means of production; *modern* refers to managerial-administrative or professional-technical occupations; *traditional* refers to clerical, sales, agricultural, or service occupations. **Professional-Technical** refers to employees in managerial-administrative and professional-technical occupations in both *public* and *private* sectors. **Informal and Self-Employed** workers do not hire any paid workers but may rely on the work of *unpaid family* labor. **Formal Wage Workers** are employees of the *public* and *private* sectors who do not own the means of production or enjoy the authority and autonomy of those in professional-technical occupations. **Political Functionaries** are employed in the political apparatus of the state, including rank and file workers as well as military, intelligence, and paramilitary forces.

segment of the labor force. Economists in the Islamic Republic often decry the persistence of informal jobs, but this phenomenon is not limited to postrevolutionary Iran. Similar countries throughout the global South, including much of Latin America, Sub-Saharan Africa, the Middle East, and South Asia, have experienced a persistence and even a relative expansion of the informal labor force.[50]

The occupational changes shown over time in table 8 do not tell us anything directly about Green Movement participation. Nevertheless, they do tell us something about how changes in social class may be experienced in contemporary Iran. Surely individuals in the informal self-employed, formal wage-labor, and professional-technical sectors are all still *workers* and could be classified as one large working class. Yet the differing lived experiences of social class, occurring at the level of both workplace and neighborhood, condition how individuals are disposed toward collective action.[51] In fact, individuals among these first two occupational classes—formal wage-labor and informal labor—have engaged in protest over the 2000s and 2010s in Iran over shared economic grievances. Labor strikes, worker petitions, and sit-ins are common enough in the country. This sort of unrest usually occurs over economic grievances, such as the nonpayment of wages, the use of temporary contracts, and the poor delivery of welfare benefits. Such protests resemble what the sociologist Beverly Silver labeled "Polanyi-type" unrest, wherein workers resist the changes in production and dismantling of manufacturing sectors brought about by "global economic transformations" and the "abandoning from above" of "established social compacts."[52] Similarly, informal-sector workers, who are often associated with urban bazaars, engaged in collective action along with shop owners against proposed tax increases by the state on retail activities. Widespread shop closings, first in October 2008 and again in 2010 and 2011, pointed to antagonisms between a state attempting to build governing capacity and an economic sector whose members struggle to avoid these regulatory practices.[53] Yet it does not follow from these sporadic episodes of protest that these occupational classes, on the whole, were linked to the political orientation of the Green Movement.

Ethnographic observation can illustrate how differences in class disposition and lived experience condition collective action. During one Green Movement demonstration in the period of peak protests between 15 and 19 June, I stood on the sidewalk as a group of hundreds of thousands of Iranians marched past me. The street was located slightly north of the Tehran Central Bazaar, lined with small shops that employed the informal workers who performed the difficult and menial tasks involved in retail and wholesale commerce. On the sidewalk with me were thousands of these workers and shop owners, milling around and gawking at the march. This particular demonstration occurred before protest participation became more dangerous as a result of intensified crowd-control tactics by the police. One could cross the street and join without any apparent cost, just as I had seen hundreds of others spontaneously join in previous marches. Therefore it was a good spot for observing how social class influences mobilization while it is taking place.

Although only a small metal barricade separated the onlookers from the marchers, no one crossed the street to join in. The microinteractional emotional energy generated by the marching protestors did not transfer over a class boundary that was deeply felt by those standing beside me. During that same week, different opposition groups issued several calls for a general strike. Even as a huge number of demonstrators poured out onto the streets, these calls for a general strike were barely heeded, including in the capital, Tehran. The experience of the Green Movement contrasts with the Egyptian and Tunisian uprisings of 2011, where labor associations were highly active. Class dispositions, embedded in observable sociocultural cues or struggles over symbolic classifications, present boundaries that can structure both the facilitation of protest and the demarcation of participation frontiers. As the economist Mohammad Majloo argued, Green Movement activists never attempted to build ties with workers outside the middle class, nor did they frame grievances along the economic and political lines that may have been important to workers.[54]

Nevertheless, even with such observations we should be cautious about describing Green Movement protestors as belonging to a narrow segment of the population. As table 8 shows, professional-technical workers have unquestionably been growing as a segment of the Iranian labor force over the lifetime of the Islamic Republic. Certainly many of the protestors, as I observed and as reported in the international media, belonged to this stratum of the labor force. Given that many of these workers are located in the public sector, possessing educational credentials and technical skills that allow them to garner higher incomes and living standards, these people can be classified as a postrevolutionary "new middle class." Relying solely on occupational classifications, however, hides several key social-structural changes that have also taken place in postrevolutionary Iran. Women, for instance, are undercounted in the labor market. While census surveys put female labor-force participation at around 15 to 17 percent, women who are classified as homemakers sometimes engage in income-generating activities. Although this would classify them as informal workers, such activities extend to high-income households and can utilize technical skills and educational credentials.[55] From my own observations, female participation in the 2009 demonstrations was almost always equal to male participation.

Also important is the expansion of secondary and tertiary education over the past two decades in Iran. In 1999, 18 percent of university-age Iranians were enrolled in tertiary education. By 2009, this level had doubled to 36 percent, with more women enrolled than men.[56] Many of the educated young Iranians who formed the militant cadres of the Green Movement were first-generation college and high-school students whose parents worked in the formal unskilled or informal sector. I spoke to numerous interlocutors who went to protests but hid their participation from families and relatives. This was not necessarily because of differences in political orientation between generations but was more out of the threat of social sanction by neighbors if participation became publicly known. Although the parents may have belonged to the working class, the children exhibited the social desires of the upwardly mobile. These social desires were nurtured by the Islamic Republic itself, especially after the end of the Iran-Iraq War.

In fact, as the Arab uprisings of 2011 again showed, the grievances of Green Movement protestors—political rights, greater social laxity, replacing the ruling elite with better-trained technocrats, separation of the private from the public sphere—are common throughout middle-income countries whenever upwardly mobile middle classes perceive themselves blocked by the state from the pathways to social power. They are educated and are cognizant of cosmopolitan habits, but they lack the political and cultural capital that would allow them to fully enjoy the middle-class lifestyle that they aspire to, free of the bureaucratic-authoritarian characteristics of the Islamic Republic. As a result of rapid class mobility over three decades, households and neighborhoods in Tehran often contain an overlap of occupational and educational levels among individuals. Divisions along class lines are not as clearly delineated as some commentators assume. For instance, I found many nonparticipants around the country who shared the grievances expressed by Green protesters. Male students with working-class backgrounds were frustrated as they became underemployed, overcredentialed members of the labor force. Women who had just exited secondary and tertiary education and entered the professional labor market often worked in clerical and service positions at occupational status levels below what their educational credentials implied. If the Green Movement can best be described as a middle-class protest, then this class was not a small elite but an increasingly large and powerful class that was largely a product of the social transformations that occurred under the Islamic Republic.

The involvement of this new class impacted the dynamics of the postelection protests. The early phase of surging mobilization created movement slogans, symbols, and emotional energy that drew in individuals from mixed-class circumstances. Yet in the demobilizational phase, the lack of organizational networks linking people with differing class dispositions exacerbated social cleavages and limited the movement's expansion. Unlike the multiple and chained mobilizations of the 2011 Arab uprisings, Iran's protestors had no diffused model to follow and adapt. It was largely a spontaneous, improvisatory effort, where face-to-face interaction rituals that transformed and charged the emotional energy of participants temporarily assuaged uncertainty and risk. The Tehran protests, at their peak, formed a cross-class coalition of millions, but the strongest ties to the movement were among the country's rising middle classes, which had expanded over the past two decades partly because of the state's developmental aspirations.

EXCLUDE OR UNIVERSALIZE? THE SWITCH FROM SUBSIDIES TO INCOME GRANTS

At least since Otto von Bismarck, if not before, states have attempted to use social policy to channel and co-opt social mobilization. From a bottom-up perspective, however, welfare policies are never solely about co-optation, even in less democratic countries. There will be always individuals in any country who decide to support a party or political association because of what the state gives them directly or indirectly. Conversely, there will also always be individuals who use state benefits as a source of social power with which to demand new rights and new opportunities from that same government. Welfare policy is not a long-term stabilizing force. In fact, social welfare often has unintended consequences in domestic politics, including on the prospects for further democratization and changes in the coalitions of ruling elites.

In Iran, as this book argues, the social compact is an arena of struggle that is up for grabs, not simply a top-down method of state control. The Islamic Republic embedded new and existing state institutions deeper in society than in any previous period of Iranian history. At the same time, new social forces, mobilized in groups or separately, have constrained and influenced the state's direction and choice of policies. Among intellectuals, critics, and even among scholars of Middle Eastern countries, welfare benefits are too often associated with populism and clientelism. The language used is reminiscent of earlier attacks on European and American welfare policies from the 1970s through the 1990s. In this view, anyone and everyone who receives something from the Islamic Republic is being bought off, co-opted, or silenced in exchange for handouts.

While a common assertion, it is historically and empirically wrong. Most Iranians are connected in some fashion, often through multiple organizations, to the welfare system in the Islamic Republic. For example, nearly all Iran's rural villages are now linked to a network of basic health-care clinics. These have helped to starkly reduce both the birthrate, because of family-planning initiatives, as well as infant and maternal mortality, because of these clinics' free services. Over the past several decades, many young villagers have migrated to Iranian cities, gone to school, and earned college degrees. A large segment obtained free scholarships to regional or national universities. In those universities, students also had access to free health care through designated hospitals. And in 2009, many of these first-generation university-educated Iranians participated in Green Movement public demonstrations. A few months after the winnowing of protests, former President Rafsanjani publicly alluded to the relationship between the Green demonstrations and the social policies implemented during the 1990s: "It is presently impossible to rule society by suppressing it, the very society that comprises three to four million students and millions of educated people. . . . Those who entered the university resist more easily and freely."[57]

By mid-2010, it appeared that Green Movement participants had lost the struggle to invalidate the 2009 presidential election results. However, as is often the case, the unrest had an impact beyond the protests themselves. We can see this impact through the process of subsidy liberalization in Iran. In order not to exclude middle- and upper-income households, a 2011 liberalization of basic-energy subsidies shifted from a targeted, pro-poor cash grant to a more nearly universal form of income transfers. Moreover, the conservative elite continued to fracture in the run-up to the 2013 election, leaving space for a surprisingly rapid mobilization that resulted in the election of Hassan Rouhani.

Back in 2005, Mahmoud Ahmadinejad seemed to hold positions on economic policy contrary to his predecessors'. The market was out; the state was back in. Yet after several years of increased state spending, notably in Iran's provinces, Ahmadinejad began to promote economic policies that sounded similar to earlier technocratic plans: merging ministries, reforming taxes, privatizing banking, boosting nonoil exports, and liberalizing the hefty price subsidies that had been in place since the end of the Iran-Iraq War. At the same time, the conservative elite that originally supported Ahmadinejad began to fracture into new oppositional coalitions that became increasingly critical of the divisive president. Even if Ahmadinejad won the 2009 election outright, the Green protests further destabilized this tenuous coalition among conservative elites. Competition ensued over which groups would implement a newly branded version of economic policies previously associated with reformist governments. As before, these policies were presented as an expert-driven, technocratic path to future economic growth. This sort of language was tailored to resonate not among Iran's poor but to the middle classes. After 2009's protests, conservative elites could no longer afford to ignore middle-class aspirations if they wanted to stay in power with any expectation of stability. One result was the Ahmadinejad government's flip-flop on plans to target cash transfers to poorer households as energy subsidies were liberalized. When the policy was finally enacted, cash transfers were extended to the entire population.

Discussions over subsidies have had a long history in Iranian politics. While some in the Rafsanjani and Khatami administrations wanted to liberalize subsidies of fuel and basic goods, it was a lesser priority than other economic reforms in the 1990s. This was party due, at the time, to lower oil prices. State subsidization of gasoline, diesel oil, or electricity was seen more as useful economic inputs for its domestic producers, including many state-owned enterprises, and less as expensive and distortionary budget items. As oil prices rose during the 2000s, peaking in 2008, these calculations changed. The government ended up paying a larger portion of its budget as it sold these goods well below the rising opportunity cost of exporting to the world market. The major users of fuel subsidies were not just industry, but consumers as well. Fuel consumption per capita in Iran—and auto-traffic levels—headed up at alarming rates. In addition, the state had security concerns about a possible United States–led embargo on gasoline imports.

Consequently, there were short-term reasons for removing subsidies on fuel, electricity, and other basic-energy inputs. But the logic behind "getting the prices right" in the Iranian economy went beyond simple crisis management. Reforming the subsidy system had been a long-standing recommendation to Iran and other Gulf states by international financial institutions such as the World Bank and the International Monetary Fund.[58] In fact, while the United States was accusing the Islamic Republic of recalcitrance in engagement with one international body—the International Atomic Energy Agency—Ahmadinejad's government was proactively engaging with International Monetary Fund economists to come up with a workable plan for subsidy liberalization. For an administration maligned in the press and opposition as nonexpert, it was the ultimate sign of technocratic respectability. Conservative opponents in the parliament in 2008–9 worriedly pondered the Ahmadinejad gambit. All agreed that something should be done about subsidies, but Ahmadinejad might get the credit if his administration pushed the process through. In 2008–9, the president hinted that the revenue saved from subsidy liberalization would be targeted at lower-income strata of the population. The parliament continued to block changes through 2009, wielding a variety of critiques. The plan was too radical or not radical enough. It would create an inflationary spiral, or it would create a group of dependent poor. This feud continued until 2009's sudden protest upsurge, which temporarily led to a semblance of conservative unity in the face of popular challenge. After the dust settled, Ahmadinejad's plan as well as conservative grumbling had shifted.

In 2010, leader and supreme jurist Ayatollah Ali Khamenei spoke in favor of subsidy liberalization. He asked that economic revitalization be the government's priority. Subsidy removals would jumpstart increased efficiencies in domestic production that could act as a linchpin in a larger set of market-friendly reforms, including a value-added tax, a revamping of the overburdened banking sector, and the privatization of Iran's large public sector. This package was largely identical to planning recommendations made in the 1990s, then opposed by conservative elites. Ahmadinejad proposed to cut subsidies over a five-year period. The revenue saved would be redistributed to lower-income households, industry, and the health-care system. Domestically produced pharmaceuticals and hospital services, notably, would remain heavily subsidized at the point of purchase.

A skeptical response arose among many middle-class Iranians. Some were certain that the liberalization of subsidies was a conspiracy against them. Having disproportionately benefited from low prices on goods and public utilities—because middle- and upper-income households consumed more—Green sympathizers believed that the subsidy cuts were a punishment for public defiance in 2009. In January 2010, a subsidy-reform bill finally passed the parliament. Iranians were told they would be placed in an income cluster that would determine eligibility for cash-transfer payments once subsidy liberalization had gone into effect. Everyone could send a mobile text message with their national identification number to a newly formed Subsidy Reform Organization and receive their cluster group via a text message. I was present in Iran during the time and watched as many individuals did so. Upon seeing their location in the wealthiest of three clusters, many stared at their mobile phones in disbelief. On this occasion, no one wanted to admit they were in the middle class.

The vocal resentment was palpable, and memories of the 2009 demonstrations were still fresh. When the president finally launched the "Targeted Subsidies Reform," in December 2010—nine months late—the targeting of income clusters had disappeared. Instead, the program had transformed into a universal cash transfer to all Iranians of 45,000 tomans per month ($40 [US] in 2011). The bill's name turned out to be a misnomer. There was no targeting to poorer-income strata. The International Monetary Fund applauded the move, admitting that the "simple compensatory scheme could win a broad-based social support for even massive price increase[s]." Moreover, the International Monetary Fund publicly noted what many Iranian politicians had discussed in private, as "denying support for the upper-income groups risked triggering public discontent among the group of the largest energy users."[59] It was technically easier to give everyone a cash grant, but this was still *far more expensive* than means-testing recipient households. The threat of renewed protest by excluded social groups was a pressing concern of the state. A major unintended consequence of the Green Movement, therefore, was to pressure a pro-market scheme into a new, universal social policy for all citizens. In welfare studies, such a program is often called a demogrant or basic-income grant.[60] Cash transfers are becoming more common around the world, whether in Brazil, China, or South Africa. A universal, or nearly universal, social policy is generally more difficult to cut or retrench than one that is narrowly targeted. Even though inflation eventually began to reduce the real value of the cash transfer, Iran's bimonthly income grant continued into the next administration, under President Rouhani.

The episode illustrated one of the contradictions of social policy in the Islamic Republic. The state could universalize welfare policies, but this inclusionary direction tends to empower and enlarge social classes that can then, in turn, make new demands on the state—demands that can be both political and economic. Alternatively, the state can weaken social policies and narrow access to welfare organizations, yet this exclusionary direction deepens the legitimation crisis of the state and reduces prospects for robust economic development. In states with narrow political elites, where political competition is highly constrained, such exclusionary policies would be easier to implement. Reliance on popular mobilization would be largely unnecessary. In postrevolutionary Iran, this has not been the case. As long as dynamics within the elite continue to remake political coalitions and provide opportunities for electoral mobilization, pushes for social inclusion in the Islamic Republic through new and existing social policies will continue.

Conclusion

Development Contradictions through
the Lens of Welfare Politics

At the outset of this book, Iran's development trajectory was placed in the overall context of wealth and welfare in the world economy. The ups and downs of Iran's economic path, I argued, were not very different from those of the majority of middle-income countries over the past five decades. Yet this path, which looked like economic stagnation—a state running fast to stay in the same place—tells us little about postrevolutionary changes in Iran. To explain these changes, I argue, the politics of social welfare can provide a useful lens. To use the lens, scholars who study commodity-producing states, or Middle Eastern states in general, must move beyond theories of rentierist politics and the relative absence of taxation.

The key institution of social policy under the Pahlavi monarchy was a corporatist welfare regime directed at formal professional and working classes. This developed as a result of two logics. First, pressure from mobilized groups from below— including nationalist intelligentsia, left-wing movements, expanding middle classes, and industrial laborers— spurred the Pahlavi monarchy to implement welfare policies in a newly coalescing nation-state. Second, however, state elites themselves utilized welfare making as a strategy for rule in order to incorporate new expanding classes as cadres in a technocratic project of state building and modernization. These welfare organizations, which took shape partly as a result of demands from below, did address the material and economic concerns of their constituencies. Other welfare efforts by the shah's state, such as land reform and rural health and education drives, however, were more a result of top-down experimentation than of social pressure. A main outcome of such efforts was the transformation of many segments of Iranian society—including those labeled as traditional, such as the peasantry, urban merchants and migrants, or the midlevel clerical establishment. The narrow form of elite politics in the Pahlavi monarchy, where little competition between rival groups occurred under the shah, resulted in less pressure to expand the welfare system to incorporate new social groups. Instead, the nationalist vision of Iran as a member of the wealthy club of countries drove state actions, entailing a certain set of priorities for economic and social policy. The overstating of the Pahlavi state's reach and power tended to mislead observers about how these policies manifested themselves in various locales, often subverted, reoriented, or utilized by individuals for their own purposes.

The 1979 revolution was a combination of the mobilization of those social groups empowered by the Pahlavi welfare system—university students, formal professionals, industrial workers, civil servants—as well as the mobilization of those groups who perceived themselves as excluded from that system—so-called traditional groups of society. The state-building modernization drives of the Pahlavi monarchy led to the politicization of the participants in this mobilizational upsurge. However, different segments of Iranian society held different visions for a modern social order, and the events of 1978–79 were, to a large degree, a struggle between confident state elites and a politicized opposition over what this order should entail and whom it should include.

This wave of social mobilization, one of the largest mass upsurges in the twentieth century, could not easily be put back in the bottle by the new postrevolutionary government. Once again, demands from below were being pushed onto the state; yet in 1978–79, it was far more forceful and widespread than in the early years of Pahlavi state building. In addition, the Islamic Republic was soon confronted with geopolitical isolation by the great powers, economic strictures on its main revenue source, and a war that imposed an existential crisis on the state's survival. Pressed by these concurrent events, the state's elites were forced to turn inward and mobilize their own population for defense, institution building, and securing the territory. Millions of Iranians did respond to the state's calls and took part in various ways during the war years, either in military institutions or in revolutionary organizations that spread throughout the country. Millions of others simply tried to make do, given the realities of wartime exigency and the fervent exclamations of state supporters who believed counterrevolutionary plots could be found under every unturned stone. Yet the survival of the new state did not rest solely on ideology, exhortation, coercion, or charisma. Something had to be promised in return, and what emerged from the mix of social pressures, state promises, and new elites positioning against each other was a warfare-welfare complex of social-policy institutions.

The components of this martyrs' welfare state most alien to Western observers, such as *bonyāds* (endowed foundations) that engaged in both welfare functions and economic production, draw attention away from the organizations that were most utilized by large segments of Iranian society that had been marginalized by the monarchy's corporatist welfare system. An expanding university system opened slots for individuals with newly acquired revolutionary credentials. The Imam Khomeini Relief Committee, a poverty-alleviation organization, gave aid to households of the rural elderly, widowed and single mothers, and refugee families. A primary-health-care clinic system spread across the countryside and trained locally embedded health workers to manage the health needs of a large segment of the population. Even the notorious *bonyāds* such as the Foundation for the Dispossessed and Martyrs provided care and income support for disabled veterans and their extended families. These were all institutional innovations that did not substantially exist before the revolution, and they contributed to a decommodification as well as a defamilization of the social reproduction of households and livelihoods. State networks of welfare partly replaced increasingly more precarious kinship and market networks of support.

The exigencies of the Iran-Iraq War locked in place reliance by new state elites on popular mobilization. Instead of fostering a single-party state, debates over wartime exigencies created new cleavages among elites in the Islamic Republic. Just as the war institutionalized popular mobilization through newly developed linkages between state and society, it also provided the space for factional divides that widened elite competition by the 1990s.

As often happens after revolutions and wars, a high degree of upward mobility occurred in the country's social structure from 1979 onward. Men and women from marginalized and poor backgrounds saw new opportunities available and often chose to pursue lives radically different from their parents' generation. The upending of status and class distinctions amid the upheavals of revolution and war assuredly did damage to thousands of households that had enjoyed decent living standards before 1979. Yet this same process also allowed numerous others to pursue a social path that had previously been blocked by overbearing parents, local elites, professional credentialing, and the old government itself. The political mobilization of revolution and war, then, resulted in the socioeconomic mobilization of millions as they took advantage of the new institutions of a welfare-welfare complex.

As the war ended and the state's elder figurehead passed away, the political elite of the Islamic Republic tussled over how to legitimate the revolution in the eyes not only of the believers but also of the world. The realization of the hard constraints of the world economy and the post-1989 rules of the game led more and more of Iran's elite to push for a reintroduction of technocratic norms and policies in order to fashion an antisystemic developmental state. For some, this was the only true route to economic independence; for others, it was a way to take the upper hand in domestic intraelite conflict. No matter the intention, nearly the entirety of the postrevolutionary elite, from stalwart cultural conservatives to former Third Worldist radicals, grudgingly came to the position that economic growth and expert knowledge were the keys to preserving the revolutionary path. Consequently, the state began to rely on and upgrade the plans and institutions of the previous Pahlavi monarchy's developmentalist push. None other than Mahmoud Ahmadinejad, a supposedly radical champion of a return to the revolution's early years, repeatedly proclaimed a main goal of his administration policies as "Iran should turn into the most advanced country in the world."[1] Within the span of three decades, the upwardly mobile Ahmadinejad and the new class of elites whom he represented repeated the bombastic promises of Mohammad Reza Shah to turn Iran into the "fifth industrial power."

In many ways, the developmentalist drive of the Islamic Republic from the 1990s onward resembled state-building efforts of the prerevolutionary era. Yet there was one crucial difference. The political elite at the top of the postrevolutionary state was far more fractious and competitive than the narrow monarchic circles of the 1960s and 1970s. These divisions meant that oppositional factions could more easily block or flank new initiatives by elites in the various branches of the state, yet in order to do so they had to mobilize various segments of society through mass politics. The intertwining of elite competition and popular mobilization invariably led to the expansion of Iran's welfare system beyond the institutions that it had inherited from the 1970s as well as those that it had invented in the 1980s. Both the monarchy and the Islamic Republic may have been authoritarian in regime type, and both may have been reliant on oil revenues, but they still produced very different welfare systems. Factional competition in the latter repeatedly provided avenues for social demands from below to become salient within elite politics, and the result was a universalizing push for social-welfare policy that has lasted up to the present.

With this expansion, however, Iran came up against two major constraints. First, as a middle-income country, alleviating absolute poverty was possible provided that the state targeted adequate resources at the task and possessed the political motivation to do so. Lessening social inequality, on the other hand, was far more challenging, partly because middle-income countries possess large informal sectors that are difficult for the state to regulate and administer. The corporatist social-insurance organizations of the past, copied from European models, could not by themselves cover the entire population, given that they largely operate through the nexus of formal employment and wage labor. Second, as absolute poverty declined and more people sought pathways for upward mobility, the social-welfare system itself became more expensive and unwieldy to operate. Long-term health care demanded more resources— both institutional and material—than did primary health care. Educational expansion resulted in credentialing hundreds of thousands of young Iranians who then demanded occupations and status commensurate with their newly acquired degrees beyond what the public and private sectors could provide. Pension funds began to strain as generous retirement pacts crafted for a smaller formal labor force and paid for via a baby-boom generation were confronted with the possibility of an aging society and a looming cost-inflection point. As new middle classes raised their expectations for welfare services, they strained and overflowed the organizational capacity of the health-care system. All these constraints are common to middle-income countries with a dual-welfare regime such as exists in Iran. The question that these constraints posed was a hard one: Does the state universalize the welfare system at a far higher cost, one that perhaps only wealthy Northern states can actually afford over the long term, or does it return to the exclusionary corporatist strategies of the past, with its unruly results? These pressures underlie not only the politics of Iran's social policy but arguably also in most middle-income countries in the twenty-first century.

The pressures indicate that Iranian society constrained the choices of the postrevolutionary state in significant ways. The government was hardly the autonomous and separate entity that many analysts tend to portray. Such constraints on the state were driven by the very developmental push that it had sponsored and encouraged over the past two decades. This push expanded the new middle class—a professional-technical stratum—and linked many other individuals through education to the possibility of a perceived middle-class lifestyle. Revolutions raise expectations, and postrevolutionary states—especially those with a highly competitive political elite and an expansive developmental project—make promises that raise those expectations even further. When these expectations do not materialize, and the cultural capital gained by millions of individuals through educational institutions over the past two decades becomes perceived as useless in the current social environment, many are willing to publicly push back on the state to hold it accountable.

This sentiment underpinned the grievances of the millions of participants in the brief but forceful Green Movement, where demands for democratization intertwined with demands for more egalitarian access to social and economic resources. Even though the protestors of 2009 were generally in the middle and upper strata of society, they were hardly the elitist upper crust that the movement's detractors portrayed them to be. Instead, these were mostly men and women who had moved upward through the Islamic Republic's own institutionalized pathways but felt blocked from the expected livelihoods that had seemed promised to them. In protesting, they were using the social power that they had gained over the course of the postrevolutionary period to push the state in a democratizing direction. The celebrated agent of democratization in European history—the independent bourgeoisie—was hardly the most active in Iran during either the 1979 revolution or the 2009 upsurge three decades later. Instead, it was the new middle class—the very cadres who were expanded and empowered to support the state—who turned against it in both instances. Over the long run, then, social and political demands became intertwined and inseparable, not antagonistically in tension with each other. The dynamic of state-society relations in Iran examined in this book runs counter to the standard portrayal of social welfare as authoritarian bribe in the rentier-state paradigm.

From this perspective, the shifts in social power over the past five decades in Iran can be placed alongside broader transformations of middle-income countries during the postcolonial era. In a 1990 essay on the politics of authoritarian middle-income countries during twentieth-century developmental projects, the sociologist Giovanni Arrighi compared the prosystemic path of Latin-American states like Argentina and Brazil and Southern European states like Spain and Portugal with the antisystemic path of the USSR and Eastern European states. The comparison between prosystemic versus antisystemic development can be interpreted in various ways, but for our purposes we can understand it as a distinction between middle-income states that enjoy support and protection from the most powerful states in the world economy and those that experience hostility and antagonism. These are all matters of degree, not categorical opposites, but in Iran we can see both paths at work. Pahlavi Iran, while still nationalistic and driven by the self-perceived interests of state elites, was generally a prosystemic actor in the Middle East from the 1950s onward, while the Islamic Republic, either by its own pronouncements or by those of its enemies, was to some extent an antisystemic actor.[2]

Prosystemic developmental efforts by authoritarian middle-income states, Arrighi argued, generated serious contradictions that could undermine the states themselves. These countries pursued industrialization by inviting in large capitalist corporations from wealthy states, building up a sizable formal working and managerial class to employ in these domestic enterprises, and securing revenue streams through international trade. In this manner, these states were able to carve out a share of economic resources from the world economy. Such states tended to distribute these resources among both elites and the small strata of technical and industrial workers who were gradually being empowered through the processes of urbanization and proletarianization that were bound up in the developmental push. The majority of the population, however, was largely excluded from this state-led process of economic and social development. Over time, many such states pursued the same strategy, and competition between them all increased. As a result of this increasing competition, subsequent economic returns in the world economy declined for these states. Nevertheless, the social and economic demands of newly empowered classes continued to increase. This led to various attempts to contain the rising social power of enlarged middle and working classes, in the form of military dictatorships or other coercive political structures. Yet repression did not permanently solve the problem. It is not a coincidence, Arrighi contended, that a wave of parliamentary democratizations across Latin America and Southern Europe in the 1970s and 1980s—what came to be labeled the Third Wave of democratization—took place among prosystemic developmental states. One can also include the democratization of South Korea and Taiwan in this process as well, as Peter Evans has shown.[3] Given the trajectory of Iranian history laid out in chapter 2, we can also include Pahlavi Iran as one more example of the contradictions of prosystemic development that eventually toppled its own political structure. Iran was not exempt from the Third Wave—not by any means. The result was not a full-fledged parliamentary democracy, but the new Islamic Republic arguably contained greater possibilities for democratization than had its predecessor, if the many electoral surprises over the past two decades are any indicator.

Antisystemic developmental states, conversely, pursued a different internal strategy. Instead of creating exclusionary social-welfare compacts and securing protection from the main geopolitical powers in the world economy, authoritarian states in the USSR and Eastern Europe created highly inclusive social-welfare systems as part of their developmental strategy. This provided a social underpinning to these regimes that, for a period, generated internal legitimacy and allowed for the pursuit of costlier internal drives for industrialization and modernization outside the ambit of large capitalist enterprises and hegemonic powers in the world. Yet this path also contained contradictions, Arrighi showed. As the social power of previously weak groups—workers and peasants under the old regime—became more nearly equalized with the livelihoods of upper strata, it became increasingly difficult to portray the authoritarian rule of state elites as a means to the protection of society. Instead, state elites came to be perceived more and more as using authoritarian means to protect their own power and privilege. To paraphrase Charles Tilly, this form of postrevolutionary social welfare compact, over time, became to resemble a rather nonrevolutionary protection racket.[4] The 1989–91 collapse of most socialist states amid a series of nationalist mobilizations was partly an outcome of the hollowing out of antisystemic bases of rule. While the Islamic Republic never engaged in social engineering on the scale of the Stalinist-era USSR and Eastern Europe, the process that has occurred over the past three decades in Iran is rather similar. Indeed, popular descriptions of the political elite in the Islamic Republic often use terms, such as *mafia,* which can be heard throughout the post-Soviet sphere.

Whether the Islamic Republic survives for another generation, or is displaced by a new regime, social processes from the country's postrevolutionary trajectory have generated a set of developmental contradictions that, at some point, will push the country down one of two paths. The first is a more exclusionary social-welfare compact and a narrower, more authoritarian political structure. The second is a more universalizing social-welfare compact and a wider, more democratic political structure. Given the breakdown of the old geopolitical order in the Middle East, it is difficult to predict which trajectory is more likely.

"Antisystemic" development does not mean much when the system is too murky even to make out proper protagonists and antagonists. Yet the tradition of contentious politics inside Iran, as well as the rising tide of global contention that we are currently experiencing, suggests that movements within Iranian society will continue to pressure, constrain, and shape the Iranian state. In that crucial sense, the popular mobilization of the 1979 revolution is still with us today.

Notes

INTRODUCTION

1. Kevan Harris, "An 'Electoral Uprising' in Iran," *Middle East Reports Online*, 19 July 2013. Online at: http://www.merip.org/mero/mero071913 (accessed 13 March 2015).

2. Jack Goldstone, "Modern Revolutions?" *Harvard International Review*, 2008. Online at: http://hir.harvard.edu/modern-revolutions/ (accessed 13 March 2015).

3. Charles Kurzman, *The Unthinkable Revolution in Iran* (Cambridge, Mass.: Harvard University Press, 2004).

4. Peter Evans, *Embedded Autonomy: States and Industrial Transformation* (Princeton: Princeton University Press, 1995); Patrick Heller, *The Labor of Development: Workers and the Transformation of Capitalism in Kerala, India* (Ithaca: Cornell University Press, 1999).

5. *Radio Free Europe/Radio Liberty Report*, 11 February 2008. Online at: http://www.rferl.org/a/1079462.html (accessed 14 June 2015).

6. Peter Evans, "Constructing the 21st Century Developmental State: Potentialities and Pitfalls," in *Constructing a Democratic Developmental State in South Africa: Potentials and Challenges,* ed. Omano Edigheji (Cape Town: HSRC Press, 2010), 9–12.

7. Jean Drèze and Amartya Sen, *Hunger and Public Action* (New York: Oxford University Press, 1989).

8. Amartya Sen, "Mortality as an Indicator of Economic Success and Failure," *The Economic Journal* 108.446 (1998): 5.

9. Ibid.: 9.

10. GDP per capita is used here because of poor data availability for gross national income (GNI); the overall trends are the same. For examining levels of inequality between countries in the world economy, as table 1 does, it is theo-

retically preferable to use GNI per capita and foreign exchange–based data (as opposed to income levels adjusted post factum for purchasing-power parity). See Giovanni Arrighi, Beverly Silver, and Benjamin Brewer, "Industrial Convergence, Globalization, and the Persistence of the North-South Divide," *Studies in Comparative International Development* 38.1 (2003): 3–31; Roberto Patricio Korzeniewicz et al., "Measuring National Income: A Critical Assessment," *Comparative Studies in Society and History* 46.3 (2004): 535–86.

11. Giovanni Arrighi, "The African Crisis: World Systemic and Regional Aspects," *New Left Review* 2.15 (2002): 5–36.

12. Farhad Nomani and Sohrab Behdad, *Class and Labor in Iran: Did the Revolution Matter?* (Syracuse: Syracuse University Press, 2006).

13. See the pioneering work of James Midgley: e.g., "Diffusion and the Development of Social Policy: Evidence from the Third World," *Journal of Social Policy* 13.2 (1984): 167–84; Anthony Hall and James Midgley, *Social Policy for Development* (London: Sage Publications, 2004).

14. John Foran, ed., *A Century of Revolution: Social Movements in Iran* (Minneapolis: University of Minnesota Press, 1994).

15. Doug McAdam, Sidney Tarrow, and Charles Tilly, *Dynamics of Contention* (Cambridge: Cambridge University Press, 2001).

16. Adam Przeworski, *Capitalism and Social Democracy* (Cambridge: Cambridge University Press, 1985), 3.

17. Jeffrey Haydu, "Making Use of the Past: Time Periods as Cases to Compare and as Sequences of Problem Solving," *American Journal of Sociology* 104.2 (1998): 339–71; idem, "Reversals of Fortune: Path Dependency, Problem Solving, and Temporal Cases," *Theory and Society* 39.1 (2010): 25–48.

18. Ching Kwan Lee, *Against the Law: Labor Protests in China's Rustbelt and Sunbelt* (Berkeley and Los Angeles: University of California Press, 2007), 266.

CHAPTER 1. CAN AN OIL STATE BE A WELFARE STATE?

1. The epigraphs to this chapter: Otto von Bismarck as quoted in Robin Blackburn, *Banking on Death, or Investing in Life: The History and Future of Pensions* (London: Verso, 2002), 31; Dirk Vandewalle, *Libya since Independence: Oil and State-Building* (Ithaca: Cornell University Press, 1998), 179. Abbās Abdi: *Āftāb-e Yazd*, 28 August 2006.

2. Hazem Beblawi and Giacomo Luciani, eds., *The Rentier State* (London: Croom Helm, 1987); Rolf Schwarz, "The Political Economy of State-Formation in the Arab Middle East: Rentier States, Economic Reform, and Democratization," *Review of International Political Economy* 15.4 (2008): 599–621. For an overview of debates on the validity of the rentier thesis for explaining authoritarianism, economic growth, and civil wars, see David Waldner and Benjamin Smith, "Rentier States and State Transformations," in Stephan Leibfried, Evelyne Huber, Matthew Lange, Frank Nullmeier, and Jonah D. Levy, eds., *The Oxford Handbook of Transformations of the State* (Oxford: Oxford University Press, 2015), 714–29.

3. Afsaneh Najmabadi, "Depoliticisation of a Rentier State: The Case of Pahlavi Iran," in Beblawi and Luciani (above, note 2), 223.

4. Interview in *Shargh*, 4 November 2006.

5. *Mardom-Sālāri*, 7 November 2007.

6. For more examples, see Kazem Alamdari, "The Power Structure of the Islamic Republic of Iran: Transition from Populism to Clientelism, and Militarization of the Government," *Third World Quarterly* 26.8 (2005): 1285–1301; Alidad Mafinezam and Aria Mehrabi, *Iran and Its Place among Nations* (Westport, Conn.: Praeger, 2008).

7. Scholarly accounts of the ideological milieu of the 1979 revolution and its lineages include Saïd Arjomand, *The Turban for the Crown: The Islamic Revolution in Iran* (New York: Oxford University Press, 1988); Hamid Dabashi, *Theology of Discontent: The Ideological Foundations of the Islamic Revolution in Iran* (New York: New York University Press, 1993); Mansoor Moaddel, *Class, Politics, and Ideology in the Iranian Revolution* (New York: Columbia University Press, 1993). For theoretical reflections on the role of ideas and culture in the revolutionary process in Iran, see Gene Burns, "Ideology, Culture, and Ambiguity: The Revolutionary Process in Iran," *Theory and Society* 25.3 (1996): 349–88; Charles Kurzman, *The Unthinkable Revolution in Iran* (Cambridge, Mass.: Harvard University Press, 2004); and John Foran, *Taking Power: On the Origins of Third World Revolutions* (Cambridge: Cambridge University Press, 2005).

8. Theda Skocpol herself wrote, "[I]f there has been a revolution deliberately 'made' by a mass-based social movement aiming to overthrow the old order, the Iranian Revolution against the Shah surely is it." In "Rentier State and Shi'a Islam in the Iranian Revolution," *Theory and Society* 11.3 (1982): 267.

9. For a collection of Khomeini's speeches and writings, see Hamid Algar, *Islam and Revolution: Writings and Declarations of Imam Khomeini* (Berkeley, Calif.: Mizan Press, 1981). More useful are the contradictory and inchoate dispositions of Iran's revolutionary coalition on display in the minutes of the debates over the 1979 constitution. See *Surat-e Mashruh-ye Mozākerāt-e Majles-e Barrasi-ye Nahā'i-ye Qānun-e Asāsi-ye Jomhuri-ye Eslāmi-ye Irān*, vols. 1–3. (Tehran: Edārah-ye Kol-e Umur-e Farhangi va Ravābet-e Omumi-ye Majles-e Showrā-ye Eslāmi, 1985).

10. Initial formulations on the USSR were by·Carl Friedrich and Zbigniew Brzezinski, *Totalitarian Dictatorship and Autocracy* (Cambridge, Mass.: Harvard University Press, 1956); Jacob Talmon, *The Origins of Totalitarian Democracy* (New York: Praeger, 1960); Hannah Arendt, *The Origins of Totalitarianism* (New York: Harcourt, 1968); whereas the critical response to the totalitarian model came from historians, historical sociologists, and economic historians such as T. H. Von Laue, *Why Lenin? Why Stalin? A Reappraisal of the Russian Revolution, 1900–1930* (Philadelphia: J. B. Lippincott, 1964); Alec Nove, *Economic Rationality and Soviet Politics; or, Was Stalin Really Necessary?* (New York: Praeger, 1964); Kenneth Jowitt, *Revolutionary Breakthroughs and National Development: The Case of Romania, 1944–1965* (Berkeley and Los Angeles: University of California Press, 1971); Stephen F. Cohen, *Bukharin and the Bolshevik Revolution: A Political Biography, 1888–1938* (Oxford: Oxford University Press, 1980); and Moshe Lewin, *The Making of the Soviet System: Essays in the Social History of Interwar Russia* (New York: Pantheon, 1985).

11. Charles King, *Extreme Politics: Nationalism, Violence, and the End of Eastern Europe* (Oxford: Oxford University Press, 2010), 82.

12. Charles Tilly uses the concepts of totalitarian and theocratic states to fashion a conceptual rubric through which authoritarian regimes temporarily absorb their populations into networks of rule. This is an ideal type for Tilly—filling the residual box in a 2 x 2 table—more than an empirical analysis of state rule apart from the case of Italian fascism, which he uses as evidence for his claim: see *Trust and Rule* (Cambridge: Cambridge University Press, 2005); idem, *Democracy* (Cambridge: Cambridge University Press, 2007). Michael Mann is more skeptical of the exceptional capacities assumed in those states defined as totalitarian, probably because his analysis of ideological power is more nuanced and sensitive to other intercutting sources of social power. See "The Autonomous Power of the State: Its Origins, Mechanisms and Results," in *States in History*, ed. John Hall (Oxford: Basil Blackwell, 1986), 131. The concept of totalitarian states re-emerged in the hotter years of the Cold War, alongside sociological research on "total institutions" such as mental hospitals and prisons. These deviant social institutions were to be contrasted with a pluralist, liberal, and voluntary association–based Western society. In this sense, totalitarian analyses partly functioned as a conceptual polemic to differentiate ideal Western societies with their ostensible geopolitical competitors. See Erving Goffman, *Asylums: Essays on the Social Situation of Mental Patients and Other Inmates* (New York: Doubleday, 1961).

13. Jan-Werner Müller, *Contesting Democracy: Political Ideas in Twentieth-Century Europe* (New Haven: Yale University Press, 2011), 108. For a revisionist theory of fascist mobilization, see Dylan Riley and Juan Fernández, "Beyond Strong and Weak: Rethinking Postdictatorship Civil Societies." *American Journal of Sociology* 120.2 (2014): 432–503.

14. Some relevant works in historical sociology are the debates between Theda Skocpol and William Sewell, Jr. (see Theda Skocpol, *Social Revolutions in the Modern World* [Cambridge: Cambridge University Press, 1994]); and the essays in Julia Adams, Elisabeth Clemens, and Ann Shola Orloff, eds., *Remaking Modernity: Politics, History, and Sociology* (Durham: Duke University Press, 2005). The ideational turn penetrated political science through the paradigm of constructivism—see programmatic statements in Rawi Abdelal, Mark Blyth, and Craig Parsons, eds., *Constructing the International Economy* (Ithaca: Cornell University Press, 2010), 1–19; Daniel Béland and Robert Cox, eds., *Ideas and Politics in Social Science Research* (Oxford: Oxford University Press), 3–15. A notable work concerning the power of ideology for organizing the Chinese communist state after 1949 is Franz Schurmann, *Ideology and Organization in Communist China* (Berkeley and Los Angeles: University of California Press, 1966).

15. Along with Arjomand and Dabashi (both above, note 7), see Ervand Abrahamian, *Khomeinism: Essays on the Islamic Republic* (Berkeley and Los Angeles: University of California Press, 1993); Vanessa Martin, *Creating an Islamic State: Khomeini and the Making of a New Iran* (London: I. B. Tauris, 2003); Behrooz Ghamari-Tabrizi, *Islam and Dissent in Postrevolutionary Iran* (London: I. B. Tauris, 2008).

16. Or, as James Scott put it, "We must keep in mind not only the capacity of state simplifications to transform the world but also the capacity of the society to modify, subvert, block, and even overturn the categories imposed upon

it": *Seeing like a State: How Certain Schemes to Improve the Human Condition Have Failed* (New Haven: Yale University Press, 1998), 49.

17. Fred Halliday and Hamza Alavi, eds., *State and Ideology in the Middle East and Pakistan* (London: Macmillan Education, 1988), 7.

18. Larry Diamond, "Why Are There No Arab Democracies?" *Journal of Democracy* 21.1 (2010): 98.

19. Hossein Mahdavy, "The Patterns and Problems of Economic Development in Rentier States: The Case of Iran," in M.A. Cook, ed., *Studies in the Economic History of the Middle East: From the Rise of Islam to the Present Day* (London: Oxford University Press, 1970), 428–67. In Iran's case, the rent is oil revenues, but any "natural" resource can apply, including foreign aid.

20. Ibid.: 466–67.

21. Homa Katouzian, "The Political Economy of Oil Exporting Countries," *Peuples Méditerranéens* 1 (1979): 3–22.

22. As Kaveh Ehsani observes, "many of the proponents of the rentier-state theory have merely 'secularized' the orientalist discourse: instead of 'Islam' being the key cultural factor explaining the essential unmodernity of the Middle East, an economic factor—oil revenues—is advanced to prove the same point." See "Social Engineering and the Contradictions of Modernization in Khuzestan's Company Towns: A Look at Abadan and Masjed-Soleyman," *International Review of Social History* 48.3 (2003): 368.

23. Beblawi and Luciani (above, note 2).

24. Ghassan Salamé, ed., *Democracy without Democrats? The Renewal of Politics in the Muslim World* (London: I.B. Tauris, 1994). For a version of the rentier argument often overlooked, see Samuel Huntington, *The Third Wave: Democratization in the Late Twentieth Century* (Norman: University of Oklahoma Press, 1991).

25. The inverse link between "productivist" states and a rentierist antithesis is no coincidence. Whereas the concept of rent-seeking returned to development theory through a neoutilitarian economic paradigm, the concept of a "productive" state was introduced in its political cousin, public choice theory. See Anne Krueger, "The Political Economy of the Rent-Seeking Society," *The American Economic Review* 64.3 (1974): 291–303; James Buchanan, *The Limits of Liberty: Between Anarchy and Leviathan* (Chicago: University of Chicago Press, 1975); as well as James Buchanan, Robert Tollison, and Gordon Tullock, eds., *Toward a Theory of the Rent-Seeking Society* (College Station: Texas A & M University Press, 1980).

26. The etymology in Persian is telling about the term's intellectual lineage. What could be simply labeled as *pārti-bāzi,* or influence peddling, is now often called *rānt-khāri,* or rent-seeking.

27. Suzanne Mettler, *The Submerged State: How Invisible Government Policies Undermine American Democracy* (Chicago: University of Chicago Press, 2011).

28. For key publications of the first generation of resource-curse theory, see Richard Auty, *Sustaining Development in Mineral Economies: The Resource Curse Thesis* (London: Routledge, 1993); idem, "The Political Economy of Resource-Driven Growth," *European Economic Review* 45.4-6 (2001): 839–46; Jeffrey Sachs and Andrew Warner, "The Curse of Natural Resources," ibid.: 827–38.

29. Christa N. Brunnschweiler, "Cursing the Blessings? Natural Resource Abundance, Institutions, and Economic Growth," *World Development* 36.3 (2008): 399–419; Victor Polterovich, Vladimir Popov, and Alexander Tonis, *Resource Abundance: A Curse or Blessing?* DESA Working Paper no. 93 (New York: United Nations Department of Economic and Social Affairs, June 2010); Kjetil Bjorvatn, Mohammad Reza Farzanegan, and Friedrich Schneider, "Resource Curse and Power Balance: Evidence from Oil-Rich Countries," *World Development* 40.7 (2012): 1308–16; Michael Herb, "No Representation without Taxation? Rents, Development, and Democracy," *Comparative Politics* 37.3 (2005): 297–316; Katharina Wick and Erwin Bulte, "The Curse of Natural Resources," *Annual Review of Resource Economics* 1.1 (2009): 139–56; Stephen Haber and Victor Menaldo, "Do Natural Resources Fuel Authoritarianism? A Reappraisal of the Resource Curse," *American Political Science Review* 105.1 (2011): 1–26.

30. Mushtaq Khan and Jomo Kwame Sundaram, eds., *Rents, Rent-Seeking and Economic Development: Theory and Evidence in Asia* (Cambridge: Cambridge University Press, 2000); Adeel Malik, "Beyond the Resource Curse: Rents and Development," in Ishac Diwan and Ahmad Galal, eds., *The Middle East Economies in Times of Transition* (London: Palgrave Macmillan, 2016), 245–58.

31. The role of Schumpeterian rents in the development of historical capitalism and the rise of Europe are discussed in Ha-Joon Chang, *Kicking Away the Ladder: Development Strategy in Historical Perspective* (London: Anthem Press, 2002); idem, *Bad Samaritans: The Myth of Free Trade and the Secret History of Capitalism* (New York: Bloomsbury Publishing USA, 2008); Erik Reinert, *How Rich Countries Got Rich and Why Poor Countries Stay Poor* (New York: Carroll & Graf, 2007). Khan and Sundaram (above, note 30) discuss the theoretical distinction between Schumpeterian rents and the neoclassical concept of rental income as deadweight loss. Many economists argue that oil income cannot be classified as a Schumpeterian rent, because the latter is temporary, whereas oil revenues are perceived as permanent by oil-producing states, which act accordingly. This may be the case in particular times and instances, but no more than can be found in the history of any large corporation that takes its supply and demand for granted. From a global perspective, the extraction, refinement, transport, and sale of oil-derived products are all economic activities that are subject to competitive pressures in the world economy. Oil companies, oil states, and non-oil states go to great lengths to generate temporary monopolies of access and supply above and beyond what is distributed by "nature." Furthermore, there have been numerous attempts over the course of the past century to buy out or prevent other sources of energy from emerging as viable alternatives to petroleum-derived resources—surely this is creative destruction of the highest order. An equivalent concept would be David Harvey's "spatial fix," as well as the various other types of "fixes" that states and capitalists undertake to generate and increase profitable returns on investment. See David Harvey, *The Limits to Capital* (Chicago: University of Chicago Press, 1982); Beverly Silver, *Forces of Labor: Workers' Movements and Globalization since 1870* (Cambridge: Cambridge University Press, 2003).

32. Giovanni Arrighi, Beverly J. Silver, and Benjamin D. Brewer. "Industrial Convergence, Globalization, and the Persistence of the North-South Divide," *Studies in Comparative International Development* 38.1 (2003): 3–31. Indeed, the United States itself may have been the most successful case of sustained economic development through intensive exploitation of domestic natural resources. See Karen Clay, "Natural Resources and Economic Outcomes," in *Economic Evolution and Revolution in Historical Time,* ed. Paul Rhode, Joshua Rosenbloom, and David Weiman (Stanford, Calif.: Stanford University Press, 2011), 27–50.

33. See Ha-Joon Chang, *Kicking Away the Ladder* (above, note 31).

34. Jonathon Moses, "Foiling the Resource Curse: Wealth, Equality, Oil and the Norwegian State," in *Constructing a Democratic Developmental State in South Africa: Potentials and Challenges,* ed. Omano Edigheji (Cape Town, South Africa: HSRC Press, 2010), 126–48.

35. Timothy Mitchell, "Carbon Democracy," *Economy and Society* 38.3 (2009): 400; idem, *Carbon Democracy: Political Power in the Age of Oil* (London: Verso, 2011).

36. K. A. Chaudhry, "The Middle East and the Political Economy of Development," *Items* 48 (1994): 41–49; idem, *The Price of Wealth: Economies and Institutions in the Middle East* (Ithaca: Cornell University Press, 1997).

37. David Waldner, *State Building and Late Development* (Ithaca: Cornell University Press, 1999).

38. Michael Herb, *All in the Family: Absolutism, Revolution, and Democracy in the Middle Eastern Monarchies* (Albany: SUNY Press, 1999).

39. Steffen Hertog, *Princes, Brokers, and Bureaucrats: Oil and the State in Saudi Arabia* (Ithaca: Cornell University Press, 2010).

40. Idem, "Defying the Resource Curse: Explaining Successful State-Owned Enterprises in Rentier States," *World Politics* 62.2 (2010): 261–301.

41. Gwenn Okruhlik, "Rentier Wealth, Unruly Law, and the Rise of Opposition: The Political Economy of Oil States," *Comparative Politics* 31.3 (1999): 296. Also see Steven Heydemann, "The Political Logic of Economic Rationality: Selective Stabilization in Syria," in *The Politics of Economic Reform in the Middle East,* ed. Henri Barkey (New York: St. Martin's Press, 1992), 11–39; Benjamin Smith, *Hard Times in the Lands of Plenty: Oil Politics in Iran and Indonesia* (Ithaca: Cornell University Press, 2007); Anne Peters and Pete Moore, "Beyond Boom and Bust: External Rents, Durable Authoritarianism, and Institutional Adaptation in the Hashemite Kingdom of Jordan," *Studies in Comparative International Development* 44.3 (2009): 256–85.

42. For the strongest case made in favor of the oil curse, see Michael Ross, *The Oil Curse: How Petroleum Wealth Shapes the Development of Nations* (Princeton: Princeton University Press, 2012).

43. Chaudhry, *Price of Wealth* (above, note 36), 191.

44. Victor Menaldo, *The Institutions Curse: Natural Resources, Politics, and Development* (Cambridge: Cambridge University Press, 2016), 57.

45. Ibid.: 58; also see Thad Dunning, *Crude Democracy: Natural Resource Wealth and Political Regimes* (Cambridge: Cambridge University Press, 2008).

46. Waldner and Smith (above, note 2), 708.

47. Roger Owen, *State Power and Politics in the Making of the Modern Middle East,* 3rd ed. (London: Routledge, 2004), xii.

48. See similar sentiments on the limits of Middle East exceptionalism in Fred Halliday, "The Middle East in International Perspective: Problems of Analysis," in *The World Order: Socialist Perspectives,* ed. Ray Bush, Gordon Johnston, and David Coates (London: Polity Press, 1987), 201–20; Simon Bromley, *Rethinking Middle East Politics* (Austin: University of Texas Press, 1994); Raymond Hinnebusch, "Toward a Historical Sociology of State Formation in the Middle East," *Middle East Critique* 19.3 (2010): 201–16.

49. A quite modern-looking bureaucratic organization within the Pahlavi state, for example, was the Planning and Budget Organization (PBO) in the 1950s, run by Abdolhasan Ebtehāj. Although it was eventually upended by the shah's insistence on micromanaging development policy, the PBO remained an "island of efficiency" for the next half-century. See Frances Bostock and Geoffrey Jones, *Planning and Power in Iran: Ebtehaj and Economic Development under the Shah* (London: Frank Cass and Co., Ltd, 1989).

50. Quoted in Hamid Dabashi, *Iran, the Green Movement and the USA: The Fox and the Paradox* (London: Zed Books, 2010), 128.

51. Hossein Bashiriyeh, *The State and Revolution in Iran, 1962–1982* (New York: St. Martin's Press, 1984), 171.

52. On the Pahlavi state as neopatrimonial, see Afsaneh Najmabadi, "Depoliticisation of a Rentier State: The Case of Pahlavi Iran," in Beblawi and Luciani (above, note 2), 211–27; Arjomand (above, note 7); Vali Nasr, "Politics within the Late-Pahlavi State: The Ministry of Economy and Industrial Policy, 1963–69," *International Journal of Middle East Studies* 32.1 (2000): 97–122; or in its sultanistic variation, H.E. Chehabi and Juan Linz, eds., *Sultanistic Regimes* (Baltimore: The Johns Hopkins University Press, 1998). For the Islamic Republic as a neopatrimonial state, usually with the office of Leader and Supreme Jurist during the tenure of Ali Khamenei replacing that of the monarch, see Akbar Ganji, "The Struggle against Sultanism," *Journal of Democracy* 16.4 (2005): 38–51; Karim Sadjadpour, *Reading Khamenei: The World View of Iran's Most Powerful Leader* (Washington, D.C.: Carnegie Endowment for International Peace, 2008); Saïd Arjomand, *After Khomeini: Iran under His Successors* (Oxford and New York: Oxford University Press, 2009).

53. Robert Merton, *Social Theory and Social Structure* (Glencoe, Ill.: Free Press, 1949), 49 (italics original).

54. Paul Taggart, *Populism* (Buckingham, Bucks: Open University Press, 2000), 4.

55. Kenneth M. Roberts, "Populism, Political Conflict, and Grass-Roots Organization in Latin America," *Comparative Politics* 38.2 (2006): 127.

56. Saïd Arjomand ("Fundamentalism, Religious Nationalism, or Populism?" *Contemporary Sociology* 23.5 [1994]: 671–75) makes this point in his criticism of Abrahamian's reading of the Islamic Republic's sharing of a "populist common denominator" with other Third World postrevolutionary states.

57. Kenneth Roberts, "Neoliberalism and the Transformation of Populism in Latin America: The Peruvian Case," *World Politics* 48.1 (1995): 84–85.

58. Kurt Weyland, "Clarifying a Contested Concept: Populism in the Study of Latin American Politics," *Comparative Politics* 34.1 (2001): 1–22.

59. Ibid., 14. This is not a result of a regional bias within Latin American studies. Paul Taggart's wide-ranging survey, which includes nineteenth-century cases in the United States and Russia, also concludes that populism is "an episodic phenomenon" that "limits itself because of its attitude towards institutions": Taggart (above, note 54), 4. Jan-Werner Müller also details the frustration with the vagueness in theories of populism: see Jan-Werner Müller, "Parsing Populism: Who Is and Who Is Not a Populist These Days?" *Juncture* 22.2 (2015): 80–89.

60. Anoushiravan Ehteshami and Emma Murphy, "Transformation of the Corporatist State in the Middle East," *Third World Quarterly* 17.4 (1996): 753–72; John Waterbury, "The Long Gestation and Brief Triumph of Import-Substituting Industrialization," *World Development* 27.2 (1999): 323–41; Alan Richards and John Waterbury, *A Political Economy of the Middle East* (Boulder: Westview Press, 2008).

61. The exceptions here are social movements identified as Islamic, which espouse a socioeconomic platform also often identified as populism. On this reading, a state might not be sufficiently populist, leaving it open to social challenge. Where Islamists are victorious, as in the Islamic Republic of Iran after 1979, populism returns as a theory to explain the long-term stability of state rule. The argument is still static and functionalist in usage.

62. In Iran, the term "populism" is often used in the negative sense, usually by liberal reformists and technocratic-leaning elites, but it also retains its earlier, positive connotation as meaning "supported by the people," which can be traced to the radical faction of the revolutionary coalition.

63. After all, in Latin America during the 1990s, populist strategies of rule were used to implement neoliberal economic policies. Scholars termed this "neopopulism," but this neologism tells us little about why neoliberal policies replaced earlier developmentalist ones.

64. Roberts (above, note 55), 145.

65. Jeffrey Winters, *Oligarchy* (Cambridge: Cambridge University Press, 2011), 17–18.

66. For the Middle East, see Jonathan Benthall and Jerome Bellion-Jourdan, *The Charitable Crescent: Politics of Aid in the Muslim World,* 2nd ed. (London: I. B. Tauris, 2009); Anne Marie Baylouny, *Privatizing Welfare in the Middle East: Kin Mutual Aid Associations in Jordan and Lebanon* (Bloomington: Indiana University Press, 2010); Janine Clark, *Islam, Charity, and Activism: Middle-Class Networks and Social Welfare in Egypt, Jordan, and Yemen* (Bloomington: Indiana University Press, 2004). For other regions, see Melani Cammett and Lauren MacLean, eds. *The Politics of Non-State Welfare* (Ithaca: Cornell University Press, 2014); and Ben Scully, "From the Shop Floor to the Kitchen Table: The Shifting Centre of Precarious Workers' Politics in South Africa," *Review of African Political Economy* 43.148 (2015): 1–17.

67. Karl Polanyi, *The Great Transformation: The Political and Economic Origins of Our Time* (Boston: Beacon Press, 1957).

68. Maurice Bruce, *The Coming of the Welfare State,* 4th ed. (London: Batsford, 1968), 31.

69. Harold L. Wilensky and Charles Nathan Lebeaux, *Industrial Society and Social Welfare: The Impact of Industrialization on the Supply and Organization of Social Welfare Services in the United States* (New York: Free Press, 1965).

70. T. H. Marshall, "Citizenship and Social Class," in *The Welfare State Reader,* ed. Christopher Pierson and Francis Castles (Cambridge: Polity Press, 2006), 31.

71. As John Stephens points out, Marshall is often misread even by scholars of the welfare state. Marshall's essays and lectures present a broad notion of social rights, defined not by specific policies but by historically determined notions of well-being and human development. Means-tested programs are not excluded from Marshall's definition, even while such programs may not be universally available for the population. For the Iranian case, as with most of the global South today, this is important for conceptualizing welfare rights, given that access to benefits can be tied to status, occupation, or class. These should not be exempted from a notion of social rights solely because they are not universal programs. See John Stephens, "The Social Rights of Citizenship," in *The Oxford Handbook of the Welfare State,* ed. Francis Castles, Stephan Leibfried, Jane Lewis, Herbert Obinger, and Christopher Pierson (Oxford: Oxford University Press, 2010), 511–25.

72. Ian Gough, *Political Economy of the Welfare State* (London: Macmillan, 1979); Frances Fox Piven and Richard Cloward, *Poor People's Movements: Why They Succeed, How They Fail* (New York: Vintage, 1978).

73. James O'Connor, *The Fiscal Crisis of the State* (New York: St. Martin's Press, 1973).

74. Claus Offe, *Contradictions of the Welfare State,* ed. John Keane (Cambridge, Mass.: MIT Press, 1984), 153.

75. Walter Korpi, *The Democratic Class Struggle* (London: Routledge & Kegan Paul, 1983).

76. Gøsta Esping-Andersen, *The Three Worlds of Welfare Capitalism* (Princeton: Princeton University Press, 1990), 15–16.

77. Ibid.: 37.

78. Idem, *Social Foundations of Postindustrial Economies* (Oxford and New York: Oxford University Press, 1999), 51.

79. Idem, "The Three Political Economies of the Welfare State," *International Journal of Sociology* 20.3 (1990): 108.

80. Carole Pateman, *The Disorder of Women: Democracy, Feminism, and Political Theory* (Stanford, Calif.: Stanford University Press, 1989). Also see Ann Orloff, "Gender and the Social Rights of Citizenship: The Comparative Analysis of Gender Relations and Welfare States," *American Sociological Review* 58.3 (1993): 303–28; Jane Lewis, "Gender and Welfare Regimes: Further Thoughts," *Social Politics: International Studies in Gender, State & Society* 4.2 (1997): 160–77; Diane Sainsbury, ed., *Gender and Welfare State Regimes* (Oxford: Oxford University Press, 1999); Julia O'Connor, Ann Orloff, and Sheila Shaver, *States, Markets, Families: Gender, Liberalism, and Social Policy in Australia, Canada, Great Britain, and the United States* (Cambridge: Cambridge University Press, 1999).

81. Theda Skocpol, *Protecting Soldiers and Mothers: The Political Origins of Social Policy in the United States* (Cambridge, Mass.: Harvard University Press, 1992).

82. Anthony Giddens, *The Third Way: The Renewal of Social Democracy* (London: Polity Press, 1998).

83. Kees van Kersbergen and Philip Manow, eds., *Religion, Class Coalitions, and Welfare States* (Cambridge: Cambridge University Press, 2009), 3.

84. A. J. P. Taylor, *English History 1914–1945* (Oxford: Oxford University Press, 1965), 455. Also see Richard Titmuss, *Commitment to Welfare* (London: Allen and Unwin, 1968).

85. Ross McKibben, *Parties and People: England 1914–1951* (Oxford: Oxford University Press, 2010), 133.

86. Andrew Abbott and Stanley DeViney, "The Welfare State as Transnational Event: Evidence from Sequences of Policy Adoption," *Social Science History*, 16.2 (1992): 245–74.

87. Wesley Widmaier, Mark Blyth, and Leonard Seabrooke, "Exogenous Shocks or Endogenous Constructions? The Meanings of Wars and Crises," *International Studies Quarterly* 51.4 (2007): 747–59.

88. Iranians tend not to link their war period of the 1980s with the welfare initiatives that continued afterwards, but neither do most Europeans and Americans. This is partly because, as the historian Bruce Porter has pointed out, liberal activists and social reformers usually "cannot accept that the welfare institutions which they regard as hallmarks of human progress could possibly have been derived in part from anything so horrendous as war." See Bruce Porter, *War and the Rise of the State: The Military Foundations of Modern Politics* (New York: Simon and Schuster, 1994), 193.

89. See comments on war and citizenship in William McNeill, *The Pursuit of Power: Technology, Armed Force, and Society since A.D. 1000* (Chicago: University of Chicago Press, 1982); John Markoff, *Waves of Democracy: Social Movements and Political Change* (Thousand Oaks, Calif.: Pine Forge Press, 1996); Silver (above, note 31); and Richard Lachmann, *States and Power* (London: Polity Press, 2009).

90. Charles Tilly, "Extraction and Democracy," in *The New Fiscal Sociology: Taxation in Comparative and Historical Perspective,* ed. Isaac Martin, Ajay Mehrotra, and Monica Prasad (Cambridge: Cambridge University Press, 2009), 182.

91. Walter Korpi, "Welfare-State Regress in Western Europe: Politics, Institutions, Globalization, and Europeanization," *Annual Review of Sociology* 29 (2003): 598.

92. Blackburn (above, note 1), 39.

93. Armando Barrientos, "Latin America: Towards a Liberal-Informal Welfare Regime," in *Insecurity and Welfare Regimes in Asia, Africa and Latin America: Social Policy in Development Contexts,* ed. Ian Gough and Geof Wood (Cambridge: Cambridge University Press, 2004), 121–68.

94. Alex Segura-Ubiergo, *The Political Economy of the Welfare State in Latin America: Globalization, Democracy, and Development* (Cambridge: Cambridge University Press, 2007).

95. Evelyne Huber and John Stephens, *Development and Crisis of the Welfare State: Parties and Policies in Global Markets* (Chicago: University of Chicago Press, 2001).

96. Ian Gough, "East Asia: The Limits of Productivist Regimes," in Gough and Wood (above, note 93), 169–201.

97. Ito Peng and Joseph Wong, "East Asia," in *The Oxford Handbook of the Welfare State*, ed. Francis G. Castles, Stephan Leibfried, Jane Lewis, Herbert Obinger, and Christopher Pierson (New York: Oxford University Press, 2010), 656–70.

98. János Kornai, *From Socialism to Capitalism: Eight Essays* (Budapest: Central European University Press, 2008), 59.

99. Claus Offe, "Epilogue: Lessons Learnt and Open Questions," in *Post-Communist Welfare Pathways: Theorizing Social Policy Transformations in Central and Eastern Europe*, ed. Alfio Cerami and Pieter Vanhuysse (Basingstoke: Palgrave Macmillan, 2009), 240.

100. Ibid.: 245.

101. Matthew Carnes and Isabela Mares, "The Welfare State in Global Perspective," in *The Oxford Handbook of Comparative Politics*, ed. Carles Boix and Susan Carol Stokes (Oxford: Oxford University Press, 2007), 868–85.

102. Sven Hort and Göran Therborn, "Citizenship and Welfare: Politics and Social Policies," in *The Wiley-Blackwell Companion to Political Sociology*, ed. Edwin Amenta, Kate Nash, and Alan Scott (Malden, Mass.: Wiley-Blackwell, 2012), 363.

103. Melani Cammett and Aytuğ Şaşmaz, "Social Policy in Developing Countries," in *The Oxford Handbook of Historical Institutionalism*, ed. Orfeo Fioretos, Tulia G. Falleti, and Adam Sheingate (Oxford: Oxford University Press, 2016), 245.

104. Isabela Mares and Matthew Carnes, "Social Policy in Developing Countries," *Annual Review of Political Science* 12 (2009): 99, based on Stephen Haber, "Authoritarian Government," in *The Oxford Handbook of Political Economy*, ed. Barry Weingast and Donald Wittman (Oxford: Oxford University Press, 2007), 688–711.

105. See Robert Bianchi, *Unruly Corporatism: Associational Life in Twentieth-Century Egypt* (New York: Oxford University Press, 1989).

106. Dan Slater, *Ordering Power: Contentious Politics and Authoritarian Leviathans in Southeast Asia* (Cambridge: Cambridge University Press, 2010).

CHAPTER 2. SEEING LIKE A KING: WELFARE POLICY AS STATE-BUILDING STRATEGY IN THE PAHLAVI MONARCHY

1. The epigraph to this chapter: Ernest Gellner, "The Struggle to Catch Up," *The Times Literary Supplement*, 9 December 1994, 14.

2. Touraj Atabaki, "Disgruntled Guests: Iranian Subalterns on the Margins of the Tsarist Empire," in *The State and the Subaltern: Modernization, Society and the State in Turkey and Iran*, ed. Touraj Atabaki (London: I.B. Tauris, 2007), 33.

3. Oliver Bast, "Disintegrating the 'Discourse of Disintegration': Some Reflections on the Historiography of the Late Qajar Period and Iranian Cultural

Memory," in *Iran in the 20th Century: Historiography and Political Culture,* ed. Touraj Atabaki (London: I. B. Tauris, 2009), 55–68.

4. Stephanie Cronin, *Reformers and Revolutionaries in Modern Iran: New Perspectives on the Iranian Left* (London and New York: RoutledgeCurzon, 2004); idem, *Tribal Politics in Iran: Rural Conflict and the New State, 1921–1941* (London and New York: Routledge, 2007); Farzin Vejdani, *Making History in Iran: Education, Nationalism, and Print Culture* (Stanford, Calif.: Stanford University Press, 2014).

5. Afshin Marashi, *Nationalizing Iran: Culture, Power, and the State, 1870–1940* (Seattle: University of Washington Press, 2008).

6. See the critique of "methodological statism" in Cyrus Schayegh, "'Seeing like a State': An Essay on the Historiography of Modern Iran," *International Journal of Middle East Studies* 42.1 (2010): 37–61.

7. Montesquieu, *Persian Letters,* ed. Andrew Kahn, trans. Margaret Mauldon (New York: Oxford University Press, 2008), 236.

8. Saïd Arjomand, *The Turban for the Crown: The Islamic Revolution in Iran* (New York: Oxford University Press, 1988).

9. Philip Abrams, "Notes on the Difficulty of Studying the State (1977)," *Journal of Historical Sociology* 1.1 (1988): 67.

10. The Pahlavi developmental dictatorship's grandiose vision is singled out in James Scott, *Seeing like a State: How Certain Schemes to Improve the Human Condition Have Failed* (New Haven: Yale University Press, 1998), 88–89.

11. Fernando Coronil, "Smelling like a Market," *The American Historical Review* 106.1 (2001): 127.

12. Charles Kurzman, *Democracy Denied, 1905–1915: Intellectuals and the Fate of Democracy* (Cambridge, Mass.: Harvard University Press, 2008).

13. Ervand Abrahamian, *A History of Modern Iran* (Cambridge: Cambridge University Press, 2008), 35–36; Vejdani (above, note 4), 8–13.

14. Benedict Anderson, *Under Three Flags: Anarchism and the Anti-Colonial Imagination* (London: Verso, 2005), 75–76.

15. Jamāl al-Din al-Afghānī, an Iranian born Shi'i theologian trained in India who then moved to Istanbul and masked his identity by claiming Sunni "Afghan" origin, was a key figure among late-nineteenth-century intellectual movements to indigenize Western concepts and reframe them for purposes of pan-Islamic unity and resistance to colonialism. In response to "Islam and Science," an 1883 lecture by Ernest Renan in which the French philologist claimed that Islam's medieval "Golden Age" actually rested on Persian and Greek learning—i.e., on "Aryan" civilization—al-Afghānī wrote a thoughtful response refuting Renan's claims. See Zachary Lockman, *Contending Visions of the Middle East: The History and Politics of Orientalism,* 2nd ed. (Cambridge: Cambridge University Press, 2010), 80–82.

16. Marashi (above, note 5), 15–16.

17. Calls for purification of the Persian language date to the mid-nineteenth century, as Mohammad Tavakoli-Targhi points out: "The movement . . . coincided with the movement for the simplification of Ottoman Turkish. Both were intimately tied to the struggle for constitutionalism. The language reform was not an after-effect of the constitutional revolutions in Iran and the Ottoman

Empire but a prelude to them." See "Historiography and Crafting Iranian National Identity," in *Iran in the 20th Century: Historiography and Political Culture*, ed. Touraj Atabaki (London: I. B. Tauris, 2009), 18.

18. Mohammad Ali Akbari, *Barnāmeh Rizi-ye Dowlati dar Howzeh-ye Ta'min-e Ejtemā'i-ye Irān (1285–1380)* (Tehran: Moassesseh-ye Ali-ye Ta'min-e Ejtemā'i, 2002).

19. Vanessa Martin, "Mudarris, Republicanism and the Rise to Power of Riza Khan, Sardar-i Sipah," in *The Making of Modern Iran: State and Society under Riza Shah, 1921–1941*, ed. Stephanie Cronin (London and New York: RoutledgeCurzon, 2003), 72–75.

20. While an east–west railroad would have been commercially more useful, the state reportedly constructed a north–south railroad from the Caspian Sea to the Persian Gulf, in order the better to shuttle troops between the most rebellious territories: Reza Ghods, "Iranian Nationalism and Reza Shah," *Middle Eastern Studies* 27.1 (1991): 35–45.

21. K. S. MacLachlan, "Economic Development, 1921–1979," in *The Cambridge History of Iran*, vol. 7, *From Nadir Shah to the Islamic Republic*, ed. Peter Avery, Gavin Hambly, and C. P. Melville (Cambridge: Cambridge University Press, 1991), 613.

22. This went well beyond Atatürk's dress codes, and their stringency helped to reinforce solidarity among the Shi'i clergy, who had, until then, been divided on supporting the monarchy.

23. Houchang Chehabi, "Dress Codes for Men in Turkey and Iran," in *Men of Order: Authoritarian Modernization under Atatürk and Reza Shah*, ed. Touraj Atabaki and Erik Zürcher (London: I. B. Tauris, 2004), 226–27.

24. Amin Banani, *The Modernization of Iran, 1921–1941* (Stanford, Calif.: Stanford University Press, 1961), 147.

25. Cronin, *Tribal Politics in Iran* (above, note 4).

26. Stephanie Cronin, "Popular Politics, the New State and the Birth of the Iranian Working Class: The 1929 Abadan Oil Refinery Strike," *Middle Eastern Studies* 46.5 (2010): 699–732.

27. Cyrus Schayegh, "The Development of Social Insurance in Iran: Technical-Financial Conditions and Political Rationales, 1941–1960," *Iranian Studies* 39 (2006): 539–68.

28. The Anglo-Iranian Oil Company created a series of company towns in southwestern Iran and recruited labor from around the country using contracted middlemen (often nomadic tribal elites). As a result of migration to these cities, a high degree of proletarianization occurred in places such as Abadan. One effect was high levels of cross-ethnic working-class unrest: see Kaveh Ehsani, "Social Engineering and the Contradictions of Modernization in Khuzestan's Company Towns: A Look at Abadan and Masjed-Soleyman," *International Review of Social History* 48.3 (2003): 361–99.

29. Andrew Abbott and Stanley DeViney, "The Welfare State as Transnational Event: Evidence from Sequences of Policy Adoption," *Social Science History* 16.2 (1992): 245–74.

30. The issue of Nazi links to the Pahlavi monarchy is convoluted, especially because of the parlance of Aryanism, which Iranian nationalists utilized for

their own peculiar inventions of tradition: Reza Zia-Ebrahimi, "Self-Orientalization and Dislocation: The Uses and Abuses of the 'Aryan' Discourse in Iran," *Iranian Studies* 44.4 (2011): 445–72. In 1922, U.S. State Department advisor Arthur Millspaugh was hired to salvage Iran's Finance Ministry, which was under great strain, and to introduce a series of economic reforms. The British and Soviets perceived this as United States' encroachment onto their spheres of influence and forced Millspaugh's delegation to be expelled in 1927: Nikolay A. Kozhanov, "The Pretexts and Reasons for the Allied Invasion of Iran in 1941," *Iranian Studies* 45.4 (2012): 479–97. The only remaining great power that could aid in Reza Shah's modernization drive was the German Reich.

31. Akbari (above, note 18).

32. Kozhanov (above, note 30).

33. Immanuel Wallerstein, *The Modern World-System*. Volume 1, *Capitalist Agriculture and the Origins of the European World-Economy in the Sixteenth Century* (Berkeley and Los Angeles: University of California Press, 2011), 136.

34. Fakhreddin Azimi, *The Quest for Democracy in Iran: A Century of Struggle against Authoritarian Rule* (Cambridge, Mass.: Harvard University Press, 2008), 121.

35. Abrahamian (above, note 13), 100.

36. Ibid.: 109.

37. Ibid.: 113.

38. Habib Ladjevardi, *Labor Unions and Autocracy in Iran* (Syracuse: Syracuse University Press, 1985).

39. In nationalist historiography, the Tudeh is almost always identified as a "Stalinist" or "Soviet-guided" party. This is an exaggeration by far: see Maziar Behrooz, *Rebels with a Cause: The Failure of the Left in Iran* (London and New York: I.B. Tauris, 1999); Afshin Matin-Asgari, "From Social Democracy to Social Democracy: The Twentieth-Century Odyssey of the Iranian Left," in *Reformers and Revolutionaries in Modern Iran: New Perspectives on the Iranian Left*, ed. Stephanie Cronin (London and New York: RoutledgeCurzon, 2004), 37–64. But the accusation stuck, since many of the Tudeh leaders fled to the USSR and other socialist countries in the 1950s and 1960s. Iran's new left organizations in the late 1960s such as the Fedāyān and the Mojāhedin mostly saw the Tudeh the same way as Parisian *soixante-huitards* saw the Parti Communiste Française. The Soviet Union kept tabs on Tudeh networks in Pahlavi Iran, which proved disastrous after the 1979 revolution. A Russian agent defected to the United Kingdom in 1982, along with a secret microfiche containing Tudeh membership rolls. The British government, eager to curry favor with the Khomeinists and prevent Soviet influence in postrevolutionary Iran after the invasion of Afghanistan, allegedly handed the list over to the Islamic Republic, which then arrested all Tudeh leaders and accused them of collaboration with the Soviets. Odd Arne Westad, *The Global Cold War: Third World Interventions and The Making of Our Times* (Cambridge: Cambridge University Press, 2005), 297–99.

40. Homa Katouzian, "The Strange Politics of Khalil Maleki," in *Reformers and Revolutionaries in Modern Iran: New Perspectives on the Iranian Left*,

ed. Stephanie Cronin (London and New York: RoutledgeCurzon, 2004), 165–88.

41. Mohammad Ali Akbari, *Barrasi-ye Barnāmeh Rizi-ye Dowlati dar Howzeh-ye Ta'min-e Ejtemā'i-ye Irān*, vol. 2, *1320–1357* (Tehran: Moassesseh-ye Ali-ye Ta'min-e Ejtemā'i, 2004); Schayegh (above, note 27).

42. Sami Zubaida usefully suggests interpreting political Islam not as a unitary civilizational blueprint for social and political action but as "an idiom in terms of which many social groups and political interests express their aspirations and frustrations, and in which ruling elites claim legitimacy." Sami Zubaida, *Beyond Islam: A New Understanding of the Middle East* (London: I. B. Tauris, 2011), 106.

43. Farhad Kazemi, "Fedā'īān-e Eslām," *Encyclopedia Iranica*, vol. 9, fasc. 5 (1999), pp. 470–74, (updated in 2012; online at: http://www.iranicaonline. org/articles/fedaian-e-esla). The assassination of seminary student–turned–lay judge Ahmad Kasravi, one of Iran's premier modern historians, by the Fedāyin-e Islām in 1946 was a shock to elites who identified with Kasravi's "integrative nationalism" and its castigation of Islamic "superstition." Ervand Abrahamian, "Kasravi: The Integrative Nationalist of Iran," *Middle Eastern Studies* 9.3 (1973): 271–95. Kasravi was an observer of the 1905 constitutional revolution himself and contributed a landmark history of the events, although he colored the revolution as chaotic and presented the coming of Reza Shah as a necessary antidote. Ahmad Kasravi, *History of the Iranian Constitutional Revolution*, trans. Evan Siegel (Costa Mesa, Calif.: Mazda Publishers, 2006).

44. Abrahamian (above, note 13), 119.

45. Mark Gasiorowski and Malcolm Byrne, eds., *Mohammad Mosaddeq and the 1953 Coup in Iran* (Syracuse: Syracuse University Press, 2004); Ervand Abrahamian, *The Coup: 1953, The CIA, and The Roots of Modern U.S.-Iranian Relations* (New Press, 2013); Ali Rahnema, *Behind the 1953 Coup in Iran: Thugs, Turncoats, Soldiers, and Spooks* (Cambridge: Cambridge University Press, 2015).

46. Akbari (above, note 41); Schayegh (above, note 27).

47. Interview at SSO head office, Tehran, March 2010.

48. Farhad Daftary, "Development Planning in Iran: A Historical Survey," *Iranian Studies* 6.4 (1973): 176–228.

49. Frances Bostock and Geoffrey Jones, *Planning and Power in Iran: Ebtehaj and Economic Development under the Shah* (London: Frank Cass and Co., Ltd, 1989).

50. The United States–based Ford Foundation, which placed a large emphasis on international development as an antidote to Third World communism, began an initiative after the ouster of Mossadeq for a pilot program in land reform. An agricultural-credit bank was set up for several farm-cooperative projects, along with village representatives trained with the latest technical knowledge. To the dismay of Foundation executives, who believed that rural development was the salvation for the Third World, the Iranian government remained uninterested in expanding the programs. While Foundation members attributed this uninterest to the backwardness of Iranian elites, the actual reason was more likely that the U.S. State Department provided far vaster sums of money to the Pahlavi state during the 1950s for the purposes of regional and

domestic "security and stability." Military spending and its symbolic power outweighed small-scale economic projects that could upset landed elites. See Victor Nemchenok, "'That So Fair a Thing Should Be So Frail': The Ford Foundation and the Failure of Rural Development in Iran, 1953–1964," *Middle East Journal* 63.2 (2009): 261–84.

51. Ali Ahmadi and Chris Harman, "What's Happening in Iran?" *Socialist Review* 6 (1978): 3–6.

52. Schayegh (above, note 27).

53. Ladjevardi (above, note 38), 228–29.

54. Schayegh (above, note 27).

55. Afshin Matin-Asgari, *Iranian Student Opposition to the Shah* (Costa Mesa, Calif.: Mazda Publishers, 2002), 40.

56. Ibid.: 44.

57. Nikki Keddie, "Ideology, Society and the State in Post-Colonial Muslim Societies," in *State and Ideology in the Middle East and Pakistan,* ed. Fred Halliday and Hamza Alavi (New York: Macmillan, 1988), 14. Also see Abbas Milani, *The Shah* (New York: Palgrave MacMillan, 2011), 206.

58. Henry Kissinger. "The White Revolutionary: Reflections on Bismarck," *Daedalus* 97.3 (1968): 889.

59. Lothar Gall, *Bismarck, the White Revolutionary* (Boston: Allen & Unwin, 1986), viii.

60. Jonathan Steinberg, *Bismarck: A Life* (Oxford: Oxford University Press, 2011), 247.

61. Ali M. Ansari, "The Myth of the White Revolution: Mohammad Reza Shah, 'Modernization' and the Consolidation of Power," *Middle Eastern Studies* 37.3 (2001): 5.

62. Hossein Bashiriyeh, *The State and Revolution in Iran, 1962–1982* (New York: St. Martin's Press, 1984), 12.

63. Victor Nemchenok, "In Search of Stability amid Chaos: U.S. Policy toward Iran, 1961–63," *Cold War History* 10.3 (2010): 353.

64. Fakhreddin Azimi, "Arsanjānī, Ḥasan" *Encyclopedia Iranica,* vol. 2, fasc. 5, (London: Routledge & Kegan Paul, 1986), 547. [Updated in 2011; online at: http://www.iranicaonline.org/articles/arsanjani-hasan-journalist-and-politician-1922–69.] (accessed 13 March 2015).

65. Abrahamian (above, note 13), 131–32.

66. For example, in the northern Iranian province of Azerbaijan, 290 large absentee landowners fell under the 1962 land-reform law, mostly consisting of merchant and government elites. Of these 290, 238 retained one village each, and the remainder sold off their holdings. In provinces to the south, where land revenues were more important sources of income, resistance by landlords was higher. Bashiriyeh (above, note 62), 22–23. Because of the paucity of provincial history for twentieth-century Iran, there is still a debate over who benefited from the land reforms. But see Hossein Mahdavy for a recollection on a village in Qazvin: "Tahavolāt-e si sāleh-ye yek deh dar dasht-e Ghazvin," *Ketāb-e Āgāh* (1982): 50–74.

67. Grace Goodell, *The Elementary Structures of Political Life: Rural Development in Pahlavi Iran* (New York: Oxford University Press, 1986).

68. Kaveh Ehsani, "Rural Society and Agricultural Development in Post-Revolution Iran: The First Two Decades," *Critique: Critical Middle Eastern Studies* 15.1 (2006): 84; also see Eric Hooglund, *Land and Revolution in Iran, 1960–1980* (Austin: University of Texas Press, 1982); Bernard Hourcade, "The Land Question and Islamic Revolution in Iran," *Comparative Studies of South Asia, Africa and the Middle East* 13.1–2 (1993): 134–47; Mostafa Azkia, "Rural Society and Revolution in Iran," in *Twenty Years of Islamic Revolution: Political and Social Transition in Iran since 1979*, ed. Eric Hooglund (Syracuse: Syracuse University Press, 2002), 96–119. For a perspective from the landlords, see Mohammad Gholi Majd, "Small Landowners and Land Distribution in Iran, 1962–71," *International Journal of Middle East Studies* 32.1 (2000): 123–53, who somewhat dramatically compares Iran's land redistribution in the 1960s to the Soviet attack on the kulaks in the 1930s. The law was extended to religious-endowment holdings in 1963, which provoked the ire of some of the high-ranking clergy.

69. Ali Mirsepassi, *Intellectual Discourse and the Politics of Modernization: Negotiating Modernity in Iran* (Cambridge: Cambridge University Press, 2000), 78. For a remarkable study on the role of the Pahlavi state in cultivating the "politics of authenticity" in the intellectual culture of prerevolutionary Iran, see Ali Mirsepassi, *Transnationalism in Iranian Political Thought: The Life and Thought of Ahmad Fardid* (Cambridge: Cambridge University Press, 2017).

70. Ervand Abrahamian, *Iran between Two Revolutions* (Princeton: Princeton University Press, 1982), 425.

71. Ruhollah Khomeini, *Sahifeh-ye Imām*, vol. 1 (Tehran: Moassesseh-ye Tanzim va Nashr-e Āsār-e Imām Khomeini, 1999), 115.

72. Lewis Namier put it this way with regard to the salience of Protestantism in the English revolution, albeit a bit bluntly: "religion is a sixteenth-century word for nationalism." Quoted in Anthony Marx, *Faith in Nation: Exclusionary Origins of Nationalism* (New York: Oxford University Press, 2003), 25.

73. MacLachlan (above, note 21), 616.

74. Bashiriyeh (above, note 62), 40. For an example, see Mohamad Tavakoli-Targhi, "Rahim Mottaghi Irvani and the Melli Industrial Group," *Iran Nameh* 30.1 (2015): 118–60.

75. Giovanni Cornia and Vladimir Popov, eds., *Transition and Institutions: The Experience of Gradual and Late Reformers*, Studies in Development Economics (Oxford and New York: Oxford University Press, 2001).

76. Ansari (above, note 61), 13.

77. Ibid., 15.

78. Michael Herb, *All in the Family: Absolutism, Revolution, and Democracy in the Middle Eastern Monarchies* (Albany: SUNY Press, 1999).

79. Bashiriyeh (above, note 62), 43.

80. Such corporatism did not "buy off" workers so much as provide them with new associational arenas where labor politics could continue. See Maral Jefroudi, "Revisiting 'the Long Night' of Iranian Workers: Labor Activism in the Iranian Oil Industry in the 1960s," *International Labor and Working-Class History* 84 (2013): 176–94.

81. Bashiriyeh (above, note 62), 42.

82. World Health Organization, *Country Studies on Health and Welfare Systems: Experiences in Indonesia, Islamic Republic of Iran, and Sri Lanka,* Health and Welfare Systems Development, Technical Report Series (Kobe: World Health Organization Center for Health Development, 2003).

83. The migrant son from the village was a trope in Dāriush Mehrjui's 1971 film *Mr. Gullible (Āghā-ye Hālu),* which drew from Italian neorealism to portray the rapid social changes occurring in Iran and their sometimes unpleasant results.

84. Annabelle Sreberny-Mohammadi and Ali Mohammadi, *Small Media, Big Revolution: Communication, Culture and the Iranian Revolution* (Minneapolis: University of Minnesota Press, 1994), 85.

85. Abrahamian (above, note 13), 134.

86. Carrie Wickham, *Mobilizing Islam: Religion, Activism, and Political Change in Egypt* (New York: Columbia University Press, 2002), 25–26.

87. David Menashri, *Education and the Making of Modern Iran* (Ithaca: Cornell University Press, 1992), 257–67.

88. Mehrzad Boroujerdi, *Iranian Intellectuals and the West: The Tormented Triumph of Nativism* (Syracuse: Syracuse University Press, 1996), 85; Ervand Abrahamian, *The Iranian Mojahedin* (New Haven: Yale University Press, 1989).

89. Matin-Asgari (above, note 55).

90. Asghar Rastegar, "Health Policy and Medical Education," in *Iran after the Revolution: Crisis of an Islamic State,* ed. Saeed Rahnema and Sohrab Behdad (London and New York: I. B. Tauris, 1995), 219.

91. Ibid.

92. Farian Sabahi, "The Literacy Corps in Pahlavi Iran (1963–1979): Political, Social and Literary Implications," *Cahiers d'Études sur la Méditerranée Orientale et le Monde Turco-Iranien* 31 (2001): 191–220.

93. Hossein Ronaghy and Steven Solter, "The Auxiliary Health Worker in Iran," *The Lancet* 302.7826 (August 1973): 428.

94. Goodell (above, note 67).

95. See the ethnographic observations of Pahlavi officials in Mary Hegland, *Days of Revolution: Political Unrest in an Iranian Village* (Stanford, Calif.: Stanford University Press, 2013).

96. Asghar Schirazi, *Islamic Development Policy: The Agrarian Question in Iran* (Boulder: Lynne Rienner Publishers, 1993), 21–22.

97. Hooglund, *Land and Revolution* (above, note 68), 135.

98. Sabahi (above, note 92).

99. In Zohreh Sullivan, "Eluding the Feminist, Overthrowing the Modern? Transformations in Twentieth-Century Iran," In *Remaking Women: Feminism and Modernity in the Middle East,* ed. Lila Abu-Lughod (Princeton, Princeton University Press, 1998), 227.

100. Ahmad Ashraf and Ali Banuazizi, "The State, Classes and Modes of Mobilization in the Iranian Revolution," *State, Culture, and Society* 1.3 (1985): 3–40.

101. Quoted in Immanuel Wallerstein, *The Modern World-System,* vol. 3, *The Second Era of Great Expansion of the Capitalist World-Economy,*

1730s–1840s (Berkeley and Los Angeles: University of California Press, 2011), 44.

102. Abrahamian (above, note 70), 496–97.

103. Ibid.: 532–33.

104. Ibid.: 526.

105. Frederick Cooper, *Colonialism in Question: Theory, Knowledge, History* (Berkeley and Los Angeles: University of California Press, 2005), 119.

106. Georgi Derluguian and Timothy Earle, "Strong Chieftaincies out of Weak States, or Elemental Power Unbound," *Comparative Social Research* 27 (2010): 51–76.

107. This can be seen in Abrahamian's own 1982 book *Iran between Two Revolutions,* which began as a study of the Tudeh Party long before the revolution. He predicted that after the charismatic effervescence of Khomeini wore off in postrevolutionary Iran, the working and middle classes would be able to take back power away from the clergy: Ervand Abrahamian, *Iran between Two Revolutions* (Princeton: Princeton University Press, 1982), 537.

108. Tim McDaniel, *Autocracy, Modernization, and Revolution in Russia and Iran* (Princeton: Princeton: Princeton University Press, 1991), 9.

109. See Charles Tilly's review of McDaniel in *American Political Science Review* 86.4 (1992): 1084–85.

110. E.g., Fernando Cardoso and Enzo Faletto, *Dependency and Development in Latin America* (Berkeley and Los Angeles: University of California Press, 1979).

111. Ahmad Ashraf, "Historical Obstacles to the Development of a Bourgeoisie in Iran," *Iranian Studies* 2.2 (1969): 54–79; Mohammad Hashem Pesaran, "The System of Dependent Capitalism in Pre- and Post-Revolutionary Iran," *International Journal of Middle East Studies* 14.4 (1982): 501–22.

112. Ibid., 511; Ashraf (above, note 111), 332.

113. See the powerful critique of the historiography of autonomous bourgeoisies as drivers of Western modernization in Vivek Chibber, *Postcolonial Theory and the Specter of Capital* (London: Verso, 2014), chaps. 2 and 3.

114. Ahmad Ashraf, "Bazaar-Mosque Alliance: The Social Basis of Revolts and Revolutions," *International Journal of Politics, Culture, and Society* 1.4 (1988): 538–67.

115. An alternative use of "dependent development" for explaining the Iranian revolution came from John Foran, who combined world-systems analysis with a *longue-durée* reading of Iranian history for a remarkable revisionist study of the country from the sixteenth century to the 1979 revolution, *Fragile Resistance: Social Transformation in Iran from 1500 to the Revolution* (Boulder: Westview Press, 1993). Yet Foran's use of "dependent development" in his studies of revolutions is problematically vague, since he broadens the concept to mean the existence of rapid development alongside "a changing social structure that creates social and economic grievances among diverse sectors of the population," which he boils down to "growth within limits": *Taking Power: On the Origins of Third World Revolutions* (Cambridge: Cambridge University Press, 2005), 19. Dependency theory was originally an explanation of economic-surplus extraction from periphery to metropole and the so-called underdeveloped

social structures that were resultantly produced in peripheral countries. Yet all states in the capitalist-world economy experience growth within limits, so the dependent/independent notion is not entirely useful as an analytic device without more precise distinctions.

116. Maurice Zeitlin and Richard Earl Radcliff, *Landlords & Capitalists: The Dominant Class of Chile.* (Princeton: Princeton University Press, 1988), 148.

117. Arang Keshavarzian, *Bazaar and State in Iran: The Politics of the Tehran Marketplace* (Cambridge: Cambridge University Press, 2007), 52.

118. Ashraf and Banuazizi (above, note 100); Val Moghadam, "Populist Revolution and the Islamic State in Iran," in *Revolution in the World-System,* ed. Terry Boswell (New York: Greenwood Press, 1989), 147–63.

119. Ervand Abrahamian, *Khomeinism: Essays on the Islamic Republic* (Berkeley and Los Angeles: University of California Press, 1993); also see the discussion of Marxist interpretations between 1979 and 1981 in Afshin Matin-Asgari, "Marxism, Historiography and Historical Consciousness in Modern Iran: A Preliminary Study," in *Iran in the 20th Century: Historiography and Political Culture,* ed. Touraj Atabaki (London: I.B. Tauris, 2009), 199–231.

120. Charles Kurzman, *The Unthinkable Revolution in Iran* (Cambridge, Mass.: Harvard University Press, 2004).

121. Stephen Jay Gould, *Full House: The Spread of Excellence from Plato to Darwin* (New York: Three Rivers Press, 1997), 24.

122. Steve Pincus, *1688: The First Modern Revolution* (New Haven: Yale University Press, 2009), 33.

123. Hooglund, *Land and Revolution* (above, note 68); Hegland (above, note 95).

124. Keshavarzian (above, note 117).

125. For an overview of how much changed in Khomeini's thought over his lifetime, see Behrooz Ghamari-Tabrizi, "The Divine, the People, and the Faqih: On Khomeini's Theory of Sovereignty," in *A Critical Introduction to Khomeini,* ed. Arshin Adib-Moghaddam (Cambridge: Cambridge University Press, 2014), 211—38.

126. Pincus (above, note 122), 40.

CHAPTER 3. CREATING A MARTYRS' WELFARE STATE: 1979, WAR, AND THE SURVIVAL OF THE ISLAMIC REPUBLIC

1. Shaul Bakhash, *The Reign of the Ayatollahs: Iran and the Islamic Revolution* (New York: Basic Books, 1986), 242.

2. The following are a few examples: "[The Islamic Republic has not] developed a comprehensive welfare program. To the contrary, it has relied on traditional Muslim institutions of philanthropy": Manoucher Parvin and Mostafa Vaziri, "Islamic Man and Society in the Islamic Republic of Iran," in *Iran: Political Culture in the Islamic Republic,* ed. Samih Farsoun and Mehrdad Mashayekhi (London: Routledge, 1992), 88. "In addition to massive propaganda and ideological indoctrination, the clerics maintain control over their followers through economic means and the provision of social welfare": Haideh

Moghissi and Saeed Rahnema, "The Working Class and the Islamic State in Iran," *Socialist Register* 37 (2001): 209. "Reliance on the export of crude oil has entrenched a rent-seeking culture among Iranians, who have come to rely on the government to bring them welfare and development": Alidad Mafinezam and Aria Mehrabi, *Iran and Its Place among Nations* (Westport, Conn.: Praeger, 2008), 89.

3. See, for instance, Mary Hegland, *Days of Revolution: Political Unrest in an Iranian Village* (Stanford, Calif.: Stanford University Press, 2013), 227–60.

4. They were Morteza Motahhari (d. 1979), Hassan Lāhouti-Eshkevari (d. 1981), Sādegh Ghotbzādeh (d. 1982), and Abolhassan Bani-Sadr (fled in 1981). The other two in the pictures were Ahmad Khomeini (d. 1995) and Sādegh Tabātabāi (lives in Tehran).

5. On how well the competition was managed between internal PRI *grupos,* see Jonathan Schlefer, *Palace Politics: How the Ruling Party Brought Crisis to Mexico* (Austin: University of Texas Press, 2009); Miguel Ángel Centeno, *Democracy within Reason: Technocratic Revolution in Mexico,* 2nd ed. (University Park, Pa.: Pennsylvania State University Press, 1997). For the manner in which personalized, informal networks are sturdily housed in a Leninist edifice with Chinese characteristics, see Andrew Nathan and Kellee Tsai, "Factionalism: A New Institutionalist Restatement," *China Journal* 34 (1995): 157–92; Lowell Dittmer and Yu-Shan Wu, "The Modernization of Factionalism in Chinese Politics," *World Politics* 47, no. 4 (1995): 467–94; Jing Huang, *Factionalism in Chinese Communist Politics* (New York: Cambridge University Press, 2000).

6. Charles Kurzman, *The Unthinkable Revolution in Iran* (Cambridge, Mass.: Harvard University Press, 2004), 121. Kurzman also gives a figure of 10 percent of the entire country for anti-shah demonstrations on 10–11 December 1978.

7. Interview, Ahvaz, November 2009. Dowlatābādi described this mobilization's dark side of revenge and recrimination as the "mad juggernaut of the revolution": Mahmoud Dowlatābādi, *The Colonel* (London: Haus Publishing, 2011), 143. Kurzman puts it more theoretically: "confusion is the recognition of deinstitutionalization, that is, the breach of routine social patterns": Kurzman, *Unthinkable Revolution* (above, note 6), 9.

8. Art Stinchcombe (below, note 9) coined the term in describing Bendix's study of postwar East Germany, but it does not appear as such in that text. See Reinhard Bendix, *Work and Authority in Industry: Managerial Ideologies in the Course of Industrialization* (New York: Wiley, 1956).

9. Arthur Stinchcombe, "Ending Revolutions and Building New Governments," *Annual Review of Political Science* 2.1 (1999): 49–73. Given that processes of mobilizing assent from below in extrainstitutional form still exist in Iran, it can be argued that the revolutionary process has never ended. How much analytical value this view provides is discussed in chapters 5 and 6.

10. Jeff Goodwin, *No Other Way Out: States and Revolutionary Movements, 1945–1991* (Cambridge: Cambridge University Press, 2001), 12.

11. See Asef Bayat, *Street Politics: Poor People's Movements in Iran* (New York: Columbia University Press, 1997), 51–52. Farhad Khosrokhavar, present during the revolution, noted for Hamadan, "the primary reasons for the birth

of the Hamadan Committee must be sought in the inability of the police of the old regime to assure the security of the city": Farhad Khosrokhavar, "The Committee in the Iranian Revolution: The Case of a Mid-Sized City: Hamadan," *Peuples Méditerranéens* 9 (1979): 85–100.

12. Dilip Hiro, *Iran under the Ayatollahs* (London: Routledge & Kegan Paul, 1987), 91.

13. The solidarity between defected armed forces and protestors seen in Egypt's 2011 revolution, for example, with elderly women pouring tea for citizen and soldier alike sitting together on tanks, can be neatly replicated in photos from the final week of the 1979 revolution. See Kaveh Golestan's street photography of such moments in Masoud Benhoud and Hojat Sepahvand, *Kaveh Golestan: Recording the Truth in Iran, 1950–2003*, ed. Malu Halasa (Ostfildern: Hatje Cantz, 2008).

14. Interview, Tehran, May 2013.

15. Ervand Abrahamian, "The Crowd in the Iranian Revolution," *Radical History Review* 105 (2009): 31.

16. Interview, Tehran, June 2006. As Abrahamian noted, "leftist groups, particularly the Feda'iyan, convinced that Bazargan was merely another Kerensky and that the 'bourgeois revolution' would inevitably be followed by a socialist one, demanded workers', peasants' and soldiers' councils, and organized unemployment demonstrations, women's rallies, factory sit-ins, and guerrilla-training sessions." Ervand Abrahamian, *The Iranian Mojahedin* (New Haven: Yale University Press, 1989), 51.

17. James Jasper, *The Art of Moral Protest: Culture, Biography, and Creativity in Social Movements* (Chicago: University of Chicago Press, 1997), 362. Cited in Kurzman, *Unthinkable Revolution* (above, note 6), 142.

18. The same headline in *Ettelāʿāt* that day featured the largest type ever used in the newspaper's 53-year history. Nasserddin Parvin, "*Eṭṭelāʿāt*," *Encyclopaedia Iranica*, vol. 9, fasc. 1, pp. 58–62, 1998, updated in 2012; online at: http://www.iranicaonline.org/articles/ettelaat. (accessed 14 April 2015).

19. Peyman Vahabzadeh, *A Guerilla Odyssey: Modernization, Secularism, Democracy, and the Fadai Period of National Liberation in Iran, 1971–1979* (Syracuse: Syracuse University Press, 2010), 68. The leftist opposition, most of which formed in the mold of the 1968-era New Left, easily found reasons to divide among themselves. The Fedāyān minority faction, for instance, reportedly left the group in June 1980 over a typographical error in the organization's magazine, *Kār*: ibid., 70–71.

20. On the Revolutionary Council, see the interview with Ezzatollāh Sahābi in Bahman Ahmadi-Amui, *Eqtesād-e Siāsi-ye Jomhuri-ye Eslāmi* (Tehran: Gam-e Now Press, 2003), 9–58. On the Islamic Republic Party, see the interview series on its origins in *Etemād*, 15 January–3 March 2014. On the 1979 constitution's alternative drafts and sundry inspirations, see Behrooz Ghamari-Tabrizi, *Islam and Dissent in Postrevolutionary Iran* (London: I.B. Tauris, 2008).

21. Asghar Schirazi, *The Constitution of Iran: Politics and the State in the Islamic Republic* (London: I.B. Tauris, 1997), 152.

22. Mohsen Nurbakhsh complained that, even though he shared the same economic views as his colleagues in the Central Bank in the early 1980s, members

of the Islamic association were able to remove him as bank chief and choose his successor: Ahmadi-Amui, *Eqtesād-e Siāsi* (above, note 20), 85–86.

23. Luckily for Khomeinists, the most forceful separatist threat, in Kurdistan, was diluted by internal divisions, just as in much of the left as a whole. Fred Halliday, well ensconced in Iran's leftist milieu at the time, argues that most of the Islamist positions on foreign and economic policy were borrowed from the left. This included the relish for petty factionalism and a hearty reliance on conspiracy theory. Within the left, "with dire consequences for the internal politics of Iran after February 1979, there was an almost universal embrace of a spirit of sectarianism that cast all who dissented from it, notably independent democratic and socialist trends, as somehow linked to, or dependent on, imperialism": Fred Halliday, "The Iranian Left in International Perspective," in *Reformers and Revolutionaries in Modern Iran: New Perspectives on the Iranian Left*, ed. Stephanie Cronin (London and New York: RoutledgeCurzon, 2004), 31.

24. Eugen Weber, *Peasants into Frenchmen: The Modernization of Rural France, 1870–1914* (Stanford, Calif.: Stanford University Press, 1976), 96.

25. Kaveh Ehsani, "The Urban Provincial Periphery in Iran: Revolution and War in Ramhormoz," in *Contemporary Iran: Economy, Society, Politics*, ed. Ali Gheissari (Oxford: Oxford University Press, 2009), 39.

26. "Goftegui-ye montasher nashodeh az shahid Bāhonar darbāreh-ye enghelāb-e farhangi: Nezām-e dāneshgāhi motnāseb bā jomhuri-ye eslāmi nabud": *Tarikh-e Irani* Web site, 13 October 2012; online at https://goo.gl/DI3hOj (accessed 12 June 2015).

27. Bakhash, *Reign of the Ayatollahs* (above, note 1), 162–89.

28. Jeffrey Winters, *Oligarchy* (Cambridge: Cambridge University Press, 2011), 16–17; On the effectiveness of socially disruptive power, see Frances Fox Piven and Richard Cloward, *Poor People's Movements: Why They Succeed, How They Fail* (New York: Vintage, 1978); also see Randall Collins, "Social Movements and the Focus of Emotional Attention," in *Passionate Politics: Emotions and Social Movements*, ed. Jeff Goodwin, James Jasper, and Francesca Polletta (Chicago: University of Chicago Press, 2001), 27–44.

29. Amir Mehryar, "Shi'ite Teachings, Pragmatism and Fertility Change in Iran," in *Islam, the State and Population*, ed. Gavin Jones and Mehtab Karim (London: Hurst, 2005), 138–40.

30. Asef Bayat, "Tehran: Paradox City," *New Left Review* 2.66 (2010): 106.

31. Cited in Ghamari-Tabrizi, *Islam and Dissent* (above, note 20), 119. For a sympathetic treatment of al-Sadr's work, see Ahmed El-Ashker and Rodney Wilson, *Islamic Economics: A Short History* (Leiden: Brill, 2006). On Bani-Sadr, see Hamid Dabashi, *Theology of Discontent: The Ideological Foundations of the Islamic Revolution in Iran* (New York: New York University Press, 1993), 367–408; Ghamari-Tabrizi, *Islam and Dissent* (above, note 20), 106–8. Dabashi's reading of Bani-Sadr's political theory posits an authoritarian tone for the book, as compared with Ghamari-Tabrizi's interpretation of a religiously inspired Francophone anarchism. For rebukes, see Mehrdad Valibeigi, "Islamic Economics and Economic Policy Formation in Post-Revolutionary Iran: A Cri-

tique," *Journal of Economic Issues* 27.3 (1993): 793–812; Sohrab Behdad, "Islam, Revivalism, and Public Policy," in *Islam and the Everyday World: Public Policy Dilemmas,* ed. Sohrab Behdad and Farhad Nomani (London: Routledge, 2006), 1–37. Another work discussed in the post-1979 era was the pseudonymous book by Islamist left intellectual Habibollah Peymān; see Habibollah Paydār, *Bardāsht-hāi Darbāreh-ye Mālekiyyat, Sarmāyeh va Kār Az Didgāh-e Eslām* (Tehran: Daftar-e Nashr-e Eslāmi, 1979).

32. Interview, Tehran, August 2009. The story told to me may be apocryphal, but it jibes with Central Bank debates as recounted by Mohsen Nurbakhsh in Ahmadi-Amui, *Eqtesād-e Siāsi* (above, note 20), 59–140. The protagonist, Behzād Nabavi, is a prime example in Iran of the ideological long march of the radical Islamist left toward social-democratic liberalism. Jailed under the shah for guerilla activities, he led the Mojāhedin of the Islamic Revolution (a breakaway group from the splintered Mojāhedin-e Khalq), was present during the U.S. Embassy takeover in 1979 at age 38, headed the Economic Mobilization Force when Ali Rajāi was prime minister (1981), served as minister of heavy industry under Mir-Hossein Mousavi's government (1985–89), played a key role in the left faction's self-critical period in the postwar wilderness while Hashemi-Rafsanjani was president (1989–97), and was elected a member of parliament in the reformist-dominated sixth parliament (2000–2004). At age 68, he was arrested after the 2009 presidential election and prosecuted in a show trial for participating in a so-called velvet revolution.

33. Hamid Enayat, *Modern Islamic Political Thought* (London: I. B. Tauris, 2005), 14.

34. Sami Zubaida, *Beyond Islam: A New Understanding of the Middle East* (London: I. B. Tauris, 2011), 73. Also see Charles Tripp, *Islam and the Moral Economy: The Challenge of Capitalism* (Cambridge: Cambridge University Press, 2006).

35. Ghamari-Tabrizi, *Islam and Dissent* (above, note 20), 55–56.

36. On these preassembly drafts, where Khomeini's position toward the role of the supreme jurist was arguably one of strategic ambiguity, see Siavush Randjbar-Daemi, "Building the Islamic State: The Draft Constitution of 1979 Reconsidered," *Iranian Studies* 46.4 (2013): 641–63.

37. *The Constitution of the Islamic Republic of Iran;* translated version available from the Foundation for Iranian Studies: http://fis-iran.org/en/resources/legaldoc/constitutionislamic (accessed 22 April 2015). As Ervand Abrahamian noted for this section of the constitution, "these clauses seem to have escaped the notice of Western journalists who claim that the Iranian Revolution was carried out in the name of rejecting the material things of this world": Ervand Abrahamian, "Khomeini: Fundamentalist or Populist?" *New Left Review* 1.186 (1991): 116–17.

38. *Surat-e Mashruh-ye Mozākerāt-e Majles-e Barrasi-ye Nahā'i-ye Qānun-e Asāsi-ye Jomhuri-ye Eslāmi-ye Irān,* vol. 1 (Tehran: Edārah-ye Kol-e Umur-e Farhangi va Ravābet-e Omumi-ye Majles-e Showrā-ye Eslāmi, 1985), 747–48.

39. According to Ezzatollāh Sahābi, Beheshti told his comrades, perhaps naively, that the wealth distribution in the country should be no more than a ratio of 1:3 between lowest and highest. He had to be informed that even in late

1970s China, income inequality stood at a 1:6 ratio. Ahmadi-Amui, *Eqtesād-e Siāsi* (above, note 20), 21–22.

40. *Surat* (above, note 38), vol. 3, 1447–70, 1474–92. The Montazeri-Beheshti exchange is on p. 1453.

41. Ibid., 1477.

42. Ibid., 1480.

43. Martin Wright and Nick Danziger, *Iran: The Khomeini Revolution* (London: Longman, 1989), 26.

44. For a comprehensive list of major and minor players on the left, see Maziar Behrooz, *Rebels with a Cause: The Failure of the Left in Iran* (London and New York: I. B. Tauris, 1999).

45. See the interview with Mohammad Hāshemi in *Tarikh-e Irani*, 21 November 2011: http://tarikhirani.ir/fa/files/38/bodyView/379 (accessed June 2015).

46. The embassy hostage crisis, spurred by Carter's admittance of the shah into the United States for cancer treatment, was one more example of the bottom-up mobilizational power of the revolution forcing the factions to position themselves vis-à-vis already-existing "facts on the ground." Though without foreknowledge, Khomeini supported the takeover by students who claimed to "follow the Imam's line," as did the Mojāhedin-e Khalq, whereas Bāzargān feared the international response. The newly negotiated Iranian constitution, which enshrined clerical oversight into the governing structure, was quickly submitted to a referendum in this environment by Khomeini's allies. As Abrahamian reasoned, although for the world the hostage affair was an international conflagration, for Iran it was therefore "predominantly an internal struggle over the constitution": Ervand Abrahamian, *A History of Modern Iran* (Cambridge: Cambridge University Press, 2008), 168.

47. Whereas many of the small leftist organizations possessed little of what could be called a mass base, the Mojāhedin-e Khalq were arguably the main competitor to Khomeini's supporters. During my fieldwork, I occasionally met young middle-class individuals who were related by kin to Tudeh or Fedāyān militants of the previous generation. Children or relatives of former Mojāhedin supporters, however, came from lower socioeconomic classes and stretched far beyond Tehran. The relative strength of the Mojāhedin as compared with other forces in those years partly explains why the state's response was particularly brutal—the number of political executions of suspected Mojāhedin members dwarfed all others in the 1980s. The Mojāhedin, however, thoroughly destroyed their own reputation inside Iran by moving to neighboring Iraq and fighting alongside the Ba'athists during the war. Their syncretism of Marxism and Shariati-inspired liberation theology rapidly morphed into a Stalinist cult of personality. See Ervand Abrahamian, *Tortured Confessions: Prisons and Public Recantations in Modern Iran* (Berkeley and Los Angeles: University of California Press, 1999).

48. Odd Arne Westad, *The Global Cold War: Third World Interventions and the Making of Our Times* (Cambridge: Cambridge University Press, 2005), 297–99.

49. Abolhassan Bani-Sadr, *Khiānat beh Omid* (Paris: n.p., 1982), 103.

50. Khomeini shared this distrust of political parties not only with many twentieth-century Iranian intellectuals, but also with Sunni revivalists such as Hasan al-Banna, who feared the divisiveness of partyism (*hizbiyya*). See Carrie Wickham, *The Muslim Brotherhood: Evolution of an Islamist Movement* (Princeton: Princeton University Press, 2013), 42, 50.

51. *Etemād*, 15 January 2014.

52. Bahman Baktiari, *Parliamentary Politics in Revolutionary Iran: The Institutionalization of Factional Politics* (Gainesville: University Press of Florida, 1996), 68–69.

53. *Etemād*, 29 January 2014.

54. Mehdi Moslem, *Factional Politics in Post-Khomeini Iran* (Syracuse: Syracuse University Press, 2002), 61. The tract was recently reprinted as Hezb-e Jomhuri-ye Eslāmi, *Mavāze'-e Mā* [Our Viewpoints] (Tehran: Islamic Republic Publishing, 2009). See the history of the Islamic Republic Party congress at http://www.beheshti.org/?p=2699 (accessed 15 January 2014).

55. One of the great counterfactuals of postrevolutionary Iran is if Beheshti had survived the cataclysms of internecine terror beyond 1981. Some saw Beheshti as equivalent to the position of Bukharin in the USSR. Had he survived into the 1990s, one wistful female university student told me in June 2008, "then reformist politics would have won." Given his emphasis on absolute organizational power, however, he might have ended up a Little Stalin instead.

56. As the Tehran political scientist Hossein Bashiriyeh categorized it, with the benefit of hindsight, "in the 1980s two parties emerged: the Party of Tradition and the Party of Khomeinists; the former supported non-intervention in economic affairs and a traditionalist jurisprudence; the latter advocated economic intervention and redistribution, as well as a dynamic jurisprudence—but this division was contained as a result of Khomeini's arbitration.": "Counterrevolution and Revolt in Iran: An Interview with Iranian Political Scientist Hossein Bashiriyeh," *Constellations* 17.1 (2010): 63.

57. Ahmadi-Amui, *Eqtesād-e Siāsi* (above, note 20), 32. See the same point made a bit more emphatically by the economist Jamshid Pazhuyān in *Donyā-ye Eqtesād*, 9 August 2012.

58. Hossein Razavi and Firouz Vakil, *The Political Environment of Economic Planning in Iran, 1971–1983: From Monarchy to Islamic Republic* (Boulder: Westview Press, 1984), 115.

59. Quoted in Foreign Broadcast Information Service Daily Report, South Asia, FBIS-SAS-85-024, from 5 February 1985, p. 12.

60. Georgi Derluguian, *Bourdieu's Secret Admirer in the Caucasus: A World-System Biography* (Chicago: University of Chicago Press, 2005), 294.

61. Ahmadi-Amui, *Eqtesād-e Siāsi* (above, note 20), 62.

62. David McLellan, *Marxism after Marx*, 4th ed. (London: Palgrave Macmillan, 2007), 126.

63. Nowshirvani and Clawson emphasize the bottom-up aspects of economic policy: "Local revolutionary organizations, more responsive to local demands and in many instances penetrated by different political factions, were

inclined to seize property even without a legal basis. The simplest way for the government to reassert its authority was to sanction these takeovers and control them through the power of the purse. Furthermore, the desire to prevent the establishment of a base by the leftist groups, rather than the threat from the economic power of a privileged group, moved the government to take immediate action. *So to some extent the expansion of state control was in response to societal pressures rather than state initiative.* Indeed, after the revolution public enterprises became a huge drain on government finances": Vahid Nowshirvani and Patrick Clawson, "The State and Social Equity in Postrevolutionary Iran," in *The Politics of Social Transformation in Afghanistan, Iran, and Pakistan,* ed. Myron Weiner and Ali Banuazizi (Syracuse: Syracuse University Press, 1994), 256; emphasis added.

64. Schirazi, *Constitution of Iran* (above, note 21), 175–205. I thank Bernard Haykel and Kristian Coates Ulrichsen for answering my inquiries on Saudi Arabia and Kuwait. See Y. Linant de Bellefonds, "Ḍarūra," *Encyclopaedia of Islam,* 2nd ed., ed. P. Bearman et al., 2012: http://referenceworks.brillonline. com/entries/encyclopaedia-of-islam-2/darura-SIM_1730 (accessed 18 August 2015).

65. Schirazi, *Constitution of Iran* (above, note 21), 182.

66. Ibid., 188.

67. Ibid., 200.

68. Fariba Adelkhah, *Being Modern in Iran* (London: Hurst, 1999), 12.

69. Ahmadi-Amui, *Eqtesād-e Siāsi* (above, note 20), 65, 90.

70. Interview, Tehran, October 2009.

71. Ahmadi-Amui, *Eqtesād-e Siāsi* (above, note 20), 9–58.

72. Arang Keshavarzian, *Bazaar and State in Iran: The Politics of the Tehran Marketplace* (Cambridge: Cambridge University Press, 2007), 105. As Nowshirvani and Clawson describe, "For some goods, the government controlled the entire market, but for others, it supplied or regulated only a segment of the market or imposed no controls at all. For instance, in the late 1980s only between 30 and 40 percent of the rice consumption was distributed by the government; similarly, extensive free markets for meat and dairy products existed alongside the controlled network mainly supplied from imports. . . . Besides these legal markets, illegal black markets also existed, for example, in ration stamps. On the whole, the most extensive black markets were not in the rationed basic commodities but in the price-controlled and government-allocated goods": "The State and Social Equity" (above, note 63), 258–59. Also see an account from the ground in Eric Hooglund, "1980–85: Political and Economic Trends," in *The Iranian Revolution and the Islamic Republic,* ed. Nikki Keddie and Eric Hooglund (Syracuse: Syracuse University Press, 1986), 17–31.

73. Interview with researcher at Ministry of Welfare and Labor, Tehran, October 2009.

74. Patrick Clawson, "Iran's Economy: Between Crisis and Collapse," *MERIP Reports* 98 (1981): 11–15. See the reminiscence of ration coupons for various goods in "Obzheh-hāye zendegi-ye ruzmareh dar daheh-ye shast," *Andisheh-ye Pouyā* 4 (2012): 76–77.

75. Dani Rodrik, "What Drives Public Employment in Developing Countries?" *Review of Development Economics* 4.3 (2000): 242.

76. Reinhold Loeffler, "Economic Changes in a Rural Area since 1979," in Keddie and Hooglund (above, note 72), 105.

77. Interview, Tabriz, February 2010. See Ezzatollāh Sahābi and Hoda Sāber, "Forsat-e ān do sāl va 'tāvān-e' ān shish sāl." *Irān-e Fardā* 58 (1999): 23–26; Setareh Karimi, "Economic Policies and Structural Changes since the Revolution," in Keddie and Hooglund (above, note 72), 32–54; and Nowshirvani and Clawson, "The State and Social Equity" (above, note 63), 247–54.

78. Interview, Tehran, May 2011. The frustrations, aspirations, and semilegal machinations that accompanied the housing boom of the 1980s can be seen in Dāriush Mehrjui's 1986 satirical film *The Lodgers*.

79. See Matthew Hunt and Heather Bullock, "Ideologies and Beliefs about Poverty," in *The Oxford Handbook of the Social Science of Poverty,* ed. David Brady and Linda Burton (Oxford: Oxford University Press, 2016), 93–117. For a psychological survey in Iran, see Dariush Hayati and Ezatollah Karami, "Typology of Causes of Poverty: The Perception of Iranian Farmers," *Journal of Economic Psychology* 26.6 (2005): 884–901.

80. Mohammad Farid Jalāli, "Barresi-ye rābeteh-ye faqr bā enherāfāt-e ejtemā'i va rāh-hāye zududan-e ān bā ta'kid bar komiteh-ye emdād-e imām Khomeini." *Faslnāmeh-ye Emdād Pazhuhān* 3.9 (2005): 45.

81. For a general overview of nonstate social-policy providers in the global South, see Ian Gough and Geof Wood, eds., *Insecurity and Welfare Regimes in Asia, Africa and Latin America: Social Policy in Development Contexts* (Cambridge: Cambridge University Press, 2004); Melani Cammett and Lauren MacLean, "Introduction: The Political Consequences of Non-state Social Welfare in the Global South," *Studies in Comparative International Development* 46.1 (2011): 1–21. On nonstate-welfare actors in Muslim-majority countries, see Siti Kusujiarti, "Pluralistic and Informal Welfare Regime: The Roles of Islamic Institutions in the Indonesian Welfare Regime," in *The Sociology of Islam: Secularism, Economy and Politics,* ed. Tugrul Keskin (Reading, Berks: Ithaca Press, 2011), 419–52; Rana Jawad and Burcu Yakut-Çakar, "Religion and Social Policy in the Middle East: The (Re)Constitution of an Old-New Partnership," *Social Policy & Administration* 44.6 (2010): 658–72; and Thomas Pierret and Kjetil Selvik, "Limits of 'Authoritarian Upgrading' in Syria: Private Welfare, Islamic Charities, and the Rise of the Zayd Movement," *International Journal of Middle East Studies* 41.4 (2009): 595–614.

82. Much of this section is based on reports and assessments of the Imam Khomeini Relief Committee published in the postwar period: *Komiteh-ye Emdād-e Imām Khomeini: Barrasi-ye Towsifi va Tahlili* (Tehran: Moassesseh-ye Ali-ye Pazhuhesh dar Barnāmeh Rizi va Towse'eh, 1994); *Komiteh-ye Emdād-e Imām Khomeini: Barnāmeh-ye Panj Sāleh-ye Dovom 1374–78* (Tehran: Mo'āvanat-e Pazhuhesh va Barnāmeh Rizi, 1995).

83. Seyyed Mahmoud Kimiāfar, *Komiteh-ye Emdād va Jang* (Tehran: Majmu'eh-ye Farhangi-ye Shahid Beheshti, 2008), 28.

84. Ibid., 29; emphasis added.

85. Ibid., 33.

86. Ibid., 33–34. On the Construction *Jihād*, see Eric Lob, "An Institutional History of the Iranian Construction Jihad," Ph.D. dissertation, Department of Near Eastern Studies, Princeton University, 2013.

87. Figures compiled from Kimiāfar, *Komiteh-ye Emdād va Jang* (above, note 83). For estimates of internal migration in Iran because of the war, see Valiollāh Rostam'alizādeh and Ali Qāsemi-Ardehā'i, "Āsār va payāmad-hāye jam'iati–ejtemā'i-ye mohājerat-hāye jang-e tahmili dar jāme'eh-ye Irān," *Pazhuheshnāmeh-ye Defā'-ye Moqadas* 1.2 (2012): 59–79.

88. Quoted in FBIS Daily Report, Near East & South Asia, FBIS-NES-90–045, 7 March 1990, p. 50.

89. For more on the Imam Khomeini Relief Committee, see Kevan Harris, "The Politics of Welfare after Revolution and War: The Imam Khomeini Relief Committee in the Islamic Republic of Iran," in *The Cup, The Gun and The Crescent: Social Welfare and Civil Unrest in Muslim Societies,* ed. Sara Crabtree, Jonathan Parker, and Azlinda Azman (London: Whiting and Birch, 2012), 134–50.

90. Farideh Farhi, "The Antinomies of Iran's War Generation," in *Iran, Iraq, and the Legacies of War,* ed. Lawrence Potter and Gary Sick (New York: Palgrave MacMillan, 2004), 104.

91. On Iraq, however, see Dina Khoury, *Iraq in Wartime: Soldiering, Martyrdom, and Remembrance* (Cambridge: Cambridge University Press, 2013). A recent French work is the best accounting thus far of the military and political dynamics of the Iran-Iraq War: Pierre Razoux, *The Iran-Iraq War,* transl. Nicholas Elliott (Cambridge, Mass.: Harvard University Press, 2015).

92. Farhi remarks on the surprisingly low number of men who served in the military during the war, conscripted or voluntary. She calculates, from various sources, between 1.5 million and 3 million combatants for a population of 45–55 million: Farhi, "Antinomies of Iran's War Generation" (above, note 90), 105. Yet participation went beyond the war front, and the category "martyr" expanded as the state designated participation "behind the lines" evidence of equally devoted sacrifice.

93. Sheila Fitzpatrick, *Everyday Stalinism: Ordinary Life in Extraordinary Times: Soviet Russia in the 1930s* (New York: Oxford University Press, 1999), 71–75.

94. We can see this discrepancy between official proclamation and popular perceptions in film itself. Several years after the war's end, Kamāl Tabrizi's 1996 film *Leili Is with Me* shocked the Iranian public. It was a black comedy about a man volunteering for the Iran-Iraq War in order to get a housing loan. When asked today, Iranians still recall the scandalous experience when first watching the movie in theaters. Tabrizi's film resonated *not* because the selfish character was unrecognizable to Iranians. On the contrary, such a common experience had never been portrayed so accurately in public. Tabrizi would go on to make *The Lizard,* a film about a thief who hides in plain sight by wearing a turban and clerical regalia to equally comic effect.

95. Nowshirvani and Clawson, "The State and Social Equity" (above, note 63), 240–42.

96. Mohammad Azizi, "Tahlil-e moshārekat-e aqshār-e mokhtalef dar defā'-ye moqadas," *Pazhuheshnāmeh-ye Defā'-ye Moqadas* 1.2 (2012): 105. This is at the higher estimate levels of war deaths in Iran. Other estimates compiled by different branches of the armed forces put the numbers between 220,000 and 183,000 deaths. As Charles Kurzman has noted, even these numbers do not appear to be in mortality data estimated from census-cohort data. For a range of estimates, see "Āmār-e vāghe'i-ye shohadā-ye jang, 190 yā 200 hezār nafar?" *Tārikh-e Irāni*, 21 September 2014: online at https://goo.gl/6kdmk3 (accessed 15 June 2015); also Charles Kurzman, "Death Tolls of the Iran-Iraq War," 31 October 2013: http://kurzman.unc.edu/death-tolls-of-the-iran-iraq-war/ (accessed 15 June 2015). For an epidemiological estimate (of 178,298 deaths, including postwar deaths from mines), see B. Mousavi et al., "Years of Life Lost among Iranian People Killed in the Iraq-Iran War: The 25-Year Perspective," *International Journal of Injury Control and Safety Promotion* 21.4 (2014): 382–87.

97. Nowshirvani and Clawson, "The State and Social Equity" (above, note 63), 251.

98. Glenn Curtis and Eric Hooglund, *Iran: A Country Study* (Washington, D.C.: Library of Congress, Federal Research Division, 2008), 136.

99. Keiko Sakurai, "University Entrance Examination and the Making of an Islamic Society in Iran: A Study of the Post-Revolutionary Iranian Approach to 'Konkur,'" *Iranian Studies* 37.3 (2004): 393–94.

100. Dilip Hiro, *The Longest War: The Iran-Iraq Military Conflict* (New York: Routledge, 1991), 243; Nowshirvani and Clawson, "The State and Social Equity" (above, note 63), 243.

101. 1 January 1989, in Foreign Broadcast Information Service Daily Report 1/3/1989, Near East & South Asia, FBIS-NES-89-001, pp. 49–54; emphasis added.

CHAPTER 4. THE REVOLUTION EMBEDDED: RURAL TRANSFORMATIONS AND THE DEMOGRAPHIC MIRACLE

1. The epigraph to this chapter is cited from Eugen Weber, *Peasants into Frenchmen: The Modernization of Rural France, 1870–1914* (Stanford, Calif.: Stanford University Press, 1976), 486.

2. Foreign household-service workers before the revolution often emigrated from the Philippines, the pioneer in late-twentieth-century Southeast Asian labor exportation. See Firouzeh Khalatbari, "Iran: A Unique Underground Economy," in *The Economy of Islamic Iran: Between State and Market,* ed. Thierry Coville (Louvain: Peeters, 1994), 118.

3. Shanta Devarajan and Lili Mottaghi, "Economic Implications of Lifting Sanctions on Iran" *Middle East and North Africa Quarterly Economic Brief* 5 (Washington, D.C.: World Bank, 2015), 14–15. Data in the report are taken from the Statistical Center of Iran.

4. Ruth Milkman, Ellen Reese, and Benita Roth, "The Macrosociology of Paid Domestic Labor," *Work and Occupations* 25.4 (1998): 483–510.

5. See the debates surrounding Gøsta Esping-Andersen, *Social Foundations of Postindustrial Economies* (Oxford and New York: Oxford University Press,

1999); and the synthesis in Ann Orloff, "Gendering the Comparative Analysis of Welfare States: An Unfinished Agenda," *Sociological Theory* 27.3 (2009): 317–43; also see Nancy Folbre, *Valuing Children: Rethinking the Economics of Family* (Cambridge, Mass.: Harvard University Press, 2008).

6. Eric Hooglund, "Changing Attitudes among Women in Rural Iran," in *Gender in Contemporary Iran: Pushing the Boundaries,* ed. Roksana Bahramitash and Eric Hooglund, 125 (London: Routledge, 2011).

7. I borrow the term "health-developmental state" from Christopher Gibson's comparative study of Brazilian primary-health-care organizations in multiple states and their varied effectiveness in health outcomes; see "Civilizing the State: Civil Society and the Politics of Primary Public Health Care in Urban Brazil," Ph.D. dissertation, Department of Sociology, Brown University, 2012; also see idem, "Sanitaristas, Petistas, and the Post-Neoliberal Public Health State in Porto Alegre," *Latin American Perspectives* 43.2 (2016): 153–71.

8. Peter Evans, "Constructing the 21st Century Developmental State: Potentialities and Pitfalls," in *Constructing a Democratic Developmental State in South Africa: Potentials and Challenges,* ed. Omano Edigheji (Cape Town: HSRC Press, 2010): 37–58.

9. Patrick Heller, *The Labor of Development: Workers and the Transformation of Capitalism in Kerala, India* (Ithaca: Cornell University Press, 1999).

10. February 2010 interview in East Azarbaijan province; also see Sara Javanparast et al., "A Policy Review of the Community Health Worker Programme in Iran," *Journal of Public Health Policy* 32.2 (2011): 263–76.

11. State investment into Iran's generic pharmaceutical industry after the revolution—a Pahlavi import-substitution strategy that was greatly expanded after the 1979 revolution—has been crucial to the state's ability to furnish low-cost medicines to the population.

12. Interview with health worker, village in Kashan Province, September 2009.

13. WHO/UNICEF, *Review of National Immunization Coverage, 1980–2007* (Geneva: World Health Organization, 2008).

14. According to U.N. Population Fund interviews with Health Ministry officials, as a result of expanding the rural health-house system, for a period the vaccination coverage in rural areas was even higher than in urban areas: UNFPA, *Family Planning Programme Report* (Tehran: United Nations Population Fund Office, 2008), 31.

15. Kiumarss Nasseri et al., "Determinants of Partial Participation in the Immunization Programmes in Iran." *Social Science & Medicine* 30.3 (1990): 379–83.

16. Mohammad Abbasi-Shavazi et al., *Return to Afghanistan? A Study of Afghans Living in Mashhad, Islamic Republic of Iran.* Afghanistan Research and Evaluation Unit (Tehran: Faculty of Social Sciences, University of Tehran, 2005).

17. Mehr News, 9 November 2009.

18. This was the case only if these young people had no connection to any villages—e.g., their grandparents and extended family all lived in large urban centers. Other young people did know of the health houses, and if they were in the room, often discussed them with those who expressed surprise.

19. Interview with former Ministry of Health official, Tehran, February 2010. As Homa Hoodfar writes, "In contrast to the provisions of basic education, which is designed primarily to benefit the regime by cultivating its ideological vision of Islamic society, improving universal access to basic health services is the main avenue through which the regime has communicated its commitment to the poor and the 'have not' regions of Iran"; see *Volunteer Health Workers in Iran as Social Activists: Can "Governmental Non-Governmental Organisations" Be Agents of Democratisation?* Occasional Papers, no. 10 (London: Women Living Under Muslim Laws, 1998), 6.

20. Data on health and welfare during the 1970s were notoriously inaccurate, and in many cases there were suspicions that the Pahlavi state inflated figures. In contrast to that assumption, data collection in the 1980s often became more accurate under the Islamic Republic because of the logistics and requirements of war.

21. Mohammad Abbasi-Shavazi, Peter McDonald, and Meimanat Hosseini-Chavoshi, *The Fertility Transition in Iran: Revolution and Reproduction* (New York: Springer, 2009), 48.

22. As Abbasi-Shavasi, McDonald, and Hosseini-Chavoshi (above, note 21), 4, write, "Iran was seen as a country in which there was a culture of high fertility, a conservative Muslim government, subjugation of women, a poorly performing economy and isolation from the West. By conventional wisdom, fertility does not fall in such circumstances."

23. These mechanisms are outlined in Abbasi-Shavasi, McDonald, and Hosseini-Chavoshi (above, note 21), 83.

24. One anecdote, related by a public health worker who had been stationed in 1970s Khuzestan, is illustrative. Mobile teams of health workers would travel to each village, set up tents, and hand out medicine in capsule form for symptoms of various ailments. The villagers would demand "ampoules"—injections—instead of pills, which they felt were ineffective. The pain of an injection was regarded as signifying its effectiveness. When told that injections would not be given and that pills were easier and less painful, the villagers would walk away irked. Upon leaving, the health workers would inevitably see a large pile of pills thrown away behind the tent (interview in Chicago, September 2010). This, incidentally, contrasts with medical consumption patterns in contemporary Iran, where pharmaceuticals are sought out for any ailment, no matter how small.

25. Richard Moore, "Family Planning in Iran, 1960–79," in *The Global Family Planning Revolution: Three Decades of Population Policies and Programs,* ed. Warren Robinson and John Ross (Washington, D.C.: The World Bank, 2007), 42.

26. Matthew Connelly, *Fatal Misconception: The Struggle to Control World Population* (Cambridge, Mass.: Harvard University Press, 2008), 220.

27. Connelly (above, note 26), 312.

28. Nitsan Chorev, *The World Health Organization between North and South* (Ithaca: Cornell University Press, 2012): chap. 3.

29. Kenneth Newell, ed., *Health by the People* (Geneva: World Health Organization, 1975).

30. M. Assar and Z. Jaksic, "A Health Services Development Project in Iran," in *Health by the People,* ed. Kenneth Newell (Geneva: World Health Organization, 1975), 112–27.

31. Hossain Ronaghy et al., "The Middle Level Auxiliary Health Worker School: The Behdar Project," *Journal of Tropical Pediatrics* 29.5 (1983): 260–64.

32. Moore (above, note 25), 36.

33. Carol Underwood, "Islam and Health Policy: A Study of the Islamic Republic of Iran," in *Islam and Social Policy,* ed. Stephen Heyneman (Nashville: Vanderbilt University Press, 2004), 184.

34. As one Iranian Health Ministry official wrote, in the 1970s, "the concept of low-cost health-care services was doomed to receive little attention because the desire to invest the huge oil revenues in grandiose endeavours was holding sway at the time." See K. Shadpour, "Primary Health Care Networks in the Islamic Republic of Iran," *Eastern Mediterranean Health Journal* 6.4 (2000): 822–25. Also see Mohammad Mirzaie, "Swings in Fertility Limitation in Iran," *Critique: Critical Middle Eastern Studies* 14.1 (2005): 25–33.

35. Chorev (above, note 28).

36. Michael Fischer, *Iran: From Religious Dispute to Revolution* (Madison: University of Wisconsin Press, 1980), 96.

37. Amir Mehryar, "Shi'ite Teachings, Pragmatism and Fertility Change in Iran," in *Islam, the State and Population,* ed. Gavin Jones and Mehtab Karim (London: Hurst, 2005), 132–33.

38. Ibid., 134–40.

39. The Iranian Women's Organization founded in 1961 was headed by the Shah's sister, Ashraf Pahlavi. This form of "state feminism" was no less politicized than the Islamic Republic's version of the ideal female role, as Parvin Paidar has argued: "The two Pahlavi Shahs saw themselves in the same light: as father of the nation who had to have total control over the women of the nation. As was the case in relation to women in the family, women of the nation, too, were not allowed to act independently and take initiatives for fear of what the unknown might bring about. The prerequisite for reform on women's political rights, then, was the Shah's control over the women's movement." See *Women and the Political Process in Twentieth-Century Iran* (Cambridge: Cambridge University Press, 1995), 142.

40. Mehryar (above, note 37), 141. Ironically, as stated in chapter 3, it was Beheshti who first pioneered the use of Islamic Associations as a method to corral revolutionary mobilization into a state-building mechanism.

41. Ibid., 138–40.

42. Moore (above, note 25), 54.

43. Akbar Aghajanian, "Post-Revolutionary Demographic Trends in Iran," in *Post-Revolutionary Iran,* ed. Hooshang Amirahmadi and Manoucher Parvin (Boulder: Westview Press, 1988), 157.

44. Wendy Goldman, *Women, the State and Revolution: Soviet Family Policy and Social Life, 1917–1936.* (Cambridge: Cambridge University Press, 1993), 106.

45. Abbasi-Shavazi, McDonald, and Hosseini-Chavoshi (above, note 21), 184.

46. Bahman Ahmadi-Amui, *Eqtesād-e Siāsi-ye Jomhuri-ye Eslāmi* (Tehran: Gam-e Now Press, 2003), 189–90.

47. Abbasi-Shavazi, McDonald, and Hosseini-Chavoshi (above, note 21), 26.

48. Homa Hoodfar, "Bargaining with Fundamentalism: Women and the Politics of Population Control in Iran," *Reproductive Health Matters* 4.8 (1996): 30–40; Homa Hoodfar and Samad Assadpour, "The Politics of Population Policy in the Islamic Republic of Iran," *Studies in Family Planning* 31.1 (2000): 19–34.

49. In fact, during the first years of the 1990s, new laws were passed that altered the standard marriage and divorce contracts; the latter even stipulated that wages for housework were to be paid upon divorce by the husband to the wife. Of course, enforcement of such provisions are difficult for women to obtain, but the legal frameworks were themselves quite progressive for the region in the early 1990s. See Homa Hoodfar, "Devices and Desires: Population Policy and Gender Roles in the Islamic Republic," *Middle East Report* 190 (1994): 11–17.

50. Mehryar (above, note 37), 149.

51. Ibid.

52. UNFPA (above, note 14), 13.

53. Mehryar (above, note 37), 151.

54. Farzaneh Roudi-Fahimi, *Iran's Family Planning Program: Responding to a Nation's Needs*, MENA Policy Brief, June (Washington, D.C.: Population Reference Bureau, 2002), 6.

55. Abbasi-Shavazi, McDonald, and Hosseini-Chavoshi (above, note 21), chap. 9.

56. This pattern is also seen in Italy, for example, where "traditional" methods are widely used, and fertility rates are very low.

57. Amir Erfani and Kevin McQuillan, "Rates of Induced Abortion in Iran: The Roles of Contraceptive Use and Religiosity," *Studies in Family Planning* 39.2 (2008): 111–22.

58. Agnes Loeffler, *Allopathy Goes Native: Traditional versus Modern Medicine in Iran* (London: I. B. Tauris, 2007).

59. Weber (above, note 1), 195.

60. Mostafa Azkia, "Rural Society and Revolution in Iran," in *Twenty Years of Islamic Revolution: Political and Social Transition in Iran since 1979*, ed. Eric Hooglund (Syracuse: Syracuse University Press, 2002), 105.

61. Kaveh Ehsani, "Rural Society and Agricultural Development in Post-Revolution Iran: The First Two Decades," *Critique: Critical Middle Eastern Studies* 15.1 (2006): 79–96.

62. Mostafa Azkia, Hossein Araghi, and Hamid Ansari, *Local Development Fund (LDF) Project: Social Assessment of Poverty Clusters in Khoozestan Province* (Tehran: Ministry of Interior and The Cooperative Company of Technical Engineering Consultants for Sustainable Development, 2004).

63. Abbasi-Shavazi, McDonald, and Hosseini-Chavoshi (above, note 21), 57–58.

CHAPTER 5. DEVELOPMENT AND DISTINCTION:
WELFARE-STATE EXPANSION AND THE POLITICS
OF THE NEW MIDDLE CLASS

1. The two epigraphs to this chapter are quoted from John Stuart Mill, "The French Revolution of 1848, and Its Assailants," *The Westminster Review* 51,

April–July (1849): 4; and from Alexander Gerschenkron, *Economic Backwardness in Historical Perspective: A Book of Essays* (Cambridge, Mass.: Belknap Press of Harvard University Press, 1962), 28–29.

2. As Chalmers Johnson described the reception of his book *MITI and the Japanese Miracle: The Growth of Industrial Policy, 1925–1975* (Stanford, Calif.: Stanford University Press, 1982), "Western ideologists want to defend Western laissez-faire capitalism against Soviet-style displacement of the market. A central ideological dimension of the cold war was to posit a 'free' market system in which the state served only as referee over and against the socialist displacement of the market for state ends. The achievements of the Japanese developmental state were inconvenient for both sides in this debate. They illustrated to the West what the state could do to improve the outcomes of market forces, and they illustrated to the Leninists that their big mistake was the displacement of the market rather than using it for developmental purposes": Chalmers Johnson, "The Developmental State: Odyssey of a Concept," in *The Developmental State,* ed. Meredith Woo-Cumings (Ithaca: Cornell University Press, 1999), 49.

3. Georgi Derluguian, *Bourdieu's Secret Admirer in the Caucasus: A World-System Biography* (Chicago: University of Chicago Press, 2005), 134.

4. See a study of the Red Queen effect in Beverly Silver, "The Contradictions of Semiperipheral Success: The Case of Israel," in *Semiperipheral States in the World Economy,* ed. William Martin (New York: Greenwood Press, 1990), 161–81.

5. Partly as a result of factional deadlocks experienced during the war, the Iranian constitution was amended in 1989 to eliminate the office of prime minister and transfer executive power to the president. Anticipating the death of Khomeini, the amendments also removed the requirement of grand ayatollah for the position of leader so that Ali Khamenei could enter the slot. This was deemed necessary since Grand Ayatollah Hossein-Ali Montazeri, who had previously been informally designated Khomeini's successor, ended up falling out with Khomeini during 1987–88—partly over the execution of thousands of political prisoners as the war neared an uncertain conclusion. In one of the Islamic Republic's many ironies, then–parliament speaker Mehdi Karroubi took part in the public shaming of Montazeri, even though twenty years later, during Green Movement protests, Karroubi claimed him as the spiritual and moral guide of the opposition. The 1989 constitutional amendments also codified the body of the Expediency Council, which had been created by Khomeini to arbitrate the political divisions of the elite. Even with all these constitutional changes, which amounted to a narrowing of the democratic process akin to the passage of the 1789 U.S. Constitutional Convention in response to the 1777 Articles of Confederation, intraelite conflict in Iran continued to spill beyond the ability of the political system to absorb it.

6. Asef Bayat, *Workers and Revolution in Iran: A Third World Experience of Workers' Control* (London: Zed Books, 1987); Peyman Jafari, "Reasons to Revolt: Iranian Oil Workers in the 1970s," *International Labor and Working-Class History* 84 (2013): 195–217.

7. Mehrdad Valibeigi, "Economy, Private Sector," in *Iran Today: An Encyclopedia of Life in the Islamic Republic,* ed. Mehran Kamrava and Manochehr Dorraj (Westport, Conn.: Greenwood Press, 2008), 159–65.

8. The charged debates over the Labor Law during the 1980s resulted in perhaps the most important *fatwa* ever issued by Khomeini, often referred to as the expediency (*maslahat*) decree. In 1987, the Labor Minister under Mousavi, in expectation of a Guardian Council veto of the Labor Bill, sent a letter to Khomeini asking for clarification of the legitimacy of the state to intervene in private contracts. Khomeini answered in the affirmative. After continued questioning from other Islamic jurists, Khomeini clarified that the interests of the Islamic Republic, as determined by its political leadership, could trump religious duties or constraints, as determined by Shi'i clergy. This *fatwa* also justified the creation of the Council for Determination of Expediency in the amendments to the 1989 Constitution for arbitrating differences between the parliament and Guardian Council. As Behrooz Ghamari-Tabrizi pointed out, "By locating the supreme authority to determine state policies in the political sphere, the unintended consequence . . . was the secularization [of the Islamic Republic's legitimation for rule]," *Islam and Dissent in Postrevolutionary Iran* (London: I. B. Tauris, 2008), 145. The Islamic Republic, in this sense, ended this particular facet of theocratic rule within less than a decade of existence.

9. Djavad Salehi-Isfahani, "Labor and the Challenge of Economic Restructuring in Iran," *Middle East Report* 210 (1999): 34–37; also Mohammad Maljoo, "Tavān-e tabāgheh-ye kārgar dar daheh-ye hashtād dar goftegu bā Mohammad Mālju," *Mehrnāmeh* 11 (2011), 39–41.

10. Behzad Yaghmaian, *Social Change in Iran: An Eyewitness Account of Dissent, Defiance, and New Movements for Rights* (Albany: SUNY Press, 2002), 173.

11. Ruth Collier and David Collier, "Inducements versus Constraints: Disaggregating 'Corporatism,'" *The American Political Science Review* 73.4 (1979): 967–86.

12. Djavad Salehi-Isfahani and Daniel Egel, *Youth Exclusion in Iran: The State of Education, Employment and Family Formation,* Middle East Youth Initiative Working Paper (Dubai: Wolfensohn Center for Development, Dubai School of Government, 2007); also International Labour Organization, *An Employment Strategy for the Islamic Republic of Iran* (New Delhi: International Labour Organization, 2004).

13. Elham Etminan and Kobra Chaker-ol-Hosseini, "Social Protection for Informal Workers: The Iranian Experience," Paper presented at the Fifth International Research Conference on Social Security, 5–7 March, Warsaw, 2007, 6–7.

14. Djavad Salehi-Isfahani, "Human Resources in Iran: Potentials and Challenges," *Iranian Studies* 38.1 (2005): 117–47.

15. Etminan and Chaker-ol-Hosseini (above, note 13), 12.

16. Majles Research Center, *Tarh-e Towse'eh-ye Eshteghāl va Ta'min-e Ejtemā'i: Koliyāt-e Motāla'ah va Sharh-e Khedamāt* (Tehran: Markaz-e Pazhuhesh-e Majles, 1996); Majles Research Center, *Mokhtasari dar Mowred-e*

Nezām-e Ta'min-e Ejtemā'i dar Irān (Tehran: Markaz-e Pazhuhesh-e Majles, 2000); Said Madani, "Cheshmāndāz-hāye farāru-ye ta'min-e ejtemā'i dar Irān: Chālesh-hā va rāhkār-hāye pishbini shodeh dar lāihe-ye nezām jāme'h-ye refāh va ta'min-e ejtemā'i." *Faslnāmeh-ye Ta'min-e Ejtemā'i* 15 (2003): 289–328; Hossein Ibrahimipour et al., "A Qualitative Study of the Difficulties in Reaching Sustainable Universal Health Insurance Coverage in Iran," *Health Policy and Planning* 26.6 (2011): 485–95; Mohammad Hajizadeh and Luke B. Connelly, "Equity of Health Care Financing in Iran: The Effect of Extending Health Insurance to the Uninsured," *Oxford Development Studies* 38.4 (2010): 461–76.

17. Interview, Tehran, October 2009. Also instructive are the documents issued by the Social Security Organization, in simple language, handed out to beneficiaries, businesses, and applicants. For background materials used in this chapter, see Social Security Organization, *Sanad-e Barnāmeh-ye Estrātezhik-e Sāzmān-e Ta'min-e Ejtemā'i* (Tehran: SSO, 2004); *Sāzmān-e Ta'min-e Ejtemā'i dar Yek Negāh* (Tehran: SSO, 2007); and *Āshenāi bā Khedamāt va Hemāyat-hāye Sāzmān-e Ta'min-e Ejtemā'i* (Tehran: SSO, 2008).

18. International Labour Organization, *ILO World Social Security Report 2010–2011* (Geneva: International Labour Organization, 2010).

19. Massoud Karshenas and Mohammad Hashem Pesaran, "Exchange Rate Unification, the Role of Markets and Planning in the Iranian Economic Reconstruction," in *The Economy of Islamic Iran: Between State and Market,* ed. Thierry Coville (Louvain: Peeters, 1994), 141–76.

20. E.g., Jāleh Shādi-Taleb, "Subsid va piāmad-hāye ejtemā'i-ye ān," *Farhang-e Towse'eh,* October–November 1992: 34–41.

21. Bahman Ahmadi-Amui, *Eqtesād-e Siāsi-ye Jomhuri-ye Eslāmi* (Tehran: Gam-e Now Press, 2003), 105.

22. Hooshang Amirahmadi, *Revolution and Economic Transition: The Iranian Experience* (Albany: State University of New York Press, 1990), 242.

23. Mohammad Quchāni, *Yaqeh Sefid-hā* (Tehran: Naqsh-o-Negār, 2000).

24. Mehdi Moslem, *Factional Politics in Post-Khomeini Iran,* (Syracuse: Syracuse University Press, 2002), 144; also see Behrooz Ghamari-Tabrizi, "Memory, Mourning, Memorializing: On the Victims of Iran-Iraq War, 1980–Present," *Radical History Review* 105 (2009): 106–21. The *hezbollāhi* dress style, with its untucked long-sleeved shirt, oversized suit, unkempt beard, and no tie, has less to do with religious orthodoxy and more to do with the various strains of post-1968 ideologies that came together in Iran in 1979. This form of dress, disposition, and language was strengthened under what Ali Gheissari and Vali Nasr have labeled the counterculture of "war fundamentalism," similar to the political climate of postrevolutionary Russia during the 1918–21 civil war. See Ali Gheissari and Vali Nasr, *Democracy in Iran: History and the Quest for Liberty* (Oxford: Oxford University Press, 2006), 78.

25. Ghamari-Tabrizi (above, note 24), 110.

26. Ibid., 147.

27. Quoted in Ghamari-Tabrizi (above, note 24), 111.

28. This critique is not wielded simply by the political elite, which is probably why the elite wields it. A common remark that I heard among former sol-

diers was that "the *basiji*s of today are not real *basiji*s." When I asked one veteran to elaborate, he explained, "A *basiji* would, upon seeing a live grenade thrown amid his brothers-in-arms, immediately jump onto the grenade. A *basiji* would also take a grenade, lie in wait under an Iraqi tank, and then pull the pin without hesitation. Today's *basiji*s are not deserving of the name" (interview, Tehran, summer 2008). This view was widely expressed, even by people who disagreed with the reformist agenda, during 2009's Green Movement demonstrations as *basij* members were used as shock troops to cause mayhem among the protestors. In other words, as is often the case with any discourse of purity wielded by state elites, the movement of principlism eventually led to dissent within former supporters of the state.

29. These two strands—the new right and the new left—had ideological overlap when Rafsanjani was still president. In 1995, Ali Akbar Mohtashemi (aka Mohtashemipour), Interior Minister between 1985 and 1989, major backer of Lebanon's Hezbollah party, and a radical supporter of Mousavi, was interviewed by the newspaper *Sobh* about the left's disqualification from the parliamentary elections in 1992 and Rafsanjani's economic policies. Mohtashemi seethed: "Liberalism in all its guises has infiltrated our lives, and whoever defends liberalism in the economy [i.e., Rafsanjani] could not withstand the manifestations of the free-market economy, the capitalists and monopolists returning to the country after the revolution threw them out, bringing with them the germs of cultural, political, and social liberalism. To make way for them, faithful revolutionary forces, trying to resist these things, must be sacrificed; and this is already happening. We are already seeing a change in priorities, with the accumulation of wealth and the enjoyment of luxury being the main goal. This society is headed for moral and social collapse, and this is what we are seeing: corruption in all its forms." *Sobh*, July 1995, in Foreign Broadcast Information Service Daily Report, Near East and South Asia, FBIS-NES-95-233, 5 December 1995, p. 87. Mohtashemi's newspaper, *Bayān*, shifted from radical views on foreign policy to moderate support of Khatami once elected. In 2009, Mohtashemi headed Mousavi's presidential campaign and vocally accused the government of election fraud in the June vote.

30. Ahmadi-Amui (above, note 21), 122.

31. E.g., World Bank, *Iran: Reconstruction and Economic Growth* (Washington, D.C.: The World Bank, 1991).

32. Ahmadi-Amui (above, note 21), 222.

33. Hassan Hakimian, "Iran's Free-Trade Zones: Back Doors to the International Economy?" *Iranian Studies* 44.6 (2011): 851–74.

34. Arang Keshavarzian, "Geopolitics and the Genealogy of Free-Trade Zones in the Persian Gulf," *Geopolitics* 15.2 (2010): 263–89.

35. Ahmadi-Amui (above, note 21), 163–64.

36. See the interview with Mohammad Maljoo on labor casualization in *Deutsche Welle Persian*, 6 February 2010, available at http://www.dw.de/dw/article/0,,5216251,00.html (accessed 13 March 2015).

37. Abdulaziz Aflakseir and Peter Coleman, "The Influence of Religious Coping on the Mental Health of Disabled Iranian War Veterans," *Mental Health, Religion and Culture* 12.2 (2009): 175–90.

38. *Resālat,* 13 November 1989. In Foreign Broadcast Information Service Daily Report, Near East & South Asia, FBIS-NES-89–235, 8 December 1989, p. 53.

39. Interview, Washington, D.C., August 2010.

40. Eric Lob, "Jehad-e Sazandegi and the End of the Iranian Revolution (1979–1983)," Paper presented at the conference "How to End a Revolution," Cambridge, Mass., 13–14 April 2012.

41. Keiko Sakurai, "University Entrance Examination and the Making of an Islamic Society in Iran: A Study of the Post-Revolutionary Iranian Approach to 'Konkur,'" *Iranian Studies* 37.3 (2004): 385–406.

42. See Kaveh Ehsani, "The Urban Provincial Periphery in Iran: Revolution and War in Ramhormoz," in *Contemporary Iran: Economy, Society, Politics,* ed. Ali Gheissari (Oxford: Oxford University Press, 2009), 38–76; this is also the case in Arab countries: see Diego Gambetta and Steffen Hertog, "Why Are There So Many Engineers among Islamic Radicals?" *European Journal of Sociology / Archives Européennes de Sociologie* 50.2 (2009): 201–30.

43. *IRNA,* 19 August 1989. In Foreign Broadcast Information Service Daily Report, Near East and South Asia, FBIS-NES-89–160, 21 August 1989, p. 61.

44. As of 2012, voluntary insurance for those in the self-employed/informal sector can be obtained at the following premiums: 12 percent of earnings for old-age pension; 14 percent for old-age and survivor benefits; or 18 percent for old-age, disability, and survivor benefits. The survivor pension can go to a widow, widower, dependent parents, and also an unmarried daughter until she marries.

45. *Resālat,* 18 July 1995. In Foreign Broadcast Information Service Daily Report, Near East & South Asia, FBIS-NES-95–160, 18 August 1995, p. 71.

46. David Robalino, *Pensions in the Middle East and North Africa: Time for Change* (Washington, D.C.: World Bank, 2005).

47. As Robalino explains, "Contrary to the gross replacement rate, the net replacement rate refers to the ratio between the net pension (that is, after taxes) and the net wage. In [most Middle Eastern pension systems], net replacement rates are higher than gross replacement rates. This is because income taxes on pensions are generally lower than income taxes on wages and because pensioners no longer pay social-security taxes. Hence, in Egypt, whereas the gross pension for the average full-career worker represents 80 percent of the gross wage, the net pension represents more than 100 percent of the net wage. Basically, in Egypt, the average worker has more disposable income after retirement than while working!" ibid., 60. In 2009, the minimum pension for SSO retirees was around $400 (US) per month, whereas the minimum unskilled wage was set at $330 per month.

48. I once was invited to lunch at the National Iranian Gas Company's "company club" in the summer of 2008. The cuisine was of a high quality but available at low, subsidized prices. In the large dining hall, I noticed women aged in their 50s and 60s eating in small groups. I discussed this with my hosts and was informed that these women all retired from positions in the Gas Company in the initial years after the revolution and had been living on pensions for over twenty years. This outcome made them quite financially independent of their husbands.

49. Farideh Farhi, "The Contending Discourses on Women in Iran," *Third World Resurgence* 94 (1998): 7.

50. Interview, former Ministry of Labor official, Tehran, May 2011.

51. There are few data on early retirement, but I suspect that some public-sector employees did not take up the offer because they did not trust the state's guarantees. A side effect is an inability for the government to merge overlapping ministries and revolutionary organizations. Redundant labor from each side could not be dismissed. See Anoushiravan Ehteshami, *After Khomeini: The Iranian Second Republic* (London: Routledge, 1995), 122.

52. Robin Blackburn, "The New Collectivism: Pension Reform, Grey Capitalism and Complex Socialism," *New Left Review* 1.233 (1999): 6.

53. *Etemād,* 22 August 2011.

54. *Āftāb,* 17 April 2011.

55. Farhad Azizi, "Medical Education in the Islamic Republic of Iran: Three Decades of Success," *Iranian Journal of Public Health* 38, Supplement 1 (2009): 19–26.

56. Seyyed Alireza Marandi, "The Integration of Medical Education and Health Care Services in the I.R. of Iran and Its Health Impacts," *Iranian Journal of Public Health* 38, Supplement 1 (2009): 5.

57. A. Khojasteh et al., "Integration of Medical Education and Healthcare Service," *Iranian Journal of Public Health* 38, Supplement 1 (2009): 29–31.

58. Marandi (above, note 56), 7.

59. *Salām,* 22 September 1995. In Foreign Broadcast Information Service Daily Report, Near East & South Asia, FBIS-NES-95-233, 5 December 1995, p. 86.

60. Interview, May 2011, London.

61. Amirhossein Takian, Arash Rashidian, and Mohammad J. Kabir, "Expediency and Coincidence in Re-Engineering a Health System: An Interpretive Approach to Formation of Family Medicine in Iran," *Health Policy and Planning* 26.2 (2011): 163–73.

62. Interview, May 2011, London.

63. Hossein Askari and Noora Arfaa, "Social Safety Net in Islam: The Case of Persian Gulf Oil Exporters," *British Journal of Middle Eastern Studies* 34.2 (2007): 177–202; Takian, Rashidian, and Kabir (above, note 61), 167–69; Hajizadeh and Connelly (above, note 16), 472–75; Ibrahimipour et al. (above, note 16), 492–93.

64. Mohammad Chaichian, "The New Phase of Globalization and Brain Drain: Migration of Educated and Skilled Iranians to the United States," *International Journal of Social Economics* 39.1–2 (2011): 18–38.

65. As the anthropologist Agnes Loeffler observed: "Physicians licensed to practice after their obligatory two years of government service previously could open a private practice in one of the larger towns or cities, but now they have to move farther and farther into rural areas to find an open niche. For example, thirty years ago the government clinic in a village in southwest Iran was served by a Pakistani physician because there was such a shortage of Iranian graduates that foreign physicians had to be imported to staff rural clinics. In 1998, the government clinic in the same village was staffed by two full-time Iranian

physicians, a recent medical-school graduate performing his obligatory medical service, and one full-time nurse, who, along with three midwives, ran the family-planning and maternal and child-care programs. There were also two private physicians' offices in the village. In addition, just forty minutes away by car, the provincial capital, which did not exist thirty-five years ago, provided the services of numerous private and government-financed generalists, specialists, clinics and hospitals." Agnes Loeffler, *Allopathy Goes Native: Traditional versus Modern Medicine in Iran* (London: I. B. Tauris, 2007), 105.

66. Ibid., 106.

CHAPTER 6. LINEAGES OF THE IRANIAN WELFARE STATE

1. The two epigraphs to this chapter are cited from International Crisis Group, *Iran: What Does Ahmadi-Nejad's Victory Mean?* Middle East Briefing (New York: International Crisis Group, 2005), 5; and from "People's Movement Will Stay Alive with Knowledge and Information: An Interview with Ahmad Batebi," Online at http://persian2english.com/?p=11421 (accessed 11 May 2012).

2. Fātemeh Sādeghi, "Khodāyān va khābgard-hā: Pirāmun-e ulum-e ensāni dar Irān." *Jomhourikhāhi Online,* 19 August 2011. Original site at: http://www.jomhourikhahi.com/2011/08/social-science-tragedy-in-iran1.html; reposted at http://www.rahesabz.net/story/41646/ (accessed 13 March 2015).

3. E.g., Elaine Sciolino, *Persian Mirrors: The Elusive Face of Iran* (New York: Free Press, 2000); Robin Wright, *The Last Great Revolution: Turmoil and Transformation in Iran* (New York: A. A. Knopf, 2000); Laura Secor, *Children of Paradise: The Struggle for the Soul of Iran* (New York: Basic Books, 2016).

4. Sādeghi (above, note 2).

5. The discussion of poverty in Iran is a political football. Factions in power tend to use very low income lines, such as the World Bank's $2-per-day line (adjusted for purchasing-power parity), whereas oppositional factions very high lines of poverty as shock tactics. The result is popular confusion, with many conflating relative inequality with absolute poverty. For example, one art-gallery owner in central Tehran, when I asked, estimated that poverty in Iran was 80 percent, without much evidence. There is no nationally determined poverty line in Iran that has been legislated by the government, such as has been instituted in neighboring Turkey, and so the discussion has never been resolved.

6. Oil-induced economic growth tends to stimulate nontradable sectors such as construction or services, and this *can* be pro-poor if unskilled labor is employed at great levels. But this is something to be investigated, not assumed, in commodity-exporting countries. See Djavad Salehi-Isfahani, "Poverty, Inequality, and Populist Politics in Iran," *Journal of Economic Inequality* 7.1 (2009): 17.

7. Roberto Patricio Korzeniewicz and Timothy Patrick Moran, *Unveiling Inequality: A World-Historical Perspective* (New York: Russell Sage Foundation, 2009).

8. Sādeghi (above, note 2).

9. Eskandar Sadeghi-Boroujerdi, "From Etelā'āti to Eslāhtalabi: Sa'id Hajjarian, Political Theology and the Politics of Reform in Post-Revolutionary Iran," *Iranian Studies* 47.6 (2014): 987–1009.

10. Ibid., 997.

11. See a survey in Hamidreza Jalāeipour, "Religious Intellectuals and Political Action in the Reform Movement," in *Intellectual Trends in Twentieth-Century Iran: A Critical Survey*, ed. Negin Nabavi (Gainesville: University Press of Florida, 2003), 136–46; also Hossein Shahidi, *Journalism in Iran: From Mission to Profession* (London: Routledge, 2007).

12. "The dynamic was simple: the reformist papers wanted more readers, and the readers wanted more news about the operation of the Iranian political system. Revealing more and more was the only way to sustain a readership in a highly competitive marketplace for the trade of 'state secrets'": Farideh Farhi, "Improvising in Public: Transgressive Politics of the Reformist Press in Postrevolutionary Iran," in *Intellectual Trends in Twentieth-Century Iran: A Critical Survey*, ed. Negin Nabavi (Gainesville: University Press of Florida, 2003), 159. Examples included Emādeddin Bāqi, *Trāzhedi-ye Demokrāsi dar Irān* [The Tragedy of Democracy in Iran] (Tehran: Nashr-e Ney, 2000); and Akbar Ganji, *'Alijenāb-e Sorkhpush va 'Alijenābān-e Khākestari: Āsibshenāsi-ye Gozār beh Dowlat-e Demokrātik-e Towse'eh-garā* [The Red Eminence and the Gray Eminences: Pathology of Transition to the Developmental Democratic State] (Tehran: Tarh-e Now, 1999).

13. Yasmin Alem, *Duality by Design: The Iranian Electoral System* (Washington, D.C.: International Foundation for Electoral Systems, 2011), 60. See Kaveh Ehsani's interview with Said Hajjāriān, "The Existing Vessels Can No Longer Contain the Movement," *Middle East Report* 212 (1999): 40–42.

14. Morad Saghafi, *Why Iran Seems So Unpredictable: Iran after 25 Years of Revolution; A Retrospective and a Look Ahead* (Washington, D.C.: Woodrow Wilson Center, 2004).

15. Interview in documentary "Terror and Tehran," *PBS Frontline*, 2 May 2002; online transcript at http://www.pbs.org/wgbh/pages/frontline/shows/tehran/interviews/raisdana.html (accessed 13 March 2015). The sixth parliament (2000–4) was majority-reformist in composition, but both a reformist executive and legislative branch were increasingly blocked by the Guardian Council and, at times, the Expediency Council, which arbitrated among them all.

16. Morad Saghafi, "The New Landscape of Iranian Politics," *Middle East Report* 233 (2004): 18.

17. Morad Saghafi, *The Reform Nobody Wants Any More: Iran's Elections*, ISIM Review (Leiden: International Institute for the Study of Islam in the Modern World, 2005), 42–43.

18. Evaleila Pesaran, *Iran's Struggle for Economic Independence: Reform and Counter-Reform in the Post-Revolutionary Era* (London: Routledge, 1999), 138.

19. Said Madani, "Cheshmāndāz-hāye farāru-ye ta'min-e ejtemā'i dar Irān: Chālesh-hā va rāhkār-hāye pishbini shodeh dar lāihe-ye nezām jāme'h-ye refāh va ta'min-e ejtemā'i," *Faslnāmeh-ye Ta'min-e Ejtemā'i* 15 (2003): 289–328.

20. Interview at Ministry of Welfare and Social Security, Tehran, August 2009; Majles Research Center, *Mokhtasari dar Mowred-e Nezām-e Ta'min-e Ejtemā'i dar Irān* (Tehran: Markaz-e Pazhuhesh-e Majles, 2000).

21. Ali Saeidi, "Dislocation of the State and the Emergence of Factional Politics in Post-revolutionary Iran," *Political Geography* 21.4 (2002): 525–46; idem, "The Accountability of Para-governmental Organizations (bonyads): The Case of Iranian Foundations," *Iranian Studies* 37.3 (2004): 479–98.

22. For example, see the projections by the Majles Research Center, *Tarh-e Towse'eh-ye Eshteghāl va Ta'min-e Ejtemā'i: Koliyāt-e Motāla'ah va Sharh-e Khedamāt* (Tehran: Markaz-e Pazhuhesh-e Majles, 1996).

23. International Labour Organization, *ILO World Social Security Report 2010–2011* (Geneva: International Labour Organization, 2010).

24. Hadi Salehi-Esfahani, "Alternative Public Service Delivery Mechanisms in Iran," *Quarterly Review of Economics and Finance* 45.2–3 (2005): 497–525.

25. Suzanne Mettler, *The Submerged State: How Invisible Government Policies Undermine American Democracy* (Chicago: University of Chicago Press, 2011).

26. This quotation and those following are from an interview with Morad Saghafi: "Bāyad 'showrā-ye hamāhangi-ye niru-hāye demokrātik' rā tashkil dād." *Shargh,* 9 July 2006.

27. Mehran Kamrava. "The Civil Society Discourse in Iran." *British Journal of Middle Eastern Studies* 28.2 (2001): 165–85.

28. For the red-engineer phenomenon in postrevolutionary Russia and China, see Stephen Kotkin, *Magnetic Mountain: Stalinism as a Civilization* (Berkeley and Los Angeles: University of California Press, 1995); Joel Andreas, *Rise of the Red Engineers: The Cultural Revolution and the Origins of China's New Class* (Stanford, Calif.: Stanford University Press, 2009).

29. Mehdi Karroubi, to his credit, did promise a basic minimum income to all Iranians to be distributed by the government if he was elected—an idea that Ahmadinejad would later borrow. Yet Karroubi was both a well-known cleric and a divisive figure on the reformist left who failed to build a broad political coalition.

30. International Crisis Group, *Iran: What Does Ahmadi-Nejad's Victory Mean?* Middle East Briefing (Washington, D.C.: International Crisis Group, 2005).

31. Ibid., 6.

32. *Poet of the Wastes* (dir. Mohammad Ahmadi, 2005).

33. Naghmeh Sohrabi, *The Power Struggle in Iran: A Centrist Comeback?* Middle East Brief (Waltham, Mass.: Crown Center for Middle East Studies, Brandeis University, July 2011).

34. Foreign and opposition media mistakenly reported that Ahmadinejad closed the Planning and Budget Organization. He did not. I often used the Planning and Budget Organization's library for archival work. Many of its employees remained and continued in an advisory capacity. They would wait for a new president in four or eight years, it seemed: one more sign that institu-

tions in the Islamic Republic never actually go away; they just get new ones built on top of them.

35. In 2011, after numerous scandals over faked university degrees emerged during the Ahmadinejad era, the parliament voted that at least a Master's Degree was necessary even to run for a parliamentary seat. This begs the question: Why revolutionaries would resort to faking degrees from foppish British universities in the first place? See *Mehr News Agency,* 2 March 2011.

36. *Jām-e Jam,* 19 January 2011.

37. Interview at SSO, Tehran, March 2010.

38. Gregory Luebbert, *Liberalism, Fascism, or Social Democracy: Social Classes and the Political Origins of Regimes in Interwar Europe* (New York: Oxford University Press, 1991); Dan Slater, *Ordering Power: Contentious Politics and Authoritarian Leviathans in Southeast Asia* (Cambridge: Cambridge University Press, 2010).

39. For a sustained critique of the use and abuse of concepts of social capital and civil society in the analysis of countries in the global South, see Bruce Cumings, "Civil Society in West and East," in *Korean Society: Civil Society, Democracy, and the State,* 2nd ed., ed. Charles Armstrong (London: Routledge, 2007), 9–32.

40. For similar observations, see Naghmeh Sohrabi and Arang Keshavarzian, "On the Eve of Iran's Presidential Elections: Report from Tehran," *Middle East Report,* 7 June 2001, online at http://www.merip.org/mero/mero060701 (accessed 11 August 2015).

41. Javier Auyero, "The Moral Politics of Argentine Crowds," *Mobilization: An International Quarterly* 9.3 (2004): 311–26.

42. Kevin O'Brien, "Neither Transgressive nor Contained: Boundary-Spanning Contention in China," *Mobilization: An International Quarterly* 8.1 (2002): 51–64.

43. Ali Kadivar, "Electoral Opportunities and Emotional Energies: Evidence from 2009 Iranian Green Movement," Presentation at the Middle East Studies Association Conference, Washington, D.C. (Washington, D.C.: Middle East Studies Association, November 2011).

44. Randall Collins, "Social Movements and the Focus of Emotional Attention," in *Passionate Politics: Emotions and Social Movements,* ed. Jeff Goodwin, James Jasper, and Francesca Polletta (Chicago: University of Chicago Press, 2001), 39.

45. Muhammad Sahimi, "Martyrs of the Green Movement," posted on *Tehran Bureau,* 19 June 2010, online at http://www.pbs.org/wgbh/pages/frontline/tehranbureau/2010/06/martyrs-of-the-green-movement.html (accessed 13 March 2015); and Misagh Parsa, "The Green Challenge to the Islamic Republic" posted on *Gozaar,* 18 November 2009; online at https://web.archive.org/web/20140528031056/http://www.gozaar.org/english/articles-en/The-Green-Challenge-to-the-Islamic-Republic.html (accessed 13 March 2015).

46. Hamid Dabashi, *The Green Movement in Iran* (New Brunswick: Transaction Publishers, 2011), 104–12.

47. Asef Bayat, "Tehran: Paradox City," *New Left Review* 2.66 (2010): 99–122.

48. Kaveh Ehsani, "Municipal Matters: The Urbanization of Consciousness and Political Change in Tehran," *Middle East Report* 212 (1999): 22–27.

49. Sohrab Behdad and Farhad Nomani, "What a Revolution! Thirty Years of Social-Class Reshuffling in Iran," *Comparative Studies of South Asia, Africa and the Middle East* 29.1 (2009): 84–104.

50. E.g., Alejandro Portes and Kelly Hoffman, "Latin American Class Structures: Their Composition and Change during the Neoliberal Era," *Latin American Research Review* 38.1 (2003): 41–82; Mike Davis, *Planet of Slums* (London: Verso, 2006). The decreasing share of unpaid family labor in Iran within the informal sector, especially in economic activities such as carpet weaving, is partly due to increased female educational levels, decreased family size, and a nuclearization of kinship structure: see Roksana Bahramitash and Hadi Salehi Esfahani, eds., *Veiled Employment: Islamism and the Political Economy of Women's Employment in Iran* (Syracuse: Syracuse University Press, 2011); for an account of changing female attitudes toward work, family, and education over two generations of Iranians living in rural areas, see Eric Hooglund, "Changing Attitudes among Women in Rural Iran," in *Gender in Contemporary Iran: Pushing the Boundaries,* ed. Roksana Bahramitash and Eric Hooglund (London: Routledge, 2011), 120–35.

51. Ira Katznelson and Aristide Zolberg, eds., *Working-Class Formation: Nineteenth-Century Patterns in Western Europe and the United States* (Princeton: Princeton University Press, 1986), 3–18.

52. Beverly J. Silver, *Forces of Labor: Workers' Movements and Globalization since 1870* (Cambridge: Cambridge University Press, 2003), 20.

53. Arang Keshavarzian, *Bazaar and State in Iran: The Politics of the Tehran Marketplace* (Cambridge: Cambridge University Press, 2007), 14–19.

54. Mohammad Maljoo, "The Green Movement Awaits an Invisible Hand," *Middle East Report,* 26 June 2010; online at: http://www.merip.org/mero/mero062610 (Accessed 13 March 2015).

55. Bahramitash and Esfahani (above, note 50), 19–23.

56. UNESCO, *Global Education Digest 2011* (Montreal: UNESCO Institute for Statistics, 2011), 204.

57. *Mehr News,* 15 December 2009.

58. E.g., Farrukh Iqbal, *Sustaining Gains in Poverty Reduction and Human Development in the Middle East and North Africa* (Washington, D.C.: World Bank Publications, 2006).

59. Dominique Guillaume, Roman Zytek, and Mohammad Reza Farzin, "Iran—The Chronicles of the Subsidy Reform," IMF Working Paper (Washington, D.C.: International Monetary Fund, 2011), 8, 14.

60. See Philippe van Parijs, *What's Wrong with a Free Lunch?* (Boston: Beacon Press, 2001).

CONCLUSION

1. E.g., *Islamic Republic News Agency,* 9 November 2011.

2. Giovanni Arrighi, "The Developmentalist Illusion: A Reconceptualization of the Semiperiphery," in *Semiperipheral States in the World-Economy,* ed. William Martin (New York: Greenwood Press, 1990), 11–42.

3. Peter Evans, *Embedded Autonomy: States and Industrial Transformation* (Princeton: Princeton University Press, 1995).

4. Charles Tilly, "State Making and War Making as Organized Crime," in *Bringing the State Back In,* ed. Peter Evans, Dietrich Rueschemeyer, and Theda Skocpol (Cambridge: Cambridge University Press, 1985), 169–91.

Bibliography

Abbasi-Shavazi, Mohammad, et al. [Abbasi-Shavazi, Mohammad, Diana Gla-
zebrook, Gholamreza Jamshidiha, Hossein Mahmoudian, and Rasoul
Sadeghi.] 2005. *Return to Afghanistan? A Study of Afghans Living in Mashhad, Islamic Republic of Iran.* Afghanistan Research and Evaluation Unit.
Tehran: Faculty of Social Sciences, University of Tehran.

Abbasi-Shavazi, Mohammad, Peter McDonald, and Meimanat Hosseini-
Chavoshi. 2009. *The Fertility Transition in Iran: Revolution and Reproduction.* New York: Springer.

Abbott, Andrew, and Stanley DeViney. 1992. "The Welfare State as Transnational Event: Evidence from Sequences of Policy Adoption." *Social Science
History* 16.2: 245–74.

Abdelal, Rawi, Mark Blyth, and Craig Parsons, eds. 2010. *Constructing the
International Economy.* Ithaca: Cornell University Press.

Abrahamian, Ervand. 1973. "Kasravi: The Integrative Nationalist of Iran."
Middle Eastern Studies 9.3: 271–95.

———. 1982. *Iran between Two Revolutions.* Princeton: Princeton University
Press.

———. 1991. "Khomeini: Fundamentalist or Populist?" *New Left Review*
1.186: 102–19.

———. 1993. *Khomeinism: Essays on the Islamic Republic.* Berkeley and Los
Angeles: University of California Press.

———. 1999. *Tortured Confessions: Prisons and Public Recantations in Modern Iran.* Berkeley and Los Angeles: University of California Press.

———. 2001. "The 1953 Coup in Iran." *Science & Society* 65.2: 182–215.

———. 2008. *A History of Modern Iran.* Cambridge: Cambridge University
Press.

———. 2009. "The Crowd in the Iranian Revolution." *Radical History Review* 105: 13–38.

———. 2013. *The Coup: 1953, The CIA, and The Roots of Modern U.S.-Iranian Relations*. New York: New Press.

Abrams, Philip. 1988. "Notes on the Difficulty of Studying the State (1977)." *Journal of Historical Sociology* 1.1: 58–89.

Adams, Julia, Elisabeth Clemens, and Ann Shola Orloff, eds. 2005. *Remaking Modernity: Politics, History, and Sociology*. Durham: Duke University Press.

Adelkhah, Fariba. 1999. *Being Modern in Iran*. London: Hurst.

Aflakseir, Abdulaziz, and Peter Coleman. 2009. "The Influence of Religious Coping on the Mental Health of Disabled Iranian War Veterans." *Mental Health, Religion & Culture* 12.2: 175–90.

Aghajanian, Akbar. 1988. "Post-Revolutionary Demographic Trends in Iran." In *Post-Revolutionary Iran*, ed. Hooshang Amirahmadi and Manoucher Parvin, 153–67. Boulder: Westview Press.

Ahmadi, Ali, and Chris Harman. 1978. "What's Happening in Iran?" *Socialist Review* 6: 3–6.

Ahmadi-Amui, Bahman. 2003. *Eqtesād-e Siāsi-ye Jomhuri-ye Eslāmi*. Tehran: Gam-e Now Press.

Akbari, Mohammad Ali. 2002. *Barnāmeh Rizi-ye Dowlati dar Howzeh-ye Ta'min-e Ejtemā'i-ye Irān (1285–1380)*. Tehran: Moassesseh-ye Ali-ye Ta'min-e Ejtemā'i.

———. 2004. *Barrasi-ye Barnāmeh Rizi-ye Dowlati dar Howzeh-ye Ta'min-e Ejtemā'i-ye Irān, Volume 2 (1320–1357)*. Tehran: Moassesseh-ye Ali-ye Ta'min-e Ejtemā'i.

Alamdari, Kazem. 2005. "The Power Structure of the Islamic Republic of Iran: Transition from Populism to Clientelism, and Militarization of the Government." *Third World Quarterly* 26.8: 1285–1301.

Alem, Yasmin. 2011. *Duality by Design: The Iranian Electoral System*. Washington, D.C.: International Foundation for Electoral Systems.

Algar, Hamid. 1981. *Islam and Revolution: Writings and Declarations of Imam Khomeini*. Berkeley, Calif.: Mizan Press.

Amirahmadi, Hooshang. 1990. *Revolution and Economic Transition: The Iranian Experience*. Albany: SUNY Press.

Anderson, Benedict. 2005. *Under Three Flags: Anarchism and the Anti-Colonial Imagination*. London: Verso.

Andreas, Joel. 2009. *Rise of the Red Engineers: The Cultural Revolution and the Origins of China's New Class*. Stanford, Calif.: Stanford University Press.

Ansari, Ali M. 2001. "The Myth of the White Revolution: Mohammad Reza Shah, 'Modernization' and the Consolidation of Power." *Middle Eastern Studies* 37.3: 1–24.

Arendt, Hannah. 1968. *The Origins of Totalitarianism*. New York: Harcourt.

Arjomand, Saïd. 1988. *The Turban for the Crown: The Islamic Revolution in Iran*. New York: Oxford University Press.

———. 1994. "Fundamentalism, Religious Nationalism, or Populism?" *Contemporary Sociology* 23.5: 671–75.

————. 2009. *After Khomeini: Iran under His Successors.* Oxford and New York: Oxford University Press.

Arrighi, Giovanni. 1990. "The Developmentalist Illusion: A Reconceptualization of the Semiperiphery." In *Semiperipheral States in the World-Economy,* ed. William Martin, 11–42. New York: Greenwood Press.

————. 2002. "The African Crisis: World-Systemic and Regional Aspects." *New Left Review* 2.15: 5–36.

Arrighi, Giovanni, Beverly J. Silver, and Benjamin D. Brewer. 2003. "Industrial Convergence, Globalization, and the Persistence of the North-South Divide." *Studies in Comparative International Development* 38.1: 3–31.

Ashraf, Ahmad. 1969. "Historical Obstacles to the Development of a Bourgeoisie in Iran." *Iranian Studies* 2.2: 54–79.

————. 1988. "Bazaar-Mosque Alliance: The Social Basis of Revolts and Revolutions." *International Journal of Politics, Culture, and Society* 1.4: 538–67.

Ashraf, Ahmad, and Ali Banuazizi. 1985. "The State, Classes and Modes of Mobilization in the Iranian Revolution." *State, Culture, and Society* 1.3: 3–40.

Askari, Hossein, and Noora Arfaa. 2007. "Social Safety Net in Islam: The Case of Persian Gulf Oil Exporters." *British Journal of Middle Eastern Studies* 34.2: 177–202.

Assar, M., and Z. Jaksic. 1975. "A Health Services Development Project in Iran." In *Health by the People,* ed. Kenneth Newell, 112–27. Geneva: World Health Organization.

Atabaki, Touraj. 2007a. "Disgruntled Guests: Iranian Subalterns on the Margins of the Tsarist Empire." In *The State and the Subaltern: Modernization, Society and the State in Turkey and Iran,* ed. Touraj Atabaki, 31–52. London: I. B. Tauris.

————, ed. 2007b. *The State and the Subaltern: Modernization, Society and the State in Turkey and Iran.* London: I. B. Tauris.

Athari, Kamal. 1994. "The Housing Sector in Iran: Market or Planning?" In *The Economy of Islamic Iran: Between State and Market,* ed. Thierry Coville, 253–60. Louvain: Peeters.

Auty, Richard. 1993. *Sustaining Development in Mineral Economies: The Resource-Curse Thesis.* London: Routledge.

————. 2001. "The Political Economy of Resource-Driven Growth." *European Economic Review* 45.4–6: 839–46.

Auyero, Javier. 2004. "The Moral Politics of Argentine Crowds." *Mobilization: An International Quarterly* 9.3: 311–26.

Azimi, Fakhreddin. 1986. "Arsanǰānī, Ḥasan." *Encyclopaedia Iranica,* vol. 2, fasc. 5, p. 547. London: Routledge & Kegan Paul. [Updated 2011; online at: http://www.iranicaonline.org/articles/arsanjani-hasan-journalist-and-politician-1922–69.] [Accessed 13 March 2015.]

————. 2008. *The Quest for Democracy in Iran: A Century of Struggle against Authoritarian Rule.* Cambridge, Mass.: Harvard University Press.

Azizi, Farhad. 2009. "Medical Education in the Islamic Republic of Iran: Three Decades of Success." *Iranian Journal of Public Health* 38, Supplement 1: 19–26.

Azizi, Mohammad. 2012. "Tahlil-e moshārekat-e aqshār-e mokhtalef dar defā'-ye moqadas." *Pazhuheshnāmeh-ye Defā'-ye Moqadas* 1.2: 97–119.

Azkia, Mostafa. 2002. "Rural Society and Revolution in Iran." In *Twenty Years of Islamic Revolution: Political and Social Transition in Iran since 1979*, ed. Eric Hooglund, 96–119. Syracuse: Syracuse University Press.

Azkia, Mostafa, Hossein Araghi, and Hamid Ansari. 2004. *Local Development Fund (LDF) Project: Social Assessment of Poverty Clusters in Khoozestan Province.* Tehran: Ministry of Interior and The Cooperative Company of Technical Engineering Consultants for Sustainable Development.

Bahramitash, Roksana, and Hadi Salehi-Esfahani, eds. 2011. *Veiled Employment: Islamism and the Political Economy of Women's Employment in Iran.* Syracuse: Syracuse University Press.

Bakhash, Shaul. 1986. *The Reign of the Ayatollahs: Iran and the Islamic Revolution.* New York: Basic Books.

Baktiari, Bahman. 1996. *Parliamentary Politics in Revolutionary Iran: The Institutionalization of Factional Politics.* Gainesville: University Press of Florida.

Banani, Amin. 1961. *The Modernization of Iran, 1921–1941.* Stanford, Calif.: Stanford University Press.

Bani-Sadr, Abolhassan. 1982. *Khiānat beh Omid.* Paris: n.p.

Bāqi, Emādeddin. 2000. *Trāzhedi-ye Demokrāsi dar Irān.* Tehran: Nashr-e Ney.

Barrientos, Armando. 2004. "Latin America: Towards a Liberal-Informal Welfare Regime." In *Insecurity and Welfare Regimes in Asia, Africa and Latin America: Social Policy in Development Contexts*, ed. Ian Gough and Geof Wood, 121–68. Cambridge: Cambridge University Press.

Bashiriyeh, Hossein. 1984. *The State and Revolution in Iran, 1962–1982.* New York: St. Martin's Press.

———. 2010. "Counter-Revolution and Revolt in Iran: An Interview with Iranian Political Scientist Hossein Bashiriyeh." *Constellations* 17.1: 61–77.

Bast, Oliver. 2009. "Disintegrating the 'Discourse of Disintegration': Some Reflections on the Historiography of the Late Qajar Period and Iranian Cultural Memory." In *Iran in the 20th Century: Historiography and Political Culture*, ed. Touraj Atabaki, 55–68. London: I. B. Tauris.

Bayat, Asef. 1987. *Workers and Revolution in Iran: A Third World Experience of Workers' Control.* London: Zed Books.

———. 1997. *Street Politics: Poor People's Movements in Iran.* New York: Columbia University Press.

———. 2010. "Tehran: Paradox City." *New Left Review* 2.66: 99–122.

Baylouny, Anne Marie. 2010. *Privatizing Welfare in the Middle East: Kin Mutual Aid Associations in Jordan and Lebanon.* Bloomington: Indiana University Press.

Beblawi, Hazem, and Giacomo Luciani, eds. 1987. *The Rentier State.* London: Croom Helm.

Behdad, Sohrab. 2006. "Islam, Revivalism, and Public Policy." In *Islam and the Everyday World: Public Policy Dilemmas,* ed. Sohrab Behdad and Farhad Nomani, 1–37. London: Routledge.

Behdad, Sohrab, and Farhad Nomani. 2009. "What a Revolution! Thirty Years of Social-Class Reshuffling in Iran." *Comparative Studies of South Asia, Africa and the Middle East* 29.1: 84–104.

Behrooz, Maziar. 1991. "Factionalism in Iran under Khomeini." *Middle Eastern Studies* 27.4: 597–614.

———. 1999. *Rebels with a Cause: The Failure of the Left in Iran.* London and New York: I. B. Tauris.

Béland, Daniel, and Robert Cox, eds. 2011. *Ideas and Politics in Social Science Research.* Oxford: Oxford University Press.

Bellefonds, Y. Linant de. 2012. "Ḍarūra." *Encyclopaedia of Islam,* 2nd ed. Ed. P. Bearman et al. [Bearman, P., T. Bianquis, C. E. Bosworth, E. van Donzel, and W. P. Heinrichs.] http://referenceworks.brillonline.com/entries/encyclo-paedia-of-islam-2/darura-SIM_1730?s.num=170&s.start=160. [Accessed 18 August 2015.]

Bendix, Reinhard. 1956. *Work and Authority in Industry: Managerial Ideologies in the Course of Industrialization.* New York: Wiley.

Benhoud, Masoud, and Hojat Sepahvand. 2008. *Kaveh Golestan: Recording the Truth in Iran, 1950–2003.* Ed. Malu Halasa. Ostfildern: Hatje Cantz.

Benthall, Jonathan, and Jerome Bellion-Jourdan. 2009. *The Charitable Crescent: Politics of Aid in the Muslim World.* 2nd ed. London: I. B. Tauris.

Bianchi, Robert. 1989. *Unruly Corporatism: Associational Life in Twentieth-Century Egypt.* New York: Oxford University Press.

Bjorvatn, Kjetil, Mohammad Reza Farzanegan, and Friedrich Schneider. 2012. "Resource Curse and Power Balance: Evidence from Oil-Rich Countries." *World Development* 40.7: 1308–16.

Blackburn, Robin. 1999. "The New Collectivism: Pension Reform, Grey Capitalism and Complex Socialism." *New Left Review* 1.233: 3–65.

———. 2002. *Banking on Death, or Investing in Life: The History and Future of Pensions.* London: Verso.

Boroujerdi, Mehrzad. 1996. *Iranian Intellectuals and the West: The Tormented Triumph of Nativism.* Syracuse: Syracuse University Press.

Bostock, Frances, and Geoffrey Jones. 1989. *Planning and Power in Iran: Ebtehaj and Economic Development under the Shah.* London: Frank Cass and Co., Ltd.

Bromley, Simon. 1994. *Rethinking Middle East Politics.* Austin: University of Texas Press.

Bruce, Maurice. 1968. *The Coming of the Welfare State.* 4th ed. London: Batsford.

Brunnschweiler, Christa N. 2008. "Cursing the Blessings? Natural Resource Abundance, Institutions, and Economic Growth." *World Development* 36.3: 399–419.

Buchanan, James. 1975. *The Limits of Liberty: Between Anarchy and Leviathan.* Chicago: University of Chicago Press.

Buchanan, James, Robert Tollison, and Gordon Tullock, eds. 1980. *Toward a Theory of the Rent-Seeking Society.* College Station: Texas A&M University Press.

Burns, Gene. 1996. "Ideology, Culture, and Ambiguity: The Revolutionary Process in Iran." *Theory and Society* 25.3: 349–88.

Cammett, Melani, and Lauren MacLean. 2011. "Introduction: The Political Consequences of Non-state Social Welfare in the Global South." *Studies in Comparative International Development* 46.1: 1–21.

———, eds. 2014. *The Politics of Non-state Welfare*. Ithaca: Cornell University Press.

Cammett, Melani, and Aytuğ Şaşmaz. 2016. "Social Policy in Developing Countries." In *The Oxford Handbook of Historical Institutionalism*, ed. Orfeo Fioretos, Tulia G. Falleti, and Adam Sheingate, 239–55. Oxford: Oxford University Press.

Cardoso, Fernando, and Enzo Faletto. 1979. *Dependency and Development in Latin America*. Berkeley and Los Angeles: University of California Press.

Carnes, Matthew, and Isabela Mares. 2007. "The Welfare State in Global Perspective." In *The Oxford Handbook of Comparative Politics*, ed. Carles Boix and Susan Carol Stokes, 868–85. Oxford: Oxford University Press.

Centeno, Miguel Ángel. 1997. *Democracy within Reason: Technocratic Revolution in Mexico*, 2nd ed. University Park: Pennsylvania State University Press.

Cerami, Alfio, and Pieter Vanhuysse, eds. 2009. *Post-Communist Welfare Pathways: Theorizing Social Policy Transformations in Central and Eastern Europe*. Basingstoke, Hants: Palgrave Macmillan.

Chaichian, Mohammad. 2011. "The New Phase of Globalization and Brain Drain: Migration of Educated and Skilled Iranians to the United States." *International Journal of Social Economics* 39.1–2: 18–38.

Chang, Ha-Joon. 2002. *Kicking Away the Ladder: Development Strategy in Historical Perspective*. London: Anthem Press.

———. 2008. *Bad Samaritans: The Myth of Free Trade and the Secret History of Capitalism*. New York: Bloomsbury.

Chaudhry, Kiren Aziz. 1994. "The Middle East and the Political Economy of Development." *Items* 48: 41–49.

———. 1997. *The Price of Wealth: Economies and Institutions in the Middle East*. Ithaca: Cornell University Press.

Chehabi, Houchang. 2004. "Dress Codes for Men in Turkey and Iran." In *Men of Order: Authoritarian Modernization under Atatürk and Reza Shah*, ed. Touraj Atabaki and Erik Zürcher, 209–37. London: I. B. Tauris.

Chehabi, Houchang E., and Juan Linz, eds. 1998. *Sultanistic Regimes*. Baltimore: The Johns Hopkins University Press.

Chibber, Vivek. 2014. *Postcolonial Theory and the Specter of Capital*. London: Verso.

Chorev, Nitsan. 2012. *The World Health Organization between North and South*. Ithaca: Cornell University Press.

Clark, Janine. 2004. *Islam, Charity, and Activism: Middle-Class Networks and Social Welfare in Egypt, Jordan, and Yemen*. Bloomington: Indiana University Press.

Clawson, Patrick. 1981. "Iran's Economy: Between Crisis and Collapse." *MERIP Reports* 98: 11–15.

Clay, Karen. 2011. "Natural Resources and Economic Outcomes." In *Economic Evolution and Revolution in Historical Time*, ed. Paul Rhode, Joshua Rosenbloom, and David Weiman, 27–50. Stanford, Calif.: Stanford University Press.

Cohen, Stephen. 1980. *Bukharin and the Bolshevik Revolution: A Political Biography, 1888–1938*. Oxford: Oxford University Press.

Collier, Ruth, and David Collier. 1979. "Inducements versus Constraints: Disaggregating 'Corporatism.'" *American Political Science Review* 73.4: 967–86.

Collins, Randall. 2001. "Social Movements and the Focus of Emotional Attention." In *Passionate Politics: Emotions and Social Movements*, ed. Jeff Goodwin, James Jasper, and Francesca Polletta, 27–44. Chicago: University of Chicago Press.

Connelly, Matthew. 2008. *Fatal Misconception: The Struggle to Control World Population*. Cambridge, Mass.: Harvard University Press.

The Constitution of the Islamic Republic of Iran. Translated version available from the Foundation for Iranian Studies: http://fis-iran.org/en/resources /legaldoc/constitutionislamic. [Accessed 22 April 2015.]

Cooper, Frederick. 2005. *Colonialism in Question: Theory, Knowledge, History*. Berkeley and Los Angeles: University of California Press.

Cornia, Giovanni, and Vladimir Popov, eds. 2001. *Transition and Institutions: The Experience of Gradual and Late Reformers*. Oxford and New York: Oxford University Press.

Coronil, Fernando. 2001. "Smelling like a Market." *American Historical Review* 106.1: 119–29.

Cronin, Stephanie. 2004. *Reformers and Revolutionaries in Modern Iran: New Perspectives on the Iranian Left*. London and New York: Routledge Curzon.

———. 2007. *Tribal Politics in Iran: Rural Conflict and the New State, 1921–1941*. London and New York: Routledge.

———. 2010. "Popular Politics, the New State and the Birth of the Iranian Working Class: The 1929 Abadan Oil Refinery Strike." *Middle Eastern Studies* 46.5: 699–732.

Cumings, Bruce. 2007. "Civil Society in West and East." In *Korean Society: Civil Society, Democracy, and the State*, 2nd ed., ed. Charles Armstrong, 9–32. London: Routledge.

Curtis, Glenn, and Eric Hooglund. 2008. *Iran: A Country Study*. Washington, D.C.: Library of Congress, Federal Research Division.

Dabashi, Hamid. 1993. *Theology of Discontent: The Ideological Foundations of the Islamic Revolution in Iran*. New York: New York University Press.

———. 2010. *Iran, the Green Movement and the USA: The Fox and the Paradox*. London: Zed Books.

———. 2011. *The Green Movement in Iran*. New Brunswick: Transaction Publishers.

Daftary, Farhad. 1973. "Development Planning in Iran: A Historical Survey." *Iranian Studies* 6.4: 176–228.

Davis, Mike. 2006. *Planet of Slums*. London: Verso.

Derluguian, Georgi. 2005. *Bourdieu's Secret Admirer in the Caucasus: A World-System Biography*. Chicago: University of Chicago Press.

Derluguian, Georgi, and Timothy Earle. 2010. "Strong Chieftaincies out of Weak States, or Elemental Power Unbound." *Comparative Social Research* 27: 51–76.

Devarajan, Shanta, and Lili Mottaghi. 2015. "Economic Implications of Lifting Sanctions on Iran." *Middle East and North Africa Quarterly Economic Brief* 5. Washington, D.C.: World Bank Publications.

Diamond, Larry. 2010. "Why Are There No Arab Democracies?" *Journal of Democracy* 21.1: 93–112.

Dittmer, Lowell, and Yu-Shan Wu. 1995. "The Modernization of Factionalism in Chinese Politics." *World Politics* 47.4: 467–94.

Dowlatabadi, Mahmoud. 2011. *The Colonel*. London: Haus Publishing.

Drèze, Jean, and Amartya Sen. 1989. *Hunger and Public Action*. New York: Oxford University Press.

Dunning, Thad. 2008. *Crude Democracy: Natural Resource Wealth and Political Regimes*. Cambridge: Cambridge University Press.

Ehsani, Kaveh. 1999a. "The Existing Vessels Can No Longer Contain the Movement." *Middle East Report* 212: 40–42. [Interview with Said Hajjāriān.]

———. 1999b. "Municipal Matters: The Urbanization of Consciousness and Political Change in Tehran." *Middle East Report* 212: 22–27.

———. 2003. "Social Engineering and the Contradictions of Modernization in Khuzestan's Company Towns: A Look at Abadan and Masjed-Soleyman." *International Review of Social History* 48.3: 361–99.

———. 2006. "Rural Society and Agricultural Development in Post-Revolution Iran: The First Two Decades." *Critique: Critical Middle Eastern Studies* 15.1: 79–96.

———. 2009. "The Urban Provincial Periphery in Iran: Revolution and War in Ramhormoz." In *Contemporary Iran: Economy, Society, Politics,* ed. Ali Gheissari, 38–76. Oxford: Oxford University Press.

Ehteshami, Anoushiravan. 1995. *After Khomeini: The Iranian Second Republic*. London: Routledge.

Ehteshami, Anoushiravan, and Emma Murphy. 1996. "Transformation of the Corporatist State in the Middle East." *Third World Quarterly* 17.4: 753–72.

El-Ashker, Ahmed, and Rodney Wilson. 2006. *Islamic Economics: A Short History*. Leiden: Brill.

Enayat, Hamid. 2005. *Modern Islamic Political Thought*. London: I.B.Tauris.

Erfani, Amir, and Kevin McQuillan. 2008. "Rates of Induced Abortion in Iran: The Roles of Contraceptive Use and Religiosity." *Studies in Family Planning* 39.2: 111–22.

Esping-Andersen, Gøsta. 1990a. "The Three Political Economies of the Welfare State." *International Journal of Sociology* 20.3: 92–123.

———. 1990b. *The Three Worlds of Welfare Capitalism*. Princeton: Princeton University Press.

———. 1999. *Social Foundations of Postindustrial Economies*. Oxford and New York: Oxford University Press.

Etminan, Elham, and Kobra Chaker-ol-Hosseini. 2007. "Social Protection for Informal Workers: The Iranian Experience." Paper presented at the Fifth Annual International Research Conference on Social Security, 5–7 March, Warsaw.

Evans, Peter. 1995. *Embedded Autonomy: States and Industrial Transformation*. Princeton: Princeton University Press.

———. 2010. "Constructing the 21st Century Developmental State: Potentialities and Pitfalls." In *Constructing a Democratic Developmental State in South Africa: Potentials and Challenges,* ed. Omano Edigheji, 37–58. Cape Town: HSRC Press.

Farhi, Farideh. 1998. "The Contending Discourses on Women in Iran." *Third World Resurgence* 94: 5–7.

———. 2003. "Improvising in Public: Transgressive Politics of the Reformist Press in Postrevolutionary Iran." In *Intellectual Trends in Twentieth-Century Iran: A Critical Survey,* ed. Negin Nabavi, 147–79. Gainesville: University Press of Florida.

———. 2004. "The Antinomies of Iran's War Generation." In *Iran, Iraq, and the Legacies of War,* ed. Lawrence Potter and Gary Sick, 101–20. New York: Palgrave MacMillan.

Fischer, Michael. 1980. *Iran: From Religious Dispute to Revolution.* Madison: University of Wisconsin Press.

Fitzpatrick, Sheila. 1999. *Everyday Stalinism: Ordinary Life in Extraordinary Times: Soviet Russia in the 1930s.* New York: Oxford University Press.

Folbre, Nancy. 2008. *Valuing Children: Rethinking the Economics of Family.* Cambridge, Mass.: Harvard University Press.

Foran, John. 1993. *Fragile Resistance: Social Transformation in Iran from 1500 to the Revolution.* Boulder: Westview Press.

———, ed. 1994. *A Century of Revolution: Social Movements in Iran.* Minneapolis: University of Minnesota Press.

———. 2005. *Taking Power: On the Origins of Third World Revolutions.* Cambridge: Cambridge University Press.

Friedrich, Carl, and Zbigniew Brzezinski. 1956. *Totalitarian Dictatorship and Autocracy.* Cambridge, Mass.: Harvard University Press.

Gall, Lothar. 1986. *Bismarck, the White Revolutionary.* Boston: Allen & Unwin.

Gambetta, Diego, and Steffen Hertog. 2009. "Why Are There So Many Engineers among Islamic Radicals?" *European Journal of Sociology / Archives Européennes de Sociologie* 50.2: 201–30.

Ganji, Akbar. 1999. '*Alijenāb-e Sorkhpush va 'Alijenābān-e Khākestari: Āsibshenāsi-ye Gozār beh Dowlat-e Demokrātik-e Towse'eh-garā.* Tehran: Tarh-e Now.

———. 2005. "The Struggle against Sultanism." *Journal of Democracy* 16.4: 38–51.

Gasiorowski, Mark, and Malcolm Byrne, eds. 2004. *Mohammad Mosaddeq and the 1953 Coup in Iran.* Syracuse: Syracuse University Press.

Gellner, Ernest. 1994. "The Struggle to Catch Up." *The Times Literary Supplement,* 9 December, 14–15.

Gerschenkron, Alexander. 1962. *Economic Backwardness in Historical Perspective: A Book of Essays.* Cambridge, Mass.: Belknap Press of Harvard University Press.

Ghamari-Tabrizi, Behrooz. 2008. *Islam and Dissent in Postrevolutionary Iran.* London: I. B. Tauris.

———. 2009. "Memory, Mourning, Memorializing: On the Victims of Iran-Iraq War, 1980–Present." *Radical History Review* 105: 106–21.

———. 2014. "The Divine, the People, and the Faqih: On Khomeini's Theory of Sovereignty." In *A Critical Introduction to Khomeini,* ed. Arshin Adib-Moghaddam, 211—38. Cambridge: Cambridge University Press.

Gheissari, Ali, and Vali Nasr. 2006. *Democracy in Iran: History and the Quest for Liberty.* Oxford: Oxford University Press.

Ghods, Reza. 1991. "Iranian Nationalism and Reza Shah." *Middle Eastern Studies* 27.1: 35–45.

Gibson, Christopher. 2012. "Civilizing the State: Civil Society and the Politics of Primary Public Health Care in Urban Brazil." Ph.D. dissertation, Department of Sociology, Brown University.

———. 2016. "Sanitaristas, Petistas, and the Post-Neoliberal Public Health State in Porto Alegre." *Latin American Perspectives* 43.2: 153–71.

Giddens, Anthony. 1998. *The Third Way: The Renewal of Social Democracy.* London: Polity Press.

Goffman, Erving. 1961. *Asylums: Essays on the Social Situation of Mental Patients and Other Inmates.* New York: Doubleday.

Goldman, Wendy. 1993. *Women, the State and Revolution: Soviet Family Policy and Social Life, 1917–1936.* Cambridge: Cambridge University Press.

Goldstone, Jack. 2008. "Modern Revolutions?" *Harvard International Review.* Online at: http://hir.harvard.edu/articles/1685. [Accessed 13 March 2015.]

Goodell, Grace. 1986. *The Elementary Structures of Political Life: Rural Development in Pahlavi Iran.* New York: Oxford University Press.

Goodwin, Jeff. 2001. *No Other Way Out: States and Revolutionary Movements, 1945–1991.* Cambridge: Cambridge University Press.

Gough, Ian. 1979. *Political Economy of the Welfare State.* London: MacMillan.

———. 2004. "East Asia: The Limits of Productivist Regimes." In *Insecurity and Welfare Regimes in Asia, Africa and Latin America: Social Policy in Development Contexts,* ed. Ian Gough and Geof Wood, 169-201. Cambridge: Cambridge University Press.

Gough, Ian, and Geof Wood, eds. 2004. *Insecurity and Welfare Regimes in Asia, Africa and Latin America: Social Policy in Development Contexts.* Cambridge: Cambridge University Press.

Gould, Stephen Jay. 1997. *Full House: The Spread of Excellence from Plato to Darwin.* New York: Three Rivers Press.

Guillaume, Dominique, Roman Zytek, and Mohammad Reza Farzin. 2011. *Iran—The Chronicles of the Subsidy Reform.* IMF Working Paper. Washington, D.C.: International Monetary Fund.

Haber, Stephen. 2007. "Authoritarian Government." In *The Oxford Handbook of Political Economy,* ed. Barry Weingast and Donald Wittman, 688–711. Oxford: Oxford University Press.

Haber, Stephen, and Victor Menaldo. 2011. "Do Natural Resources Fuel Authoritarianism? A Reappraisal of the Resource Curse." *American Political Science Review* 105.1: 1–26.

Habibi, Nader. 1989. "Allocation of Educational and Occupational Opportunities in the Islamic Republic of Iran: A Case Study in the Political Screening of Human Capital." *Iranian Studies* 22.4: 19–46.

Hajizadeh, Mohammad, and Luke B. Connelly. 2010. "Equity of Health-Care Financing in Iran: The Effect of Extending Health Insurance to the Uninsured." *Oxford Development Studies* 38.4: 461–76.

Hakimian, Hassan. 2011. "Iran's Free-Trade Zones: Back Doors to the International Economy?" *Iranian Studies* 44.6: 851–74.

Hall, Anthony, and James Midgley. 2004. *Social Policy for Development*. London: Sage Publications.

Halliday, Fred. 1987. "The Middle East in International Perspective: Problems of Analysis." In *The World Order: Socialist Perspectives,* ed. Ray Bush, Gordon Johnston, and David Coates, 201–20. London: Polity Press.

———. 2004. "The Iranian Left in International Perspective." In *Reformers and Revolutionaries in Modern Iran: New Perspectives on the Iranian Left,* ed. Stephanie Cronin, 19–36. London and New York: RoutledgeCurzon.

Halliday, Fred, and Hamza Alavi, eds. 1988. *State and Ideology in the Middle East and Pakistan*. London: Macmillan.

Harris, Kevan. 2012a. "The Politics of Welfare after Revolution and War: The Imam Khomeini Relief Committee in the Islamic Republic of Iran." In *The Cup, The Gun and The Crescent: Social Welfare and Civil Unrest in Muslim Societies,* ed. Sara Crabtree, Jonathan Parker, and Azlinda Azman, 134–50. London: Whiting and Birch.

———. 2012b. "The Brokered Exuberance of the Middle Class: An Ethnographic Analysis of Iran's 2009 Green Movement." *Mobilization* 17.6: 435–55.

———. 2013. "An 'Electoral Uprising' in Iran." *Middle East Reports Online,* 19 July. Online at: http://www.merip.org/mero/mero071913. [Accessed 13 March 2015.]

Harvey, David. 1982. *The Limits to Capital*. Chicago: University of Chicago Press.

Hayati, Dariush, and Ezatollah Karami. 2005. "Typology of Causes of Poverty: The Perception of Iranian Farmers." *Journal of Economic Psychology* 26.6: 884–901.

Haydu, Jeffrey. 1998. "Making Use of the Past: Time Periods as Cases to Compare and as Sequences of Problem Solving." *American Journal of Sociology* 104.2: 339–71.

———. 2010. "Reversals of Fortune: Path Dependency, Problem Solving, and Temporal Cases." *Theory and Society* 39.1: 25–48.

Hegland, Mary. 2013. *Days of Revolution: Political Unrest in an Iranian Village*. Stanford, Calif.: Stanford University Press.

Heller, Patrick. 1999. *The Labor of Development: Workers and the Transformation of Capitalism in Kerala, India*. Ithaca: Cornell University Press.

Herb, Michael. 1999. *All in the Family: Absolutism, Revolution, and Democracy in the Middle Eastern Monarchies*. Albany: SUNY Press.

———. 2005. "No Representation without Taxation? Rents, Development, and Democracy." *Comparative Politics* 37.3: 297–316.

Hertog, Steffen. 2010a. "Defying the Resource Curse: Explaining Successful State-Owned Enterprises in Rentier States." *World Politics* 62.2: 261–301.

———. 2010b. *Princes, Brokers, and Bureaucrats: Oil and the State in Saudi Arabia*. Ithaca: Cornell University Press.

Heydemann, Steven. 1992. "The Political Logic of Economic Rationality: Selective Stabilization in Syria," in *The Politics of Economic Reform in the Middle East*, ed. Henri Barkey, 11–39. New York: St. Martin's Press.

Hezb-e Jomhuri-ye Eslāmi. 2009. *Mavāze'-e Mā*. Tehran: Islamic Republic Publishing.

Hinnebusch, Raymond. 2010. "Toward a Historical Sociology of State Formation in the Middle East." *Middle East Critique* 19.3: 201–16.

Hiro, Dilip. 1987. *Iran under the Ayatollahs*. London: Routledge & Kegan Paul.

———. 1991. *The Longest War: The Iran-Iraq Military Conflict*. New York: Routledge.

Hoodfar, Homa. 1994. "Devices and Desires: Population Policy and Gender Roles in the Islamic Republic." *Middle East Report* 190: 11–17.

———. 1996. "Bargaining with Fundamentalism: Women and the Politics of Population Control in Iran." *Reproductive Health Matters* 4.8: 30–40.

———. 1998. *Volunteer Health Workers in Iran as Social Activists: Can "Governmental Non-Governmental Organisations" Be Agents of Democratisation?* Occasional Papers, no.10. London: Women Living under Muslim Laws.

Hoodfar, Homa, and Samad Assadpour. 2000. "The Politics of Population Policy in the Islamic Republic of Iran." *Studies in Family Planning* 31.1: 19–34.

Hooglund, Eric J. 1982. *Land and Revolution in Iran, 1960–1980*. Austin: University of Texas Press.

———. 1986. "1980–85: Political and Economic Trends." In *The Iranian Revolution and the Islamic Republic*, ed. Nikki Keddie and Eric Hooglund, 17–31. Syracuse: Syracuse University Press.

———. 2011. "Changing Attitudes among Women in Rural Iran." In *Gender in Contemporary Iran: Pushing the Boundaries,* ed. Roksana Bahramitash and Eric Hooglund, 120–35. London: Routledge.

Hort, Sven, and Göran Therborn. 2012. "Citizenship and Welfare: Politics and Social Policies." In *The Wiley-Blackwell Companion to Political Sociology,* ed. Edwin Amenta, Kate Nash, and Alan Scott, 360–71. Malden, Mass.: Wiley-Blackwell.

Hourcade, Bernard. 1993. "The Land Question and Islamic Revolution in Iran." *Comparative Studies of South Asia, Africa and the Middle East* 13.1–2: 134–47.

Huang, Jing. 2000. *Factionalism in Chinese Communist Politics*. New York: Cambridge University Press.

Huber, Evelyne, and John Stephens. 2001. *Development and Crisis of the Welfare State: Parties and Policies in Global Markets*. Chicago: University of Chicago Press.

Hunt, Matthew, and Heather Bullock. 2016. "Ideologies and Beliefs about Poverty." In *The Oxford Handbook of the Social Science of Poverty*, ed. David Brady and Linda Burton, 93–117. Oxford: Oxford University Press.

Huntington, Samuel. 1991. *The Third Wave: Democratization in the Late Twentieth Century*. Norman: University of Oklahoma Press.

Ibrahimipour, Hossein, et al. [Ibrahimipour, Hossein, Mohammad-Reza Maleki, Richard Brown, Mohammadreza Gohari, Iraj Karimi and Reza Dehnavieh.] 2011. "A Qualitative Study of the Difficulties in Reaching Sustainable

Universal Health Insurance Coverage in Iran." *Health Policy and Planning* 26.6: 485–95.

International Crisis Group. 2005. *Iran: What Does Ahmadi-Nejad's Victory Mean?* Middle East Briefing. New York: International Crisis Group.

International Labour Organization. 2004. *An Employment Strategy for the Islamic Republic of Iran.* New Delhi: ILO Press.

———. 2010. *ILO World Social Security Report 2010–2011.* Geneva: International Labour Organization.

Iqbal, Farrukh. 2006. *Sustaining Gains in Poverty Reduction and Human Development in the Middle East and North Africa.* Washington, D.C.: World Bank Publications.

Jafari, Peyman. 2013. "Reasons to Revolt: Iranian Oil Workers in the 1970s." *International Labor and Working-Class History* 84: 195–217.

Jalāeipour, Hamidreza. 2003. "Religious Intellectuals and Political Action in the Reform Movement." In *Intellectual Trends in Twentieth-Century Iran: A Critical Survey,* ed. Negin Nabavi, 136–46. Gainesville: University Press of Florida.

Jalāli, Mohammad Farid. 2005. "Barresi-ye rābeteh-ye faqr bā enherāfāt-e ejtemā'i va rāh-hāye zududan-e ān bā ta'kid bar komiteh-ye emdād-e imām Khomeini." *Faslnāmeh-ye Emdād Pazhuhān* 3.9: 37–54.

Jasper, James. 1997. *The Art of Moral Protest: Culture, Biography, and Creativity in Social Movements.* Chicago: University of Chicago Press.

Javanparast, Sara, et al. [Javanparast, Sara, Fran Baum, Ronald Labonte, David Sanders, Gholamreza Heidari, and Sakineh Rezaie.] 2011. "A Policy Review of the Community Health Worker Programme in Iran." *Journal of Public Health Policy* 32.2: 263–76.

Jawad, Rana, and Burcu Yakut-Çakar. 2010. "Religion and Social Policy in the Middle East: The (Re)Constitution of an Old-New Partnership." *Social Policy & Administration* 44.6: 658–72.

Jefroudi, Maral. 2013. "Revisiting 'the Long Night' of Iranian Workers: Labor Activism in the Iranian Oil Industry in the 1960s." *International Labor and Working-Class History* 84: 176–94.

Johnson, Chalmers. 1982. *MITI and the Japanese Miracle: The Growth of Industrial Policy, 1925–1975.* Stanford, Calif.: Stanford University Press.

———. 1999. "The Developmental State: Odyssey of a Concept." In *The Developmental State,* ed. Meredith Woo-Cumings, 32–60. Ithaca: Cornell University Press.

Jowitt, Kenneth. 1971. *Revolutionary Breakthroughs and National Development: The Case of Romania, 1944–1965.* Berkeley and Los Angeles: University of California Press.

Kadivar, Ali. 2011. "Electoral Opportunities and Emotional Energies: Evidence from 2009 Iranian Green Movement." Paper presented at the Middle East Studies Association Conference, Washington, D.C.

Kamrava, Mehran. 2001. "The Civil Society Discourse in Iran." *British Journal of Middle Eastern Studies* 28.2: 165–85.

Karimi, Setareh. 1986. "Economic Policies and Structural Changes since the Revolution." In *The Iranian Revolution and the Islamic Republic,* ed. Nikki Keddie and Eric Hooglund, 32–54. Syracuse: Syracuse University Press.

Karshenas, Massoud, and Mohammad Hashem Pesaran. 1994. "Exchange-Rate Unification, the Role of Markets and Planning in the Iranian Economic Reconstruction." In *The Economy of Islamic Iran: Between State and Market*, ed. Thierry Coville, 141–76. Louvain: Peeters.

Kasravi, Ahmad. 2006. *History of the Iranian Constitutional Revolution.* Trans. Evan Siegel. Costa Mesa, Calif.: Mazda Publishers.

Katouzian, Homa. 1979. "The Political Economy of Oil-Exporting Countries." *Peuples Méditerranéens* 1: 3–22.

———. 2004. "The Strange Politics of Khalil Maleki." In *Reformers and Revolutionaries in Modern Iran: New Perspectives on the Iranian Left,* ed. Stephanie Cronin 165–88. London and New York: RoutledgeCurzon.

Katznelson, Ira, and Aristide Zolberg, eds. 1986. *Working-Class Formation: Nineteenth-Century Patterns in Western Europe and the United States.* Princeton: Princeton University Press.

Kazemi, Farhad. 1999. "Fedā'īān-e Eslām." *Encyclopaedia Iranica*, vol. 9, fasc. 5, pp. 470–74. London: Routledge & Kegan Paul. [Updated 2012; online at: http://www.iranicaonline.org/articles/fedaian-e-esla.] [Accessed 13 March 2015.]

Keddie, Nikki. 1988. "Ideology, Society and the State in Post-Colonial Muslim Societies." In *State and Ideology in the Middle East and Pakistan,* ed. Fred Halliday and Hamza Alavi, 9–30. New York: Macmillan.

Kersbergen, Kees van, and Philip Manow, eds. 2009. *Religion, Class Coalitions, and Welfare States.* Cambridge: Cambridge University Press.

Keshavarzian, Arang. 2007. *Bazaar and State in Iran: The Politics of the Tehran Marketplace.* Cambridge: Cambridge University Press.

———. 2010. "Geopolitics and the Genealogy of Free-Trade Zones in the Persian Gulf." *Geopolitics* 15.2: 263–89.

Khalatbari, Firouzeh. 1994. "Iran: A Unique Underground Economy." In *The Economy of Islamic Iran: Between State and Market,* ed. Thierry Coville, 113–38. Louvain: Peeters.

Khan, Mushtaq, and Jomo Kwame Sundaram, eds. 2000. *Rents, Rent-Seeking and Economic Development: Theory and Evidence in Asia.* Cambridge: Cambridge University Press.

Khojasteh, A., et al. [Khojasteh, A., N. Momtazmanesh, A. Entezari, and B. Einollahi.] 2009. "Integration of Medical Education and Healthcare Service." *Iranian Journal of Public Health* 38, Supplement 1: 29–31.

Khomeini, Ruhollah. 1999. *Sahifeh-ye Imām,* volume 1. Tehran: Moassesseh-ye Tanzim va Nashr-e Āsār-e Hazrat-e Imām Khomeini.

Khosrokhavar, Farhad. 1979. "The Committee in the Iranian Revolution: The Case of a Mid-Sized City: Hamadan." *Peuples Méditerranéens* 9: 85–100.

Khoury, Dina. 2013. *Iraq in Wartime: Soldiering, Martyrdom, and Remembrance.* Cambridge: Cambridge University Press.

Kimiāfar, Seyyed Mahmoud. 2008. *Komiteh-ye Emdād va Jang.* Tehran: Majmu'eh-ye Farhangi-ye Shahid Beheshti.

King, Charles. 2010. *Extreme Politics: Nationalism, Violence, and the End of Eastern Europe.* Oxford: Oxford University Press.

Kissinger, Henry. 1968. "The White Revolutionary: Reflections on Bismarck." *Daedalus* 97.3: 888–924.

Komiteh-ye Emdād-e Imām Khomeini: Barrasi-ye Towsifi va Tahlili. 1994. Tehran: Moassesseh-ye Ali-ye Pazhuhesh dar Barnāmeh Rizi va Towse'eh.

Komiteh-ye Emdād-e Imām Khomeini: Barnāmeh-ye Panj Sāleh-ye Dovom 1374–78. 1995. Tehran: Mo'āvanat-e Pazhuhesh va Barnāmeh Rizi.

Kornai, János. 2008. *From Socialism to Capitalism: Eight Essays.* Budapest: Central European University Press.

Korpi, Walter. 1983. *The Democratic Class Struggle.* London: Routledge & Kegan Paul.

———. 2003. "Welfare-State Regress in Western Europe: Politics, Institutions, Globalization, and Europeanization." *Annual Review of Sociology* 29: 589–609.

Korzeniewicz, Roberto Patricio, et al. [Korzeniewicz, Roberto Patricio, Angela Stach, Vrushali Patil, and Timothy Patrick Moran.] 2004. "Measuring National Income: A Critical Assessment." *Comparative Studies in Society and History* 46.3: 535–86.

Korzeniewicz, Roberto Patricio, and Timothy Patrick Moran. 2009. *Unveiling Inequality: A World-Historical Perspective.* New York: Russell Sage Foundation.

Kotkin, Stephen. 1995. *Magnetic Mountain: Stalinism as a Civilization.* Berkeley and Los Angeles: University of California Press.

Kozhanov, Nikolay A. 2012. "The Pretexts and Reasons for the Allied Invasion of Iran in 1941." *Iranian Studies* 45.4: 479–97.

Krueger, Anne. 1974. "The Political Economy of the Rent-Seeking Society." *American Economic Review* 64.3: 291–303.

Kurzman, Charles. 2004. *The Unthinkable Revolution in Iran.* Cambridge, Mass.: Harvard University Press.

———. 2008. *Democracy Denied, 1905–1915: Intellectuals and the Fate of Democracy.* Cambridge, Mass.: Harvard University Press.

———. 2013. "Death Tolls of the Iran-Iraq War." 31 October: http://kurzman.unc.edu/death-tolls-of-the-iran-iraq-war/. [Accessed 15 June 2015.]

Kusujiarti, Siti. 2011. "Pluralistic and Informal Welfare Regime: The Roles of Islamic Institutions in the Indonesian Welfare Regime." In *The Sociology of Islam: Secularism, Economy and Politics,* ed. Tugrul Keskin, 419–52. Reading, Berks: Ithaca Press.

Lachmann, Richard. 2009. *States and Power.* London: Polity Press.

Ladjevardi, Habib. 1985. *Labor Unions and Autocracy in Iran.* Syracuse: Syracuse University Press.

Lee, Ching Kwan. 2007. *Against the Law: Labor Protests in China's Rustbelt and Sunbelt.* Berkeley and Los Angeles: University of California Press.

Lewin, Moshe. 1985. *The Making of the Soviet System: Essays in the Social History of Interwar Russia.* New York: Pantheon.

Lewis, Jane. 1997. "Gender and Welfare Regimes: Further Thoughts." *Social Politics: International Studies in Gender, State & Society* 4.2: 160–77.

Lob, Eric. 2012. "Jehad-e Sazandegi and the End of the Iranian Revolution (1979–1983)." Paper presented at the conference "How to End a Revolution?" Harvard University, 13–14 April.

———. 2013. "An Institutional History of the Iranian Construction Jihad." Ph.D. dissertation, Department of Near Eastern Studies, Princeton University.

Lockman, Zachary. 2010. *Contending Visions of the Middle East: The History and Politics of Orientalism*. 2nd ed. Cambridge: Cambridge University Press.

Loeffler, Agnes. 2007. *Allopathy Goes Native: Traditional versus Modern Medicine in Iran*. London: I. B. Tauris.

Loeffler, Reinhold. 1986. "Economic Changes in a Rural Area since 1979." In *The Iranian Revolution and the Islamic Republic*, ed. Nikki Keddie and Eric Hooglund, 93–107. Syracuse: Syracuse University Press.

Luebbert, Gregory. 1991. *Liberalism, Fascism, or Social Democracy: Social Classes and the Political Origins of Regimes in Interwar Europe*. New York: Oxford University Press.

MacLachlan, K. S. 1991. "Economic Development, 1921–1979." In *The Cambridge History of Iran*, vol. 7, *From Nadir Shah to the Islamic Republic*, ed. Peter Avery, Gavin Hambly, and C. P. Melville, 608–38. Cambridge: Cambridge University Press.

Madani, Said. 2003. "Cheshmāndāz-hāye farāru-ye ta'min-e ejtemā'i dar Irān: Chālesh-hā va rāhkār-hāye pishbini shodeh dar lāihe-ye nezām jāme'h-ye refāh va ta'min-e ejtemā'i." *Faslnāmeh-ye Ta'min-e Ejtemā'i* 15: 289–328.

Mafinezam, Alidad, and Aria Mehrabi. 2008. *Iran and Its Place among Nations*. Westport, Conn.: Praeger.

Mahdavy, Hossein. 1970. "The Patterns and Problems of Economic Development in Rentier States: The Case of Iran." In *Studies in the Economic History of the Middle East: From the Rise of Islam to the Present Day*. ed. M. A. Cook, 428–67. London: Oxford University Press.

———. 1982. "Tahavolāt-e si sāleh-ye yek deh dar dasht-e Ghazvin." *Ketāb-e Āgāh*: 50–74.

Majd, Mohammad Gholi. 2000. "Small Landowners and Land Distribution in Iran, 1962–71." *International Journal of Middle East Studies* 32.1: 123–53.

Majles Research Center. 1996. *Tarh-e Towse'eh-ye Eshteghāl va Ta'min-e Ejtemā'i: Koliyāt-e Motāla'ah va Sharh-e Khedamāt*. Tehran: Markaz-e Pazhuhesh-e Majles.

———. 2000. *Mokhtasari dar Mowred-e Nezām-e Ta'min-e Ejtemā'i dar Irān*. Tehran: Markaz-e Pazhuhesh-e Majles.

Malik, Adeel. 2016. "Beyond the Resource Curse: Rents and Development." In Ishac Diwan and Ahmad Galal, eds., *The Middle East Economies in Times of Transition*, 245–58. London: Palgrave Macmillan.

Maljoo, Mohammad. 2010a. "The Green Movement Awaits an Invisible Hand." *Middle East Report*. Online at http://www.merip.org/mero/mero062610 [Accessed 13 March 2015.]

———. 2010b. Interview with Mohammad Maljoo. *Deutsche Welle Persian*, 6 February 2010; available at http://www.dw.de/dw/article/0,,5216251,00.html [Accessed 13 March 2015.]

———. 2011. "Tavān-e tabāgheh-ye kārgar dar daheh-ye hashtād dar goftegu bā Mohammad Mālju." *Mehrnāmeh* 11: 39–41.

Mann, Michael. 1986. "The Autonomous Power of the State: Its Origins, Mechanisms and Results." In *States in History*, ed. John Hall, 109–36. Oxford: Basil Blackwell.

Marandi, Seyyed Alireza. 2009. "The Integration of Medical Education and Health Care Services in the I.R. of Iran and Its Health Impacts." *Iranian Journal of Public Health* 38, Supplement 1: 4–12.

Marashi, Afshin. 2008. *Nationalizing Iran: Culture, Power, and the State, 1870–1940*. Seattle: University of Washington Press.

Mares, Isabela, and Matthew Carnes. 2009. "Social Policy in Developing Countries." *Annual Review of Political Science* 12: 93–113.

Markoff, John. 1996. *Waves of Democracy: Social Movements and Political Change*. Thousand Oaks, Calif.: Pine Forge Press.

Marshall, T. H. 2006. "Citizenship and Social Class." In *The Welfare State Reader*, ed. Christopher Pierson and Francis Castles, 30–39. Cambridge: Polity Press.

Martin, Vanessa. 2003a. *Creating an Islamic State: Khomeini and the Making of a New Iran*. London: I. B. Tauris.

———. 2003b. "Mudarris, Republicanism and the Rise to Power of Riza Khan, Sardar-i Sipah." In *The Making of Modern Iran: State and Society under Riza Shah, 1921–1941*, ed. Stephanie Cronin, 67–80. London and New York: RoutledgeCurzon.

Marx, Anthony. 2003. *Faith in Nation: Exclusionary Origins of Nationalism*. New York: Oxford University Press.

Matin-Asgari, Afshin. 2002. *Iranian Student Opposition to the Shah*. Costa Mesa, Calif.: Mazda Publishers.

———. 2004. "From Social Democracy to Social Democracy: The Twentieth-Century Odyssey of the Iranian Left." In *Reformers and Revolutionaries in Modern Iran: New Perspectives on the Iranian Left*, ed. Stephanie Cronin, 37–64. London and New York: RoutledgeCurzon.

———. 2009. "Marxism, Historiography and Historical Consciousness in Modern Iran: A Preliminary Study." In *Iran in the 20th Century: Historiography and Political Culture*, ed. Touraj Atabaki, 199–231. London: I. B. Tauris.

McAdam, Doug, Sidney Tarrow, and Charles Tilly. 2001. *Dynamics of Contention*. Cambridge: Cambridge University Press.

McDaniel, Tim. 1991. *Autocracy, Modernization, and Revolution in Russia and Iran*. Princeton: Princeton University Press.

McKibben, Ross. 2010. *Parties and People: England, 1914–1951*. Oxford: Oxford University Press.

McLellan, David. 2007. *Marxism after Marx*. 4th ed. London: Palgrave Macmillan.

McNeill, William. 1982. *The Pursuit of Power: Technology, Armed Force, and Society since A.D. 1000*. Chicago: University of Chicago Press.

Mehryar, Amir. 2005. "Shi'ite Teachings, Pragmatism and Fertility Change in Iran." In *Islam, the State and Population*, ed. Gavin Jones and Mehtab Karim, 118–56. London: Hurst.

Menaldo, Victor. 2016. *The Institutions Curse: Natural Resources, Politics, and Development*. Cambridge: Cambridge University Press.

Menashri, David. 1992. *Education and the Making of Modern Iran.* Ithaca: Cornell University Press.

Merton, Robert. 1949. *Social Theory and Social Structure.* Glencoe, Ill.: Free Press.

Mettler, Suzanne. 2011. *The Submerged State: How Invisible Government Policies Undermine American Democracy.* Chicago: University of Chicago Press.

Midgley, James. 1984. "Diffusion and the Development of Social Policy: Evidence from the Third World." *Journal of Social Policy* 13.2: 167–84.

Milani, Abbas. 2011. *The Shah.* New York: Palgrave MacMillan.

Milkman, Ruth, Ellen Reese, and Benita Roth. 1998. "The Macrosociology of Paid Domestic Labor." *Work and Occupations* 25.4: 483–510.

Mill, John Stuart. 1849. "The French Revolution of 1848, and Its Assailants." *The Westminster Review* 51 (April–July): 1–26.

Mirsepassi, Ali. 2000. *Intellectual Discourse and the Politics of Modernization: Negotiating Modernity in Iran.* Cambridge: Cambridge University Press.

———. 2017. *Transnationalism in Iranian Political Thought: The Life and Thought of Ahmad Fardid.* Cambridge: Cambridge University Press.

Mirzaie, Mohammad. 2005. "Swings in Fertility Limitation in Iran." *Critique: Critical Middle Eastern Studies* 14.1: 25–33.

Mitchell, Timothy. 2009. "Carbon Democracy." *Economy and Society* 38.3: 399–432.

———. 2011. *Carbon Democracy: Political Power in the Age of Oil.* London: Verso.

Moaddel, Mansoor. 1993. *Class, Politics, and Ideology in the Iranian Revolution.* New York: Columbia University Press.

Moghadam, Val. 1989. "Populist Revolution and the Islamic State in Iran." In *Revolution in the World-System,* ed. Terry Boswell, 147–63. New York: Greenwood Press.

Moghissi, Haideh, and Saeed Rahnema. 2001. "The Working Class and the Islamic State in Iran." *Socialist Register* 37: 197–218.

Montesquieu, Baron de. 2008. *Persian Letters.* Ed. Andrew Kahn. Trans. Margaret Mauldon. New York: Oxford University Press.

Moore, Richard. 2007. "Family Planning in Iran, 1960–79." In *The Global Family Planning Revolution: Three Decades of Population Policies and Programs,* ed. Warren Robinson and John Ross, 33–57. Washington, D.C.: World Bank Publications.

Moses, Jonathon. 2010. "Foiling the Resource Curse: Wealth, Equality, Oil and the Norwegian State." In *Constructing a Democratic Developmental State in South Africa: Potentials and Challenges,* ed. Omano Edigheji, 126–48. Cape Town: HSRC Press.

Moslem, Mehdi. 2002. *Factional Politics in Post-Khomeini Iran.* Syracuse: Syracuse University Press.

Mousavi, B., et al. [Mousavi, B., M. Moradi-Lakeh, M. Karbakhsh, and M. Soroush.] 2014. "Years of Life Lost among Iranian People Killed in the Iraq–Iran War: The 25-Year Perspective." *International Journal of Injury Control and Safety Promotion* 21.4: 382–87.

Müller, Jan-Werner. 2011. *Contesting Democracy: Political Ideas in Twentieth-Century Europe.* New Haven: Yale University Press.

———. 2015. "Parsing Populism: Who Is and Who Is Not a Populist These Days?" *Juncture* 22.2: 80–89.

Najmabadi, Afsaneh. 1987. "Depoliticisation of a Rentier State: The Case of Pahlavi Iran." In *The Rentier State,* ed. Hazem Beblawi and Giacomo Luciani, 211–27. London: Croom Helm.

Nasr, Vali. 2000. "Politics within the Late-Pahlavi State: The Ministry of Economy and Industrial Policy, 1963–69." *International Journal of Middle East Studies* 32.1: 97–122.

Nasseri, Kiumarss, et al. [Nasseri, Kiumarss, Mehdi Latifi, Firooz Azordegan, Forough Shafii, and Reza All-E-Agha.] 1990. "Determinants of Partial Participation in the Immunization Programmes in Iran." *Social Science & Medicine* 30.3: 379–83.

Nathan, Andrew, and Kellee Tsai. 1995. "Factionalism: A New Institutionalist Restatement." *China Journal* 34: 157–92.

Nemchenok, Victor. 2009. "'That So Fair a Thing Should Be So Frail': The Ford Foundation and the Failure of Rural Development in Iran, 1953–1964." *Middle East Journal* 63.2: 261–84.

———. 2010. "In Search of Stability amid Chaos: U.S. policy toward Iran, 1961–63." *Cold War History* 10.3: 341–69.

Newell, Kenneth, ed. 1975. *Health by the People.* Geneva: World Health Organization.

Nomani, Farhad, and Sohrab Behdad. 2006. *Class and Labor in Iran: Did the Revolution Matter?* Syracuse: Syracuse University Press.

Nove, Alec. 1964. *Economic Rationality and Soviet Politics; or, Was Stalin Really Necessary?* New York: Praeger.

Nowshirvani, Vahid, and Patrick Clawson. 1994. "The State and Social Equity in Postrevolutionary Iran." In *The Politics of Social Transformation in Afghanistan, Iran, and Pakistan,* ed. Myron Weiner and Ali Banuazizi, 228–69. Syracuse: Syracuse University Press.

O'Brien, Kevin. 2002. "Neither Transgressive nor Contained: Boundary-Spanning Contention in China." *Mobilization: An International Quarterly* 8.1: 51–64.

O'Connor, James. 1973. *The Fiscal Crisis of the State.* New York: St. Martin's Press.

O'Connor, Julia, Ann Orloff, and Sheila Shaver. 1999. *States, Markets, Families: Gender, Liberalism, and Social Policy in Australia, Canada, Great Britain, and the United States.* Cambridge: Cambridge University Press.

Offe, Claus. 1984. *Contradictions of the Welfare State.* Ed. John Keane. Cambridge, Mass.: MIT Press.

———. 2009. "Epilogue: Lessons Learnt and Open Questions." In *Post-Communist Welfare Pathways: Theorizing Social Policy Transformations in Central and Eastern Europe,* ed. Alfio Cerami and Pieter Vanhuysse, 237–47. Basingstoke, Hants: Palgrave Macmillan.

Okruhlik, Gwenn. 1999. "Rentier Wealth, Unruly Law, and the Rise of Opposition: The Political Economy of Oil States." *Comparative Politics* 31.3: 295–315.

Orloff, Ann. 1993. "Gender and the Social Rights of Citizenship: The Comparative Analysis of Gender Relations and Welfare States." *American Sociological Review* 58.3: 303–28.

———. 2009. "Gendering the Comparative Analysis of Welfare States: An Unfinished Agenda." *Sociological Theory* 27.3: 317–43

Owen, Roger. 2004. *State Power and Politics in the Making of the Modern Middle East.* 3rd ed. London: Routledge.

Paidar, Parvin. 1995. *Women and the Political Process in Twentieth-Century Iran.* Cambridge: Cambridge University Press.

Parijs, Philippe van. 2001. *What's Wrong with a Free Lunch?* Boston: Beacon Press.

Parsa, Misagh. 2009. "The Green Challenge to the Islamic Republic." Posted on *Gozaar,* 18 November. Online at: http://www.gozaar.org/english/articles-en/The-Green-Challenge-to-the-Islamic-Republic.html. [Accessed 13 March 2015.]

Parvin, Manoucher, and Mostafa Vaziri. 1992. "Islamic Man and Society in the Islamic Republic of Iran." In *Iran: Political Culture in the Islamic Republic,* ed. Samih Farsoun and Mehrdad Mashayekhi, 80–91. London: Routledge,

Parvin, Nasserddin. 1998. "*Ettelā'āt.*" *Encyclopaedia Iranica,* vol. 9, fasc. 1, pp. 58–62. Updated in 2012. Online at: http://www.iranicaonline.org/articles/ettelaat. [Accessed 13 March 2015.]

Pateman, Carole. 1989. *The Disorder of Women: Democracy, Feminism, and Political Theory.* Stanford, Calif.: Stanford University Press.

Paydār, Habibollah [Habibollah Peymān]. 1979. *Bardāsht-hāi Darbāreh-ye Mālekiyyat, Sarmāyeh va Kār Az Didgāh-e Eslām.* Tehran: Daftar-e Nashr-e Eslāmi.

Peng, Ito, and Joseph Wong. 2010. "East Asia." In *The Oxford Handbook of the Welfare State,* ed. Francis G. Castles, Stephan Leibfried, Jane Lewis, Herbert Obinger, and Christopher Pierson, 656–70. New York: Oxford University Press.

Pesaran, Evaleila. 2011. *Iran's Struggle for Economic Independence: Reform and Counter-Reform in the Post-Revolutionary Era.* London: Routledge.

Pesaran, Mohammad Hashem. 1982. "The System of Dependent Capitalism in Pre- and Post-Revolutionary Iran." *International Journal of Middle East Studies* 14.4: 501–22.

Peters, Anne, and Pete Moore. 2009. "Beyond Boom and Bust: External Rents, Durable Authoritarianism, and Institutional Adaptation in the Hashemite Kingdom of Jordan." *Studies in Comparative International Development* 44.3: 256–85.

Pierret, Thomas, and Kjetil Selvik. 2009. "Limits of 'Authoritarian Upgrading' in Syria: Private Welfare, Islamic Charities, and the Rise of the Zayd Movement." *International Journal of Middle East Studies* 41.4: 595–614.

Pincus, Steve. 2009. *1688: The First Modern Revolution.* New Haven: Yale University Press.

Piven, Frances Fox, and Richard Cloward. 1978. *Poor People's Movements: Why They Succeed, How They Fail.* New York: Vintage.

Polanyi, Karl. 1957. *The Great Transformation: The Political and Economic Origins of Our Time*. Boston: Beacon Press.

Polterovich, Victor, Vladimir Popov, and Alexander Tonis. 2010. *Resource Abundance: A Curse or Blessing?* DESA Working Paper no. 93. New York: United Nations Department of Economic and Social Affairs.

Porter, Bruce. 1994. *War and the Rise of the State: The Military Foundations of Modern Politics*. New York: Simon and Schuster.

Portes, Alejandro, and Kelly Hoffman. 2003. "Latin American Class Structures: Their Composition and Change during the Neoliberal Era." *Latin American Research Review* 38.1: 41–82.

Przeworski, Adam. 1985. *Capitalism and Social Democracy*. Cambridge: Cambridge University Press.

Quchāni, Mohammad. 2000. *Yaqeh Sefid-hā*. Tehran: Naqsh-o-Negār.

Rahnema, Ali. 2015. *Behind the 1953 Coup in Iran: Thugs, Turncoats, Soldiers, and Spooks*. Cambridge: Cambridge University Press.

Randjbar-Daemi, Siavush. 2013. "Building the Islamic State: The Draft Constitution of 1979 Reconsidered." *Iranian Studies* 46.4: 641–63.

Rastegar, Asghar. 1995. "Health Policy and Medical Education." In *Iran after the Revolution: Crisis of an Islamic State*, ed. Saeed Rahnema and Sohrab Behdad, 218–28. London and New York: I.B. Tauris.

Razavi, Hossein, and Firouz Vakil. 1984. *The Political Environment of Economic Planning in Iran, 1971–1983: From Monarchy to Islamic Republic*. Boulder: Westview Press.

Razoux, Pierre. 2015. *The Iran-Iraq War*. Transl. Nicholas Elliott. Cambridge, Mass.: Harvard University Press.

Reinert, Erik. 2007. *How Rich Countries Got Rich and Why Poor Countries Stay Poor*. New York: Carroll & Graf.

Richards, Alan, and John Waterbury. 2008. *A Political Economy of the Middle East*. Boulder: Westview Press.

Riley, Dylan, and Juan Fernández. 2014. "Beyond Strong and Weak: Rethinking Postdictatorship Civil Societies." *American Journal of Sociology* 120.2: 432–503.

Robalino, David. 2005. *Pensions in the Middle East and North Africa: Time for Change*. Washington, D.C.: World Bank Publications.

Roberts, Kenneth. 1995. "Neoliberalism and the Transformation of Populism in Latin America: The Peruvian Case." *World Politics* 48.1: 82–116.

———. 2006. "Populism, Political Conflict, and Grass-Roots Organization in Latin America." *Comparative Politics* 38.2: 127–48.

Rodrik, Dani. 2000. "What Drives Public Employment in Developing Countries?" *Review of Development Economics* 4.3: 229–43.

Ronaghy, Hossain, et al. [Ronaghy, Hossain, J. Mehrabanpour, B. Zeighami, E. Zeighami, S. Mansouri, M. Ayatolahi, and N. Rasulnia.] 1983. "The Middle Level Auxiliary Health Worker School: The Behdar Project." *Journal of Tropical Pediatrics* 29.5: 260–64.

Ronaghy, Hossain, and Steven Solter. 1973. "The Auxilary Health Worker in Iran." *The Lancet* 302.7826 (August): 427–29.

Ross, Michael. 2012. *The Oil Curse: How Petroleum Wealth Shapes the Development of Nations*. Princeton: Princeton University Press.

Rostam'alizādeh, Valiollāh, and Ali Qāsemi-Ardehā'i. 2012. "Āsār va payāmad-hāye jam'iati–ejtemā'i-ye mohājerat-hāye jang-e tahmili dar jāme'eh-ye Irān," *Pazhuheshnāmeh-ye Defā'-ye Moqadas* 1.2: 59–79.

Roudi-Fahimi, Farzaneh. 2002. *Iran's Family Planning Program: Responding to a Nation's Needs.* MENA Policy Brief (June). Washington, D.C.: Population Reference Bureau.

Sabahi, Farian. 2001. "The Literacy Corps in Pahlavi Iran (1963–1979): Political, Social and Literary Implications." *Cahiers d'Études sur la Méditerranée Orientale et le Monde Turco-Iranien* 31: 191–220.

Sachs, Jeffrey, and Andrew Warner. 2001. "The Curse of Natural Resources." *European Economic Review* 45.4–6: 827–38.

Sādeghi, Fātemeh. 2011. "Khodāyān va khābgard-hā: Pirāmun-e ulum-e ensāni dar Irān." *Jomhourikhāhi Online*, 19 August. Original site at: http://www.jomhourikhahi.com/2011/08/social-science-tragedy-in-iran1.html; Reposted at http://www.rahesabz.net/story/41646/ [Accessed 13 March 2015.]

Sadeghi-Boroujerdi, Eskandar. 2014. "From Etelā'āti to Eslāhtalabi: Sa'id Hajjarian, Political Theology and the Politics of Reform in Post-Revolutionary Iran." *Iranian Studies* 47.6: 987–1009.

Sadjadpour, Karim. 2008. *Reading Khamenei: The World View of Iran's Most Powerful Leader.* Washington, D.C.: Carnegie Endowment for International Peace.

Saeidi, Ali. 2002. "Dislocation of the State and the Emergence of Factional Politics in Post-Revolutionary Iran." *Political Geography* 21.4: 525–46.

———. 2004. "The Accountability of Para-governmental Organizations (*bonyads*): The Case of Iranian Foundations." *Iranian Studies* 37.3: 479–98.

Saghafi, Morad. 2004a. "The New Landscape of Iranian Politics." *Middle East Report* 233: 16–23.

———. 2004b. *Why Iran Seems So Unpredictable: Iran after 25 Years of Revolution; A Retrospective and a Look Ahead.* Washington, D.C.: Woodrow Wilson Center.

———. 2005. *The Reform Nobody Wants Any More: Iran's Elections.* ISIM Review. Leiden: International Institute for the Study of Islam in the Modern World.

Sahābi, Ezzatollāh, and Hoda Sāber. 1999. "Forsat-e ān do sāl va 'tāvān-e' ān shish sāl." *Irān-e Fardā* 58: 23–26.

Sahimi, Muhammad. 2010. "Martyrs of the Green Movement," posted on *Tehran Bureau*, 19 June. Online at: http://www.pbs.org/wgbh/pages/frontline/tehranbureau/2010/06/martyrs-of-the-green-movement.html. [Accessed 13 March 2015.]

Sainsbury, Diane, ed. 1999. *Gender and Welfare State Regimes.* Oxford: Oxford University Press.

Sakurai, Keiko. 2004. "University Entrance Examination and the Making of an Islamic Society in Iran: A Study of the Post-Revolutionary Iranian Approach to 'Konkur.'" *Iranian Studies* 37.3: 385–406.

Salamé, Ghassan, ed. 1994. *Democracy without Democrats? The Renewal of Politics in the Muslim World.* London: I. B. Tauris.

Salehi-Esfahani, Hadi. 2005. "Alternative Public Service Delivery Mechanisms in Iran." *Quarterly Review of Economics and Finance* 45.2–3: 497–525.

Salehi-Isfahani, Djavad. 1999. "Labor and the Challenge of Economic Restructuring in Iran." *Middle East Report* 210: 34–37.

———. 2005. "Human Resources in Iran: Potentials and Challenges." *Iranian Studies* 38.1: 117–47.

———. 2009. "Poverty, Inequality, and Populist Politics in Iran." *Journal of Economic Inequality* 7.1: 5–28.

———. 2016. "Long Term Trends in Poverty and Inequality in Iran." *Tyranny of Numbers Blog,* 29 March. Online at: https://djavadsalehi.com/2016/03/29/long-term-trends-in-poverty-and-inequality-in-iran/ [Accessed 1 April 2016.]

Salehi-Isfahani, Djavad, and Daniel Egel. 2007. *Youth Exclusion in Iran: The State of Education, Employment and Family Formation.* Dubai: Wolfensohn Center for Development, Dubai School of Government.

Schayegh, Cyrus. 2006. "The Development of Social Insurance in Iran: Technical-Financial Conditions and Political Rationales, 1941–1960." *Iranian Studies* 39: 539–68.

———. 2010. "'Seeing like a State': An Essay on the Historiography of Modern Iran." *International Journal of Middle East Studies* 42.1: 37–61.

Schirazi, Asghar. 1993. *Islamic Development Policy: The Agrarian Question in Iran.* Boulder: Lynne Rienner Publishers.

———. 1997. *The Constitution of Iran: Politics and the State in the Islamic Republic.* London: I. B. Tauris.

Schlefer, Jonathan. 2009. *Palace Politics: How the Ruling Party Brought Crisis to Mexico.* Austin: University of Texas Press.

Schurmann, Franz. 1966. *Ideology and Organization in Communist China.* Berkeley and Los Angeles: University of California Press.

Schwarz, Rolf. 2008. "The Political Economy of State-Formation in the Arab Middle East: Rentier States, Economic Reform, and Democratization." *Review of International Political Economy* 15.4: 599–621.

Sciolino, Elaine. 2000. *Persian Mirrors: The Elusive Face of Iran.* New York: Free Press.

Scott, James. 1998. *Seeing like a State: How Certain Schemes to Improve the Human Condition Have Failed.* New Haven: Yale University Press.

Scully, Ben. 2015. "From the Shop Floor to the Kitchen Table: The Shifting Centre of Precarious Workers' Politics in South Africa." *Review of African Political Economy* 43.148: 1–17.

Secor, Laura. 2016. *Children of Paradise: The Struggle for the Soul of Iran.* New York: Basic Books.

Segura-Ubiergo, Alex. 2007. *The Political Economy of the Welfare State in Latin America: Globalization, Democracy, and Development.* Cambridge: Cambridge University Press.

Sen, Amartya. 1998. "Mortality as an Indicator of Economic Success and Failure." *The Economic Journal* 108.446: 1–25.

Shādi-Taleb, Jāleh. 1992. "Subsid va piāmad-hāye ejtemā'i-ye ān." *Farhang-e Towse'eh* October–November: 34–41.

Shadpour, Kaveh. 2000. "Primary Health Care Networks in the Islamic Republic of Iran." *Eastern Mediterranean Health Journal* 6.4: 822–25.

Shahidi, Hossein. 2007. *Journalism in Iran: From Mission to Profession*. London: Routledge.

Silver, Beverly J. 1990. "The Contradictions of Semiperipheral Success: The Case of Israel." In *Semiperipheral States in the World Economy*, ed. William Martin, 161–81. New York: Greenwood Press.

———. 2003. *Forces of Labor: Workers' Movements and Globalization since 1870*. Cambridge: Cambridge University Press.

Skocpol, Theda. 1979. *States and Social Revolutions: A Comparative Analysis of France, Russia, and China*. Cambridge: Cambridge University Press.

———. 1982. "Rentier State and Shi'a Islam in the Iranian Revolution." *Theory and Society* 11.3: 265–83.

———. 1992. *Protecting Soldiers and Mothers: The Political Origins of Social Policy in the United States*. Cambridge, Mass.: Harvard University Press.

———. 1994. *Social Revolutions in the Modern World*. Cambridge: Cambridge University Press.

Slater, Dan. 2010. *Ordering Power: Contentious Politics and Authoritarian Leviathans in Southeast Asia*. Cambridge: Cambridge University Press.

Smith, Benjamin. 2007. *Hard Times in the Lands of Plenty: Oil Politics in Iran and Indonesia*. Ithaca: Cornell University Press.

Social Security Organization. 2004. *Sanad-e Barnāmeh-ye Estrātezhik-e Sāzmān-e Ta'min-e Ejtemā'i*. Tehran: SSO.

———. 2007. *Sāzmān-e Ta'min-e Ejtemā'i dar Yek Negāh*. Tehran: SSO.

———. 2008. *Āshenāi bā Khedamāt va Hemāyat-hāye Sāzmān-e Ta'min-e Ejtemā'i*. Tehran: SSO.

Sohrabi, Naghmeh. 2011. *The Power Struggle in Iran: A Centrist Comeback?* Middle East Brief. Waltham, Mass.: Crown Center for Middle East Studies, Brandeis University.

Sohrabi, Naghmeh, and Arang Keshavarzian. 2001. "On the Eve of Iran's Presidential Elections: Report from Tehran." *Middle East Report* 7 June. Online at: http://www.merip.org/mero/mero060701. [accessed 11 August 2015.]

Sreberny-Mohammadi, Annabelle, and Ali Mohammadi. 1994. *Small Media, Big Revolution: Communication, Culture and the Iranian Revolution*. Minneapolis: University of Minnesota Press.

Steinberg, Jonathan. 2011. *Bismarck: A Life*. Oxford: Oxford University Press.

Stephens, John. 2010. "The Social Rights of Citizenship." In *The Oxford Handbook of the Welfare State*, ed. Francis Castles et al. [Francis Castles, Stephan Leibfried, Jane Lewis, Herbert Obinger, and Christopher Pierson], 511–25. Oxford: Oxford University Press.

Stinchcombe, Arthur. 1999. "Ending Revolutions and Building New Governments." *Annual Review of Political Science* 2.1: 49–73.

Sullivan, Zohreh. 1998. "Eluding the Feminist, Overthrowing the Modern? Transformations in Twentieth-Century Iran." In *Remaking Women: Feminism and Modernity in the Middle East*, ed. Lila Abu-Lughod, 215–42. Princeton: Princeton University Press.

Surat-e Mashruh-ye Mozākerāt-e Majles-e Barrasi-ye Nahā'i-ye Qānun-e Asāsi-ye Jomhuri-ye Eslāmi-ye Irān. 1985. Vols. 1–3. Tehran: Edārah-ye Kol-e Umur-e Farhangi va Ravābet-e Omumi-ye Majles-e Showrā-ye Eslāmi.

Taggart, Paul. 2000. *Populism.* Buckingham, Bucks: Open University Press.

Takian, Amirhossein, Arash Rashidian, and Mohammad J. Kabir. 2011. "Expediency and Coincidence in Re-Engineering a Health System: An Interpretive Approach to Formation of Family Medicine in Iran." *Health Policy and Planning* 26.2: 163–73.

Talmon, Jacob. 1960. *The Origins of Totalitarian Democracy.* New York: Praeger.

Tavakoli-Targhi, Mohamad. 2009. "Historiography and Crafting Iranian National Identity." In *Iran in the 20th Century: Historiography and Political Culture,* ed. Touraj Atabaki, 5–21. London: I. B. Tauris.

———. 2015. "Rahim Mottaghi Irvani and the Melli Industrial Group." *Iran Nameh* 30.1: 118–60.

Taylor, A. J. P. 1965. *English History, 1914–1945.* Oxford: Oxford University Press.

Tilly, Charles. 1985. "State Making and War Making as Organized Crime." In *Bringing the State Back In,* ed. Peter Evans, Dietrich Rueschemeyer, and Theda Skocpol, 169–91. Cambridge: Cambridge University Press.

———. 1992. Review of *Autocracy, Modernization, and Revolution in Russia and Iran,* by Tim McDaniel. *American Political Science Review* 86.4: 1084–85.

———. 2005. *Trust and Rule.* Cambridge: Cambridge University Press.

———. 2007. *Democracy.* Cambridge: Cambridge University Press.

———. 2009. "Extraction and Democracy." In *The New Fiscal Sociology: Taxation in Comparative and Historical Perspective,* ed. Isaac Martin, Ajay Mehrotra, and Monica Prasad, 173–82. Cambridge: Cambridge University Press.

Titmuss, Richard. 1968. *Commitment to Welfare.* London: Allen and Unwin.

Tripp, Charles. 2006. *Islam and the Moral Economy: The Challenge of Capitalism.* Cambridge: Cambridge University Press.

Underwood, Carol. 2004. "Islam and Health Policy: A Study of the Islamic Republic of Iran." In *Islam and Social Policy,* ed. Stephen Heyneman, 181–206. Nashville: Vanderbilt University Press.

United Nations Educational, Scientific and Cultural Organization. 2011. *Global Education Digest 2011.* Montreal: UNESCO Institute for Statistics.

United Nations Industrial Development Organization. 1995. *Non-Farm Employment for Rural Poverty Alleviation: A Report on the Regional Seminar, Pilot Projects, and Country Papers.* Vienna: United Nations Industrial Development Organization.

United Nations Population Fund Office. 2008. *Family Planning Programme Report.* Tehran: United Nations Population Fund Office.

Vahabzadeh, Peyman. 2010. *A Guerilla Odyssey: Modernization, Secularism, Democracy, and the Fadai Period of National Liberation In Iran, 1971–1979.* Syracuse: Syracuse University Press.

Valibeigi, Mehrdad. 1993. "Islamic Economics and Economic Policy Formation in Post-Revolutionary Iran: A Critique." *Journal of Economic Issues* 27.3: 793–812.

———. 2008. "Economy, Private Sector." In *Iran Today: An Encyclopedia of Life in the Islamic Republic*, ed. Mehran Kamrava and Manochehr Dorraj, vol. 1, 159–65. Westport, Conn.: Greenwood Press.

Vandewalle, Dirk. 1998. *Libya since Independence: Oil and State-Building*. Ithaca: Cornell University Press.

Vejdani, Farzin. 2014. *Making History in Iran: Education, Nationalism, and Print Culture*. Stanford, Calif.: Stanford University Press.

Von Laue, T. H. 1964. *Why Lenin? Why Stalin? A Reappraisal of the Russian Revolution, 1900–1930*. Philadelphia: J. B. Lippincott.

Waldner, David. 1999. *State Building and Late Development*. Ithaca: Cornell University Press.

Waldner, David, and Benjamin Smith. 2015. "Rentier States and State Transformations." In Stephan Leibfried et al. [Stephan Leibfried, Evelyne Huber, Matthew Lange, Frank Nullmeier, and Jonah D. Levy], eds., *The Oxford Handbook of Transformations of the State*, 714–29. Oxford: Oxford University Press.

Wallerstein, Immanuel. 2011a. *The Modern World-System*. Volume 1, *Capitalist Agriculture and the Origins of the European World-Economy in the Sixteenth Century*. Berkeley and Los Angeles: University of California Press.

———. 2011b. *The Modern World-System*. Volume 3, *The Second Era of Great Expansion of the Capitalist World-Economy, 1730s–1840s*. Berkeley and Los Angeles: University of California Press.

Waterbury, John. 1999. "The Long Gestation and Brief Triumph of Import-Substituting Industrialization." *World Development* 27.2: 323–41.

Weber, Eugen. 1976. *Peasants into Frenchmen: The Modernization of Rural France, 1870–1914*. Stanford, Calif.: Stanford University Press.

Westad, Odd Arne. 2005. *The Global Cold War: Third World Interventions and The Making of Our Times*. Cambridge: Cambridge University Press.

Weyland, Kurt. 2001. "Clarifying a Contested Concept: Populism in the Study of Latin American Politics." *Comparative Politics* 34.1: 1–22.

Wick, Katharina, and Erwin Bulte. 2009. "The Curse of Natural Resources." *Annual Review of Resource Economics* 1.1: 139–56.

Wickham, Carrie. 2002. *Mobilizing Islam: Religion, Activism, and Political Change in Egypt*. New York: Columbia University Press.

———. 2013. *The Muslim Brotherhood: Evolution of an Islamist Movement*. Princeton: Princeton University Press.

Widmaier, Wesley, Mark Blyth, and Leonard Seabrooke. 2007. "Exogenous Shocks or Endogenous Constructions? The Meanings of Wars and Crises." *International Studies Quarterly* 51.4: 747–59.

Wilensky, Harold L., and Charles Nathan Lebeaux. 1965. *Industrial Society and Social Welfare: The Impact of Industrialization on the Supply and Organization of Social Welfare Services in the United States*. New York: Free Press.

Winters, Jeffrey. 2011. *Oligarchy*. Cambridge: Cambridge University Press.

World Bank. 1991. *Iran: Reconstruction and Economic Growth*. Washington, D.C.: World Bank Publications.

World Bank. 2016. *World Development Indicators Database*. Washington, D.C.: World Bank.

World Health Organization. 2003. *Country Studies on Health and Welfare Systems: Experiences in Indonesia, Islamic Republic of Iran, and Sri Lanka.* Kobe: World Health Organization Center for Health Development.

World Health Organization / United Nations Children's Fund. 2008. *Review of National Immunization Coverage, 1980–2007.* Geneva: World Health Organization.

Wright, Martin, and Nick Danziger. 1989. *Iran: The Khomeini Revolution.* London: Longman.

Wright, Robin. 2000. *The Last Great Revolution: Turmoil and Transformation in Iran.* New York: A.A. Knopf.

Yaghmaian, Behzad. 2002. *Social Change in Iran: An Eyewitness Account of Dissent, Defiance, and New Movements for Rights.* Albany: SUNY Press.

Zeitlin, Maurice, and Richard Earl Radcliff. 1988. *Landlords & Capitalists: The Dominant Class of Chile.* Princeton: Princeton University Press.

Zia-Ebrahimi, Reza. 2011. "Self-Orientalization and Dislocation: The Uses and Abuses of the 'Aryan' Discourse in Iran." *Iranian Studies* 44.4: 445–72.

Zubaida, Sami. 2011. *Beyond Islam: A New Understanding of the Middle East.* London: I.B. Tauris.

Index

Abadan Crisis, 53, 56
Abdi, Abbās, 23
Abrahamian, Ervand, 56, 65, 74–75
absolutism, and Pahlavi monarchy, 47–48
Ādeli, Mohammad-Hossein, 155
al-Afghāni, Jamāl al-Din, 50
Afghans, 108, 124, 195
agricultural sector: agrarian reforms, 33,
    49; Ministry of Agriculture, 87, 88tab.5;
    self-sufficiency, 101
Ahmad, Jalal al-e, 66
Ahmadi, Mohammad, 191
Ahmadinejad, Mahmoud: candidacy of,
    158, 175, 188; charismatic authority of,
    14; criticism of, 199–200; election of, 2,
    4, 11, 175–76, 181, 189; reelection of,
    198fig.17, 212; support for, 189–91,
    212
Ahmadinejad administration: agenda of,
    191–92; economic policies, 192–93,
    212; and IKRC, 195; Labor Law and,
    149–50; manufacturing sector and, 195;
    postwar support of, 188–96; poverty
    rate, 177, 178fig.4, 179; social-insur-
    ance expansion, 151, 195; social justice,
    175–76; and SSO, 195; subsidies, 30,
    54, 154, 196, 212–15; taxation and,
    193, 212, 214; technocrats, 194. See
    also Green Movement
AIOC (Anglo-Iranian Oil Company). See
    Anglo-Iranian Oil Company (AIOC)

Alavi, Hamza, 26
Alavi-Tabār, Ali Rezā, 24
Albania, 85
Algeria, 93, 153, 153tab.6
Amini, Ali, 62, 64–65
Anglo-Iranian Oil Company (AIOC),
    53–54, 56–58
anticlericalism, 51
anti-imperialism, 74
antisystemic developmental state, 3–4, 14,
    222–25
anti-Western sentiment, 26
Arab uprisings of 2011, 43, 49, 210
Argentina, 7tab.1, 153, 153tab.6, 201, 222
Arrighi, Giovanni, 222–23
assassinations: Beheshti, 98; IRP and,
    97–98; Motahhari, 97; by Navvāb
    Safavi, 57; Pahlavi attempt, 57;
    Rafsanjani attempt, 97; Rajāi, 98;
    Razmara, 58; state assassinations,
    49–50
Association of Militant Clerics, 100
Atatürk, Kemal, 52, 62
Athāri, Kamal, 105
authoritarianisms, 33, 42, 46
Auyero, Javier, 201
awqāf (endowment holdings), 64
Azerbaijan, 56–57

Ba'athist Iraq. See Iraq, Ba'athist
Baenani, Amin, 52